T0189425

Lecture Notes in Computer Science   14033

The series Lecture Notes in Computer Science (LNCS), including its subseries Lecture Notes in Artificial Intelligence (LNAI) and Lecture Notes in Bioinformatics (LNBI), has established itself as a medium for the publication of new developments in computer science and information technology research, teaching, and education.

LNCS enjoys close cooperation with the computer science R & D community, the series counts many renowned academics among its volume editors and paper authors, and collaborates with prestigious societies. Its mission is to serve this international community by providing an invaluable service, mainly focused on the publication of conference and workshop proceedings and postproceedings. LNCS commenced publication in 1973.

Aaron Marcus · Elizabeth Rosenzweig ·
Marcelo M. Soares
Editors

Design, User Experience, and Usability

12th International Conference, DUXU 2023
Held as Part of the 25th HCI International Conference, HCII 2023
Copenhagen, Denmark, July 23–28, 2023
Proceedings, Part IV

 Springer

Editors
Aaron Marcus
Aaron Marcus and Associates
Berkeley, CA, USA

Elizabeth Rosenzweig
World Usability Day and Bubble Mountain
Consulting
Newton Center, MA, USA

Marcelo M. Soares
Southern University of Science
and Technology – SUSTech
Shenzhen, China

ISSN 0302-9743   ISSN 1611-3349 (electronic)
Lecture Notes in Computer Science
ISBN 978-3-031-35707-7   ISBN 978-3-031-35708-4 (eBook)
https://doi.org/10.1007/978-3-031-35708-4

This Springer imprint is published by the registered company Springer Nature Switzerland AG
The registered company address is: Gewerbestrasse 11, 6330 Cham, Switzerland

Foreword

Human-computer interaction (HCI) is acquiring an ever-increasing scientific and industrial importance, as well as having more impact on people's everyday lives, as an ever-growing number of human activities are progressively moving from the physical to the digital world. This process, which has been ongoing for some time now, was further accelerated during the acute period of the COVID-19 pandemic. The HCI International (HCII) conference series, held annually, aims to respond to the compelling need to advance the exchange of knowledge and research and development efforts on the human aspects of design and use of computing systems.

The 25th International Conference on Human-Computer Interaction, HCI International 2023 (HCII 2023), was held in the emerging post-pandemic era as a 'hybrid' event at the AC Bella Sky Hotel and Bella Center, Copenhagen, Denmark, during July 23–28, 2023. It incorporated the 21 thematic areas and affiliated conferences listed below.

A total of 7472 individuals from academia, research institutes, industry, and government agencies from 85 countries submitted contributions, and 1578 papers and 396 posters were included in the volumes of the proceedings that were published just before the start of the conference, these are listed below. The contributions thoroughly cover the entire field of human-computer interaction, addressing major advances in knowledge and effective use of computers in a variety of application areas. These papers provide academics, researchers, engineers, scientists, practitioners and students with state-of-the-art information on the most recent advances in HCI.

The HCI International (HCII) conference also offers the option of presenting 'Late Breaking Work', and this applies both for papers and posters, with corresponding volumes of proceedings that will be published after the conference. Full papers will be included in the 'HCII 2023 - Late Breaking Work - Papers' volumes of the proceedings to be published in the Springer LNCS series, while 'Poster Extended Abstracts' will be included as short research papers in the 'HCII 2023 - Late Breaking Work - Posters' volumes to be published in the Springer CCIS series.

I would like to thank the Program Board Chairs and the members of the Program Boards of all thematic areas and affiliated conferences for their contribution towards the high scientific quality and overall success of the HCI International 2023 conference. Their manifold support in terms of paper reviewing (single-blind review process, with a minimum of two reviews per submission), session organization and their willingness to act as goodwill ambassadors for the conference is most highly appreciated.

This conference would not have been possible without the continuous and unwavering support and advice of Gavriel Salvendy, founder, General Chair Emeritus, and Scientific Advisor. For his outstanding efforts, I would like to express my sincere appreciation to Abbas Moallem, Communications Chair and Editor of HCI International News.

July 2023   Constantine Stephanidis

HCI International 2023 Thematic Areas and Affiliated Conferences

Thematic Areas

- HCI: Human-Computer Interaction
- HIMI: Human Interface and the Management of Information

Affiliated Conferences

- EPCE: 20th International Conference on Engineering Psychology and Cognitive Ergonomics
- AC: 17th International Conference on Augmented Cognition
- UAHCI: 17th International Conference on Universal Access in Human-Computer Interaction
- CCD: 15th International Conference on Cross-Cultural Design
- SCSM: 15th International Conference on Social Computing and Social Media
- VAMR: 15th International Conference on Virtual, Augmented and Mixed Reality
- DHM: 14th International Conference on Digital Human Modeling and Applications in Health, Safety, Ergonomics and Risk Management
- DUXU: 12th International Conference on Design, User Experience and Usability
- C&C: 11th International Conference on Culture and Computing
- DAPI: 11th International Conference on Distributed, Ambient and Pervasive Interactions
- HCIBGO: 10th International Conference on HCI in Business, Government and Organizations
- LCT: 10th International Conference on Learning and Collaboration Technologies
- ITAP: 9th International Conference on Human Aspects of IT for the Aged Population
- AIS: 5th International Conference on Adaptive Instructional Systems
- HCI-CPT: 5th International Conference on HCI for Cybersecurity, Privacy and Trust
- HCI-Games: 5th International Conference on HCI in Games
- MobiTAS: 5th International Conference on HCI in Mobility, Transport and Automotive Systems
- AI-HCI: 4th International Conference on Artificial Intelligence in HCI
- MOBILE: 4th International Conference on Design, Operation and Evaluation of Mobile Communications

List of Conference Proceedings Volumes Appearing Before the Conference

1. LNCS 14011, Human-Computer Interaction: Part I, edited by Masaaki Kurosu and Ayako Hashizume
2. LNCS 14012, Human-Computer Interaction: Part II, edited by Masaaki Kurosu and Ayako Hashizume
3. LNCS 14013, Human-Computer Interaction: Part III, edited by Masaaki Kurosu and Ayako Hashizume
4. LNCS 14014, Human-Computer Interaction: Part IV, edited by Masaaki Kurosu and Ayako Hashizume
5. LNCS 14015, Human Interface and the Management of Information: Part I, edited by Hirohiko Mori and Yumi Asahi
6. LNCS 14016, Human Interface and the Management of Information: Part II, edited by Hirohiko Mori and Yumi Asahi
7. LNAI 14017, Engineering Psychology and Cognitive Ergonomics: Part I, edited by Don Harris and Wen-Chin Li
8. LNAI 14018, Engineering Psychology and Cognitive Ergonomics: Part II, edited by Don Harris and Wen-Chin Li
9. LNAI 14019, Augmented Cognition, edited by Dylan D. Schmorrow and Cali M. Fidopiastis
10. LNCS 14020, Universal Access in Human-Computer Interaction: Part I, edited by Margherita Antona and Constantine Stephanidis
11. LNCS 14021, Universal Access in Human-Computer Interaction: Part II, edited by Margherita Antona and Constantine Stephanidis
12. LNCS 14022, Cross-Cultural Design: Part I, edited by Pei-Luen Patrick Rau
13. LNCS 14023, Cross-Cultural Design: Part II, edited by Pei-Luen Patrick Rau
14. LNCS 14024, Cross-Cultural Design: Part III, edited by Pei-Luen Patrick Rau
15. LNCS 14025, Social Computing and Social Media: Part I, edited by Adela Coman and Simona Vasilache
16. LNCS 14026, Social Computing and Social Media: Part II, edited by Adela Coman and Simona Vasilache
17. LNCS 14027, Virtual, Augmented and Mixed Reality, edited by Jessie Y. C. Chen and Gino Fragomeni
18. LNCS 14028, Digital Human Modeling and Applications in Health, Safety, Ergonomics and Risk Management: Part I, edited by Vincent G. Duffy
19. LNCS 14029, Digital Human Modeling and Applications in Health, Safety, Ergonomics and Risk Management: Part II, edited by Vincent G. Duffy
20. LNCS 14030, Design, User Experience, and Usability: Part I, edited by Aaron Marcus, Elizabeth Rosenzweig and Marcelo Soares
21. LNCS 14031, Design, User Experience, and Usability: Part II, edited by Aaron Marcus, Elizabeth Rosenzweig and Marcelo Soares

22. LNCS 14032, Design, User Experience, and Usability: Part III, edited by Aaron Marcus, Elizabeth Rosenzweig and Marcelo Soares
23. LNCS 14033, Design, User Experience, and Usability: Part IV, edited by Aaron Marcus, Elizabeth Rosenzweig and Marcelo Soares
24. LNCS 14034, Design, User Experience, and Usability: Part V, edited by Aaron Marcus, Elizabeth Rosenzweig and Marcelo Soares
25. LNCS 14035, Culture and Computing, edited by Matthias Rauterberg
26. LNCS 14036, Distributed, Ambient and Pervasive Interactions: Part I, edited by Norbert Streitz and Shin'ichi Konomi
27. LNCS 14037, Distributed, Ambient and Pervasive Interactions: Part II, edited by Norbert Streitz and Shin'ichi Konomi
28. LNCS 14038, HCI in Business, Government and Organizations: Part I, edited by Fiona Fui-Hoon Nah and Keng Siau
29. LNCS 14039, HCI in Business, Government and Organizations: Part II, edited by Fiona Fui-Hoon Nah and Keng Siau
30. LNCS 14040, Learning and Collaboration Technologies: Part I, edited by Panayiotis Zaphiris and Andri Ioannou
31. LNCS 14041, Learning and Collaboration Technologies: Part II, edited by Panayiotis Zaphiris and Andri Ioannou
32. LNCS 14042, Human Aspects of IT for the Aged Population: Part I, edited by Qin Gao and Jia Zhou
33. LNCS 14043, Human Aspects of IT for the Aged Population: Part II, edited by Qin Gao and Jia Zhou
34. LNCS 14044, Adaptive Instructional Systems, edited by Robert A. Sottilare and Jessica Schwarz
35. LNCS 14045, HCI for Cybersecurity, Privacy and Trust, edited by Abbas Moallem
36. LNCS 14046, HCI in Games: Part I, edited by Xiaowen Fang
37. LNCS 14047, HCI in Games: Part II, edited by Xiaowen Fang
38. LNCS 14048, HCI in Mobility, Transport and Automotive Systems: Part I, edited by Heidi Krömker
39. LNCS 14049, HCI in Mobility, Transport and Automotive Systems: Part II, edited by Heidi Krömker
40. LNAI 14050, Artificial Intelligence in HCI: Part I, edited by Helmut Degen and Stavroula Ntoa
41. LNAI 14051, Artificial Intelligence in HCI: Part II, edited by Helmut Degen and Stavroula Ntoa
42. LNCS 14052, Design, Operation and Evaluation of Mobile Communications, edited by Gavriel Salvendy and June Wei
43. CCIS 1832, HCI International 2023 Posters - Part I, edited by Constantine Stephanidis, Margherita Antona, Stavroula Ntoa and Gavriel Salvendy
44. CCIS 1833, HCI International 2023 Posters - Part II, edited by Constantine Stephanidis, Margherita Antona, Stavroula Ntoa and Gavriel Salvendy
45. CCIS 1834, HCI International 2023 Posters - Part III, edited by Constantine Stephanidis, Margherita Antona, Stavroula Ntoa and Gavriel Salvendy
46. CCIS 1835, HCI International 2023 Posters - Part IV, edited by Constantine Stephanidis, Margherita Antona, Stavroula Ntoa and Gavriel Salvendy

47. CCIS 1836, HCI International 2023 Posters - Part V, edited by Constantine Stephanidis, Margherita Antona, Stavroula Ntoa and Gavriel Salvendy

https://2023.hci.international/proceedings

Preface

User experience (UX) refers to a person's thoughts, feelings, and behavior when using interactive systems. UX design becomes fundamentally important for new and emerging mobile, ubiquitous, and omnipresent computer-based contexts. The scope of design, user experience, and usability (DUXU) extends to all aspects of the user's interaction with a product or service, how it is perceived, learned, and used. DUXU also addresses design knowledge, methods, and practices, with a focus on deeply human-centered processes. Usability, usefulness, and appeal are fundamental requirements for effective user-experience design.

The 12th Design, User Experience, and Usability Conference (DUXU 2023), an affiliated conference of the HCI International conference, encouraged papers from professionals, academics, and researchers that report results and cover a broad range of research and development activities on a variety of related topics. Professionals include designers, software engineers, scientists, marketers, business leaders, and practitioners in fields such as AI, architecture, financial and wealth management, game design, graphic design, finance, healthcare, industrial design, mobile, psychology, travel, and vehicles.

This year's submissions covered a wide range of content across the spectrum of design, user-experience, and usability. The latest trends and technologies are represented, as well as contributions from professionals, academics, and researchers across the globe. The breadth of their work is indicated in the following topics covered in the proceedings.

Five volumes of the HCII 2023 proceedings are dedicated to this year's edition of the DUXU Conference:

- Part I addresses topics related to design methods, tools and practices, as well as emotional and persuasive design.
- Part II addresses topics related to design case studies, as well as creativity and design education.
- Part III addresses topics related to evaluation methods and techniques, as well as usability, user experience, and technology acceptance studies.
- Part IV addresses topics related to designing learning experiences, as well as design and user experience of chatbots, conversational agents, and robots.
- Part V addresses topics related to DUXU for cultural heritage, as well as DUXU for health and wellbeing.

The papers in these volumes were included for publication after a minimum of two single–blind reviews from the members of the DUXU Program Board or, in some cases, from Preface members of the Program Boards of other affiliated conferences. We would like to thank all of them for their invaluable contribution, support, and efforts.

July 2023   Aaron Marcus
                                                                    Elizabeth Rosenzweig
                                                                      Marcelo M. Soares

12th International Conference on Design, User Experience and Usability (DUXU 2023)

Program Board Chairs: **Aaron Marcus**, *Aaron Marcus and Associates, USA*, **Elizabeth Rosenzweig**, *World Usability Day and Bubble Mountain Consulting, USA*, and **Marcelo M. Soares**, *Southern University of Science and Technology – SUSTech, P.R. China*

Program Board:

- Sisira Adikari, *University of Canberra, Australia*
- Claire Ancient, *University of Winchester, UK*
- Eric Brangier, *Université de Lorraine, France*
- Tian Cao, *Nanjing University of Science & Technology, P.R. China*
- Silvia de los Ríos, *Indra, Spain*
- Romi Dey, *Lowe's India Pvt Ltd, India*
- Cristina Pires Dos Santos, *Polytechnic Institute of Beja, Portugal*
- Marc Fabri, *Leeds Beckett University, UK*
- Guneet Ghotra, *Wayne State University, USA*
- Michael Gibson, *University of North Texas, USA*
- Hao He, *Central Academy of Fine Arts, P.R. China*
- Wei Liu, *Beijing Normal University, P.R. China*
- Zhen Liu, *South China University of Technology, P.R. China*
- Keith Owens, *University of North Texas, USA*
- Gunther Paul, *James Cook University, Australia*
- Francisco Rebelo, *University of Lisbon, Portugal*
- Christine Riedmann-Streitz, *MarkenFactory GmbH, Germany*
- Patricia Search, *Rensselaer Polytechnic Institute, USA*
- Dorothy Shamonsky, *Brandeis University, USA*
- David Sless, *Communication Research Institute, Australia*
- Maksym Tkachuk, *service.so, Ukraine*
- Elisângela Vilar, *Universidade de Lisboa, Portugal*
- Wei Wang, *Hunan University, P.R. China*
- Haining Wang, *Hunan University, P.R. China*

The full list with the Program Board Chairs and the members of the Program Boards of all thematic areas and affiliated conferences of HCII2023 is available online at:

http://www.hci.international/board-members-2023.php

HCI International 2024 Conference

The 26th International Conference on Human-Computer Interaction, HCI International 2024, will be held jointly with the affiliated conferences at the Washington Hilton Hotel, Washington, DC, USA, June 29 – July 4, 2024. It will cover a broad spectrum of themes related to Human-Computer Interaction, including theoretical issues, methods, tools, processes, and case studies in HCI design, as well as novel interaction techniques, interfaces, and applications. The proceedings will be published by Springer. More information will be made available on the conference website: http://2024.hci.international/.

General Chair
Prof. Constantine Stephanidis
University of Crete and ICS-FORTH
Heraklion, Crete, Greece
Email: general_chair@hcii2024.org

https://2024.hci.international/

Contents – Part IV

Designing Learning Experiences

The Attention of Students in the Metaverse: Practical Application   3
    Layane Araújo, Marcelo M. Soares, Romero Tori, and Yijing Zhang

Interactive Design of Immersive First Aid Skills Teaching Based
on Multimedia Devices   24
    Yunfei Chen

Interactive Video: Application in Narrative Competence Education of 1st
to 3rd Grade Primary School Children   39
    Wei-na Chien and Mang-mang Zhang

Optimization Strategy of Guidance Methods of Online Education
Information Transmission   58
    Jimiao Dong, Jian Wang, Jing Tan, Ziye Wang, and Jiahao Sun

Multimedia and Multisensory International Learning: Making a Case
for Going Beyond the Screen During Creative Virtual Exchanges   77
    Denielle J. Emans and Kelly M. Murdoch-Kitt

A Focused Exploration About How Technologically Enhanced Educational
Approaches Can Positively Foster Early Childhood to Young Adult
Learning and Creativity   88
    Michael R. Gibson and Keith M. Owens

VR and AR Application in Academia, Overview in the Middle East
Universities   98
    Rund Hiyasat, Lindita Bande, Khaled Galal Ahmed, Baraah Hamdoon,
    Jose Lopez Berengueres, and Abdul-Aziz Banawi

Study on the Tangible User Interface Jigsaw Puzzle for Curing
ADHD/ADD Children   111
    Qian Lai, Chun Yu, Yuanchun Shi, and Yingqing Xu

VPlaytime: Face-to-Face Recess in Virtual Reality Classrooms   120
    Xin Li, DanDan Yu, Min Wang, and WenJing Li

Transdisciplinary Teaching and Learning in Summer Camp by Service
Design 131
   Manhai Li, Lianyu Huang, and Yingxuan Li

Chinese Character Learning and Platform Tool Development for Junior
Primary School Student Based on Orthographic Awareness 142
   Zhen Liu and Ziyu Lin

Pair-Teamwork Effect on First Semester IT Students to Achieve
Collaborative Learning Through Social Relations 154
   Jan P. Nees and XiaoLei Bi

Potential Attempt to Treat Attention Deficit/Hyperactivity Disorder
(ADHD) Children with Engineering Education Games 166
   Zhiya Tan, Zhen Liu, and Shiqi Gong

Playable Modeling: Interactive Learning Process in Science and Art 185
   Qi Tan

A Study on the Effect of Teaching Effectiveness of Online Courses
and the Number of Bullet Screen 200
   Gengyi Wang, Wenda Tian, and Qianhang Qin

Research on Undergraduate Classroom Teaching Quality Assurance
System Based on Student Experience 212
   Qiong Yang

Research on the Application of Interaction Design in the Digital Education
of Traditional Crafts 221
   Hai'ou Yang

Trends in Research Related to Product Design for Rural Teaching
from 2012 to 2022: A Bibliometric and Knowledge Mapping Analysis 239
   Xing Yuan, Yang Zhao, Yixin Xie, Liuyi Wu, and Tiantian Wang

A Study on the Fogg Behavior Model in Designing Educational Apps
for Children 249
   Youtian Zhou, Qianhang Qin, Bo Tang, and Wenda Tian

Teaching Design Practice of Statistics Course for Economics
and Management Majors Based on Humanized Participation Mode Model
Technology 262
   Jixu Zhu, Xiaoshi Chen, and Zhichao Liu

Chatbots, Conversational Agents and Robots: Design and User Experience

Exploring Emotions in Avatar Design to Increase Adherence to Chatbot
Technology 273
    Bernardo Cortes, Júlia Teles, and Emília Duarte

Rethinking Interaction with Conversational Agents: How to Create
a Positive User Experience Utilizing Dialog Patterns 283
    Marvin Heuer, Tom Lewandowski, Joffrey Weglewski, Tom Mayer,
    Max Kubicek, Patrick Lembke, Simon Ortgiese, and Tilo Böhmann

Towards Effective Conversational Agents: A Prototype-Based Approach
for Facilitating Their Evaluation and Improvement 302
    Marvin Heuer, Tom Lewandowski, Emir Kučević, Jannis Hellmich,
    Michael Raykhlin, Stefan Blum, and Tilo Böhmann

Towards Validating a Chatbot Usability Scale 321
    Samuel Holmes, Raymond Bond, Anne Moorhead, Jane Zheng,
    Vivien Coates, and Michael McTear

Exploring Active and Critical Engagement in Human-Robot Interaction
to Develop Programming Skills: A Pilot Study 340
    Deepti Mishra, Yavuz Inal, Karen Parish, Guillermo Arroyo Romero,
    and Rumi Rajbhandari

A Comparative Analysis of Real Time Open-Source Speech Recognition
Tools for Social Robots 355
    Akshara Pande, Bhanu Shrestha, Anshul Rani, and Deepti Mishra

It's a Long Way to Neutrality. An Evaluation of Gendered Artificial Faces 366
    Oronzo Parlangeli, Paola Palmitesta, Leonardo Masi,
    Michele Tittarelli, and Stefano Guidi

Author Index 379

Designing Learning Experiences

The Attention of Students in the Metaverse: Practical Application

Layane Araújo[1]([⊠]), Marcelo M. Soares[2,3], Romero Tori[4], and Yijing Zhang[5]

[1] Federal University of Pernambuco, Recife, Brazil
layane.araujo@ufpe.br
[2] SUSTech – Southern University of Science and Technology, Shenzhen, People's Republic of China
[3] Post Graduate Program of Design, Federal University of Pernambuco, Recife, Brazil
soaresmm@gmail.com
[4] University of São Paulo, USP, São Paulo, Brazil
tori@usp.br
[5] Southern University of Science and Technology, Shenzhen, People's Republic of China
12010839@mail.sustech.edu.cn

Abstract. It is known that the new global paradigms have been modifying the teaching and learning relationships. Soon, educational activities broke the boundaries of the physical classroom and headed to the virtual field, like the metaverse. Knowing that attention plays a fundamental role in the construction of knowledge, a pilot experiment was carried out with a class of undergraduate design students from the Southern University of Science and Technology of China in the teaching space of the metaverse hosted in the Frame VR software, with the objective of to identify the students' attention during the class given. To assess attention, images correlated to the class content and 3D models outside the classroom at specific moments of the class were presented. As a result, students performed better in terms of focused attention while watching videos in class, as they did not identify which 3D models were placed outside the room for them to identify at those times. Regarding the images, most students did not respond to the teacher's commands to look at screens and identify the images presented, proving that they did not have focused attention in class at these times. However, all students reported that they found the experience unprecedented and that the immersive environment of the metaverse has elements that divert the attention of the class. This article aims to present a guiding experience of a doctoral thesis in progress in the Design course at the Federal University of Pernambuco, Brazil, which proposes to present ergonomic design guidelines to assist teaching activities that take place in metaverse spaces. This experience will serve as a guide for future experiments to follow in other teaching scenarios in the metaverse and with different audiences.

Keywords: Design · Teaching Environment · Attention · Metaverse

1 Introduction

It is known that the new global paradigms have been modifying the teaching and learning relationships. However, Sarmento (2018) argues that in the current context, the school environment, which features rowed desks arranged in front of the traditional blackboard, does not correspond, in technology, comfort, and quality, to the demands of the new relationships between students, teaching and digital culture.

In fact, according to the author, the new paradigm is based on Hybrid Education, or blended learning. Part of the learning that takes place online via the internet, allowing the student to maximize their individual potential, develop new skills to solve real life issues.

With the COVID-19 pandemic, "distance learning" intensified, and "on-site" teaching decreased. From one moment to the next, a multitude of online school activities promoted by teachers was announced. As a result, teachers and students enrolled in courses that were previously face-to-face migrated to networked educational activities (Couto et al. 2020).

Soon, educational activities broke the boundaries of the physical classroom and headed to the virtual field, like the metaverse. Metaverse is a multi-user online interactive digital environment in which people participate and interact, with the environment and other users, through their avatars. These entities represent the students and are controlled by them. The gamified interface of these environments is relatively easy to use and pleasant for students.

Design is a multidisciplinary field encompassing social, anthropological, psychological, marketing, and ergonomic aspects. Given this, the designer can provide a space that helps in its user's behavior, conduct, and performance. Concerning the environment and learning relationship, Kastrup (2004); Araujo (2020); Lima, Queiroz, and Sant'anna (2018), emphasize that attention plays a fundamental role in the construction of knowledge.

It was observed that there is already some research dedicated to understanding the relationship between attention and learning and the physically built environment for teaching (Bernardes and Vergara, 2021; Araujo, 2020). Motivated by this fact, this study, which is part of a doctoral thesis in Design from the Federal University of Pernambuco, Brazil, aims to understand the relationship between attention and the teaching environment in metaverse virtual reality.

To this end, a teaching activity was carried out in a metaverse, in partnership with the School of Design, SUSTech – Southern University of Science and Technology, China. The class was taught to a group of seven students in the FRAME VR software, which allows the creation of immersive collaboration spaces that run from the browser on desktop, mobile, or VR. For this experiment, it was decided not to use equipment such as Virtual Reality glasses.

2   Design, Ergonomics, and Teaching in the Metaverse

To better understand the concepts of Design, Ergonomics, and Metaverse, this topic aims to establish a relationship between them and teaching environments.

Design means to develop and conceive (Bürdek, 2010). In this case, the designer creates artifacts, environments, and services. To this end, Ergonomics must be an integral part of this process since ergonomics is an area that aims to transform and adapt not only the work but also the space to the different needs of human beings, taking into account their limitations and characteristics.

According to Soares (2021, p. 47), Ergonomics can contribute to the generation of design concepts, providing designers with an understanding of users' physical and cognitive needs to generate solutions compatible with the function to be performed.

Thus, combining Design and Ergonomics in social and educational interventions is necessary. According to Iida and Guimarães (2016), ergonomic requirements allow for maximizing user comfort, satisfaction, and safety.

Harrison et al. (2019) state that Design interventions in the educational environment can improve the quality of teaching and learning. According to Barrett et al. (2013; 2015; 2017), teaching environments interfere with student performance. For example, physical comfort factors such as light, temperature, noise, the flexibility of layout, complexity, and color, and issues related to belonging directly influence student learning.

Araujo (2020), corroborating with the author, states that the educational space is configured in a social environment, where human relationships, users' cultural context, preferences, and satisfaction interfere with the activity.

Thus, Ahmad, Osman, and Halim (2013) state that students perform better when they appreciate their educational environment. Therefore, human perception of the environment should be one of the determining factors in the development of space design.

According to Bins Ely (2003) and Paiva (2018), the influence of the built environment on the individual's behavior is related to both the requirements of the task performed in the environment and the characteristics and needs of the user. The activities performed in physical spaces are mediated by human cognition and perception to optimize users' physical, psychological, and emotional needs for these environments.

In the case of the teaching environment, the main tasks performed are teaching and learning, and being "attention" a predictor of learning (Araújo, 2018; Lima, Queiroz and Sant'anna, 2018), these tasks will be used in the metaverse to evaluate the student-teaching environment and performance relationship.

According to Iida and Guimarães (2016), attention is the concentration of perception on a subject, enhancing information processing. Sternberg (2008) defines attention as the phenomenon by which an individual processes a limited amount of the total information available in the environment through the sense organs, stored memories, and other cognitive processes.

In their studies, Kaplan and Kaplan (1982) investigate how the properties of environments, natural or built, can restore fatigue and attention to their users. For the authors, the environment can enable the renewal of directed attention and, consequently, the reduction of mental fatigue; that is, the space must provide a means by which this attention reaches a state of equilibrium.

In this study, concentrated, divided, and alternating attention was evaluated. The first kind of attention (concentration) is the ability to select only one source of information in the face of multiple distracting stimuli in a given period (Rueda, 2017). The second one (divided attention) is the ability to focus on two or more stimuli simultaneously (Rueda and de Castro, 2010). Finally, the third kind of attention (alternating attention) is the ability to focus sometimes on one stimulus, sometimes on another, alternately, during a given period (Rueda, Castro, Sisto, 2010).

But does this also apply to online learning?

Over the years, several scientific studies have found no significant differences in students' academic performance when comparing the effectiveness of remote and traditional teaching (Machtmes and Asher, 2000; Bernard et al., 2004; Lou, Bernard and Abrami, 2006).

Siemens et al. (2015), in their comparative studies between distance and traditional teaching, state that distance learning is more effective, or at least as effective as instruction given in the traditional classroom (Siemens et al. 2015, p. 34). Thus, Ortega-Rodriguez (2022) stresses the importance of implementing emerging technologies in the education of the future in order to improve the teaching-learning process.

Sarmento (2018) discusses the change in social paradigms, the inclusion of hybrid teaching (classes in physical and virtual teaching environments), and technological tools in the learning process. For the author, this type of teaching allows shared learning, with broad access to information at any time, a profound change in the roles played by teachers and students, and the flexibilization of pre-established concepts (Sarmento, 2018, p. 21).

In this way, educational activities broke the boundaries of the physical classroom. They headed to the virtual field, such as the metaverse:

In a metaverse-type environment, it is the avatar that appears in place of the person, which makes them more at ease, without the other classmates feeling more distant because they have the feeling of all being together in the same environment. In addition, the gamified interface of these environments is quite enjoyable and easy to use for current generations of students, even graduate students (Tori, 2022, p. 53).

According to Schlemmer and Backes (2008), the metaverse presents real character and public and private utility because it is an extension of the real space of the physical world within a virtual environment on the internet. That is, it is a replication of the physical world.

Thus, due to its characteristic of replicating a real environment or creating an immersive environment, ensuring ease of access for students in remote and online modes. As a result, educational activities have been developed in these metaverse spaces, such as military training (Siyaev and Jo, 2021), health educational activities (Koo, 2021), science education (Jovanovic and Milosavljevic, 2022; Tori, 2022), artistic activities (Tasa and Gorgulu, 2010; Choi and Kim, 2017), among others.

Lee et al. (2022) demonstrated that using the Metaverse platform in university education could enhance the active participation of students in classes, thus allowing the extension of traditional learning. Schlemmer and Backes (2015) explain that the development of online education in the metaverse can contribute to raising the quality of education in the world educational scenario through pedagogical proposals.

A class was conducted within a metaverse platform aiming to understand the use of the metaverse in teaching activities. Afterward, tests were carried out to analyze the performance and attention of the participating students. The experiment will be better detailed in the following topic.

3   The Experiment

The experiment was conducted in partnership with the School of Design, SUSTECH – Southern University of Science and Technology, China. The class was about Design for Augmented and Virtual Reality, in the course "Usability for Products and Systems" for a class of seven students, in the 3rd year, of the Design undergraduate course of the referred university.

The space chosen was the campus, developed for the Frame VR platform, beta version (Fig. 1). It was chosen because it is already active and simulates a university campus. In addition, the intention was to study a space already used for teaching activities.

Fig. 1. Campus – Frame VR beta version. Source: authors (2022).

The primary purpose was to understand the relationship between the space and the elements of its composition chosen for the analysis, the educational activity developed and its users, identifying through observational methods (observation and recordings of the action) during the teaching activity, and interactional (applied questionnaire), after the class given. The experiment aimed to show how the environment and surrounding elements can influence the students' attention and improve the didactics used in the classroom.

3.1   Technical Details

The software used was FRAME VR, the beta version. The number of individuals allowed in the virtual space was a maximum of 15 individuals interacting in the space with their avatars, and a maximum of 15 spectators, with no direct interaction in the activity. Students were instructed to access tutorials for using the software and create their avatars before the class started.

The subjects were also instructed to use computers to access the environment. Smartphones and other equipment were not allowed for this experiment, so that everyone could share the same experience.

The experiment lasted 1 h and 50 min. The class content, which theme was Design for Augmented and Virtual Reality, comprised 32 slides containing six videos, three 3D models, and five illustrative images.

Attention tests were conducted during the lecture. Three types of attention were evaluated: Concentrated Attention, Divided Attention, and Alternate Attention.

3.2   Activity Script

The class started at 2:00 pm and finished at 3:50 pm Shenzhen time, China, equivalent to 3:00 am to 4:50 am Recife time, Brazil.

Students were instructed to arrive at least 15 min early to test their Avatars (previously created) in the teaching space.

Two assistants (one of them a student of the course), a teacher, and an observer participated the experiment activities on the virtual campus. The assistants directed the students inside the space to the location chosen for the lesson. The activities for each assistant and the observer were:

- One assistant helped the teacher during the lesson by adding or changing elements of the scenario relative to the content and testing the experiment at specific times.
- The other assistant helped students when required.
- The observer did not use an avatar, remaining invisible and without communication during the class. She only observed the students' positioning during the experiment.

Once in the previously prepared space, the teacher displayed his slide presentation and began the lesson. The position of the teacher in the virtual space can be seen in Fig. 2:

Fig. 2. The position of the teacher in the classroom was created by Frame VR – campus – beta version. Source: authors (2022).

The space chosen within the campus presented is a classroom with a maximum capacity of 12 individuals positioned at each bench.

This space was chosen because of its favorable positioning for the experiment. It has a large glass window that allows students to see outside the room, as is usually the case in traditional classrooms, which have a window to the outside of the space.

Three sliding screens were used – one in front of the desk and two on the left and right sides, with the landscape on the left side shown through the large glass window.

The side screens displayed images presented during the lesson, correlating with the experiment's content.

The experiment took place in three distinct parts: (1) display of images relating to the content on the side screens, (2) display of 3D models walking around in the garden outside the classroom, and (3) presentation of a quiz. The first two parts occurred at alternating times during the class.

The First Part of the Experiment: Display of Images Relating to the Content on the Side Screens.

During the lesson, at a specific moment, the teacher asked the students to look at the screen on the right and, at a certain moment, the screen on the left.

It was observed whether the students had their attention focused on the lesson and complied with the teacher's command to turn to the right and left screen at the requested time and returned their gaze to the main screen when the teacher continued the lesson. It took an average of 2 s for the image to be displayed on the indicated screens, and the image remained on the screen for 10 s.

This activity allowed the analyses of the students' Concentrated Attention and Alternate Attention. The moments observed are arranged in the order in Table 1, which follows.

Table 1. Observed moments of part 1 of the experiment

Observed moments	
First observation	The students turned at the exact moment of the teacher's prompt (2 s)
Second observation	The students turned only at the moment the image appeared on the screen
Third observation	The students turned the wrong way
Fourth observation	The students did not see the picture

Below, we describe the five images, their relationship to the lesson content, and the position in which it was shown.

The first image (Fig. 3) was displayed at the end of slide 3. Lesson content: What is virtual reality, and what interactive devices are used for virtual reality? Was the image displayed on the right screen?

Fig. 3. Virtual reality glasses. Source: google images (2022).

The second image (Fig. 4) was displayed at the end of slide 6. Lesson content: Fundamental concepts for VR. The image was displayed on the left screen.

Fig. 4. Man wearing a virtual reality glasses. Source: google images (2022).

The third image (Fig. 5) was presented at the end of slide 10. Lesson content: What is Augmented Reality? – image displayed on left screen (pattern break).

Fourth image (Fig. 6): at the end of slide 20. Lesson content: Considerations for the VR Design Process: Safety and Comfort – image displayed on the right screen.

Fig. 5. Augmented reality. Source: google images (2022).

Fig. 6. Menu inside a virtual reality. Source: google images (2022).

Fifth image (Fig. 7): at the end of slide 26. Lesson content: Assessing Human Behaviors – image displayed on the right screen (pattern break).

Fig. 7. Medical training in virtual reality. Source: google images (2022).

At the end of displaying each image, students should turn their attention to the main slide, allowing the analysis of alternating attention.

The Second Part of the Experiment: The Display of 3D Models Walking Around in the Garden Outside the Classroom

In this step of the experiment, it was observed whether the student's paid attention to the lesson and the 3D objects simultaneously, allowing the evaluation of divided attention.

Three 3D models were arranged outside the classroom during the lesson and at specific times. The students could view the objects through the glass window of the classroom. At a particular interval of time, the objects were excluded.

Since the software notifies those present when a new object is added to the space, the models were inserted into the environment before the students started the class. To assess divided attention, at these moments, the teacher continued explaining the content, and the video of the exact moment of the model's appearance continued to be shown on the main screen. It was verified, through a questionnaire applied after the class, if the students could look at the model and understand the content presented at that exact moment of its appearance.

The models were, respectively, a dog, a dinosaur, and a car. The moments in which the models appeared are described below:

First 3D model, dog (Fig. 8): shown, on slide 4, during the video, showed the virtual reality to explore human organs.

Fig. 8. First 3D model: a dog. Source: Sketchfab (2022).

The second 3D model was a dinosaur (Fig. 9): shown on slide 13 of the video named "This is Why Mixed Reality or MR is a Big Deal".

Fig. 9. Second 3D model: a dinosaur. Source: Sketchfab (2022).

The third 3D model was a sports car (Fig. 10): shown during slide 23, during the video that presents how McLaren Automotive uses virtual reality to design its sports cars and supercars.

Fig. 10. Third 3D model: a sports car. Source: Sketchfab (2022).

After these experiment steps, the students were given a questionnaire displayed on the room's main screen. Then, they were required to read the questions, answer them, and send the answers later by email.

The Third Part of the Experiment: Presentation of a Quiz
The displayed quiz had nine questions. The first five were related to the images presented during the class on the side screens, left and right. The questions had the following format: Q1. What was the first image presented? After that, two images were presented on the screen similar in complexity to the image initially presented, as shown in Table 2.

Table 2. Questions and respective images were presented to students to choose their answers.

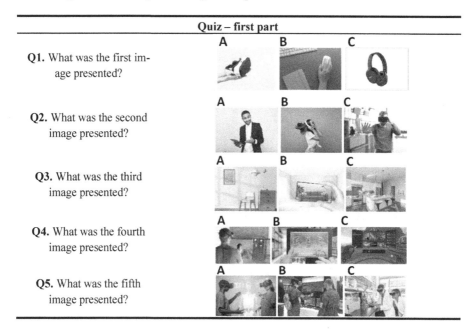

After this first block of questions, three questions were presented regarding the 3D models shown outside the classroom, in the garden. The questions are shown in Table 3.

The last question, presented at the end of the questionnaire, asked the students about their general understanding of the content presented in class. The question was: **Q9** – What is the difference between Virtual Reality, Augmented Reality, and Mixed Reality?

Table 3. Questions were posed to students regarding the 3D models seen in the space.

Quiz – Second part
Q6 – In the video that showed the human organs seen in Virtual Reality, did you observe any 3D models from outside the virtual room?   Answer YES or NO. If yes, what did you see?
Q7 – In the video that introduced mixed reality, did you observe any 3D models from the outside of the virtual room?   Answer YES or NO. If yes, what did you see?
Q8 – In the video that showed the use of virtual reality in car design at McLaren Automotive, did you observe any 3D models from outside the virtual room?   Answer YES or NO. If yes, what did you see?

After the experiment, the data collected was analyzed and presented in the following topic.

4 Results and Discussion

The participants were previously informed that this experiment would be carried out during the class. Therefore, the movements made by the students' avatars during the class were observed to analyze attention in the teaching space. For this, it was initially necessary to understand how the movement of the avatars occurs in the FRAME VR software.

4.1 Avatar Movements

In the Frame VR platform, the avatar moves according to the user's direction. This factor was crucial for the analysis of attention in the classroom. If the user, even standing still, looks to one side, that is, only positions the mouse or touchpad to the place in which he wishes to observe, left, right, up, or down and the avatar will also turn its head to the side in which the user was looking. For example, if the user positions the mouse to the right side, the avatar will also turn its head to this side.

The user can also use the directional keypads, which can be the arrow keys on the keyboard, left, right, up(front), and down(back), or the keys of the letters W(front), A(left), S(back), D(right). Again, the avatar will move in the direction indicated, turning the whole "body" in this case. To better elucidate this explanation refer to Figs. 11 and 12.

To evaluate the participants' attention on the metaverse used, it was checked which way each student's avatar was directed during the moments specified in the previous topic of the lesson.

At the beginning of the lesson (Fig. 13) students were told in advance that they should look at screen number 1 or number 2, their right and left sides, respectively, facing the main screen. This action must occur when the teacher has notified them.

Fig. 11. Image sequence showing the avatar looking up, down, and forward, respectively. Source: authors (2022).

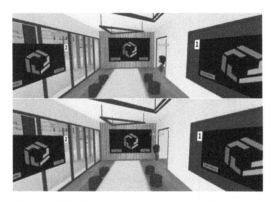

Fig. 12. Avatar turns the whole body to look at the left and right sides. Source: authors (2022).

Fig. 13. Beginning of the class. Source: authors (2022).

The next step analyzes each part of the experiment:

Analyzing the First Part of the Experiment: Display of Images Relating to the Content on the Side Screens

It was verified for each of the images presented during the class, the items that indicate the moments observed in Table 1. In addition, the number of students who performed the expected movements was checked, as shown in Table 4.

There was a technical delay in the display of the first image (Fig. 14). Despite this, one student turned at the exact moment of the teacher's command to the correct side, showing that he was paying attention in class, while another turned to the wrong side. The others did not follow the teacher's command to look at the image on screen number 1, so we can suppose that they were not paying attention to the content.

However, on the quiz, four students stated that they saw the first image, accenting it among the options presented.

For the second image, it was observed that two students turned the wrong way at the time of its display. The remaining students did not respond to the teacher's command. Therefore, none of the students saw the second image.

For the third image, it was observed that one student responded to the teacher's command. However, he turned to the wrong side. The conclusion of the observation is that none of the students saw image number 3.

Four students got images 3 and 4 right among the options presented in the questionnaire. The classroom observation results can be seen in Fig. 15, which follows.

For the fourth image (Fig. 16), none of the students turned in at the requested time. Therefore, none of the students saw the presented image. But in the quiz, one student got image four right out of the options shown.

For the fifth and last image, it was concluded that two students viewed the image (Fig. 17). Initially, the first student turned to the wrong side and then turned to the correct side, while the other student immediately turned to the correct side as instructed by the teacher. The other students did not respond to the given command. In the quiz, two students got image five right out of the choices presented.

Since the images were displayed near the slides' beginning, middle, and end, through the observational method, it was noted that the greatest number of student distractions occurred in the middle part of the lesson, demonstrating that students were mainly distracted by their surroundings. Some students did not respond to any of the commands given.

However, according to the questionnaire responses, the highest number of hits was on the first images presented, showing that the student's attention was lost throughout the lesson. Most students were dispersed during the 45 min lesson, not paying attention to the teacher's commands to look at images 4 and 5.

Analyzing the Second Part of the Experiment: The Display of 3D Models Walking Around in the Garden Outside the Classroom

As stated earlier, the second part of the experiment took place alternately with the first part. While the teacher was showing videos during the class, outside the room, through the window, three 3D models were shown. They slowly walked along the sidewalk outside.

The purpose of this part of the experiment was to check the alternating attention and divided attention of the students concerning the models presented and the lesson content.

Table 4. Observed moments of part 1 of the experiment.

Pictures	Observed moments		Number of students who executed this movement from (0 to 7)
First Image	**First observation**	The students turned at the exact moment of the teacher's prompt (2 s)	1
	Second observation	The students turned only at the moment the image appeared on the screen	1
	Third observation	The students turned the wrong way	0
	Fourth observation	The students did not see the picture	5
Second Image	**First observation**	The students turned at the exact moment of the teacher's prompt (2 s)	0
	Second observation	The students turned only at the moment the image appeared on the screen	0
	Third observation	The students turned the wrong way	2
	Fourth observation	The students did not see the picture	7
Third Image	**First observation**	The students turned at the exact moment of the teacher's prompt (2 s)	0
	Second observation	The students turned only at the moment the image appeared on the screen	0
	Third observation	The students turned the wrong way	1
	Fourth observation	The students did not see the picture	7
Fourth image	**First observation**	The students turned at the exact moment of the teacher's prompt (2 s)	0
	Second observation	The students turned only at the moment the image appeared on the screen	0

(*continued*)

Table 4. (*continued*)

Pictures	Observed moments		Number of students who executed this movement from (0 to 7)
	Third observation	The students turned the wrong way	0
	Fourth observation	The students did not see the picture	7
Fifth image	**First observation**	The students turned at the exact moment of the teacher's prompt (2 s)	1
	Second observation	The students turned only at the moment the image appeared on the screen	0
	Third observation	The students turned the wrong way	1
	Fourth observation	The students did not see the picture	5

Fig. 14. Only two students respond to the teacher's command. Source: authors (2022).

Fig. 15. Two students turning the wrong way in the display of image 2, figure on the right, and a student turning the wrong way in the display of image 3, figure on the left. Source: authors (2022).

The students answered an evaluative questionnaire to see if they saw the models during the lesson, and the result is presented in Table 5.

Fig. 16. None of the students turned during the display of the fourth image. Source: authors (2022).

Fig. 17. Two students viewed the fifth image. Source: authors (2022).

Table 5. Observed moments of part 2 of the experiment.

3D Models	How many students saw the models through the window outside the room? (From 0 to 7 students.)
Model 1 – dog	None of the students saw the dog
Model 2 – dinosaur	A student saw a dinosaur
Model 3 – sports car	None of the students saw the sports car

The moments of the 3D model display are shown in Figs. 18, 19, and 20.

Fig. 18. None of the students saw the dog. Source: authors (2022).

One of the students further stated that he saw the assisting green robot placed in the field to move the 3D objects, which were camouflaged in the landscape, but did not see any of the 3D objects.

Another student said that he zoomed in on the screen to get a better view of the displayed videos, thus overlooking the distracting elements of the environment.

Fig. 19. A student claimed to see the dinosaur. Source: authors (2022).

Fig. 20. None of the students saw the sports car. Source: authors (2022).

It was concluded that most students who did not see the objects were focused on the videos.

Analyze the Third Part of the Experiment: Presentation of a Quiz
The result of the quiz was presented in those provided above, through a method of comparative observational analysis of the students' actions during the experiment and the answers given by them in the quiz.

After applying the quiz, a final interview was conducted with the students so they could give their reports about the experiment.

Some students stated that they could not concentrate on the lesson in the metaverse since everything in the immersive environment was inviting. One student commented that he had to consciously make an effort to be able to pay attention to the class content. Another student pointed out that one of the reasons for their lack of concentration was precisely the distracting elements (3D models) purposely placed for the experiment outside the classroom window.

After only thirteen minutes of class, the students started playing in the space, applying effects to the environment, and changing the appearance of their avatars, as illustrated in Fig. 21.

Fig. 21. Students applied effects in space on the left and changed the appearance of their avatars on the right. Source: authors (2022).

Technical problems occurred during the experiment concerning the connection between some students and the participating teacher. This problem caused the students to become disoriented halfway through the class and to take a while to regain concentration on the content. So, when the teacher was out of the room, the students started adding 3D models to the space and other effects (Fig. 22), even though they were told that at the end of the class they could interact freely with the space.

Fig. 22. Students added 3D models and applied effects in the room. Source: authors (2022).

One student also stated that he felt dizzy from the metaverse experience, even though he was using a computer and not wearing virtual immersion goggles.

One of the main complaints was related to the videos presented. It occurred due to the instability of the connection and showed delays in the display of the content.

However, all the students said it was an exciting and innovative lesson, and they approved of the experience. Figure 23 shows the chart signed by all participants at the end of the class.

Fig. 23. Students signed a board at the end of class on the left and freely enjoyed the space on the right. Source: authors (2022).

In the end, the students were let out to explore the campus (Fig. 21), and the students were able to interact with the environment and have fun in the space. They freely placed effects in the courtyard and other 3D models.

5 Conclusion

After analyzing the students' attention, it was identified that they showed more concentrated attention during the videos since they did not identify the 3D models that were shown in the scenario. Given this, they showed low divided and alternating attention performance in this activity.

For the presented images, students showed low performance in focused attention regarding the content and the lesson explanation since they did not follow the teacher's commands to turn and observe the images on the screens at the suggested times. In addition, they also failed to alternate attention since they could not keep their attention on the content and identify the images presented.

The results of this experiment will guide new experiments that will be developed and applied during the preparation of the thesis that aims to answer what a suitable virtual reality learning environment would be like for carrying out educational activities. Thus, it was observed that the experiment carried out had some flaws, which we hope to correct for subsequent experiments of this type to be carried out, such as the connection problems presented.

It is intended to do another test, still with undergraduate students, in the same campus metaverse presented, but in classrooms with no visualization of the external environment, to compare the results.

Another group that we intend to evaluate will be graduate students. It is expected that the activities developed with this group will be more effective due to the maturity of this public.

The authors wish to thank the Foundation for the Support of Science and Technology of the State of Pernambuco (FACEPE), Brazil, for the financial support of the research.

References

Che Ahmad, C.N., Osman, K., Halim, L.: Physical and psychosocial aspects of the learning environment in the science laboratory and their relationship to teacher satisfaction. Learn. Environ. Res. **16**(3), 367–385 (2013). https://doi.org/10.1007/s10984-013-9136-8

Araujo, M.C.: O papel do ambiente construído sobre a educação: a influência sobre a atenção e a relação com o aprendizado. Tese (Doutorado) – Universidade Federal de Pernambuco. Centro de Artes e Comunicação. Programa de Pós-Graduação em Design (2020)

Barrett, P., et al.: A holistic, multi-level analysis identifying the impact of classroom design on pupils' learning. Build. Environ. **59**, 678–689 (2013)

Barrett, P., et al.: The impact of classroom design on pupils' learning: Final results of a holistic, multi-level analysis. Build. Environ. **89**, 118–133 (2015)

Barrett, P., et al.: The holistic impact of classroom spaces on learning in specific subjects. Environ. Behav. **49**(4), 425–451 (2017)

Bernardes, M., Vergara, L.G.L.: Attention in the classroom: how can restorative environments contribute? Oculum Ensaios **19** (2021)

Bernard, R.M., et al.: How does distance education compare with classroom instruction? A meta-analysis of the empirical literature. Rev. Educ. Res. **74**(3), 379–439 (2004)

Bins Ely, V.H.M.: Ergonomia + Arquitetura: buscando um melhor desempenho do ambiente físico. In: 3th Congresso Internacional de Ergonomia e Usabilidade de Interfaces Humano-Tecnologia: Produtos, Programas, Informação, Ambiente Construído. LEUI/PUC-Rio, Rio de Janeiro (2003)

Bürdek, B.E.: História, Teoria e Prática do Design de Produtos. Tradução Freddy Van Camp. Edgard Blücher, São Paulo (2010)

Choi, H.S., Kim, S.H.: A content service deployment plan for metaverse museum exhibitions – centering on the combination of beacons and HMDs. Int. J. Inf. Manage. **37**(1), 1519–1527 (2017)

Couto, E.S., Couto, E.S., de Cruz, I.M.P.: Stay home: education in the Covid-19 pandemic. Education **8**(3), 200–217 (2020)

Harrison, J.R., Soares, D.A., Rudzinski, S., Johnson, R.: Attention deficit hyperactivity disorders and classroom-based interventions: evidence-based status, effectiveness, and moderators of effects in single-case design research. Rev. Educ. Res. **89**(4), 569–611 (2019)

Iida, I., Guimarães, L.B.M.: Ergonomics: Design and Production, 3rd edn. Edgard Blucher, São Paulo (2016)

Jovanovic, A., Milosavljevic, A.: VoRtex metaverse platform for gamified collaborative learning. Electronics **11**(3), 317 (2022)

Kaplan, S., Kaplan, R.: Cognition and Environment: Functioning in an Uncertain World. Praeger, New York (1982)

Kastrup, V.: The learning of attention in inventive cognition. Psychol. Soc. **16**(3), 7–16 (2004)

Koo, H.: Training in lung cancer surgery through the metaverse, including extended reality, in the smart operating room of Seoul National University Bundang Hospital. J. Educ. Éval. Health Prof. 18 (2021)

Lee, I., Sung, Y., Kim, T.: The Expanding Role of Metaverse Platform in College Education. ICIC Express Letters, Part B: Applications 13 (2022)

Lima, C.L., Queiroz, E.C.S.B., Sant'anna, G.J.: The relationship between concentration and learning: the use of TIDC for learning to learn. Multidiscipl. Sci. J. Nucleus Knowl. **5**(11), 161–186 (2018)

Lou, Y., Bernard, R.M., Abrami, P.C.: Media and pedagogy in undergraduate distance education: a theory-based meta-analysis of empirical literature. Educ. Technol. Res. **54**(2), 141–176 (2006)

Machtmes, K., Asher, J.W.: A meta-analysis of the effectiveness of telecourses in distance education. Am. J. Dist. Educ. **14**(1), 27–46 (2000)

Ortega-Rodríguez, P.J.: De La Realidad Extendida al Metaverso: una Reflexión Crítica sobre las Aportaciones a La Educación. Teoría De La Educación. Revista Interuniversitaria **34**(2), 189–208 (2022)

Paiva, M.M.B.: Percepção de salas residenciais por idosos: uso das técnicas de seleção visual, realidade virtual e eletroencefalografia. Tese (Doutorado) – Universidade Federal de Pernambuco, Centro de Artes e Comunicação. Programa de Pós-Graduação em Design (2018)

Rueda, F.J.M.: Relationship between Concentrated Attention Tests (TEACO-FF) and Divided Attention Tests (AD). Psychol. Argument **28**(62), 225–234 (2017)

Rueda, F.J.M., de Castro, N.R.: Convergent construct validity evidence for the divided attention test – TEADI. Interdiscipl. Stud. Psychol. **1**(2), 141–158 (2010)

Rueda, F.J.M., de Castro, N.R., Sisto, F.F.: Validity evidence for the Alternating Attention Test – TEALT. Res. Psychol. **4**(1), 40–49 (2010)

Sarmento, T.F.C.S.: Modelo conceitual de ambiente de aprendizagem adequado a práticas com blended learning para escolas de ensino médio. Tese (Doutorado) – Universidade Federal de Pernambuco, Centro de Artes e Comunicação. Design (2018)

Schlemmer, E., Backes, L.: Online education in metaverse: novelty or innovation? Learning in metaverses: co-existing in real virtuality, IGI Global 183–214 (2015)

Sternberg, R.J.: Cognitive Psychology. 4th ed. Artmed, Porto Alegre (2008)

Siemens, G., Gašević, D., Dawson, S.: Preparing for the Digital University: A Review of the History and Current State of Distance, Blended and Online Learning, p. 234. Athabasca University Press, Athabasca, AB, Canada (2015)

Siyaev, A., Jo, G.S.: Neuro-symbolic speech understanding in aircraft maintenance metaverse. IEEE Access **9**, 154484–154499 (2021)

Soares, M.M.: Ergodesign Methodology for Product Design: A Human-Centered Approach. CRC Press, Boca Rotan (2022)

Tasa, U.B., Gorgulu, T.: Meta-art: art of the 3-D user-created virtual worlds. Digit. Creat. **21**(1), 100–111 (2010)

Tori, R.: Educação sem distância: mídias e tecnologias na educação a distância, ensino híbrido e na sala de aula, 3rd edn. Artesanato Educacional, São Paulo (2022)

Interactive Design of Immersive First Aid Skills Teaching Based on Multimedia Devices

Yunfei Chen[✉]

Royal College of Art, London SW11 4AY, UK
`yunfei.chen@network.rca.ac.uk`

Abstract. Many young people are currently dealing with long-term health issues as a result of an increasingly competitive environment and high work pressure. According to the WHO report, more than one-third of adults over 25 worldwide have hypertension, putting a lot of people at risk for sudden death from high blood pressure. The prevalence of sudden cardiac death is rising, first aid training is a top priority for many businesses and organizations, and the epidemic is making individuals more conscious of their health. Immediate CPR before the AED arrives improves survival chances. However, the life-saving use of CPR + AEDs might be delayed by emotional and psychological barriers to action, such as fear, especially in China, where CPR + AED prevalence is low. The purpose of this paper is to investigate the use of new media (such as smartphones and VR devices) as first aid teaching tools to help learners improve their first aid and emergency response skills. It also suggests a strategy for designing low-cost, ordinary first aid interactions so that more individuals may get the essential first aid skills in a more practical manner.

Keywords: Firs aid · AR · Learning kit · Motion recognition · Mediapipe

1 Introduction

1.1 Background of My Thesis

More than 9 million people worldwide die suddenly each year from conditions such as sudden heart attacks or strokes with high blood pressure. From WHO's report [1], more than a third of the world's population over the age of 25 has a condition known as hypertension, so many people are at risk of sudden death due to high blood pressure. Especially in China the prevalence of CPR + AED is very low [2]. Also, in next few generations, first aid training in public will continue in both high/low prevalence areas. So, it is very important to promote first aid education with high quality.

1.2 CPR and AED Bystander First Aid

Starting immediate CPR is vital as it keeps blood and oxygen circulating to the brain and around the body to prevent severe and irreversible brain damage because of the lack

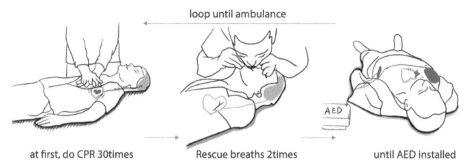

Fig. 1. Process of AED installation.

of blood flow to the entire brain. Below are the implementation of CPR and AED when the incidence of a cardiac arrest happens [3] (Fig. 1).

After cardiac arrest, survival is reduced by 7–10% for every minute that passes, causing severe damage after 4–6 min, immediate CPR improves survival by 2.5 times [2] (Table 1).

Table 1. Chance of survival from cardiac arrest.

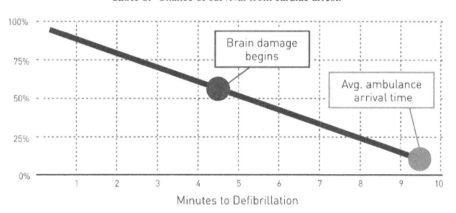

1.3 Key Factors on AED Learning

Based on the literature study the most relevant factors which affect the chances of delivering a successful defibrillation were recognized [4]:

Time: The most crucial factor for the successful defibrillation is the time from SCA to the first shock. For that reason, shock from an AED must be provided with the minimum of delay. Survival rates decrease approximately 7% to 10% with every minute that defibrillation is delayed. Delays can be caused by the user, device design, or location of

AED. The usage of AED includes also providing CPR between shots. It is recommended to minimize the interruption in chest compression as much as it is possible.

Education: Although AEDs can be correctly operated without prior experience, even minimal training improves performance, timeliness, and efficacy, which is crucial in sudden cardiac arrest. Moreover, there are studies which highlight the need to improve public knowledge and confidence in the use of AED. Positioning the pads correctly or following the correct safety procedures are recognized as the common mistakes within untrained subject which can affect the successful intervention. In addition, bystanders who used AED in a cardiac arrest, found the first aid course essential for feeling comfortable with using the AED.

Teamwork: In many sudden cardiac arrest cases, bystanders describe the resuscitation attempt as a team effort. When there is more than one responder task can be distributed. For example, CPR can be provided continuously, while AED is brought and power on and pads are placed. Good teamwork helps bystanders taking actions, delegating tasks, not interrupting each other, and staying calm.

Emotions: Emotional factors which stop or delay initiating first aid include panic, a fear of litigation, causing harm, or not performing it correctly for both trained and untrained bystanders [5]. When bystander overcome initial hesitation to act, the reason for declining to use AED is fear of legal liability or removing a stranger's shirt can be present [6].

Physical AED Design: AED user interface and features can significantly influence the ability of untrained caregivers to appropriately place pads and quickly deliver a shock. Also, number of steps to deliver shock can affect it efficiency, for example the need to plug the electrodes into the AED. Further research is recommended to making devices user-friendly and robust to untrained layperson [6].

1.4 Conclusion

Cardiac arrest can happen to anyone at any time and remains a leading cause of death in Europe and the United States. Nevertheless, the combination of immediate CPR and use of AED can provide the survival rate as high as 50–70%. As the AED devices became easily accessible, the general awareness of defibrillator and their benefits has increased. However, they can be operated without prior training, education is a crucial factor which helps to increase the chances of successful defibrillation and minimize delays. Victims brain has 4–6 min from the cardiac arrest before the irreversibly damaged will occur. AED training improves the speed with which the electric shock is delivered. Besides, it has also a positive influence on other vital elements. It boosts bystander confidence and comfort, which can affect the willingness to provide first aid and use AED. Moreover, it provides knowledge about AED interface and how to use it in combination with CPR. Nowadays, AED is considered an integral component of training in basic life support.

2 Methods

2.1 Research Methods

As part of the research, multiple methods were used, including interviews, observation and autoethnography to gather relevant information from multiple stakeholders and understand different perspectives. Also, research was conducted in multiple locations including on-site training and zoom meetings.

Literature and desktop research (1): The literature review and desktop research were done to gain a holistic perspective about the legal, user and market requirements of training and equipment. It also gave an understanding of the current conditions of training by including different fields such as psychology, sociology, medical science. I also learnt about the different ways in which CPR is available in different regions and the market demand for training aids. The market status in China is also included.

Questionnaires with *questionnairestar* & *monkeysurvey* (2): The literature review and desktop research were done to gain a holistic perspective about the legal, user and market requirements of AED training and equipment. It also gave an understanding of the current conditions of training by including different fields such as psychology, sociology, medical science. I also learnt about the different ways in which CPR is available in different regions and the market demand for training aids.

Observation study with China's red cross (3): Two different courses were observed at St John Ambulance. The first was the AED course, and the second one was the first aid in workplace course. These observation studies gave insight into methods used for teaching, course dynamics and the interaction between instructor, participants, and the equipment.

Interview with St John Ambulance instructors, London, the United Kingdom
Interview with Chinese instructors, Zoom (4): During two days of the visit, five semi structured interviews were conducted with certified instructors from St John Ambulance. Participants were selected based on the availability and experience in providing diverse courses which include training. Interview questions were prepared with the aim to understand instructors' perspective on the course, teaching methods, and evaluate training devices. Besides, instructors need, and aims were defined.

Focus groups with participants and two instructors (5): Short, semi structured interviews were conducted with seven participants. Participants were selected based on their knowledge about AED and experience with first AED training. The purpose of the interviews was to understand the perspective of potential bystanders before and after exposure to the training.

We worked together with some post-it notes to sort and narrow down the final key steps in training and in the real CPR first aid process.

2.2 Design Methods

The Double Diamond [7]: This project is a systematic work that involves multi-stakeholders and have many touch points from online and offline, so I use the Double Diamond method to discover, define, develop, and deliver my product and service (Fig. 2).

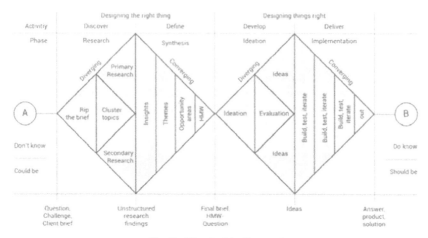

Fig. 2. The double diamond

Planet Centred Design [8]: For regenerative consideration, a toolkit provided by *planetcentricdesign* is added as a design tool on this project. This toolkit was designed to help you create products and services that do not harm the planet. It will help you create concepts that are desirable and profitable, but also put the planet in the center of the design process.

Seventh Generation Principle [9]: Based on the Seventh Generation Principle, based on the Great Law of the Haudenosaunee (founding document of the Iroquois Confederacy) is the indigenous culture to designate people to 'take on the role of future generations' and have them stand in for future generations.

2.3 Conclusion

As part of the research, multiple methods were used, including interviews, observation and autoethnography to gather relevant information from multiple stakeholders and understand different perspectives. Also, research was conducted in multiple locations including on-site training and zoom meetings. The goal of the literature study and desk research was to develop a comprehensive understanding of the requirements for training and equipment from a legal, user, and market viewpoint. To gain insight into teaching strategies, course dynamics, and interactions between the instructor, students, and equipment, two sets of interviews with both Chinese and British instructors will be conducted. User journeys were also used to identify the main characteristics of touchpoints during human-computer interaction as well as the demands of learners for low-cost instructional tools. When developing strategies, keep planet-centered design methodology in mind. The prototypes are partially dependent on python programming.

3   Design Research

3.1   Current Situation of AED Learning

82 questionnaires from *questionnairestar* and 76 questionnaires from *monkeysurvey* were collected to analyze, the problems in both China & UK based on the results of questionnaire are as below:

AEDs can be correctly operated without prior experience, and before AED arrived, CPR should be done immediately. However, emotional, and psychological barriers to action, such as fear, can delay or prevent AED's lifesaving use. The best way to gain willingness and confidence to do rescue in cardiac arrest and save someone's life is AED training. Nevertheless, this kind of training is complex and dynamic. Multiple participants perform the exercises at the same time. It is challenging for the instructor as it requires to assess multiple students simultaneously by keeping track of their actions and the device instructions. Moreover, when the instructor interacts with participants to provide feedback, he/she loses track of the rest of the class. As a result, an instructor is stressed and overwhelmed, and participants can receive limited or incorrect feedback. Also, with a higher quality of the training, participants will become more confident. It will affect the reaction speed, increasing victims' chances of survival.

3.2   Market Research on AED Teaching Aid

And CPR popularization and teaching very important material is the training with the dummy, the bad training need simulation, and popularization need cost control, even now such a dummy need about 199 lb cost, so even at that time that twenty people teaching class, the class is only two dummies can practice, which reduces the efficiency, not good to be carried (Fig. 3).

Fig. 3. High price of AED course on St John Ambulance & high price of manikins on Amazon

3.3   Problems and Needs: Why Both Participants and Instructors Feel Inefficient?

The typical problem is that the training resources are very limited. The manikins are too expensive, and it should be replaced every 5–7 years. Even worse, the training mode is too rigid. There is no aid of tech for the AED course. China is short in trainer supply and trainers are already overworked. Then, it will limit the number that the training centers and *Red Cross* can train each year. For the perspective on users, the users who haven't learn about AED usually have less motivation and awareness to learn AED. It is because of less opportunity and time.

In recent years, Laerdal, the leading AED company, has also launched some AED teaching aids for home contact. I have also conducted product tests on this, selected three men and women, and recorded their reactions when using them, to help me find design opportunities (Table 2).

Table 2. Records on *MiniAnne*'s (AED learning kit) tests.

user	gender	weight	placement	compression	expressions
Kyle	male	56kg	correct	Enough	Imconficdent and tired
lingyu	female	48kg	correct	Not enough	Tired and hesitant
nick	male	63kg	correct	Enough but too fast	Tired

We discussed and found that there is no feedback when user compress enough pressure. Also, everyone wasted a lot of time to do the low-quality rescue breath to manikin. Using a lot of disposable items in this kit is not a regenerative way for the planet.

To summaries, limited amount of equipment and few full-time professionals, resulting in fewer opportunities, less efficient training, and less hands-on opportunities, so afraid to do it.

From the part of potential users, those who want to learn AED, we define the needs for participants and their learning goals based on the user journey on AED learning process of potential users,

Needs:

– A safe and friendly learning environment.
– Guidance in the education process.
– Simple and clear instructions.
– Assurance that the exercise is performed correctly. – Assurance of rescue safety.
– Understand how CPR works.
– Experience the use of CPR in the scenario – Positive feedback.

Learning goals:

– Be able to use CPR
– Achieve the mastery of skills – Gain confidence
– Remember the information presented in the course.

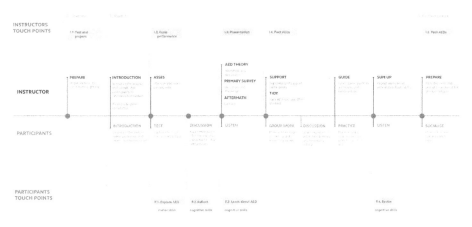

Fig. 4. User journey

– Receive a certificate

From the part of protecting the planet, the supply chain for original manikins is taking into consideration. We can provide a learning kit with less pressure on recycling and lower carbon emission. Instead of relying on a limited number of expensive and non-recyclable manikins, can we combine AR and posture recognition ai technology to create a low-cost training environment with items around us and increase the frequency of training to make CPR training more like a normal thing in our everyday lives, thus increasing the confidence of learners (Fig. 4).

3.4 Technical Feasibility

I was also inspired by the physical exercise game on the iPad, which uses the front-facing camera to recognize people's posture in real time as an input to the game. Its feedback is displayed on the screen in real time. The feedback information is usually based on positive encouragement, with appropriate suggestions, which provides users with accurate and effective self-learning information. Such interactive behavior can also be well applied in the self-learning process of AED.

In the future developing about the solution, we set up. We need recognition algorithm with machine learning, which can provide more accurate feedback when training. Therefore, I investigated the existing background servers and commonly used pose recognition algorithms. Among them, OpenCV [11] and Mediapipe [10] are the most frequently used resource libraries (Figs. 5 and 6).

Fig. 5. Screenshots on app (active arcade).

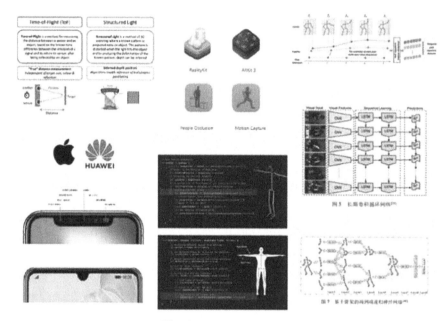

Fig. 6. Technical research.

3.5　Conclusion

First aid training in public will continue in both high- and low-prevalence areas for future generations. However, this type of teaching is dynamic and complicated, and to make matters worse, several learners exercise on the same manikin. The instructors have a challenging work since they must evaluate several students at the same time while keeping track of their behaviors. The main source of this dilemma is that the expensive manikins and infrequent exercises performed throughout the training process undermine the participants' trust. Regular training in simulated emergencies is the best way to build motivation and confidence to perform rescues and to minimize psychological barriers when a cardiac arrest happens. The development of interactive, flexible scenario-based training models may be done with multimedia tools. This might be an innovative way to improve the training quality. Then, with better training, the reaction time will change, improving the chances of survival for victims.

4 Product Design of Interactive Design of Immersive First Aid Skills Teaching

Design brief: *Savebeats* creates a new interactive process for learning CPR that is every day, gamified learning platform that relies on AR and deep learning algorithms to give users more effective CPR training and certification, giving the planet low-cost reproducible CPR training.

4.1 Prototype and Focus Group

I tested with things I could see in the house, pillows, toys of Jelly cat, many bottles. I found that the coke bottle was the most suitable and then I tested it with sensors and found that it was the most similar react as the manikins do (Fig. 7).

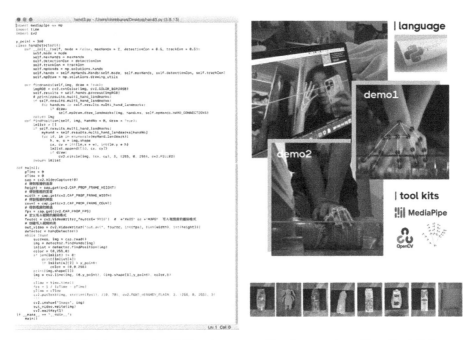

Fig. 7. Quick prototyping CPR posture recognition (programing with python). link

From the previous research, the training process has a lot of step-by-step content, which can make it difficult to get the focus, and this will not be beneficial in our search for a living, everyday training approach. So, I organized a focus group with one of the students and the instructor (from St john's ambulance) after attending the onsite AED training. Together we drew storyboards and narrowed down key CPR training elements (Fig. 8).

Here are some problems should be put attention in learning outcomes:

i. Knowing how to analyze the situations;
ii. Placement and posture of Hands;
iii. Frequency and depth of compressions;
iv. hands-only CPR is allowed.

Fig. 8. Focus group on user flow.

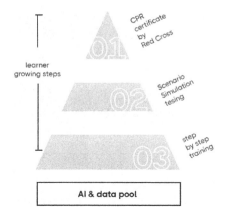

Fig. 9. Overview on training steps.

4.2 Function Design of the Savebeats

Learner Growing Steps: The user enters the teaching process through the app end of Savebeats, and the ai combined with the mobile phone hardware camera will become the tutor to regulate your actions. The teaching of Savebeats is gradual and divided into three levels: first, users will standardize their actions through daily training. When the actions reach a certain proficiency and training time, they will move to the next level; Secondly, Savebeats will test the user's resilience and self-confidence through simulation assessment, and the image will be integrated into the assessment process to simulate the real emergency, so that the user can be in the scene and make his own judgment. After meeting the assessment criteria, it will move to the next level; Finally, the user will get Savebeats (Figs. 9, 10 and 11).

Fig. 10. Information structure.

Fig. 11. Low-fi wireframe.

4.3 Key Functions

Preparing Suitable Bottle: User who have the suitable bottle scan the barcode to check the type of the bottle and adjust the parameter values to fit it. After DIY your own AED learning aid by the bottle following the guide on Savebeats, the user begin the trip on Savebeats. I design a IP called Kumo, which is used as a key role of this training game to get closer with the audience, and the game-based setting makes the whole daily training process have a sense of achievement and interest (Fig. 12).

Fig. 12. Registration part of UI interfaces. link

Gamification: At the beginning, the world of user Savebeats has only one tree. There are training mode and test mode in teaching. The training mode is the daily frequency. When the daily training reaches a certain length of time and integral, and is recorded as an effective CPR, a tree will be obtained. The test mode is locked at the beginning. When users accumulate ten trees, they can unlock the test mode. The test mode is to simulate the real emergency scene. If the simulation test game determines that the user rescue is successful, add a love icon (Fig. 13).

Fig. 13. Rewards part of UI interfaces.

Training Mode: When starting the training mode, users first select their preferred songs. At the beginning of the training, move the bottle to the range shown on the screen. After recognizing the posture, find the appropriate press rhythm according to the music rhythm. AI will judge and feedback your posture and press depth (Fig. 14).

Testing Mode: Users will be faced with a variety of emergency simulations, with live images presented and brought in on the screen. Users make their own judgments through voice interaction and action recognition (such as whether to call an ambulance, whether the check action before CPR is complete, etc.), and Savebeats will record your choice and give a score (Fig. 15).

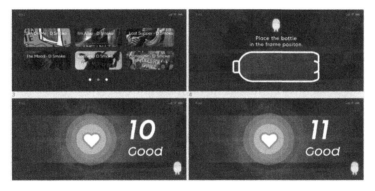

Fig. 14. Training part of UI interfaces.

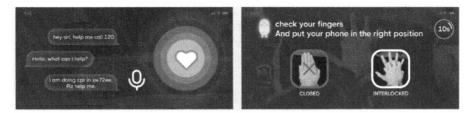

Fig. 15. Testing part of UI interfaces.

Certificate and Mini Tutorials: Users will have digital certification after passing the tests, and there will be some first aid online tutorials on Savebeats (Fig. 16).

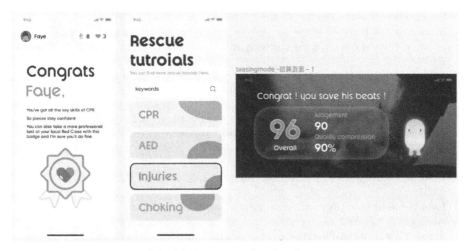

Fig. 16. Score part of UI interfaces.

4.4 Conclusion and Value

Savebeats is a design practice that incorporates the practice of multimedia teaching first aid. The aim is to create a new interactive process of learning on a low-threshold gamified platform that relies on smart hardware and deep learning algorithms to give users more effective CPR training and certification, bringing low-cost repeatable CPR training to the planet. Instead of learning in a single area with few teaching resources, it creates a self-directed learning experience. In near future, Savebeats can also be used on VR application, multimedia will have more chance to innovate the interaction way with the AED learning aid.

In the post-epidemic era, physical and mental health are issues that affect all facets of society, and there is an increased need for first aid and medical education. The production of low-cost, immersive daily learning scenarios is made possible by multimedia tools. Utilizing multimedia tools and machine learning algorithms to the fullest extent is a novel effort, but accuracy testing and iterative testing of the learning models used to evaluate the training effects are ongoing to provide improved outcomes.

References

1. Tsao, C.W., et al.: Heart disease and stroke statistics—2022 update: a report from the American Heart Association. Circulation **145**, e153–e639 (2022)
2. Yan, S., et al.: Willingness to attend cardiopulmonary resuscitation training and the associated factors among adults in China. Crit. Care **24**, 457 (2020)
3. Strogilos, V., Lim, L., Binte Mohamed Buhari, N.: Differentiated instruction for students with SEN in mainstream classrooms: contextual features and types of curriculum modifications. Asia Pac. J. Educ. 1–17 (2021)
4. Kaur, L., Bala, N.: A Study to Assess the Effectiveness of Teaching Programme on Knowledge and Skills Regarding Automated External Defibrillation (AED) Among Staff Nurses in Selected Hospitals of Jalandhar, Punjab Lovesampuranjot Kaur. **7**, (2021)
5. Sondergaard, K.B., et al.: Bystander cardiopulmonary resuscitation and long-term outcomes in out-of-hospital cardiac arrest according to location of arrest. Eur. Heart J. **40**, 309–318 (2019)
6. Ijuin, S., et al.: Successful interhospital transfer for extracorporeal cardiopulmonary resuscitation of a patient who had a cardiac arrest after cesarean section. Acute Med. Surg. **8**, e701 (2021)
7. Integrating Open Innovation Process with the Double Diamond Design Thinking Model – ProQuest. https://www.proquest.com/openview/f8449f687b3b10d63f02f95032bb86f1/1?pq-origsite=gscholar&cbl=1796412
8. https://planetcentricdesign.com/. Accessed 21 Apr 2022
9. Reed, B.: Shifting from "Sustainability" to regeneration. Build. Res. Inf. **35**(6), 674–680 (2007)
10. https://www.resus.org.uk/public-resource/how-we-save-lives/lifesaver-learning/lifesaver-vr. Accessed 21 Apr 2022
11. Zhang, F., et al.: MediaPipe Hands: On-device Real-time Hand Tracking (2020). Preprint at https://doi.org/10.48550/arXiv.2006.10214
12. https://docs.opencv.org/4.x/d9/df8/tutorial_root.html. Accessed 17 May 2022
13. https://en.wikipedia.org/wiki/Uncanny_valley. Accessed 20 May 2022

Interactive Video: Application in Narrative Competence Education of 1st to 3rd Grade Primary School Children

Wei-na Chien and Mang-mang Zhang[✉]

Tsinghua University, Haidian District, Beijing 100084, People's Republic of China
zhangmangth@126.com

Abstract. This paper discusses the impact of interactive videos on the narrative competence education of primary school children from grades 1st to 3rd. It explores the relationship between interactive videos and interactive movie games, and how they can improve children's language proficiency, socialization, and cognitive abilities. The author conducted a study in Taiwan and used Toulmin's model of argument and the Oral Narrative Content Dimension for testing subjects' oral textual content analysis. The study found that children between the ages of 7 to 9 are the most practical group for using interactive videos for narrative competence education. The author also compared the test results of different narrative types of interactive video and proposed some recommendations for enhancing the impact of interactive videos on children's narrative competence education.

Keywords: interactive video · interactive movie games · interactive video education · narrative competence · primary education · children's narrative development · narrative education

1 Research Motivation and Background

1.1 The Importance of the Development of Children's Narrative Ability

The development of narrative ability has a profound impact on children's growth. Children can express their needs and ideas through narratives and retell books or video clips they have read. Children between the ages of 7–9 begin to narrate more frequently, communicate with others or clearly express their opinions and learning outcomes, and their range of interactions usually includes parents, peers, and teachers. Many Chinese and foreign studies have indicated that the development of children's narrative ability is one of the predictive factors for the future academic achievement of both normally developing children and children with learning disabilities (Cameron et al. 1988; Feagans and Applebaum 1986; Fazio et al. 1996; Hughes et al. 1997; Mehta et al. 2005; Yeh 2011). The development of children's narrative ability not only affects their oral expression ability but also affects the development of future interpersonal and social relationships. Therefore, the education and training of children's narrative development is an essential part of children's education.

A. Marcus et al. (Eds.): HCII 2023, LNCS 14033, pp. 39–57, 2023.
https://doi.org/10.1007/978-3-031-35708-4_3

According to research on the development of children's narrative ability, children aged 5–7 are in the "True Narratives" stage. Children at this age can tell a complete story, and the narrative framework includes the subject of the story (Protagonist), the theme of the story, the motivations and goals of the subject's behavior, and the ending of the story. Children aged 7–12 are in the complex narrative stage "Complex narratives" stage. In addition to the basic narrative framework, the children in this age group can present a slightly richer narrative tension and plot, and the narrative may increase the emotions and thoughts of the subject. They can even use more details to describe the plot of the story. In addition, children in the "Complex narratives" stage not only describe the narrative content subjectively but also add objective analysis, making the overall narrative framework more complete (Applebee 1978). Based on the research of scholar Applebee, the author divided the research subjects into primary school children in grades 1st -3rd (7–9 years old), who are between the late stage of "True Narratives" and the early stage of "Complex narratives".

1.2 The Relationship and Impact of Interactive Video and Narrative Education

In this era of thriving information and development in technology, children's education requires more application of technology and techniques to assist children in learning. Humans receive more and more intense sensory stimulation each day, and various electronic devices, even some of the immersive entertainment technologies like virtual reality are becoming increasingly mature. The mainstream mode of children's education needs to be adjusted with various new technology devices from different aspects, to explore new core educational values. In the past, traditional cramming education was relatively single-output, and children's learning mode was passive information reception with low interactivity and initiative. In Asia, most children only receive information passively, and are difficult to make some reaction and express their own opinions and feelings. Children in the early narrative stage are unable to express their opinions and thoughts without assistance. The delayed development of narrative competence development can lead children to obstacles in interpersonal and social relationships in their later life. "Edutainment" means teaching with entertainment projects. Compared with traditional prescriptive education, edutainment is more like a game-style educational method, which can improve the interactivity and initiative of children during learning. Edutainment is a kind of immersive education model that organizes academic knowledge, using rich language descriptions, colors, images, and interesting story themes to enhance children's initiative. Among them, edutainment dominated through video is more common and it is easier to convey educational content through video media.

Traditional children-oriented videos are mostly linear narratives, which have a limited effect on enhancing children's creativity and critical thinking skills. Interactive video, on the other hand, allows children to participate actively in the learning process, make choices, and explore possibilities. It can stimulate children's curiosity and creativity, and enhance their critical thinking skills. Interactive videos integrate video, animation, and interactive games. It provides children with a more interesting, interactive, and immersive learning experience. Interactive videos can also help children develop a variety of skills, such as communication skills, problem-solving skills, and teamwork skills. In short, interactive videos can play an important role in promoting children's comprehensive development and enhancing their learning experience (Zhou 2022).

2   Core Concept Definition

2.1   Core Concept and Development Overview of Interactive Video

The core concept of interactive video is to make traditional linear narrative videos interactive, allowing audiences to participate in the development of video content and directing different outcomes based on the audience's different choices. Video creators will build the main storyline of the video and design interactive nodes at different plot points, allowing audiences to choose some of the story branches. Currently, research shows that the earliest interactive video concept can be traced back to the 1967 Czech film "Kinoautomat". The interaction mode of this film is that each seat in the theater is equipped with a remote control with red and green buttons. When the video reaches a plot divergence point, it is paused to make the audience choose the next step of the main character. The story continues to develop based on the majority choice, then it leads to different outcomes. Even though this film doesn't have real interaction with the audience, and the buttons pressed by the audience cannot affect the story development, it was just a method for director Radúz Cincera to express his political slant. Nevertheless, this film work still presents the concept of interactive video and breaks the rule of passively receiving information in traditional linear narrative films.

Interactive video is becoming increasingly sophisticated, with many streaming platforms offering interactive movies or series. One of the more well-known platforms is "Netflix". The audience can participate in the development of story content while watching the video. This immersive experience can lead the audience to focus on every aspect and element of the video. In 2016, Netflix issued the first children-oriented interactive video named "Puss in Book: Trapped in an Epic Tale". And the most famous interactive movie on the platform is "Black Mirror: Bandersnatch," with 312 min of footage, but due to the different interactive choices made by audiences, each person can only watch about 90 min of the story plot. Many audiences repeat watching and interacting with the movie to experience every storyline. This work enhances the recognition and stickiness of the audiences for the whole video production. Besides, there have been several interactive movies coming out in theaters in recent years, such as "Late Shift". The audiences must download the interactive application on their phones and make choices on the app during the interactive nodes in the movie and the story develops with the majority of choices. This interactive movie has a more mature interactive narrative design than previous interactive videos, with 180 choices and 7 endings. Many audiences go to the theater multiple times to experience all the story plots and endings. Even though the audience experiences many times, the story develops only with the majority of choices, and it is a main pain point in interactive video design.

2.2   Core Concepts and Development of Interactive Movie Games

The core themes of interactive movie games are mostly Adventure. Many of the game scenes adopt high-quality film production videos, replacing basic animated graphics. Interactive movie games focus on the story experience of the player, rather than the single interaction function of the game character. The player mainly operates the character related to the development of the story plot of the game. Interactive movie games are usually well-designed for characteristic backgrounds as well as story layouts.

The concept of early interactive movie games can be traced back to "Dragon's Lair," produced by former Walt Disney animator Don Bluth in 1983. In this game, players can control some of the actions of the protagonist, usually in dangerous situations. If the player makes the wrong choice, the game will choose an animation display of "losing a life," until the player chooses the correct behavior at the right time point to make the story continue. Although this game defines the player's interactive choice nodes, not every choice can continue the story. Only by choosing the options designed by the game designer can make the story proceed. However, this work has developed the core concept of interactive video. With related technologies, the development of interactive movie games has rapidly progressed in terms of narrative mode and picture quality. Notable works include "Beyond: Two Souls" and "Detroit: Become Human," both developed by the French electronic game company Quantic Dream. In these two games, players can experience the emotions and thoughts of the characters, making choices that will affect the story. The graphics of the games are very realistic and vivid, making the player fully immersed in the game world.

In China, notable works include "The Invisible Guardian" developed by New One Studio, and "Change Profession" developed by Xinhua. These games use the "live-action video interactive drama" technique and mostly graphic interpretations present by real-person performances. The refined picture presentation, rich plot, and complete character background design make the player fully immersed in the game.

2.3   Relationship and Characteristics of Interactive Video and Interactive Movie Games

Interactive video and interactive movie games are both interactive products that combine video and electronic games. Both aim to immerse the audience in the work, creating the illusion that the audience can direct the development and end of the story. In interactive movies, the director will try to collect the audience's cognition in a database and pre-determine some paths (Wang 2021). In interactive video, if the audience does not make any choice in time, the default choice will advance the story. In interactive movie games, if the player hesitates, the game will pause to wait for a choice. If the player chooses an option other than the game designed or is invalid, the game will be stuck. From the perspective of children as the audience, interactive video is easier to understand due to its simpler interactive instruction. Both interactive video and interactive movie games are highly engaging, allowing the audience to be more immersed in the work and improving their efficiency in receiving information about the work. The distinction between the two is becoming increasingly blurred, with interactive video becoming more diverse in its narrative types and increasingly similar to game design, while interactive movie games are getting closer to high-quality movie presentation. In the future, the technology and content of both interactive entertainment works will be more mature, becoming essential Edutainment projects. This study only focuses on the influence and efficacy of children's interactive video on their narrative education and thus only uses children's interactive video as a test tool.

2.4 The Core Concept of Narrative Competence

The concept of narrative competence refers to an individual's ability to express organized and coherent discourse, commonly known as extended discourse. This language ability is commonly observed in young children when they utter multiple sentences in succession (Wang 2017). Previous studies have emphasized the importance of narrative in children's language development. It can impact academic performance, interpersonal relationships, and the overall development of children. (Cameron et al. 1988; Feagans and Applebaum 1986; Fazio et al. 1996; Hughes et al. 1997; Mehta et al. 2005; Yeh 2011).

This study focuses on the manifestation of narrative competence as oral narratives, emphasizing the structure of the oral narratives of the tested subject. Previous research has established that oral narratives are complex linguistic activities that require the use of memory, knowledge, vocabulary, and sentence structure to effectively encode and articulate the events, characters, and themes of a narrative (Chi 2004). To analyze the oral narratives of the children, this study employs a framework that evaluates three dimensions of the narrative: the total number of words, the number of unique words, and the integrity of the narrative structure, which includes the story background, triggering events, goals, actions, and results, etc. (Yeh 2011).

2.5 Structure of Interactive Narratives Types

Interactive videos are a combination of linear and non-linear narrative types, whereas traditional videos without interactivity are typically linear in nature. Linear narratives focus on maintaining the unity of the story, coherence of time and space, and the integrity of the plot. In contrast, non-linear narratives emphasize the psychological aspects of the characters and are characterized by elements such as disjointed time and space, fragmented plots, and open-ended stories.

With the growth of the digital entertainment industry, traditional linear narratives have been combined with non-linear narrative forms to create interactive videos. This format transforms the passive role of the audience in traditional videos into an active participant, who can make choices that shape the outcome of the story. The narrative structure of interactive videos can be divided into linear and non-linear forms based on the level of interactivity. Unlike traditional linear narratives, interactive videos offer multiple interactive plot points that allow the audience to actively shape the outcome of the story through their choices.

The author synthesizes the three primary interactive video narrative types discussed by previous researchers (Lu 2019), modifying them to align with the author's understanding. These types include:

Multi-ending Choice Type: This is a linear narrative that incorporates interactive nodes at various points in the story. It typically focuses on the psychological changes and growth of characters. The author sets up interactive choices at key story points, which lead to different endings depending on the audience's choices (Fig. 1).

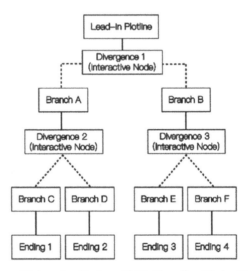

Fig. 1. Design of Interactive Nodes with Multi-ending Choice Type Narrative

Multi-cue Viewpoint Type: This is a non-linear narrative that allows the audience to experience events from different characters' or perspectives' points of view. The audience can enter the story from different roles and perspectives and better understand how events unfold from different perspectives, thereby deepening the immersive experience (Fig. 2).

Sequential Recombination Type: This type of narrative completely breaks linear timing by rearranging the sequence of events. The story is divided into modules, allowing the audience to choose which part to experience and thus re-create the story context and timeline.

It is worth noting that the majority of interactive videos currently available belong to the Multi-ending Choice Type, as this type has a greater emphasis on clues, viewpoints, and time sequence reorganization. (Hu 2020) (Fig. 3).

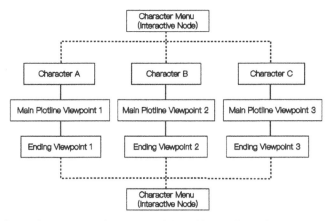

Fig. 2. Design of Interactive Nodes with Multi-cue Viewpoint Type Narrative

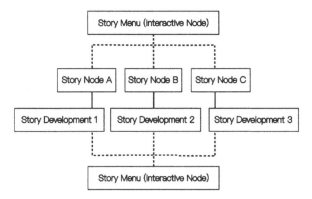

Fig. 3. Design of Interactive Nodes with Sequential Recombination Type Narrative

2.6 Comparison of Development of Video and Interactive Video for Children in China and Abroad

Interactive Videos for Children. Themes and Types Interactive videos for children have grown in popularity and now offer a range of themes, including adventure, family, magic, and character development. These videos engage children's desire to play and learn, making them a powerful tool for education. The interactive nature of the videos enhances immersion and learning outcomes. As a result, interactive videos are becoming increasingly popular in the field of children's education for their ability to impart academic knowledge and values efficiently (Table 1).

Table 1. Comparison of Development of Interactive Video for Children in China and Abroad

Nation Area	Development status	Development characteristics	Mainstream interactive video platforms	Pain points
China	Interactive video for adults is well developed, but there are fewer options for children	Streaming platforms allow for diverse homemade interactive videos to be uploaded and provide the making instruction. (bilibili, IQIYI, URL)	bilibili, IQIYI, Tencent Video, YOUKU, etc	High-cost productions typically focus on scenarios for young adults and adults rather than children, lacking strong story packaging for educational content
Overseas:	Interactive video has matured with the advancement of technology, including virtual reality, and places emphasis on a well-developed plot with educational content presented in an engaging way	Interactive videos emphasize the development of the plot and present the story theme and intended implications in a metaphorical way. Children-oriented interactive videos are mostly official productions with similar themes. Suggesting to allow for diverse homemade interactive videos to be uploaded on streaming platforms	Netflix, Disney, Eko, etc	Currently, children's interactive videos are mainly official fundraising productions with similar stories, such as adventures and magic. It may be suggested that main streams platforms can encourage their users to create their own interactive videos, increasing the breadth and depth of story themes

3   Experimental Details

3.1   Research Design

This research experiment aims to explore the impact of children-oriented interactive videos on the narrative education of elementary school students in the 1st to 3rd grades. The study employs the children's cartoon "The Last Boy on Earth: Happy Doom" available on Netflix as the interactive video experiment tool. The author has extracted several video clips and edited them into three different interactive video narrative versions: multi-ending choice narrative, multi-clue viewpoint narrative, and time sequence reconstruction narrative. The video interaction tool is facilitated by YouTube's built-in node settings, which guide the promotion function of the user's channel or another video, and children under test are provided with a click operation. Different groups of subjects were tested with different interactive video narrative versions, and their understanding of the video content description and the operation process was analyzed for narrative analysis after viewing.

The oral narrative texts of the tested children were analyzed using two narrative-level deconstruction methods, Toulmin's model of argument and the Oral Narrative Content Dimension. Toulmin's model of argument (Hamby 2012), proposed by British philosopher Stephen Toulmin, is a method for effectively proving and explaining one's point of view, and is widely used in logical arguments in the fields of law. The author first used Toulmin's model of argument to frame and list the reasons for the children's choices at each interaction node and then analyzed the children's oral narrative corpus using the analysis framework from previous studies to form a summary of the oral narrative content. The three dimensions analyzed were the number of words, the number of different words, and the completeness of the story's background, events leading to it, problems or goals, actions taken, and results. The scores of the three dimensions were calculated and the impact of different interactive video narrative types on children's narrative ability was compared. The author has adapted the narrative model concept from previous studies and organized it as follows (Figs. 4 and 5):

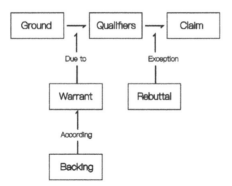

Fig. 4. Toulmin's model of argument

3.2 Research Questions

The study seeks to understand the overall differences and situations of different groups of children in the test for interactive videos with different narrative types by using Toulmin's model of argument to deconstruct the narrative expressions of the subjects, and then analyzing the deconstructed texts with three dimensions of spoken narrative (total words, different words, and completeness), and using two narrative analysis tools to count the scores of the subjects' narrative corpus.

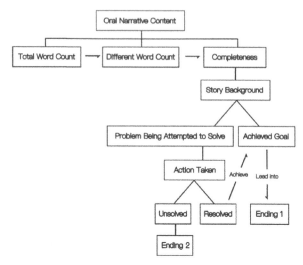

Fig. 5. Model of Oral Narration Dimension

3.3 Research Hypothesis

This study hypothesizes that children's interactive videos with different narrative types will have different levels of impact on the narrative education and development of children.

3.4 Participants

Due to pandemic-related restrictions, the author conducted remote online tests with students from the first to third grades of some elementary schools in Taiwan, using 3–4 students from each grade, for a total of 10 children. Each child participated in an online intelligence test and was confirmed to have normal language ability and intelligence levels for their age group (7–9 years old). The data from a total of 10 children is valid. The information on the tested children is as follows (Table 2):

Table 2. Participant Information

Grade	Age	Male	Female	Total
1	7	2	1	3
2	8	1	2	3
3	9	3	1	4
		6	4	10

3.5   Research Materials and Procedures

Research Tools. The research experiment utilized the interactive video test tool in the children's adventure animation "The Last Boy on Earth: Happy Doom," which was played on the Netflix platform. This video, based on Max Brallier's book series of the same name, premiered on September 17, 2019. To ensure the accuracy and fairness of the experiment, a simple interview was conducted to confirm that each child tested had not previously seen the video.

The story of the video revolves around the end of the world and the zombie monsters that have taken over. The main characters, Jack and his friends Quint, Baker, and June, are a group of 13-year-olds who, despite the danger, want to stick together. The video follows the friends as they go on an adventure to celebrate June's birthday. The content of the video is highly narrative and presents a level of complexity suitable for the age group of the children being tested (7 years and older). The author analyzed the narrative text of the video and extracted several test clips (Fig. 6).

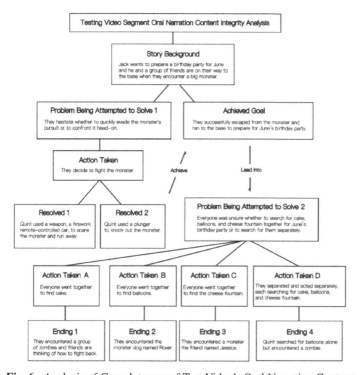

Fig. 6. Analysis of Completeness of Test Video's Oral Narration Content

The video was originally an interactive video with multiple endings, but the author edited it into a general linear narrative version, a point-of-view narrative version, and a timing reorganization narrative version, all based on the same plot segments. The analysis of the narrative types of each version of the test video is as follows (Figs. 7, 8 and 9):

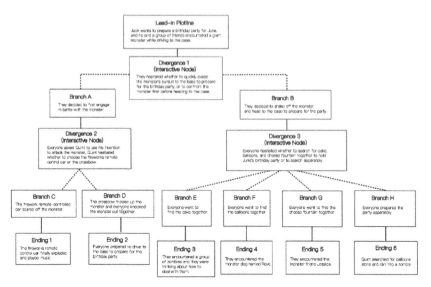

Fig. 7. Analysis of Test Video's Multi-ending Choice Type Narrative

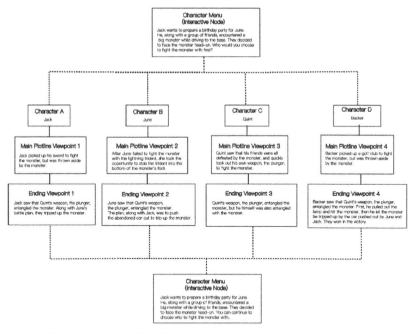

Fig. 8. Analysis of Test Video's Multi-cue Viewpoint Type Narrative

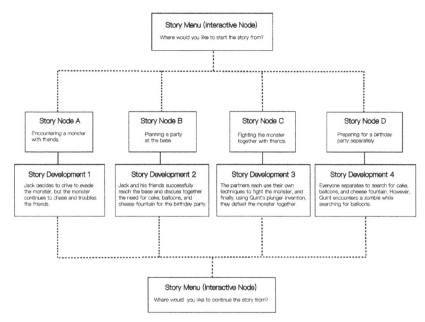

Fig. 9. Analysis of Test Video's Sequential Recombination Type Narrative

The Testing Process for the Research Experiment. The interactive video test tool for this research experiment was utilized in the children's adventure animation interactive video "The Last Boy on Earth: Happy Doom", which was played on Netflix. Based on Max Brallier's book series of the same name, the video was premiered.

Four test groups were assigned to each grade, with the parents of the test subjects assisting in opening the test video. The subjects were then allowed to operate the video independently, guided by the instructions contained within. After viewing the test video, the parents acted as the primary testers, asking questions and guiding the subjects to answer. The entire test completed operates in Chinese. The subjects' responses speaking were recorded through the recording function of mobile phones (Table 3).

Narrative Corpus Transcription and Scoring. In this test, a total of 1343 words were collected from the narrative corpus transcriptions of 10 children aged 7 to 9, with the parental guides (e.g. "then, what else, why, etc.") removed. The author applied Toulmin's model of argument to deconstruct the narrative expression of the reasons for the selection of interactive nodes and then analyzed the deconstructed text using three dimensions of oral narrative: total word count, unique word count, and completeness (Table 4).

Table 3. Testing Group Allocation Information

Narrative Type	Interactive Type	Test Group	Number of Participants in the Test Group
Multi-ending Choice Narrative	Selection of narrative content development at specific plot points by choosing any of the options A, B, C, D, etc	1st -3rd Grade Group A	4
Multi-cue Viewpoint Type Narrative	Experience of narrative content from the perspective of any of the story characters selected from the main menu	1st -3rd Grade Group B	3
Sequential Recombination Type Narrative	Entering the narrative content by selecting any of the story nodes from the main menu	1st -3rd Grade Group C	3

Table 4. Example of Text Transcription of Subject X's Oral Narration Corpus

Analysis of Interactive Videos Narrative Type	Multi-cue Viewpoint Type Narrative
Test Group	3rd Grade Group B
Text Transcription of Oral Narration Corpus	At first, they met a big monster and then they needed to avoid the monster but the monster kept chasing them. They were in a car and had to choose between going to a birthday party or fighting the monster. I chose to fight the monster because the monster was scary and kept chasing them. Fighting the monster was hard at first and they got knocked down by the monster. Then a dark-skinned boy had a weapon. I helped him choose a weapon between a plunger and a fireworks car. I chose the plunger because I thought it was more powerful. The weapon had a rope that came out and tripped the monster, they won and they could hit the monster on its body and knock it out, then they won

Toulmin's model of argument deconstruction scoring method for the reasons for the selection of interactive nodes was as follows: If the subject's oral narrative corpus explained the reasons for the selection of interactive nodes and met any of the following six conditions - Ground, Claim, Qualifier, Warrant, Backing, and Rebuttal - a score of 1 was given. The minimum score was 0 and the maximum score was 6 (Fig. 10).

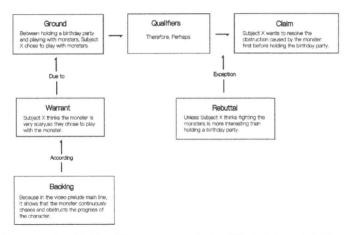

Fig. 10. Example of Subject X's response analysis of Toulmin's model of argument

As an example, the oral narrative corpus of a 9-year-old child (Subject X) in 3rd-grade group A was analyzed and explained. The reason for Subject X to choose one of the interactive nodes (holding a birthday party or fighting monsters) satisfied the six deconstruction conditions of Toulmin's model of argument, thus scoring 6 points at this stage. The average value was calculated by dividing the sum of the scores of all interactive nodes that met the six deconstruction conditions of Toulmin's model of argument by the total number of interactive nodes.

The three dimensions of analysis of the oral narrative content were the total number of words, the number of unique words, and the completeness of the story (story background, triggering events, problems attempted to be solved or goals achieved, actions taken, results). If the text transcription of the oral narrative corpus satisfied any of the items in the story's completeness, a score of 1 was given, with additional points for repeated items. The score was increased based on the complexity of the children's explanations (Fig. 11).

The oral narrative corpus text transcription of Subject X satisfied the completeness of the story, scoring 1 point for the story background, 2 points for the problem to be solved, 2 points for the action taken, 1 point for the solved goal, 1 point for the achieved goal, and 1 point for the ending. Thus, Subject X scored 8 points in this stage. The oral narrative consisted of 184 words, 76 unique words, and 5 sentences.

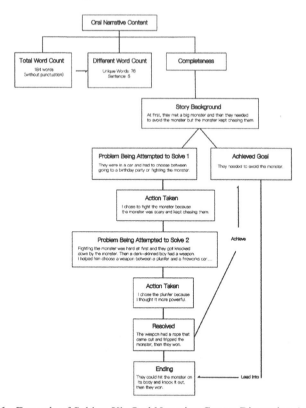

Fig. 11. Example of Subject X's Oral Narration Corpus Dimension Analysis

Based on the reason for the selection of interactive nodes, the sample of the oral narrative corpus analysis, and the scoring method, the score results for each child were calculated and tabulated (Table 5).

Statistical Analysis Results of Test Scores. The results of a statistical analysis of test scores are presented in this report. The data was collected from the narrative corpus transcriptions of 10 children aged 7–9, and the parental guides (such as "then," "what else," and "why," among others) were removed. The scores of the subjects' narrative corpus were counted using two types of narrative analysis tools. The author compares the results to the research hypotheses and preliminary calculates the impact of different interactive video narrative types on the development of the narrative ability of children in grades 1st to 3rd.

The study found that interactive videos with multiple endings and a selective narrative type can improve the active cognition of children and increase their focus on video content. Most of the children tested were able to clearly describe the main storyline and the choices they made, and they were also able to guide themselves through the interaction according to the video. In later interviews, all children reported that there were no operation links that they did not understand.

Table 5. Statistical Analysis of Reason for Interactive Node Selection and Score of Subject X's Oral Narration Corp

Participant Information	Test Group	Narrative Type of Test Interactive Video	Score of Toulmin Model of Reason for Interactive Node Selection	Score of Completeness of Oral Narration Content	Total Number of Words	Different Number of Words
1st Grade Female	A	Multi-ending Choice Type	5	3	117	Unique Words: 43 Sentence: 3
1st Grade Male	B	Multi-cue Viewpoint Type	3	2	73	Unique Words: 23 Sentence: 1
1st Grade Male	C	Sequential Recombination Type	0 (no reason)	2	57	Unique Words: 12 Sentence: 1
2nd Grade Female	A	Multi-ending Choice Type	6	8	223	Unique Words: 78 Sentence: 4
2nd Grade Female	B	Multi-cue Viewpoint Type	6	7	167	Unique Words: 74 Sentence: 3
2nd Grade Male	C	Sequential Recombination Type	3	5	126	Unique Words: 29 Sentence: 2
3rd Grade Female	C	Sequential Recombination Type	6	10	197	Unique Words: 83 Sentence: 5
3rd Grade Male	A	Multi-ending Choice Type	6	8	184	Unique Words: 76 Sentence: 5
3rd Grade Male	A	Multi-ending Choice Type	6	6	106	Unique Words: 52 Sentence: 2
3rd Grade Male	B	Multi-cue Viewpoint Type	5	6	93	Unique Words: 44 Sentence: 2

The research results show that subjects in Group A, who operated the multi-ending «choice narrative type, scored higher in Toulmin's model of argument and the completeness of oral narrative content. They also had a higher total number of words in the narrative corpus and a higher number of different words compared to other test groups. These findings suggest that interactive videos of different narrative types may have a significant impact on the narrative development of children. The results also indicated that the high-scoring age group was 9-year-old children in 3rd grade, and female subjects scored higher than male subjects. These results suggest that children of different grades and genders may have differences in understanding the same interactive video narrative type and gaps in the narrative ability within the experimental scope of grades 1st to 3rd.

4   Research Conclusions and Educational Recommendations

4.1   Research Conclusions

Innovations of the Research. The present study aimed to explore the impact of different types of interactive videos on the narrative ability of children in the first to third grades of elementary school. The findings indicate that children exhibit high acceptance of and willingness to operate and engage with interactive videos. According to the statistical results, the use of interactive videos with multiple endings and selective narratives can improve children's active cognition and increase their focus on the video content. The majority of the children in the multi-ending choice narrative group were able to clearly describe the main storyline and the choices they made after watching the video. They also expressed their feelings and opinions during the narrative process, such as "the monster is so scary" or "this prop looks more powerful". These results suggest that this type of interactive video has a positive impact on the narrative ability of children.

On the other hand, the results of the multi-cue viewpoint narrative and sequence recombination narrative groups were not as strong. The children in these groups were vague when describing the main storyline and only remembered specific elements such as the character they chose or the story node they entered. These interactive narratives are non-linear and fragmented, making it difficult for children to fully understand the storylines. As a result, the impact on their narrative ability and interaction, and the initiative was weaker. The study also revealed that children of different grades and genders have different levels of understanding and narrative ability.

Insufficiency and Prospects of Research. The study was conducted online and remotely due to pandemic-related restrictions, which posed challenges. The author had to communicate with each parent in advance and relied on them to guide their children through the different interactive videos. Some older parents encountered difficulties such as not being able to start the video or missing interactive nodes. The small sample size of the study limits the accuracy and representativeness of the conclusions. The author plans to continue the research offline in the future, using modified methods and tools to improve the accuracy and referentiality of the conclusions.

Educational Recommendations for Improving Children's Narrative Ability. Based on the research findings, it is recommended that interactive videos with multi-ending choice narratives be used to promote children's immersion and focus on the video content. When operating this type of interactive video, children tend to think about the information before making a choice, rather than passively receiving it. Additionally, the author suggests combining the design of "select the characters" from multi-cue viewpoint narratives with the multi-ending choice narratives to increase children's interest and involvement in the video content, ultimately aiding in the development of their narrative competence.

References

Cameron, C.A., Hunt, A.K., Linton, M.J.: Medium effects on children's story rewriting and story retelling. First Language **8**(22, Pt 1), 3–18 (1988). https://doi.org/10.1177/014272378 800802201

Feagans, L., Appelbaum, M.I.: Validation of language subtypes in learning disabled children. J. Educ. Psychol. **78**(5), 358–364 (1986). https://doi.org/10.1037/0022-0663.78.5.358

Fazio, B.B., Naremore, R.C., Connell, P.J.: Tracking children from poverty at risk for specific language impairment: a 3-year longitudinal study. J. Speech Hear. Res. **39**(3), 611–624 (1996). https://doi.org/10.1044/jshr.3903.611. Hughes, McGillivray,&Schmidek,1997

Mehta, P.D., Foorman, B.R., Branum-Martin, L., Taylor, W.P.: Literacy as a unidimensional multilevel construct: validation, sources of influence, and implications in a longitudinal study in grades 1 to 4. Sci. Stud. Read. **9**(2), 85–116 (2005). https://doi.org/10.1207/s1532799xssr 0902_1

Yeh, C.-Y.: Using story-mapping to improve the oral narrative skills for children with intellectual disabilities. (School of Nursing. National Taipei University of Nursing and Health Sciences. Master Thesis) National Digital Library of Theses and Dissertations in Taiwan (2011). https:// hdl.handle.net/11296/4d8kpc。

Applebee, A.N.: The Child's Concept of Story: Ages Two to Seventeen, pp. 143–144. The University of Chicago Press, Chicago (1978)

Zhou, R.: Research and countermeasures of interactive narrative communication mode in children's programming education. J. Qiqihar University (Phi & Soc Sci), **300**(02), 146–149 (2022).https://doi.org/10.13971/j.cnki.cn23-1435/c.2022.02.033

Wang, G.: Hu Dong Dian Ying, Dian Ying You Xi Yu Hu Dong Shi Dian Ying You Xi: Ji Yu Guan Zhong (Yong Hu) Xu Shi Can Yu Du De Yi Zhong Kao Cha. Dian Ying Xin Zuo, **254**(02), 152–156 (2021)

Wang, H.: 5-6 Sui You Er Xu Shi Neng Li Fa Zhan Te Dian Ji Qi Yu Yan Ying Xiang. Shaanxi Normal University (2017)

Cameron, S.: The impact of video recorders on cinema attendance. J. Cult. Econ. **12**(1), 73–80 (1988)

Chi, P.-H.: Story grammar abilities in children with poor reading abilities. Bull. Special Educ. **26** 247–269 (2004). (TSSCI)

Lu, W.: Branch points in interactive narrative: structure, weight and context. School of Information Management, Wuhan University, Wuhan, **27**(05), 90–98 (2019). https://doi.org/10.13363/j.pub lishingjournal.2019.05.015.

Hu, Y.: Research on the AR game design of children's safety education based on interactive narrative. Jang Su University (2020). https://doi.org/10.27170/d.cnki.gjsuu.2020.000948

Hamby, B.: Toulmin's "Analytic Arguments." Inf. Logic **32**(1), 116–131 (2012)

Interactive video production instruction (bilibili). https://www.bilibili.com/video/av58324327/? vd_source=8445043c34d107a2dc82ea2397fc2aab

Interactive video production instruction (IQIYI). https://www.iqiyi.com/ivg/#%E6%A6%82% E8%BF%B0

Optimization Strategy of Guidance Methods of Online Education Information Transmission

Jimiao Dong(✉) 📵, Jian Wang📵, Jing Tan📵, Ziye Wang📵, and Jiahao Sun📵

School of Design Art, Changsha University of Science and Technology, Changsha, China
xxxdxixi@163.com

Abstract. The innovation of immersion tools and online platforms provides more possibilities for the development of online education. Information guidance is a key part of information translation for online education information providers and directly affects the information translation into the receiver, so a more profound discussion and design of guidance methods are needed to optimize the effectiveness of online education information transmission. This study expands the guidance methods by dividing them into traditional guidance and multidimensional guidance according to different interaction modes of online education. Forty subjects were screened by a basic information questionnaire and a two-factor intergroup experimental design with 2 guidance methods (traditional and multidimensional) × 2 digital media (smartphone and tablet) was conducted. Learners evaluated and provided feedback on the experimental material from cognitive and affective goals through questionnaires. The results of the questionnaire analysis showed that the effectiveness of online educational transfer Learners learn better when educators use multidimensional guidance; multidimensional guidance increases learner engagement, thus effectively improving the effectiveness of information transmission. Learners learn better when digital media with large screen sizes are used; educators always improve online learning satisfaction better when they use tablets as digital media when conducting instruction. This finding enriches the research on the influence of guidance methods and digital media on information delivery in synchronous online teaching, where the research on the innovation of guidance methods provides the basis for the innovation and application of interactive technologies in online education.

Keywords: Online Education · Guidance Method · Learning Effect · Online Learning Satisfaction · Online Learning Commitment

1 Introduction

With the popularity of the Internet and the development of newer technologies, almost everyone has their own digital media devices, and education has broken through the traditional limitations of time and space, developing from offline to online and forming a new education ecosystem. In his keynote speech at the International Council for Open and Distance Education (ICDE) World Congress on Online Learning, Nelson pointed out that "the global online education market is still in its infancy ". At the same time, the Newcastle pneumonia pandemic has affected education on multiple levels, and it has made online learning a common way of teaching and learning around the world. This change has led to a greater focus on the future of online education. We should not simply look at online education as Emergency Remote Teaching in response to the epidemic [1], but we need to take a longer-term view of online education.

The Swiss pedagogue Johan Heinrich Pestalozzi pointed out that "information processing ability is the basic condition for learning", which, from the modern informatics point of view, initially indicates the generation of information transmission ideas. The information transmission model can also be applied to the field of on-line education in the light of the actual on-line teaching process. The seven elements in the information dissemination model correspond to those in online education: educator, instructional design, digital media, learner, learning effect, and the difference of each subject. The difference of each subject element and the interaction between the subject elements affect the learning effect of the learners, and the learning effect as the feedback will affect the educator's teaching design. That is, the learning effect represents the effect of information transmission in the whole education process, and it will also influence the improvement of the next information transmission. Interaction has gained attention as the scale of the online education business has expanded.

Interaction in the educational process includes both human interaction and human-computer interaction. It has been pointed out that interactivity is a fundamental guarantee of active and meaningful online learning [2]. Research has been conducted to demonstrate the processing theory of instructional humor, revealing the mechanisms underlying the influence of verbal humor on learner engagement in educators' instructional design [3]. However, the focus on interaction is often too idealized with respect to the "human" factor, resulting in less existing research. Mayer et al. have shown that when educators are intentionally guided during the teaching process, learners' learning outcomes are enhanced [4]. Mayer also divided guidance cues into visual and verbal categories, with visual cues including colors, gestures, etc., and verbal cues including changing topics and emphasizing phonological content [5]. Focusing on the synchronous form of online learning, the visual and auditory guidance in it becomes more limited and missing compared to the asynchronous form of online education. There is a large literature on asynchronous learning prior to the New Coronary Crisis. Research has shown that "asynchronous forms of online education have received more attention than synchronous forms" [6]. Asynchronous interactions were the basis for most online learning before the new coronary crisis [7]. However, there has been a significant increase in synchronous forms of online education due to the adoption of emergency distance learning instead of the original face-to-face classroom instruction. At the same time, teaching through synchronous online platforms such as Tencent Meetings and Zoom often limits the flexibility of online learning interactions and the effectiveness of information transmission. Therefore, this paper studies the guidance methods in educators' instructional design and conducts user experience research on guidance methods with the purpose of optimizing information transmission effectiveness.

In addition, the development and application of digital tools are proliferating, making interaction more immersive. With the development of digital education ecology, digital media of various sizes carrying knowledge and information have emerged as information dissemination media and become an important part of learners' process of acquiring knowledge and information through online learning. Gourlay illustrates the increasingly complex relationship between humans and technology from a socio-material perspective, pointing out that learning is "in person" even when learning alone at home through a digital screen. " [8]. In contrast, a large body of research in the field of communication and human-computer interaction suggests that increasing screen size often has a positive effect on user perceptions, including a sense of reality, presence, and immersion [9–11]. Because online education requires longer screen use and students use digital devices with different screen sizes, this leads to differences in learning outcomes for learners taking the same online course. Studies comparing the effectiveness of screen sizes have existed in research on online education, but no studies have addressed the effectiveness of optimizing information transmission through changes in guidance methods when using digital devices with different screen sizes. Therefore, this paper will investigate the effect of the difference in screen size of the terminal digital media device chosen by learners for receiving information in the process of online education on the learning effectiveness of learners under different educator guidance methods. From the above research analysis, we will provide strategies for optimizing the guidance method of online education information transmission.

2 Theoretical Basis

2.1 Information Transmission in Online Education

Online education did not appear out of nowhere; it was only the pandemic of the new crown epidemic that propelled it more directly into the limelight. In terms of the space in which learning occurs, learners can engage in formal in-class learning on campus, out-of-class learning on campus, formal off-campus classroom learning, and off-campus out-of-class learning, and these four forms are interwoven through digital leakage (digital leakage) in the form of a digital learning ecosystem [12]. Nowadays, the digital learning ecosystem with no fixed space, time and people relying on the Internet shows the development trend of both integration, expansion, opening and diversity [13] (Fig. 1).

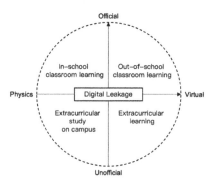

Fig. 1. Digital Learning Ecology

The "5W" model proposed by Lasswell was the first to clearly divide the communication process into five elements, and to define control analysis, content analysis, media analysis, audience analysis, and effect analysis as the five areas of communication research [14], which effectively described communication and planned communication research, and provided a dimension for thinking about education and teaching. Claude Shannon & Warren Weaver proposed the "Shannon-Weaver model of communication" in their article "A Mathematical Theory of Communication" [15]. This model divides the communication process into a two-way communication model consisting of seven elements, which provides important inspiration for the study of the communication process. The seven elements of the model are: educator, instructional design, digital media, learner, learning effect, and the difference of each subject. The educator transmits the knowledge and information of the brain to the learners through certain digital media through instructional design, and the learners choose the digital media they need to receive the information on their own and give feedback to the educator in the form of learning effects. After analyzing and judging, the educator adjusts the output information and teaching design, and this cycle forms the information transmission mode of online education.

2.2 Interaction Guidance

Picciano states that interactivity is a fundamental guarantee of active and meaningful online learning [2]. Moore proposes three kinds of interactions, defining instructional interactions as the interactions between the learner and the teacher, the learner, and the learning content [16]. Anderson, in the interaction equivalence principle, suggests that. "As long as one of the three interactions is at a high level, it can support active and meaningful learning. At this point, even if the other two interactions do not occur, the quality of the educational experience is not diminished" [17]. When focusing on online educational interactions, we tend to focus on the development of technology and are overly idealistic about the human factor; Brown notes that the use of digital technology alone does little to improve online learning interactivity and that specific instructional practices depend on how teachers and students choose to interact [12]. It has been noted that "learners learn better when guided by teachers who draw pictures on the board while explaining (the dynamic drawing principle), look at the students and then at the board (the gaze guidance principle), and provide prompts for summarizing and explaining content (the generative activity principle) during instruction" [18]. To ensure that active and meaningful learning occurs, online education needs to be more accurately designed and guided, and Valenzeno et al. compared the differences in visual attention and learning outcomes for learners with and without physical guidance from the instructor and concluded that learners learn better with physical guidance from the instructor [19]. Mayer divided the guidance cues into two categories, visual and verbal, with visual cues including colors, gestures, etc. and verbal cues including changing topics and emphasizing phonological content [5]. Jiang Yanling et al. found that adding mouse guidance in instructional videos without focused presentation helped learners learn, but learning was instead better in instructional videos with focused presentation without mouse guidance [20]. Li explored the effect of the teacher's guidance style in instructional videos on learning outcomes and learning satisfaction, etc. [21]. In contrast to the asynchronous form of online education, the synchronous form is more limited and lacking in visual and auditory guidance. Among the many new interaction technologies, eye-tracking has been applied in live entertainment, where the live streamer's line of sight is directly reflected on the screen, which both better guides audience interaction and increases the entertainment of the live stream. Based on the study of eye-tracking technology and online education, this paper summarizes the teacher's guidance according to the difference of interaction forms of synchronous online courses. It also classifies the guidance methods of educators in online education into traditional guidance and multidimensional guidance (Figs. 2 and 3).

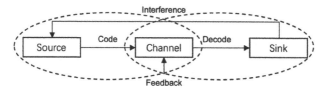

Fig. 2. The Shannon Weaver Model

Guiding Mode	Interactive Form	Interaction Cue	Transmission Characteristics	Practical Manifestation
Multidimensional Guidance	Passive Interaction (traditional Guidance)	Acoustic Cue	Linguistic Input	teachers output instructional focus information through active verbalization
			Auditory Output	learners listen to the instructor's guidance and understand the instructional information
		Visual Cue	Gesture Input	through active gesture operation, teachers output key teaching information instruction in the screen
			Visual Output	learners follow the mouse instructions and focus on the information area of the screen
	Active Interaction	Visual Cue	Eye Movement Input	actively carry out real-time visual output of teachers' eye movement trajectory
			Visual Output	the teacher's eye trajectory guides the learner's continuous attention to the information area on the screen

Fig. 3. Guidance based on different forms of interaction

2.3 Digital Media Screen Size Difference

As digital technology continues to be updated and most people own smartphones or tablets, learners can choose from different digital media to receive information delivered during online learning. The difference in screen size is a prominent physical structural feature of digital media, and Kim et al. studied the effect of different screen sizes on learners' vocabulary learning and concluded that larger screen sizes facilitate learners' vocabulary learning compared to smaller screen sizes [22]. One study found that screen size affects the level of message elaboration and thus information transfer [23]. Wibirama et al. noted that mobile devices with large screen sizes produce a significantly more immersive experience than mobile devices with small screen sizes [24]. The audiovisual process of learners in online learning requires digital media as a mediator for information transfer, and the presentation of digital media of different sizes has different effects on online learning information transmission. Studies comparing the effectiveness of screen sizes have existed in research on online education, but no studies have addressed the optimization of information transmission effects through changes in guidance when using digital devices with different screen sizes. Based on this, this study limits the transmission media in online education transmission to smartphones and tablets based on size differences based on the digital media commonly used by learners.

3 Research Method

Based on the above literature compilation, it is known that previous studies have been conducted on educator guidance as an influential factor in online education research, but they have failed to analyze the impact of changes deeply and innovatively among subject factors on the information transmission effect in the online education process from the perspective of information transmission. This study will use information dissemination theory to show the educator guidance differences in the different sizes of digital devices used by learners from the perspective of Design and analyze learner learning effect differences to derive information transmission effect differences, so that strategies can be given for different online education elements to improve the overall information transmission effect of online education. The study is divided into five steps: 1. Confirm the connection between the theoretical core and each element; 2. Select appropriate research method indicators as the measure of information transmission effectiveness; 3. Sort out the research logic and design experiments; 4. Analyze the data obtained from the experiments and draw conclusions; 5. Propose design suggestions and optimization strategies based on the conclusions drawn from the experiments.

Based on Shannon-Weaver's information dissemination theory, this study divided the online education information transmission tripartite into educators, remote digital media, and learners, and used a two-factor intergroup experimental design of 2 guidance methods (traditional guidance, multidimensional guidance) × 2 digital media (smart-phones, tablets). The learning effect of the learner's Illustrator (hereafter referred to as AI) online synchronous course was also used as the dependent variable of the experiment. The learning effect measures included two dimensions of affective goals (learning satisfaction, learning engagement) and cognitive goals (learning retention and learning transfer effects, time-bound task completion effects), and the specific research methods were as follows.

3.1 Prior Knowledge

Prior knowledge is knowledge that precedes experience, and the term has been used in research since early times, with some common descriptions such as "preexisting knowledge," "experiential knowledge," and "background knowledge" [25]. Filip et al. defined prior knowledge as "all of one's knowledge" and constructed a concept map.

They argue that prior knowledge helps them to analyze and solve problems in new situations and is essential for task completion [26]. It has also been shown that the level of learners' prior knowledge affects their cognitive processing and attention allocation patterns, which in turn affects their learning outcomes [27]. Thus, the definition of prior knowledge in this paper is the collection of knowledge and information accumulated by the learner over a certain period that precedes experience.

3.2 Learning Effect

Learning effectiveness refers to the outcome of learning, and learning effectiveness has different classifications based on different dimensions. Homer et al. classified learning effectiveness into retention and transfer effects based on the level of understanding and mastery of knowledge [28]. The degree of change in the learner's knowledge and skills is generally reflected through the learner's academic performance. The retention effect is the learner's ability to recognize and remember, and it mainly examines the subject's understanding of the basic information and core concepts extracted from the content learned. The transfer effect is the learners' comprehension ability, which mainly examines the subjects' ability to apply what they have learned to new situations. In this paper, the learning effect is measured from the perspective of knowledge, skills and learning experience, and the retention effect and transfer effect of learners' knowledge are examined. This study designs moderately difficult knowledge quizzes and time operations around the explanatory content of the video. Learners' errors in practice operations will trigger a correction method, which will increase the length of practice operations and thus affect the efficiency of practice. Therefore, the completion of the practice tasks from the limited operation time can understand the learners' learning of knowledge and skills from the side of operation proficiency and task completion.

3.3 Learning Satisfaction

Satisfaction generally refers to the psychological state in which a person's expectations are met with varying degrees of pleasure. Studies have combined psychology and education to show that learning activities are influenced by a combination of internal and external conditions, and that the conditions are mutually constraining and influencing each other [29]. Many scholars have conducted studies. Huei et al. explored the mediating effects between online learning perceptions, online learning readiness, online course satisfaction, and online learning performance and found that online self-efficacy mediated the relationship between online learning perceptions, online discussion performance, and course satisfaction [30]. According to Xiong et al. learning satisfaction reflects students' overall positive assessment of their learning experience and is a direct reflection of the difference between learners' own learning expectations and the actual implementation of instruction [31]. Researchers commonly describe learning satisfaction in terms of both needs and perceptions of learning. Hu defines learning satisfaction in detail from two perspectives: from the perspective of need, learning satisfaction is the gap between learners' needs or expectations for learning and the actual results, and the smaller the gap, the more satisfied they will become; and from the perspective of cognition, learning satisfaction is learners' feelings or attitudes toward learning activities [32]. Online learners, as evaluation subjects, come to give feedback on the teaching and learning process according to their knowledge and skill learning and emotional needs. In this paper, learning satisfaction refers to the degree of satisfaction of learning activities on learners' learning needs and perceptions: when learners' interactive needs are satisfied or learning reaches its goal in learning activities, they have a pleasant feeling psychologically. Based on this, this study integrates the four dimensions of teacher teaching quality, course content characteristics, teacher-student interaction support, and platform equipment form to construct the influencing factors of online learning satisfaction questionnaire.

3.4 Learning Engagement

According to Reeve, learning engagement refers to "the extent to which learners are actively engaged in learning activities and are consistently active" [33], and according to Philp et al., learning engagement includes four dimensions: behavioral, cognitive, emotional, and social engagement. Online learning engagement is developed on top of the concept of learning engagement [34]. Online learning engagement is influenced by multiple variables such as teachers, courses, learning platforms, and learners, and its unique "weak control" puts higher demands on learners' motivation and willpower [35]. Sun et al. developed a distance learning student engagement questionnaire based on the classroom engagement scale for elementary school students [36]. Deng et al. conceptualized MOOC learning engagement into four dimensions: behavioral, cognitive, affective, and social engagement, and developed the MOOC engagement scale (MES) [37]. The questionnaire in this study was revised from this scale.

4 Research Design

The main purpose of this study is to investigate the effect of different guidance methods of educators on learners' learning outcomes in synchronous online education courses when learners use different screen sizes of transmission devices. The questionnaire used in the study consisted of five sections: basic personal information, prior knowledge, learning effectiveness test, online learning satisfaction scale, and online learning engagement scale. To exclude unfamiliarity with the use of digital devices, the questionnaire was distributed to groups of college students and graduate students (18–28 years old). A random sample of 80 questionnaires was distributed using the questionnaire star, and 68 valid questionnaires were collected by excluding incomplete information and inattentive questionnaires. Excluding 28 software professionals who did not meet the requirements of the experimental setup, the actual experimental staff was 40. Among them, 28 were female, 12 were male, 22 were bachelor's degree holders, 18 were master's degree holders, 27 had online learning experience, and 13 had no online learning experience.

4.1 Experimental Materials

The experimental materials of this study were screened by professionals proficient in Illustrator software (AI software hereafter) for online teaching course contents, then the professionals made the teaching materials of theoretical courses, drew the teaching contents of practical courses, and finally taught in online form through Tencent conference software. The video course is the basic teaching of theoretical knowledge and practical operation of AI software. According to the different teaching guidance methods summarized by the research, two versions of teaching courses were conducted to present the effect. The first one is the traditional guidance mode, in which the educator passively guides the teaching through voice and manual interaction. The second was a multidimensional guidance model (passive + active guidance), i.e., the former model was supplemented by an active guidance approach featuring the educator's eye trajectory as an interaction. The experiment was conducted by grouping two groups for simultaneous online learning to investigate whether the active guidance mode with eye-tracking interaction can optimize the effect of online education information transmission. Second, in addition to the difference in guidance methods, the electronic devices used by the learners for online teaching were also one of the objects of this experiment. The digital media devices used to transmit information were divided into smartphones and tablets according to the size difference, and groups were selected to use different digital media for online learning, to analyze whether the difference in the screen size ratio of digital media is one of the factors influencing the effectiveness of online education information transmission and its influence on the guidance method. The duration of both versions of online education was limited to 12 min, and the content taught was identical except for the difference in educator guidance. The screen sizes of the two electronic devices (IPHONE 13 and IPAD PRO 2021) were 6.1 inches and 11 inches, respectively. The teachers who conducted the instruction were professional teachers who were proficient in AI software and had rich knowledge base and teaching experience in AI software (Fig. 4).

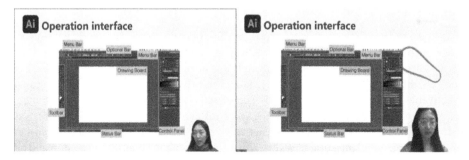

Fig. 4. Two types of online education teacher guidance

4.2 Experimental Procedures

The basic information questionnaire was first distributed online to screen out non-professionally related interested persons who had basic knowledge about the software, and the final subjects totaled 40. To improve the content validity and reliability of the post-test questionnaire, a pre-experiment was conducted, and the questionnaire was finalized for the study after minor changes were made to the order and dimensions of the questions. The study was specifically divided into two parts. Part I: Subjects entered the laboratory and were randomly assigned to participate in one of the online course learning groups, i.e., traditional guided + smartphone format, traditional guided + tablet format, multidimensional guided + smartphone format, and multidimensional guided + tablet format. At the end of the study, the subjects completed the required learning tasks. Part 2: Subjects fill out three questionnaires. The duration of the whole experiment was about 50 min.

The questionnaire 1 is a prior knowledge questionnaire. With reference to the basic operation of Illustrator software and the required teaching content of the experiment, this study developed its own prior knowledge testing questionnaire. The quiz consists of 2 multiple choice questions and 10 single choice questions. The quiz examined the basic theoretical knowledge of AI software and the mastery of AI software interface and tools, respectively. The total score of the test is 100, and the higher the score, the higher the mastery of AI software.

The questionnaire 2 is a learning effectiveness test. The questionnaire was designed in two dimensions: knowledge retention and transfer [38], and the knowledge points covered in the test were taken from the learning content taught in the online course. The questionnaire consisted of 12 single-choice questions, 3 multiple-choice questions and 1 practical question. The total score of the quiz is 100 points, of which the practical questions are worth 25 points. Learners completed illustrations based on the course content, and their work was evaluated by two professionals and graded on the following five dimensions: (1) proficiency: whether it was completed within the time limit; (2) shape: whether it was mastered using the rectangle, ellipse and path finder-shape mode - union tools; (3) color: whether it was mastered using the straw tool; (4) detail: whether it was mastered using the shape generator, scissors (5) Innovation: innovation in the overall effect of composition, etc. Each dimension was scored out of 5.

The questionnaire 3 is a learning satisfaction questionnaire. The questionnaire in this study was revised from the Computer Classroom Learning Satisfaction Scale developed by Wang [39], which includes four dimensions of teacher teaching, classroom content, teacher-student interaction, and learning equipment, with 18 question options. The scale was rated on a 5-point Likert scale, and subjects were asked to record their level of agreement with the question statement using five response levels.

The MOOC engagement scale (MES) was developed by Deng et al. [37]. The questionnaire in this study was modified from this scale and includes four dimensions: behavioral, cognitive, affective, and social, with 12 question options. The scale is rated on a 5-point Likert scale, and the total score of the scale indicates the level of engagement in online learning (Figs. 5 and 6).

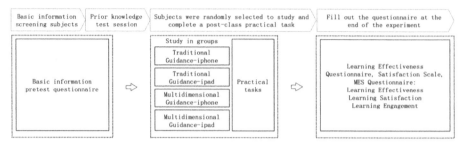

Fig. 5. Experimental process

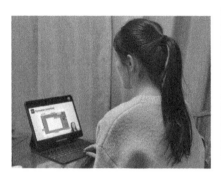

Fig. 6. Two kinds of experimental equipment situation

5   Research Results

SPSS 28.0 was used to test the reliability, validity, and structural validity of the four measurement instruments. Also, descriptive statistics and correlation tests were conducted on the collected data with the help of SPSS 28.0 and AMOS 26.0. By conducting descriptive statistics on the collected data, the effects of different teacher guidance on the effectiveness of information delivery when learners use different screen sizes of transmission devices were then examined.

5.1   Results of Analysis of Covariance for Learning Effects

The means and standard deviations of the total scores of the four groups on the posttest questionnaires, i.e., the retention test and the migration test, are shown in the table. The original hypothesis of "equal variance of the dependent variable in each group" was tested by the Levin equivalence test of the error variance. The probability of being equal is 54.1%, which is not a small probability event and can be subjected to analysis of covariance. The purpose of the between-subjects effect test is to test whether each factor influences the variance of the data, i.e., whether there is a difference in the mean of the data between different levels of a particular factor. Analysis of the data showed that the "group number" factor $F = 3.448$, $P = 0.028 < 0.05$, was statistically significant, meaning that the four different groupings did influence the posttest total score (there was a linear relationship between the two), and the data differed by group; the pre-test total score factor $F = 4.447$, $P = 0.043 < 0.05$, was statistically significant. 0.05, which is statistically significant, i.e., the subjects' own knowledge base influences the posttest scores. Therefore, the data means were not equal among the groups, i.e., changes in guidance mode and digital media had significant effects on data changes; the data means were not equal among different prior knowledge levels, i.e., changes in prior knowledge levels had some effects on data changes.

The results of the above analysis showed that the data means between the four groups were not equal, and to investigate the differences between the groups, a two-way comparison of the means of the four groups was needed. The number of cases in each group was 10, and the mean of group 1 was 71.35, group 2 was 67.45, group 3 was 86.25, and group 4 was 83.7. The final mean comparison results were group 3 > group 4 > group 1 > group 2. The results of the data analysis showed that the mean of the total posttest scores in the group using tablets as digital media was greater than that in the group using smartphones. Among the groups using tablets, the mean of the total posttest scores of the groups in which the educators used multidimensional guidance was higher than that of the groups using traditional guidance (Table 1).

Table 1. Between-subjects effect test

Source	Class III sum of squares	DOF	Mean square	F	Significance
Modified model	3780.025[a]	7	540.004	6.935	0
Intercept	4758.561	1	4758.561	61.11	0
Group number	805.45	3	268.483	3.448	0.028
Pretest score	346.284	1	346.284	4.447	0.043
Group number * total pre-test score	443.213	3	147.738	1.897	0.15
Error	2491.818	32	77.869		
Total	244588.3	40			
Total after amendment	6271.844	39			

[a]R-squared = .603 (adjusted R-squared = .516)

5.2 ANOVA Results of Learning Satisfaction

According to the results of the online learning satisfaction scale, the mean values of the four dimensions of teacher teaching, classroom content, teacher-student interaction and learning equipment range from 4.12 to 4.35, which are between 4 ("agree relatively") and 5 ("agree strongly"). This indicates that the online learning course is reasonably designed, and the learners are satisfied with the online learning. In terms of the total online learning satisfaction scores, the different groups of samples did not

Table 2. The mean and standard deviation of learning effect

Number and group	N	Average value	Standard deviation
1. Multi-dimensional guidance + iPhone	10	71.35	10.36835
2. Traditional guidance + iPhone	10	67.45	12.72454
3. Multi-dimensional guidance + iPad	10	86.25	10.10019
4. Traditional guidance + iPad	10	83.7	6.62151
Total	40	77.1875	12.68134

show significant differences in the total learning satisfaction scores ($p > 0.05$). However, the mean total satisfaction scores of traditional guided-smartphone, multidimensional guided-smartphone, traditional guided-tablet, and multidimensional guided-tablet showed a trend from low to high. In contrast, the mean total satisfaction score of the group of subjects using multidimensional guidance was higher than that of the group of subjects using traditional guidance ($78.55 > 73.15$). In the group of subjects using multidimensional guidance, the group using tablets as a digital media was more satisfied than the group using smartphones ($81.90 > 77.20$).

One-way ANOVA was used to study the effects of different teacher guidance styles on online learning satisfaction under different digital media presentation methods from the variability of four dimensions: teacher teaching, classroom content, teacher-student interaction, and learning equipment. The table below shows that the sample does not show significance ($p > 0.05$) for a total of 14 items (A1, A2, A3, A4, A5, B1, B2, B3, B4, B5, C3, C4, D2, D3) for different teacher guidance styles in different digital media presentation methods, and not post hoc test analysis is needed. There was no significant effect of different teacher guidance styles on learners' learning satisfaction in the classroom content dimension under different digital media presentation. In addition, the sample with different teacher guidance methods in different digital media presentation methods showed significant ($p < 0.05$) for a total of four items, A6 teacher teaching, C1 teacher-student interaction, C2 teacher-student interaction, and D1 learning equipment, with differences that can be specifically analyzed by post hoc test. Specific LSD methods: samples for A6 teacher teaching showed a 0.05 level of significance ($F = 2.932$, $p = 0.047$), there are more significant differences in the group mean score comparison results show: "iPhone – multi-dimensional guidance > iPhone - traditional guide; iPad - multi-dimensional guidance > iPhone - traditional guide ", i.e., multidimensional guidance is better for increasing online learning satisfaction when using smartphones as digital media. The sample showed 0.01 level of significance ($F = 5.231$, $p = 0.004$) for C2 student-teacher interaction, with more significantly different group mean scores comparing the results showing that "iPad - multi-dimensional guidance > iPhone – multi-dimensional guidance; iPad - traditional guide > iPhone – multi-dimensional guidance; iPad - multi-dimensional guidance > iPhone - traditional guide; iPad - traditional guide > iPhone - traditional guide", i.e., teachers' satisfaction with online learning is better when using tablets as digital media when conducting multidimensional guidance.

The sample showed a 0.05 level of significance ($F = 4.278$, $p = 0.011$) for D1 learning devices, with more significantly different group mean scores comparing the results showing that "iPad - traditional guide > iPhone – multi-dimensional guidance; iPad - multi-dimensional guidance > iPhone - traditional guide; iPad - traditional guide > iPhone - traditional guide", i.e., teachers are always better able to increase online learning satisfaction by using tablets as digital media when conducting guidance (Table 3).

Table 3. The variance results of learning satisfaction. (Mean $\pm$ standard deviation)

	iPhone – multi-dimensional guidance (n = 10)	iPhone - traditional guide (n = 10)	iPad - multi-dimensional guidance (n = 10)	iPad - traditional guide (n = 10)	F	p
A1 Teacher teaching	4.60 ± 0.70	4.30 ± 0.82	4.30 ± 0.67	4.80 ± 0.42	1.333	0.279
A2 Teacher teaching	4.60 ± 0.52	4.30 ± 0.67	4.60 ± 0.97	4.90 ± 0.32	1.367	0.268
A3 Teacher teaching	4.60 ± 0.70	3.90 ± 1.10	4.00 ± 0.94	4.50 ± 0.53	1.721	0.180
A4 Teacher teaching	4.40 ± 0.52	4.00 ± 1.05	4.40 ± 0.97	4.60 ± 0.52	0.983	0.412
A5 Teacher teaching	4.30 ± 0.82	3.60 ± 1.35	4.30 ± 0.67	4.70 ± 0.67	2.453	0.079
A6 Teacher teaching	4.30 ± 0.48	3.50 ± 1.18	4.60 ± 0.70	4.20 ± 0.92	2.932	0.047*
B1 Course content	4.10 ± 0.88	4.30 ± 0.48	4.40 ± 0.97	4.80 ± 0.42	1.642	0.197
B2 Course content	4.10 ± 0.74	3.90 ± 0.88	4.20 ± 1.03	4.40 ± 0.70	0.605	0.616
B3 Course content	4.40 ± 0.97	3.60 ± 0.97	4.00 ± 0.82	3.50 ± 0.53	2.407	0.083
B4 Course content	4.40 ± 0.70	3.50 ± 1.18	4.50 ± 0.71	4.30 ± 0.82	2.738	0.058
B5 Course content	4.00 ± 0.82	3.70 ± 1.06	4.40 ± 0.70	4.30 ± 0.82	1.353	0.273
C1 Student-teacher interaction	3.90 ± 0.74	3.00 ± 1.25	4.00 ± 1.15	4.30 ± 0.82	3.049	0.041*
C2 Student-teacher interaction	3.60 ± 0.97	3.60 ± 0.97	4.50 ± 0.71	4.70 ± 0.48	5.231	0.004**
C3 Student-teacher interaction	4.10 ± 0.57	3.90 ± 0.74	4.50 ± 0.97	4.70 ± 0.48	2.609	0.066
C4 Student-teacher interaction	4.60 ± 0.52	3.60 ± 1.65	4.40 ± 0.97	4.50 ± 0.85	1.806	0.164

(*continued*)

Table 3. (*continued*)

	iPhone – multi-dimensional guidance (n = 10)	iPhone - traditional guide (n = 10)	iPad - multi-dimensional guidance (n = 10)	iPad - traditional guide (n = 10)	F	p
D1 Learning facilities	3.40 ± 1.35	2.90 ± 1.60	4.30 ± 0.67	4.50 ± 0.71	4.278	0.011*
D2 Learning facilities	4.10 ± 0.88	4.10 ± 0.74	4.70 ± 0.67	4.70 ± 0.48	2.400	0.084
D3 Learning facilities	4.50 ± 0.53	4.10 ± 0.74	4.40 ± 1.07	4.70 ± 0.48	1.131	0.350

* $p < 0.05$ ** $p < 0.01$.

5.3 ANOVA Results for Learning Engagement

According to the results of the Online Learning Engagement Scale, the mean values of the four dimensions range from 3.15 to 4.1, which are between 3 ("average") and 5 ("perfect"), indicating that the overall online learning engagement is in the middle to upper range. In addition, although the mean scores of online learning engagement in the cognitive dimension (3.72), behavioral dimension (3.75), social dimension (3.82) and affective dimension (4.0) showed a trend from low to high, there was no significant difference between the subjects' online learning engagement in the cognitive, behavioral and social dimensions, and the online engagement in the affective dimension was significantly higher than the other three dimensions, indicating that the online education mode learners are more emotionally engaged and satisfied with the online learning process (Table 4).

One-way ANOVA was used to study the effects of different teacher guidance styles on online learning engagement under different digital media presentation methods in terms of the variability of four dimensions: behavioral, cognitive, affective, and social. From the above table (see Table 2), we can see that there is no significance ($p > 0.05$) in the affective dimension of learners' engagement in online learning under different teacher-led approaches and different digital media presentation methods, which showed consistency and did not require post-hoc test analysis. On the other hand, the four items of A1 Behavior, B2 Cognition, D1 Sociality, and D2 Sociality were significant ($p < 0.05$), implying that the sociality dimension of learners' online learning engagement was significantly different under different teacher-led and digital media presentation methods, and could be analyzed by post-hoc tests. The LSD method analysis of specific items shows that: different teacher-guided approaches, under different digital media presentation methods, present a 0.05 level of significance ($F = 2.876$, $p = 0.049$) for A1 behavior, and the comparison results of the mean scores of groups with more significant differences show that: "smartphone-multi-dimensional guidance > smartphone-traditional guidance; tablet computer-multidimensional guidance > smartphone-traditional guidance", i.e., multidimensional guidance is better at increasing the engagement of online learning behavior dimensions when using smartphones as digital media. The comparison of the mean scores of the groups with more significant differences between different teacher guidance methods, with different digital media presentations, for B2

Table 4. The variance result of learning engagement.

	iPhone – multi-dimensional guidance (n = 10)	iPhone - traditional guide (n = 10)	iPad - multi-dimensional guidance (n = 10)	iPad - traditional guide (n = 10)	F	p
A1 behavior	3.70 ± 1.34	2.70 ± 0.82	4.00 ± 0.82	3.50 ± 1.08	2.876	0.049*
A2 behavior	4.30 ± 0.67	3.50 ± 0.71	4.20 ± 1.03	4.10 ± 0.99	1.716	0.181
A3 behavior	3.60 ± 1.07	3.40 ± 1.07	4.50 ± 0.71	3.50 ± 1.43	2.110	0.116
B1 cognize	4.30 ± 0.82	3.50 ± 1.27	4.10 ± 0.88	4.00 ± 0.94	1.175	0.333
B2 cognize	3.30 ± 1.16	2.30 ± 1.06	3.50 ± 0.85	3.50 ± 0.85	3.375	0.029*
B3 cognize	4.40 ± 0.70	3.60 ± 0.84	4.20 ± 1.03	3.90 ± 0.99	1.505	0.230
C1 emotion	4.10 ± 0.74	3.40 ± 0.84	4.20 ± 0.63	4.30 ± 1.06	2.400	0.084
C2 emotion	4.10 ± 0.57	3.40 ± 1.26	4.00 ± 0.82	4.00 ± 0.94	1.179	0.331
C3 emotion	4.20 ± 1.14	3.50 ± 1.27	4.50 ± 0.53	4.20 ± 1.32	1.466	0.240
D1 sociality	3.70 ± 0.95	2.90 ± 0.88	4.10 ± 0.74	3.80 ± 1.03	3.203	0.035*
D2 sociality	3.60 ± 0.84	3.20 ± 0.92	4.20 ± 0.79	4.20 ± 0.79	3.429	0.027*
D3 sociality	4.00 ± 0.94	3.40 ± 1.07	4.50 ± 0.71	4.20 ± 0.79	2.726	0.058

* $p < 0.05$ ** $p < 0.01$.

cognition showed 0.05 level of significance (F = 3.375, p = 0.029), showing that "smartphone-multidimensional guidance > smartphone -traditional guidance; tablet-multidimensional guidance > smartphone-traditional guidance; tablet-traditional guidance > smartphone-traditional guidance", i.e., when using smartphones as digital media, multidimensional guidance is better to improve the engagement of cognitive dimensions of online learning. In summary: under different digital media presentation methods, learners' engagement in online learning is higher under multi-dimensional guidance of educators than under traditional guidance. And when instructors were guided, using tablets as digital media always improved online learning satisfaction better.

6 Conclusion

With the development of technology and social changes, online education has become a hot topic of social development. Online education has broken the limitations of traditional teaching in terms of time and space, but how to ensure efficient transmission of educational information remains a problem. Although digital tools are an important factor in optimizing the interactive effect of online education, rich interaction cannot be achieved without careful pedagogical design by educators and active and efficient participation of learners. The lack of interaction is more evident in synchronous forms of online learning, where teachers and students often teach unilaterally and other interfering factors such as network latency make it difficult to achieve efficient interaction.

Currently, there is not enough research on the effectiveness of information transfer in online education, especially on the effect of differences in various factors on information transfer. Studies have shown that cues influence people's visual attention. Interactions realized by teachers through different dimensional features have a guiding effect and are one of the important factors that influence learners' perception of information. Meanwhile, many studies quantify the immersion experience through the Immersion Experience Questionnaire (IEQ) and find that the screen size of digital media affects the intensity of people's immersion. Learners choose to use common mobile digital devices of different sizes for terminal information reception, and the difference between devices is also one of the important factors affecting learners' perception of information. Therefore, in this study, we demonstrated the effects of different guidance methods (traditional guidance and multidimensional guidance) and different digital media screen sizes (6.1 inches and 11 inches for IPHONE 13 and IPAD PRO 2021, respectively) on online educational information delivery through differences in two dimensions of learners' affective and cognitive goals. 40 subjects were enrolled in the experiment on a voluntary basis. The Learning Effectiveness Checklist, Online Learning Satisfaction Questionnaire, and Online Learning Engagement Questionnaire (IEQ) were used to quantify the effect of information delivery in online education.

According to the findings, it was found that the most significant variability in the effectiveness of each information delivery was reflected in the cognitive goals of the learners, and less variability was shown in the affective goals of the learners. Learners' learning outcomes and engagement in the affective dimension were always better when educators used multidimensional guidance. When educators used different guidance methods, learners' learning outcomes were always better and learners' learning satisfaction was always higher when using large screen size mobile devices. Moreover, digital media with large screen size gave more significant engagement than digital media with small screen size ($p < 0.05$).

In summary, this study has expanded the guidance methods of teachers in synchronous online education by dividing and organizing them according to the differences in interaction forms. At the same time, the output results will help to develop intervention strategies for designing online education interactions, to better optimize the effect of online education information transmission. Although the data are from China, the cognitive level and digital ability of the subject group are consistent with the average level, and the findings in the study are to some extent applicable to other countries as well. In addition, our experimental results suggest that eye-tracking technology could be a direction to explore for future research on educator guidance methods. Future research work is necessary to confirm the correlation between different forms of eye movements (e.g., speed, size, color differences) and the effectiveness of educational message transmission. This study is an exploratory study with limitations such as moderate reliability and sample limitations. Future research work needs to increase the coverage of the valid sample as much as possible, involving different types of learning groups of different age groups and different cultural backgrounds, to improve the applicability and generalizability of the study.

References

1. Hodges, C.B., Moore, S., Lockee, B.B., et al.: The difference between emergency remote teaching and online learning (2020)
2. Picciano, A.G.: Theories and frameworks for online education: seeking an integrated model. Online Learn. **21**(3) (2017)
3. Qiyang, G., Peiyao, C., Yong, W., Runfeng, L.: The effect of teacher humor on learning engagement in online learning environments: a multilevel structural equation analysis. Psychol. Sci. **45**(04), 879–887 (2022). https://doi.org/10.16719/j.cnki.1671-6981.20220415
4. Mayer, R.E., Sobko, K., Mautone, P.D.: Social cues in multimedia learning: role of speaker's voice. J. Educ. Psychol. **95**(2), 419–425 (2003)
5. Mayer, R.E.: The Cambridge Handbook of Multimedia Learning. Cambridge University Press, Cambridge (2005)
6. Siemens, G., Gasevic, D., Dawson, S.: Preparing for the digital university (2015). https://linkresearchlab.org/PreparingDigitalUniversity.pdf
7. Verenikina, I., Jones, P.T., Delahunty, J.: The guide to fostering asynchronous online discussion in higher education (2017). http://www.fold.org.au/docs/TheGuide_Final.pdf
8. Gourlay, L.: There is no 'virtual learning': the materiality of digital education. J. New Approach. Educ. Res. **9**(2), 57 (2021)
9. Kim, K.J., Sundar, S.S.: Can interface features affect aggression resulting from violent video game play? An examination of realistic controller and large screen size. Cyberpsychol. Behav. Soc. Newt. **16**(5), 329–334 (2013)
10. Matthew, L., Theresa, D.: At the heart of it all: the concept of presence. J. Computer-mediated Commun. **3**(2) (2010)
11. Detenber, B.H., Reeves, B.: A bio-informational theory of emotion: motion and image size effects on viewers. J. Commun. **46**(3), 66–84 (2010)
12. Brown, M.: Looking over the horizon: new learning platforms, old technology debates. In: Mooney, B. (ed.) Education Matters: Shaping Ireland's Education Landscape, pp. 40–48. Educatio n Matters, Galway (2015)
13. Brown, M., Costello, E., Donlon, E., Junhong, I.: Five trends affecting online learning: a multi-focused perspective on possible future developments. China Dist. Educ. **569**(06), 21–35+7677 (2022). https://doi.org/10.13541/j.cnki.chinade.2022.06.003
14. Lasswell, H.D.: The structure and function of communication in society. In The Communication of Ideas; The Institute for Religious and Social Studies, New York (1948)
15. Qingguang, G.: Tutorial on Communication. People's University of China Press, Beijing (1999)
16. Moore, M.G.: Three types of interaction. Am. J. Dist. Educ. **3**(2), 1–7 (1989)
17. Anderson, T.: Getting the mix right again: an updated and theoretical rationale for interaction. Int. Rev. Res. Open Dist. Learn. **4**(2), 65 (2003)

18. Mayer, R.E., Fiorella, L., Stull, A.: Five ways to increase the effectiveness of instructional video. Educ. Technol. Res. Dev. **68**(3), 837–852 (2020). https://doi.org/10.1007/s11423-020-09749-6

19. Valenzeno, L., Alibali, M.W., Klatzky, R.: Teachers' gestures facilitate students' learning: a lesson in symmetry. Contemp. Educ. Psychol. **28**(2), 187–204 (2003)

20. Jiang, Y., Li, W., Liu, Y., Gu, D.: An eye-movement study on the effect of presentation of important and difficult points on learning effect in teaching videos. Telev. Technol. **42**(03), 86–92 (2018). https://doi.org/10.16280/j.videoe.2018.03.014

21. Li, L.: The effects of teacher gestures and gaze guidance on learners' learning in instructional videos: the experience reversal effect. Huazhong Normal University (2019)

22. Kim, D., Kim, D.J.: Effect of screen size on multimedia vocabulary learning. Br. J. Educ. Technol. **43**(1), 62–70 (2012)

23. Joon, K.K.: Shape and size matter for smartwatches: effects of screen shape, screen size, and presentation mode in wearable communication. J. Comput.-Mediat. Commun. **2017**(3), 124–140 (2017)

24. Wibirama, S., Nugroho, H.A.: Towards understanding addiction factors of mobile devices: an eye tracking study on effect of screen size. In: International Conference of the IEEE Engineering in Medicine & Biology Society, pp. 2454–2457. IEEE (2017)

25. Neisser, U.: Cognitive psychology. (Book Reviews: Cognition and Reality. Principles and Implications of Cognitive Psychology). Science, **198**, 816–817 (1977)

26. Dochy, F.J.R.C., Alexander, P.A.: Mapping prior knowledge: a framework for discussion among researchers. Eur. J. Psychol. Educ. **10**(3), 225–242 (1995)

27. Kalyuga, S.: Expertise reversal effect and its implications for learner-tailored instruction. Educ. Psychol. Rev. **19**(4), 509–539 (2007)

28. Homer, B.D., Plass, J.L., Blake, L.: The effects of video on cognitive load and social presence in multimedia-learning. Comput. Human Behav. **24**(3), 786–797 (2008)

29. Gagnewritten, R.: The Conditions of Learnig, 3rd edn. Holt Rinehart and Winston, Austin (1977)

30. Wei, H.C., Chou, C.: Online learning performance and satisfaction: do perceptions and readiness matter? (2020)

31. Xiong, Y., Wu, Q.: A survey on online learning satisfaction of secondary school students in the context of "no classes, no school": a survey analysis of 27, 199 secondary school students. China Vocat. Tech. Educ. **753**(29), 40–48 (2020)

32. Hu, X.: Preliminary development of a learning satisfaction scale for elementary school students. Hunan Normal University (2010)

33. Reeve, J.: A Self-determination Theory Perspective on Student Engagement. Springer, New York (2012)

34. Philp, J., Duchesne, S.: Exploring engagement in tasks in the language classroom. Ann. Rev. Appl. Linguist. **36**, 50–72 (2016)

35. Lepper, M.R., Malone, T.W.: Intrinsic motivation and instructional effectiveness in computer-based education (1999)

36. Sun, C.Y., Rueda, R.: Situational interest, computer self-efficacy and self-regulation: Their impact on student engagement in distance education. Br. J. Educ. Technol. **43**(2), 191–204 (2012)

37. Deng, R., Benckendorff, P., Gannaway, D.: Learner engagement in MOOCs: scale development and validation. Br. J. Edu. Technol. **2020**(5), 1–18 (2020)

38. Mayer, R.E.: Multimedia Learning, 2nd edn. Cambridge University Press, Cambridge (2009)

39. Wang, X.: Research on the influence of information presentation and self-efficacy on learning effectiveness. Liaoning Normal University (2013)

Multimedia and Multisensory International Learning: Making a Case for Going Beyond the Screen During Creative Virtual Exchanges

Denielle J. Emans[1]([✉]) [iD] and Kelly M. Murdoch-Kitt[2] [iD]

[1] Roger Williams University, Bristol, RI 02809, USA
demans@rwu.edu
[2] The University of Michigan, Ann Arbor, MI 48103, USA

Abstract. Accelerated by the effects of a global pandemic, higher education has rapidly integrated technology-facilitated learning and hybrid models of instruction—or blended learning—that mix face-to-face and online experiences in pre-K through university-level classrooms [1]. Project-based virtual exchanges between students and faculty in different countries spanning multiple time zones have also become more frequent in creative and educational spaces. This type of learning is called Collaborative Online International Learning (COIL) [2]. Typical media utilized in COIL exchanges range from real-time or synchronous forms imbued with high social presence (e.g., videoconferencing) to asynchronous media imbued with low social presence (email) [3]. Because people learn, respond, and take in information differently [4], media with high and low "social presence" are essential to the effective implementation and sustenance of COIL. The inherent reliance of COIL on remote communication and collaboration tools, therefore, creates a need to interrogate the different effects and outcomes of multimedia and multisensory learning in these collaborations. This paper examines how different media interactions may affect individual or shared experiences in COIL. In addition to relevant literature, the authors draw from more than 12 years of their ongoing research in developing, testing, and operating visual thinking methods that support remote Intercultural Design Collaborations (IDC). The authors argue that a successful COIL exchange relies on technology that supports rich communication [5], meaningful collaboration [6], and co-creation [7] while also allowing time and affording opportunities for individual reflection and growth.

Keywords: Multisensory Learning · Collaborative Online International Learning (COIL) · Technology-Enhanced Learning · Intercultural Design Collaboration · Social Presence · Virtual Exchange

1 Introduction

Today's creative industries—such as design; the fine and performing arts; and video, film, and gaming—demand more accrued abilities and knowledge from students and young professionals than technical skills and software training alone. University-level students must also learn to be critical thinkers who can effectively identify, frame, and solve problems in addition to skilled makers of artifacts, systems, policies, and more. Together, these skills are essential to attaining roles in design agencies or, increasingly, in international efforts dedicated to addressing wicked problems such as sustainability, climate change, poverty, and homelessness [8].

Today's design students need to be prepared to work in future scenarios that span all four of what Richard Buchanan first articulated as "the four orders of design," which encompass visual symbols, physical things, actions and interactions, and systems thinking [9]. At the same time, industry professionals encourage students to think of themselves as influential creators and storytellers who can lead change not only as individuals but as collaborators and team members [10, 11, 12]. Technical proficiency without critical thinking is precarious. Designers may create work without an awareness of, or assuming responsibility for, its effects or ramifications. Therefore, designers must learn how to develop a systemic awareness and unbiased analysis to guide their judgment and actions.

Collaboration is a skill that can be both deliberately learned and acquired through various experiences and interactions with others, perhaps most especially with those unlike oneself. Intercultural competence can be acquired and constructed as people actively seek to compare and comprehend other cultures' social, political, and behavioral expectations and norms. The development of both collaboration and intercultural competence requires self-awareness and practice. Virtual exchange presents opportunities for students to reflectively practice these skills and sensibilities within the context of productive communication and teamwork.

The authors' study focuses on Collaborative Online International Learning (COIL). COIL facilitates virtual exchanges between two or more geographically distinct classrooms. COIL utilizes communication types (e.g., private, one-to-one, one-to-team; written, visual, oral) and qualities (e.g., synchrony, richness, social presence, sensory inputs) which collectively affect how students receive and then understand information as they work together. While the authors' research examines University-level COIL, it and other forms of virtual exchange are also gaining interest in K–12 curricula. The specific type of COIL that the authors research and practice is Intercultural Design Collaboration (IDC). The visual thinking activities they have developed to support IDC have been tried, tested, and refined with over 400 participants from seven academic institutions and more than 24 countries. These activities help students explore differences, understand complex topics (such as the UN Sustainable Development Goals), share ideas, and co-create projects.

The authors' research simultaneously introduces visual thinking within disciplines that typically engage in international exchange, such as language courses, world cultures, and other humanities disciplines, while advocating for international learning to become part of more university-level design curricula. Their work in improving IDC has helped to bridge gaps between the discipline of design and more typical realms of virtual exchange, historically limited to language-learning classrooms. This visual thinking research has also been implemented within COIL initiatives by other university-level and K–12 educators across various disciplines (such as biology, urban planning, physical education, mathematics, English Language Arts, engineering, performing arts, and more).

The authors' research focuses on developing and implementing visual thinking activities—and how to best deliver these through various online and digitally enabled communication platforms and media. Through implementing these activities in an intercultural context, they have observed increased levels of critical thinking, curiosity, and engagement in their cohorts of COIL students compared to cohorts who did not utilize these approaches [13]. This is noted through measurements such as the Intercultural Development Inventory (IDI), discussed in Sect. 2.1.

2   Media Benefits and Limitations in Virtual Exchange

As a novel approach to COIL, the authors' Intercultural Design Collaborations (IDC) incorporate visual thinking, collaborative design methods, and a tailored approach to planning and operating communication tools. The virtual exchanges within their study transpire between students working within two or more geographically distinct design classrooms. IDC provides a stimulating context for developing and strengthening various skills and bases of knowledge necessary to facilitate collaborative project-based work. Some examples of these skills include critical thinking, open-mindedness, communication, creative ideation (the joint development of creative ideas), and iteration (exploration and refinement of those ideas). These skills converge as teams from geographically dispersed classrooms work together to define and execute design projects. With the support of experienced faculty, IDC at the university level provides students with the opportunity to take responsibility for iteratively developing collaborative projects with intercultural partners.

Compared to traditional study abroad programs, the remote cultural learning opportunities made possible by COIL are accessible to many more students. Moreover, unless living with a host family, the global average of 2% of college and university students who study abroad [14] often have limited opportunities for direct communication or collaboration with local people in their host country [15]. Remote collaboration with peers in a culture outside their own gives COIL students a rare opportunity to work closely with someone whose experientially informed knowledge and understandings may differ from their own. This experience can help prepare students to have more meaningful intercultural opportunities in their future studies abroad.

While screen-based environments initially enable the facilitation of COIL, they present limitations regarding how students learn and perceive opportunities for collaboration. According to neuroscientist-turned-teacher Judy Willis, one of the best ways to overcome such limitations is to employ multisensory experiences to benefit learning [16]. Thus, the authors advocate for virtual exchanges imbued with multi-channel, multimodal, and multi-sensory learning experiences that incorporate tangible practices that cannot take place solely within a digital realm. They examine the positive and negative effects of technologically mediated learning within the context of IDC to make a case for going beyond the screen during creative virtual exchanges. Participants in long-distance intercultural collaborations need to be aware of the ways the digital world both enhances and limits their learning through primarily visual and verbal channels. Thus, educators need to better understand how multimedia and multisensory factors influence the student experiences that occur during IDC exchanges.

2.1 Using the Intercultural Development Inventory (IDI) in COIL

One tool the authors have found to be a useful gauge to measure the effectiveness of Intercultural Design Collaboration (IDC) is the Intercultural Development Inventory (IDI). The IDI is a quantitative self-assessment tool designed to help its users better understand their own cultural competence [17]. Created by Mitch Hammer and Milton Bennett, the IDI is a 50-question survey based on Bennett's Developmental Model of Intercultural Sensitivity (DMIS). It has been used globally among a broad and diverse variety of participants and is available in 18 languages.

Consistent improvements in each cohort's initial and final IDI scores between the start and conclusion of an IDC exchange demonstrate the value of multichannel, multisensory, and multimodal learning (i.e., acquiring or constructing knowledge via more than one method). The IDI is typically utilized within the context of in-person experiences, such as assessing competencies developed through participation in study abroad programs or internally by companies working to improve their team dynamics and inclusion practices. The authors' use of IDI to measure improvements in intercultural competency within IDC virtual exchange environments is a pioneering application of this assessment tool.

3 Multimedia and Multisensory Intercultural Learning

3.1 Multimedia Learning Theory

Developed by educational psychologist Richard E. Mayer, multimedia learning theory is based on the idea that encountering visual and verbal information together enables humans to learn more effectively than when they encounter this information separately. In this context, the visual encompasses any kind of static image, including photographs and drawings, or moving images, such as animations, videos, or immersive visual environments. The verbal includes all manner of spoken or written words [18].

Multimedia learning theory relies on the assumption of dual-channel or multichannel learning, which means that verbal and visual information is processed by different pathways, or channels, within the brain [19]. It posits that the brain first processes written words in the same area that deals with other types of visual information before the part of the brain that deals with language. According to Mayer's theory, multichannel learning occurs when the learner can "construct a mental representation… Based on the words and pictures [she, he, or they perceive]." Mayer also refers to this representation as a "mental model." Mayer's theory is an inherent aspect of typical teaching and learning experiences in many classroom settings, such as the slide-lecture format predominant in higher education.

Understanding multimedia learning theory aids in virtual and intercultural partnerships. [7] During an IDC, multimedia learning helps students to critique their existing mental models of other cultures. In doing so, students consciously build new definitions of other cultures based on the knowledge they construct as they contribute to the operation of team structures, partnerships, and interactions. At the same time, approaches confined to the usage of a particular set of screen-based devices (e.g., phones, laptops, projection screens) can create barriers to natural verbal and visual exchange.

In an asynchronous learning environment where students are separated—by distance, time, or both—channels of information are often separated. For example, learners may only encounter verbal information (via email or other online forums), then later encounter a related visual representation (such as photographs)—or vice versa. When such a separation of visual and verbal information occurs, the disconnected information is less memorable. Thus, multichannel learning is relevant to the larger discussion of COIL and IDC as a foundation to build new mental models and memorable information. From this starting point, the authors describe the importance of multisensory experiences that further engage the senses and mind.

3.2 Multisensory Experiences Go Beyond Multichannel Learning

A *multisensory experience* occurs when humans engage in sensorimotor activities that extend beyond the verbal and visual channels. Sensorimotor modalities include the visual and auditory, but expand to include taste, smell, haptics (recognizing objects through touch), and kinesthetics (learning through movement and one's bodily motion). Sensory modalities are not to be confused with teaching modalities, which are defined in this paper as in-person, remote, and hybrid. Sensorimotor stimulation engages people across their range of senses and thus improves learning [16], but it is often taken for granted within in-person, or "face-to-face," learning environments where these modalities tend to occur more naturally.

Many K–12 learning environments, specifically early elementary education, are oriented toward facilitating multisensory learning, which leverages these students' natural tendencies toward mobility, interest in materials, and response to sensory stimuli. This is a primary reason why project-based learning (PBL) is becoming widely adopted in K–12 curricula [20]. PBL and other forms of experiential learning lean into and rely upon various planned and spontaneous multisensory experiences, such as site visits; spatial interactions; using physical materials or tactile elements; preparing or sampling foods; experiencing smells associated with the environment; or handling and using materials. The learning outcomes of experiential learning are usually more varied and personalized than a typical paper or report, and better integrate the student's interests, research, experiences, and/or collaboration efforts. More broadly speaking, multisensory teaching approaches like PBL invite students to participate and contribute more expansively to the development of their own learning experiences by sourcing and utilizing a variety of inputs and media. This aligns with Gardner's theory of multiple intelligences [21], which seeks to honor multiple modalities of learning and diverse abilities.

Intercultural Design Collaboration (IDC) is a complex form of PBL. In this context, student teams determine opportunities to develop design work as the outcomes of their learning processes. The deliberate combination of multi-channel visual and verbal activities, in combination with multisensory stimulation improves the learning experience and the quality of outcomes [7]. Multisensory learning physically creates more pathways within the brain as someone engages with a concept or problem using different sensory inputs [16]. Over their 12 years of evolving research on IDC, the authors have observed the effects of limiting and expanding channels of communication and teamwork. When a virtual exchange is limited only to visual and verbal channels within remote instruction, students miss out on the learning benefits of utilizing their full range of senses and the memories associated with that sensory input.

Thus, the authors argue that a multisensory experience in a virtual exchange must bring visual and verbal information together with other sensory experiences, such as tactile or spatial. In other words, a virtual exchange is more effective when activities and interactions are not limited to videoconferencing tools. This means that online interactions should not only be driven by visual activities but also engage with experiential and tangible activities. Willis reinforces this finding in that repeated stimulation—specifically, that which is "relational, emotional, personally relevant, learner-participatory, and experiential" improves memory retrieval [16].

3.3 Media Richness and Social Presence

In discussing multisensory and multichannel learning in virtual exchanges, *media richness,* and *social presence* play essential roles. *Media richness theory* describes the amount and perceived quality of information conveyed via different forms of media, clarifying how some tools convey more information than others. Here, "information" refers to the subject matter and any kind of communication or content that influences the reader or receiver's experience with the medium. Some forms of media communicate higher levels of information than others. The extent of the information available to the receiver in a media interaction indicates its level of "richness" [22].

Social presence is one of the types of content considered in media richness. A particular medium's capability of communicating the physical presence of another person is its relative *social presence* [3]. More information-dense forms of media are more capable of conveying social presence. Social presence theory works together with media richness theory. Indicators of social presence include facial expressions, tone of voice, and contextual cues such as lighting and audio quality. *Rich media*, such as video, contain more embedded information and, with it, can convey a *higher social presence.* Meanwhile, *lean media* with a *low social presence*, such as email, generally convey less information.

"Low social presence" media include many asynchronous forms of communication; again, email is a prime example. However, the decreased social presence typically associated with asynchronous, lean media may cause some COIL participants to find these modes less inspiring. At the same time, Robert and Dennis' Cognitive Model of Media Choice [23] suggests some positive attributes for lean media—like writing and emailing. Drawing parallels between the authors' research and study observations, when used strategically, lean media can encourage concentration and critical thinking, leading to more articulate contributions [7].

Meanwhile, videoconferencing, in-person meetings, and voice conversations are all synchronous forms of communication with "high social presence." "Asynchronous" does not necessarily equate to "lean," though, and media "richness" does not necessarily equate to an ideal learning experience for COIL participants. For example, participants can benefit from both high social presence and asynchrony through pre-recorded video exchanges. This format communicates physical presence while enabling learners to take their time and be reflective of the viewing experience.

In pre-recorded videos, high social presence features could include facial expressions, gestures, and tone of voice to convey a sense of personalized, one-to-one communication. For students communicating in different languages, taking their time to pause, rewind, rewatch, and reflect can reduce stress and improve their ability to receive information. But in this case, the real-time, responsive nature of a live conversation is missing. After all, one cannot ask a question to a person in a pre-recorded video.

Dialogue and exchange are key benefits of synchronous communication that are difficult to replicate with asynchronous media. With real-time synchronous exchange comes excitement, stimulation, and conversation at best [7]—and, at its worst, stress, awkward silences, misunderstandings, or even conflict. [13].

Because both synchronous and asynchronous approaches come with benefits and challenges, the authors advocate for using both asynchronous and synchronous forms of communication and embedding both high and low social presence media into COIL. A combined approach supports the technical needs of IDC alongside the needs of multiple intelligences and the affordances of multisensory learning. The ideal mix of media and platforms may vary depending on the disciplinary orientation of the participants, the duration of the collaboration, and the desired outcomes.

4   The Medium is Still the Message—And the Motivation

As discussed, the authors have found that activities simultaneously engaging multiple senses are instrumental to intercultural learning, team building, and project-based learning (PBL). Multisensory approaches encourage broad exploration of and experiences with information sharing amongst partners, cultivating an ability to see one's culture from an outside perspective. Sharing and discussing these perspectives promotes a sense of camaraderie among teammates who begin to understand and appreciate each other as embodied beings. For example, they can go out into the world to learn about and document various phenomena in their own environments and share them back with their remote teammates. Virtual partners can then begin to think of each other as embodied beings, not merely as two-dimensional rectangular representations on a screen.

Robert and Dennis' Cognitive Model of Media Choice [23] evokes the work of media theorist Marshall McLuhan. In his seminal book, *The Medium is the Message*, McLuhan developed the idea that the stories we tell about ourselves are linked to the medium through which we tell them—and, by extension, the technologies that enable those mediums [24]. McLuhan's point for COIL is that establishing which form of media work best for the collaboration also entails understanding how the format itself may contribute to (or detract from) individual and shared experience. As such, technologically facilitated classrooms can affect students' learning and creative potential.

Donald Norman expands somewhat on McLuhan's famous thesis in his book, *The Things that Make Us Smart*. Consistent with the authors' trials and findings within Intercultural Design Collaborations, Norman observes the positive and negative powers of technological mediation:

"Technologies are not neutral. They affect the course of society, aiding some actions, impeding others, independent of the morality or necessity of those actions.

Technology also has its side effects, both physical and mental. Technology can aid as much as it can detract. It really is up to us, both as individuals and as a society, to decide which course we shall take." [25]

Along these lines, faculty must mindfully chart a course when integrating technology, tools, and experiences into a virtual exchange. Awareness of additional inputs beyond the screen is especially important for COIL and IDC because these choices make the work feel real and not entirely screen dependent. Making choices about materiality, working methods, use of physical space, and collaborative tools are even more critical in this context because these decisions make the difference between an abstract experience and one that feels grounded in reality.

The authors argue that when students are solely focused on screen-based instruction, without tangible components to facilitate their learning, they become less engaged, and their participation, accountability, and morale decrease. At the same time, students' perceptions of the value or purpose of the experience decrease. In contrast, these aspects of the student experience improve by including multisensory learning that spans media and teaching modalities (for example, regularly scheduled in-person meetings and remote work sessions).

Educators who pivoted to remote instruction during the 2020 COVID lockdowns can attest: when courses only meet online, a teacher cannot observe and reinforce the physical components of typical classroom interactions. For example, one cannot quickly scan the room and see who is prepared or unprepared, sleepy or alert, happy or sad. It becomes much harder to know when the class needs a boost, and impossible to physically shift them—to their feet, to another side of the room, to a new space—to change the energy when needed. Small talk is also lost in the awkwardness of videoconferencing, which increases the conceptual distance from student to student, and from student to teacher. In the face-to-face classroom, however, a teacher can feel the energy of motivation, see when students are completing the work, or realize when the pace of instruction needs to slow down.

Relationships are built through unspoken interactions and observations, side conversations, and off-topic jokes—and these spontaneous interactions are lost in the artificial world of videoconferencing. Because relationship-building and trust are key to COIL's success, interspersing in-person experiences with remote class sessions is essential to students' success. Students within the same institutional cohorts can then get to know each other. Instructors can set a tone for openness and model the relationship-building behaviors that students will need to replicate on their own within their remote teams.

4.1 Recent Case Study Findings

The authors' long view of synchronous and asynchronous communication tools demonstrates that technological changes also change the nature of their students' interactions and collaborations in several ways. Their most recent IDC case study offers an illustrative example of the ways multiple tools, senses and modalities facilitate deeper understanding. Recent comparative data gathered through implementing the Intercultural Development Inventory (IDI) demonstrates the value of multichannel learning in these COIL contexts. The need for reflective practice is amplified during IDC, because it is critical to understand oneself and one's relationship to the world before working in collaborative teams [26, 27]. A foundation of self-understanding enables students to better appreciate differences and collaborate effectively with intercultural partners.

Per the authors' study, without the intentional and spontaneous multisensory inputs embedded within in-person instruction, there are additional casualties of purely virtual COIL exchanges. In addition to minimized self-reflection capabilities, when COIL takes place completely online, students' motivation, energy, and group analysis capabilities are endangered. Compared to the authors' IDC studies that included a balance of in-person and virtual instruction and interactions, their studies of exclusively virtual IDCs shared common challenges including decreased motivation, oversaturation, diminished reflective capability, and reduced creativity.

Four Critical Challenges of Exclusively Virtual IDC

1. **Decreased motivation:** Without less social presence embedded in learning activities, there is often disconnection, distrust, and lack of motivation among team members.
2. **Oversaturation:** Because certain digital tools require more effort to convey social presence, they can also be taxing and stressful to use. Students (and faculty) can become overwhelmed by the cognitive and emotional energy demands of certain platforms, like videoconferencing.
3. **Diminished reflective capability:** Group processing and the decompression space that happens in distinct classroom spaces often naturally occur with in-person learning. There is value in helping students cultivate an individual reflective practice in virtual collaborations and creating time and space for them to pause and reflect. Additionally, language barriers can be stressful and can benefit from pause/reflection time to ease the pressure of response time.
4. **Reduced creativity:** When produced in a purely remote instructional environment, using only digital tools, IDC student projects are often less sophisticated and polished. Other researchers exploring the intersection of remote/digital vs. in-person/tactile creative practices, such as Shen and Sanders, note that, in their study of co-creation modalities, purely digital methods of creation and expression "haven't shown the same levels of creativity and elaboration as the hand-drawn ones." [28]

These findings reinforce self-understanding as a necessary foundation for acceptance of others' differences and that one can develop an intercultural mindset through multisensory virtual exchange [7]. Accordingly, the authors' approach to COIL encourages participants to take responsibility for their own participation and learning in intercultural collaboration. While Mayer's discussion of multimedia learning emphasizes the need for a facilitator or instructor, students must learn to become stewards of their own relationships, professionally and developmentally: in the classroom, at home, at work, and in their communities. Ultimately, when evolving technologies are used strategically to provide students with communication options and multisensory experiences, they can help students learn and apply intercultural competence [4].

5 Conclusion

The authors of this paper are writing from a unique perspective. They have incorporated technological communication tools into their Intercultural Design Collaborations and pedagogical research since 2011, before videoconferencing was widely available. Based on their long-term observations of and experiments with virtual exchanges, they argue that technological supports are ideally *additive* to in-person classroom experiences. While these digital tools are not a full replacement for multisensory learning, technology plays an essential role in communication, especially within virtual exchange courses. However, when virtual tools are used exclusively (without a multisensory approach), they detract from the learning experience—decreasing student motivation, creativity, and reflective capabilities—while increasing oversaturation.

Consequently, their research advocates for multisensory learning opportunities that ground otherwise virtual learning experiences in the tangible experience of real life and thus make their relationships with collaborators feel less abstract. To enhance communication and trust among teammates, these collaborative opportunities enhance project-based learning by using low-stakes visuals (such as sketches) and tangible hands-on activities (such as using physical materials to visualize data related to the project). [7] Through such visual thinking activities and processes, students can explore the potential of multichannel information to improve intercultural exchange and experiences. While remote collaboration broadens horizons and reminds students that we are all citizens of the world, structured in-person interactions and multisensory experiences remind us how to be human within that widened world. Each is an antidote to the other.

References

1. Lederman, D.: What have we learned about online learning? https://www.insidehighered.com/news/2022/07/06/what-have-we-learned-about-online-learning
2. SUNY coil student guide. https://slcny.libguides.com/sunycoil
3. Short, J., Williams, E., Christie, B.: Social Psychology of Telecommunications. Wiley, London (1976)
4. Mansilla, V.B., Jackson, A.: Educating for global competence: learning redefined for an interconnected world. In: Mastering Global Literacy, pp. 5–27. Solution Tree, New York (2013)
5. Daft, R.L., Lengel, R.H.: Organizational information requirements, media richness and structural design. Manag. Sci. **32**, 554–571 (1986). https://doi.org/10.1287/mnsc.32.5.554
6. Lane, M.M., Tegtmeyer, R. (eds.): Collaboration in Design Education. Bloomsbury Publishing, London (2020)
7. Murdoch-Kitt, K.M., Emans, D.J.: Intercultural Collaboration by Design: Drawing From Differences, Distances and Disciplines Through Visual Thinking. Routledge, Milton Park (2020)
8. Egenhoefer, R.B. (ed.): Routledge Handbook of Sustainable Design. Routledge, London (2017)
9. Buchanan, R.: Design research and the new learning. Des. Issues **17**, 3–23 (2001)
10. Pater, R.: The Politics of Design: A (Not So) Global Manual for Visual Communication. BIS Publishers, Amsterdam (2017)

11. Brown, T., Katz, B.: Change by design: how design thinking transforms organizations and inspires innovation. HarperCollins (2019)
12. Fry, T.: Design Futuring: Sustainability, Ethics and New Practice. Bloomsbury Visual Arts, London (2019)
13. Murdoch-Kitt, K., Emans, D.: Improving intercultural collaboration with visual thinking. In: LearnxDesign 2021: Engaging with Challenges in Design Education (2021). https://doi.org/10.21606/drs_lxd2021.09.235
14. NAFSA: Trends in U.S. study abroad. https://www.nafsa.org/policy-and-advocacy/policy-resources/trends-us-study-abroad
15. Hammer, M.R.: The Intercultural development inventory: a new frontier in assessment and development of intercultural competence. In: Berg, M.V., Paige, R.M. (eds.) Student Learning Abroad: What our Students Are Learning, What They're Not, and What We Can Do About It, pp. 115–136. Stylus, Sterling Va (2012)
16. Willis, J.: Research-based strategies to IGNITE student learning: insights from a neurologist and classroom teacher. ASCD Association for Supervision and Curriculum Development (2006)
17. Hammer, M.R.: Additional cross-cultural validity testing of the intercultural development inventory. Int. J. Intercult. Relat. **35**, 474–487 (2011)
18. Mayer, R.E.: Multimedia learning. Psychol. Learn. Motiv., 85–139 (2002). https://doi.org/10.1016/S0079-7421(02)80005-6
19. Anzalone, S.J.: Multichannel Learning: Connecting All to Education. Education Development Center, Washington, D.C (1995)
20. Markula, A., Aksela, M.: The key characteristics of project-based learning: how teachers implement projects in K-12 science education. Discip. Interdiscip. Sci. Educ. Res. **4** (2022)
21. Gardner, H.: Multiple Intelligences: New Horizons. BasicBooks, New York (2006)
22. Dennis, A.R., Kinney, S.T.: Testing media richness theory in the new media: the effects of cues, feedback, and task equivocality. Inf. Syst. Res. **9**, 256–274 (1998). https://doi.org/10.1287/isre.9.3.256
23. Robert, L., Dennis, A.R.: Paradox of richness: a cognitive model of media choice. IEEE Trans. Prof. Commun. **48**, 10–21 (2005)
24. Fiore, Q., McLuhan, M.: The Medium is the Message, pp. 126–128. Bantam, New York (1967)
25. Norman, D.A.: Things That Make Us Smart: Defending Human Attributes in the Age of the Machine. Addison-Wesley Pub. Co., Reading (1993)
26. Baxter Magolda, M.B.: Making their own way: narratives for transforming higher education to promote self-development. Stylus, Sterling, VA (2004)
27. Kegan, R.: In Over Our Heads: The Mental Demands of Modern Life. Harvard University Press, Cambridge (1994)
28. Shen, Y., Sanders, E.B.N.: Visualizing stress – in-person and virtual co-designing with chart-based tools. In: Bruyns, G., Wei, H. (eds.) IASDR 2021, pp. 2693–2705. Springer, Singapore (2022). https://doi.org/10.1007/978-981-19-4472-7_173

A Focused Exploration About How Technologically Enhanced Educational Approaches Can Positively Foster Early Childhood to Young Adult Learning and Creativity

Michael R. Gibson[✉] [iD] and Keith M. Owens[iD]

The University of North Texas, Denton, TX 76201, USA
{michael.gibson,keith.owens}@unt.edu

Abstract. The critical focus of this co-authored paper will be to examine research approaches, design processes, and the analyses of their outcomes that address how and why technologically enhanced teaching and learning strategies and methods can positively affect the knowledge construction and critical thinking abilities of a wide range of learners, as well as those who teach them. More specifically, this paper will interrogate and examine how technologically facilitated learning and creativity nurturing affects the conceptualization, learning, instruction, immersion in design processes, and educational reforms that are evolving (or that perhaps need to evolve) in educational spaces designed to meet the needs of this set of learners. We propose to present information-cum-knowledge gleaned from over fifteen years of our own research in and around this area, as well as pertinent scholarship from several others who are and have been working in this space, that explore and interrogate two key foci. The first entails an examination of how interactive technologies could be leveraged to help students in these age ranges chart more meaningful and effective *learning paths* for themselves by enabling them to intertwine the knowledge and skills necessary to understand a given concept, phenomenon, or domain. Second, this paper will critically examine how *information and communication technologies,* or ICT (and the pedagogical approaches that these both affect and are affected by), might be used to pierce the siloed nature of the conceptually and methodologically constrained, subject-based teaching that pervades so much of the K-12 and university-level learning paradigms.

Keywords: technology enhanced learning · information and communication technologies · learning paths · educational reforms · Improving learning experiences

1 Introduction

The idea that the effects of technology enhanced approaches to the facilitation of teaching and learning in the K–12 and post-secondary education spaces have been as profoundly transformational in these arenas as they have been in finance, medicine and healthcare, law enforcement, and management is not new. There is general consensus about this among the academic communities that have explored and published scholarship about this over the past two decades [1, 2]. (In the context of this article, *technology* refers to the operation of computationally structured, digitally operated systems that allow instructors and learners to, "rapidly collect data, represent knowledge, share perspectives, digitally construct, and collaborate from almost any location." [3]) What has not been broadly agreed upon is whether using technology in these ways actually improves the learning experiences of students while improving the performances of those who teach them. A key question to pose regarding this is, *"what advantages or benefits accrue to learners who are immersed in technologically enhanced learning situations?"*.

This article examines how particular strategies and tactics for designing and utilizing technology can improve learning processes and outcomes for students while strengthening the teaching abilities of educators. More specifically, it will explore how technologically facilitated learning and nurtured creativity could affect the conceptualization, learning, instruction, immersion in design processes, and—more broadly—educational reforms that are evolving in educational spaces. (In the context of this piece, *design processes* refer to phased, recursive-rather-than-linear methods that support and bolster decision-making, as well as new ways of doing or making.) To support the attainment of these objectives, the authors will present knowledge constructed and gleaned from over five years of their research in and around this area, and support this with pertinent scholarship from others who have also worked within it. Specifically, this piece has been structured to analyze two key foci.

The first examines how interactive technologies could be leveraged to help students chart more meaningful and effective *learning paths* by enabling them to intertwine diverse knowledge and skills necessary to better understand a given concept, phenomenon, or domain. A *learning path* refers to a sequential set of learning activities that occur in small steps, and that accounts for the personal characteristics of the learner, such as his, her, or their temperaments, interests, goals, socio-cultural beliefs, attitudes, and general abilities [4]. Planning and operating a learning path invites an educator and a student to engage in an ongoing relationship that requires the educator to coach as much as teach, and, as necessary, partner with the student as a given learning experience evolves. It also requires that the student assume a large portion of responsibility for his, her or their own learning. Learning paths that weave both knowledge and skills together are crucial to constructing the consciousness and abilities necessary to engage in *critical thinking,* [5] which requires enough background knowledge of or about a concept, phenomenon, or domain to *comprehend* why and how it exists, functions and is generally understood, and deep enough knowledge to *analyze* it and, if asked, suggest and enact changes to its existence, functionality, and contextualization.

The second involves a critical examination of how technology in the classroom generally, and, more specifically, information and communication technologies, or ICT (and the pedagogical approaches that it both affects and is affected by) in particular, might be used in some way to pierce the siloed nature of conceptually and methodologically constrained, subject-based teaching that pervades so much of the K–12 and university-level learning paradigms.

2 Using Technology to Devise and Navigate Learning Paths: Better Beginnings and Approaches

From Kindergarten through the doctoral level, we have reached the point in the evolution of teaching and learning practices where the kinds of learning paths that help guide students through experiences tend to involve using an online search platform such as *Google* to begin their inquiries. While these powerful tools, or toolkits, can be said to have greatly enhanced students' abilities to find information that could perhaps prove useful to them, they do not operate, nor have they been designed to operate, in ways that encourage or facilitate their abilities to formulate probative questions that ask *"how might we (improve ____?____)," or "what if ____?____ instead of (that which currently exists)."*

Nor can search technology, *per se*, intellectually or emotionally equip learners with the abilities necessary to examine or speculate about the contextual factors and phenomena that cause particular effects, or that at least correlate them. They cannot imbue learners with the abilities necessary to question information presented to them as facts, or help them engage in or lead scaffolded dialogue—the kind that requires active listening and empathy—with others (especially those unlike themselves), or consider given situations or sets of circumstances from multiple perspectives, or, more simply, not "fall in love" with the first idea they generate (or pirate, or use generative AI such as *ChatGPT* to create). Although these search engines do not directly transform information into either knowledge or understandings in the minds of those who use them, many in the education community plan and operate teaching and learning experiences as if this is case. In short, knowing how to use *Google, DuckDuckGo, Bing, Baidu, Yahoo!* and *Yandex* does not mean a specific student can engage in critical thinking, or "analyze, reason and communicate effectively" [6]. Knowing how to use these search engines also cannot be said to definitively improve student learning outcomes or teaching practices, as the authors have documented and published in their own research [7].

Over the past two decades, much has been written across the educational canon about the limitations that supplanting learning activities that foster critical thinking and questioning have on learners and on those who teach them with those that merely ask them to obtain data or information. Effective *learning* is guided by the ability to deploy knowledge and understandings that have been constructed or gleaned from experience [8]. It also requires that a necessary skill or skills have been acquired to facilitate this intellectual activity. Information provides the contextual framework within which this skill-abetted deployment of knowledge and understandings occurs.

Effective *teaching* requires the strategic formulation and actuation of experiences that span a broad spectrum. These range from step-by-step instruction to challenges rooted in problem identification, framing, and addressing (and perhaps resolution), to more complex knowledge construction activities. These call for the intermingling of intelligences that span multiple disciplines or ways of thinking and doing to guide the development, testing and implementation of products, systems, services, and experiences. Teaching can facilitate learning to good effect in modes that are both passive, such as assigning readings and then discussing them, or active, which might entail leading a group of learners through their operation of an experiment, or the development of a prototype that may require several iterations to successfully complete.

2.1   Utilizing Technology to Open Effective Learning Paths

This brief, contextualized overview of teaching and learning is offered to preface the argument that using technology to enhance learning and teaching on behalf of students ranging from pre-Kindergarten to those who are engaged in post-doctoral study is dependent on several factors. One of them is the need for educators who endeavor to use technology to enhance their students' learning experiences to cultivate a broadly informed, thoroughly explored set of understandings about how and *why* using technology could potentially be effective. Support for this argument was recently articulated as follows by Matthew Bower in his book *Design of Technology-Enhanced Learning: Integrating Research and Practice*:

> "As technologies change, it is crucial that educators… respond in a principled fashion based on a deep understanding of pedagogical issues, rather than haphazardly based on intuitive or superficial reasoning. Maintaining a focus on pedagogical issues means that educators can avoid being distracted by the novelty of new technologies and concentrate upon how each technology is influencing interaction and learning." [3]

Further, when students and educators work together to thoughtfully and systematically utilize technology to guide their learning partnerships, they greatly improve their abilities to mutually develop and evolve viable strategies for operating learning paths that are adaptable to how different individuals and groups learn (and teach) [9]. When this occurs, this type of technologically abetted activity becomes rooted in *co-design,* which means that the sequences of events that transpire as learning experiences progress—tutorials, hands-on, project-based endeavors, and opportunities for documentation and storytelling or reporting—guide these learning paths in ways that allow students to become much more adept at thinking about how and why they think as they do. This technology abetted reflectiveness also allows them to become more inquisitive and elaborative as particular learning paths initiate, branch out, intersect, and even loop back on themselves. Connective technologies such as ZOOM provide opportunities for feedback to extend beyond classroom environs and between (for example) project participants in rural and urban settings, or across social class divides, or across geographic and logistical barriers of the types that allow teams of students and educators that are disparately located to work on group projects.

Utilizing technology to allow students and educators to weave together elements of learning that are self-paced and self-regulated, and that foster knowledge acquisition and construction in situations that combine online-learning with face-to-face interactions, "…leads to better student experiences and outcomes, and more efficient teaching and course management practices…" [10] This type of so-called *blended learning* creates favorable circumstances for students to and their educator-partners to work together not only to attempt to address and resolve problems that have been identified and framed for them by others, but to do so themselves. In this way, students are allowed to create their own content, and are thus more likely to be engaged in not only learning about the essential ideas and domains of knowledge that inform it, but in how and why they choose to perceive and understand it as they do. They also tend to choose more synthetic approaches when examining content that has relevance to their own lives, or to those who inhabit their lives, and this can be (and has been) facilitated in ways that do not compromise whatever siloed curriculum or topic-based standards must be met to satisfy applicable accrediting bodies [11].

Individual students and learning teams who become adept at using technology to chart and navigate specific learning paths also become adept at *competency-based learning* [12]. This means that not only can they demonstrate their abilities to appropriately apply knowledge and skills in particular areas, but—more importantly—they can demonstrate their abilities to learn *how to learn*, which involves knowing how, why and when to access resources available to them through whatever knowledge sources they have access to, and, how, why and when to, as necessary, engage in observational research and analysis, or to iteratively develop and test prototypes. This also becomes quite advantageous when learners are challenged to engage in actually solving the problems they will have learned to identify and frame by engaging in blended learning. When enhanced by mindful, broadly informed usage of interactive technology, blended and competency-based learning also yield opportunities for students and educators to work effectively in and across teams, and to fulfill various roles within them that span the spectrum from project management to testing and troubleshooting to content creation. As these scenarios play out, team members engage in *active learning* as they interact with one another virtually and in person, and, in so doing, learn that having to explain and articulate rationales to support specific project-based decision-making tends to increase self-awareness and the ability to assess methods and outcomes. Perhaps most importantly, and this reflects a reality that the authors have observed to play out as they have engaged in and facilitated over two hundred project-based, technology enhanced learning endeavors with their design students over the past 20 years, is how sharply their students critical, analytical, and productive abilities increase when they come to understand that there is no "good idea" on any computer keyboard, and that their knowledge of software and how to engage with social media is not likely to improve on these either.

While the evidence that technologically supported education can lead to rich and effective blended and competency-based learning paths is compelling and continues to accrue, one longstanding structural reality of K-12 learning persistently acts as a barrier to these types of technology abetted approaches—siloed, subject based curriculum and teaching approaches. The second section of this paper briefly outlines this conundrum and suggests how Information Communication Technology (ICT) can offer remedies.

3   Educational Siloing: Its Critics, and Responses

Why does K-12 education continue to rest upon siloed curricula when complex modern life often requires understandings and actions based on synthesis rather than simplification and deconstruction? Historically there are many reasons, but two stand out. First, siloing knowledge into individual areas of expertise such as biology or math allows educators to focus on information relevant to a primary topic, simplifies the classroom learning environment, and aligns well with the widely accepted and rarely questioned scientific method (i.e., to break down complex phenomena into more easily understood and controllable variables). Second, this approach to segmenting and disseminating knowledge makes it easier for schools to develop curricula and, in an age of stricter accounting for student learning, track student progress using discreet, compartmentalized knowledge and proficiency acquisition markers.

"More often than not, it has been the voices of science and economics that have shaped the curriculum. [13] Industrial efficiency studies and scientific thinking characterized by objective, quantifiable measurement has led to the assumption 'that complex tasks become more manageable (i.e., easier) once broken down into their so-called basic parts." [14, 15]

Proponents of siloed curricula cite its ease of implementation and structural reliance on long-accepted scientific methods for understanding complex phenomena. Curricular variations of this approach are known by the following, subject-centered, descriptors: subject-area, common content, back-to-basics, perennialist, and essentialist. However, detractors consider siloed, skill-centric curricular and pedagogical approaches such as these to be antiquated and deeply flawed.

"Critics, however, claim that the subject centered curriculum is fragmented, a mass of facts and concepts learned in isolation. They see this kind of curriculum as deemphasizing life experiences and failing to consider adequately the needs and interests of students. The emphasis, such critics argue, is on the teaching of knowledge [or simple] recall of facts." [16]

Nor is this criticism a recent phenomenon. Debate over the efficacy of siloed versus integrated curricula has been a prime focal point in educational discourse for over eighty-plus years—and it continues.

"Coordinating disciplines has been a primary feature of curriculum planning since the turn of the [20th] century when Herbart's notion of 'apperceptive mass' changed the way theorists conceptualized the sequencing of learning. Since then, articulation within the disciplines and across the K-12 curriculum has been a prime focal point of educational discourse [17]." [15]

A sampling of the many contemporary expressions of integrated curriculum that have been developed and championed as antidotes to the limitations posed by siloed teaching approaches include interdisciplinary studies and cross-disciplinary correlation—two or more disciplines taught in conscious relation to each other; problem-based learning—providing students with 'complex, real-world' problems for them to engage with sans deconstruction and with an eye toward synthesis and solution finding; and constructivist approaches—a paradigm of learning that assumes the locus of new knowledge construction should be the ever-evolving individual, rather than external subject matter [18]. Salient studies focused on these learning methods suggest their effectiveness at opening *learning paths* that can engender student engagement, hone critical thinking skills, and foster students' ability to deal with complexity by teaching them engage in effective analysis and synthesis. Moreover, these approaches have been shown to encourage disciplinary transcendence by providing learners with ways to search for self-directed knowledge coherence and personal meaning.

3.1 Information Communication Technology (ICT): Curricular Facilitation and Scaffolding

Proponents of ICT in the classroom believe it offers a variety of important benefits for learners, teachers, and educational institutions. Among these are higher levels of student engagement and motivation, more active collaboration between students, more fluid integrative learning across subject areas, increased communication between students (peer-to-peer learning) and between students and teachers (mentor/mentee), and more developed cognitive discernment arising out of engagement with real-world, real-time content. Students also note the benefits of ICT and learning.

> "…students report that, as a result of using technology to support learning, they are realizing improved academic outcomes, developing future-ready skills, and enjoying a more personalized learning experience. For example, 59% of middle school students say they have better grades and test scores as a result of having access to digital tools, content, and resources to support schoolwork" [20]

These benefits, however, are generally believed to arise most often when ICT is thoughtfully paired with student-centered, integrative learning, and when it enjoys broad-based, institutional support, rather than when it is simply used to empirically track and assess student progress against external metrics such as state mandated learning objectives. A recent McKinsey & Company analysis of a 2018 Program for International Student Assessment (PISA), survey published in December 2019 by the Organization for Economic Co-operation and Development (OECD) reaffirmed this view:

> "…Taken together, these [survey] results suggest that systems that take a comprehensive, data-informed approach may achieve learning gains from thoughtful use of technology in the classroom. The best results come when significant effort is put into ensuring that devices and infrastructure are fit for [the] purpose (fast enough internet service, for example), that software is effective and integrated with curricula, that teachers are trained and given time to rethink lesson plans integrating technology, that students have enough interaction with tech to use it effectively, and that technology strategy is cognizant of the system's position on the school-system reform journey." [21]

Echoing the same sentiment:

A report issued by the Higher Education Funding Council for England (HEFCE) in 2009 and cited more recently by Adrian Kirkwood and Linda Price, utilizing technology to facilitate learning can be qualified as beneficial for the following reasons:

- It allows for existing processes that guide enterprises as broadly construed as curriculum planning or as narrowly construed as day-to-day lesson and activity planning to be carried out in ways that are more *efficient* in terms of time-on-task, financial expenditure, and resource allocation.

- It affords opportunities to *improve* existing processes that guide the inherent functionality and management of educator training, the successful realization of student learning outcomes, and the infrastructure necessary to effectively facilitate these.
- It provides the means necessary to plan and implement *transformations* to existing processes, or the inventions of new processes, as deemed necessary by educators and those who learn from them [22].

Thus, while several studies have demonstrated the efficacy of the strategic implementation of ITC *in the classroom, institutional and personnel barriers* can negatively affect its broader impact. "Both infrastructure and [educator] competencies are required for the successful implementation of ICT in a school" [23]. Moreover, "[t]he case studies suggest further that the less that ICT is part and parcel of a concerted effort in the school to drastically change teaching practices, ICT has relatively little impact on such practices" [24].

4 Technology Enhanced Education: A Practical Reflection

The two co-authors have amassed extensive experience over the past two decades working with a wide variety of educators and educational administrators in these educational settings. These experiences have taught them some fundamental tenets.

First, that worthwhile learning paths can be opened through the thoughtful consideration and implementation of certain Information Communication Technologies (ICT) in the classroom. However, success cannot rest on the use of ICT alone. True educational attainment must be based on coupling these technologies with curricula that span rather than is bounded by siloed subject matter. Paramount to this realignment is understanding new learning opportunities exist *across* disciplines as much as within them. Our personal experience, along with other investigators' studies, have shown that, working in tandem, the strategic pairing between technology and cross-subject orientations can and do support effective blended and competency-based learning experiences, environments, and outcomes.

Second and more broadly, classroom implementation of technologically facilitated learning must be supported by the host institution through funding, enhanced educator training and a foundational commitment to transforming legacy teaching approaches into more nimble, forward-thinking strategies. And finally, in order for investigators or other outside experts or consultants to have any hope of success within extant K-12 learning institutions and their unique dynamics, a clearly formulated precursor agreement needs to be in place prior to operating, or attempting to operate, learning opportunities that employ new technologies and that span disciplines withing existing institutional frameworks. This subtle but vital differentiation can be expressed as the strategic and tactical differences between playing the game by an extant set of rules better than the other team versus creating new rules to guide new kinds of play as they are required.

References

1. Sarker, M., Wu, M., Qian, C., Alam, G.M.M., Li, D.: Leveraging digital technology for better learning and education: a systematic literature review. Int. J. Inf. Educ. Technol. **9**(7), 453–461 (2019)

2. Villatoro, S., de-Benito, B.: Self-regulation of learning and the co-design of personalized learning pathways in higher education: a theoretical model approach. J. Interact. Media Educ. 1(6), 1–16 (2022). https://jime.open.ac.uk/articles/10.5334/jime.749/. Accessed 19 Jan 2023

3. Bower, M.: Design of Technology-Enhanced Learning: Integrating Research and Practice. Emerald Publishing, Bingley (2017)

4. Lindín, C., Steffens, K., Bartolomé, A.: Experiencing edublocks: a project to help students in higher education to select their own learning paths. J. Interact. Media Educ. 7, 1–16 (2022)

5. Willingham, D.: Knowledge matters: restoring wonder and excitement to the classroom. Arts Educ. Policy Rev. 109(4), 21–32 (2010)

6. Marczak, M.: Using technology to teach critical thinking skills. Digit. Learn. Collab. (2019). https://www.digitallearningcollab.com/blog/2019/1/16/using-technology-to-teach-critical-thinking-skills. Accessed 22 Jan 2023

7. Gibson, M.R., Owens, K.M., Hyland, P., Donaldson, C.: Preparing to introduce design thinking in middle schools. In: Bohemia, E., Nielsen, M.N., Pan, L., Börekçi, N.A.G.Z., Zhang, Y. (eds.) Proceedings of the Design Research Society Learn x Design 2021 Conference: Engaging with Challenges in Design Education, the 6th International Conference for Design Education Researchers, Jinan, China, 24–26 September 2021, pp. 405–413. The Design Research Society, London (2021). https://www.researchgate.net/publication/357381548_Volume_4_Proceedings_of_the_DRS_LEARN_X_DESIGN_2021_6th_International_Conference_for_Design_Education_Researchers. Accessed 27 Jan 2023

8. Organisation for Economic Co-Operation and Development: Understanding the Brain: The Birth of a Learning Science, p. 42. OECD Publishing, Paris, France (2007)

9. Moral, S.V., Crosseti, B.d-B.: Self-regulation of learning and the co-design of personalized learning pathways in higher education: a theoretical model approach. J. Interact. Media Educ. 6, 1–16 (2022). https://jime.open.ac.uk/articles/10.5334/jime.749/. Accessed 25 Jan 2023

10. Serrano, D.R., Dea-Ayula, M.A., Gonzalez-Burgos, E., Serrano-Gil, A.L.: Technology-enhanced learning in higher education: how to enhance student engagement through blended learning. Eur. J. Educ. Res. Dev. Policy 54, 273–286 (2019). https://onlinelibrary.wiley.com/doi/10.1111/ejed.12330. Accessed 17 Jan 2023

11. Sackstein, S.: Authentic learning begins with student-designed curriculum education week. Education Week (2018). https://www.edweek.org/leadership/opinion-authentic-learning-begins-with-student-designed-curriculum/2018/03#:~:text=Implications%20of%20student-generated%20curriculum%3A%201%20Students%20are%20more,a%20culture%20of%20success%20and%20interest.%20More%20items. Accessed 16 Jan 2023

12. Sarker, Md.N.I., Wu, M., Qian, C., Alam, G.M.M., Li, D.: Leveraging digital technology for better learning and education: a systematic literature review. Int. J. Inf. Educ. Technol. 9(7), 453–461 (2019)

13. Cohen, A.M., Hill, A.: Instructional Practices in the Sciences, Spring 1978. Center for the Study of Community Colleges, Los Angeles, CA, USA, 1 September 1978. Chrome-extension://efaidnbmnnnibpcajpcglclefindmkaj/. https://files.eric.ed.gov/fulltext/ED160144.pdf. Accessed 1 Feb 2023

14. Iran-Nejad, A.: The global coherence context in educational practice: a comparison of piecemeal and whole-themed approaches to learning and teaching. Res. Sch. 1(1), 63–76 (1994)

15. Mathison, S., Freeman, M.: The logic of interdisciplinary studies. Report series 2.33. Paper presented at the Annual Meeting of the American Educational Research Association, Chicago, IL, USA, 24–28 March 1997. Published by the National Research Center on English Learning and Achievement, Albany, NY, USA. Sponsored by The Office of Educational Research and Improvement (ED) (1998). Chrome-extension://efaidnbmnnnibpcajpcglclefindmkaj/. https://files.eric.ed.gov/fulltext/ED418434.pdf. Accessed 1 Feb 2023

16. Ornstein, A.: Curriculum contrasts: a historical overview. Phi Delta Kappan, February 1982, pp. 404–408. Chrome-extension://efaidnbmnnnibpcajpcglclefindmkaj/. http://www.projec t2061.org/publications/designs/online/pdfs/reprints/2_ornstn.pdf. Accessed 1 Feb 2023

17. Harvill, H.: Origins of the core concept. Soc. Educ. **18**(4), 161–164 (1954)

18. Jonassen, D.H.: Objectivism versus constructivism: do we need a new philosophical paradigm? Educ. Technol. Res. Dev. **39**(3), 5–14 (1991)

19. Rideout, V., Robb, M.B.: The common sense census: media use by tweens and teens. Common Sense (2019). https://www.commonsensemedia.org/research/the-common-sense-census-media-use-by-tweens-and-teens-2019. Accessed 1 Feb 2023

20. Evans, J.: Digital Learning: Peril or Promise for Our K-12 Students? Project Tomorrow Speak Up Research Initiative Congressional Briefing, p. 7 (2019). https://tomorrow.org/Speakup/spe akup2018-19-Digital-Learning-Peril-or-Promise-october2019.html. Accessed 1 Feb 2023

21. Bryant, J. Child, F. Dorn, E., Hall, S.: New global data reveal education technology's impact on learning. McKinsey Company Educational Report, 15 June 2020. https://www.mckinsey.com/industries/education/our-insights/new-global-data-reveal-education-technologys-impact-on-learning. Accessed 22 Dec 2022

22. Kirkwood, A., Price, L.: Technology-enhanced learning and teaching in higher education: what is 'enhanced' and how do we know? A critical literature review. Learn. Media Technol. **39**(1), 6–36 (2014)

23. Venezky, R., Davis, C.: Quo vademus? The transformation of schooling in a networked world. OECD/CERI, Version 8c, Paris, France, 6 March (2002). https://www.oecd.org/innovation/research/2073054.pdf. Accessed 2 Feb 2023

24. Conroy, M.: ICT in Education: possibilities and challenges. inaugural lecture of the 2004–2005 academic year. Universitat Oberta de Catalunya (2004). http://www.uoc.edu/inaugu ral04/dt/eng/carnoy1004.pdf. Accessed 3 Jan 2023

VR and AR Application in Academia, Overview in the Middle East Universities

Rund Hiyasat[1], Lindita Bande[2(✉)], Khaled Galal Ahmed[2], Baraah Hamdoon[2], Jose Lopez Berengueres[2], and Abdul-Aziz Banawi[3]

[1] Design Department, College of Arts and Creative Enterprises, Zayed University, Abu Dhabi, United Arab Emirates
rund.hiyasat@zu.ac.ae
[2] Architectural Engineering Department, College of Engineering, United Arab Emirates University , Al Ain, Abu Dhabi, United Arab Emirates
lindita.bande@uaeu.ac.ae
[3] University of North Dakota, Grand Forks, USA

Abstract. VR and AR is a technology that is being applied in various Universities in Middle East. The application in laboratories is done with the aim to contribute to the modelling of buildings and structure in different Departments such as Architecture, Civil-Mechanical-Electrical Engineering, and others. In each of these disciplines the VR and AR have different purposes. However, the overall aim is to assist the students in the learning process of the complex environment of construction.

The methodology to be followed in this study is as per the below steps:

1. Literature review on current application of VR and AR in universities in Middle East
2. Current application of VR and AR in UAE Universities,
3. Application of VR in design Courses in AE, COE, UAEU
4. Findings and results

The aim of this study is to increase the application of VR and AR in the academic environment in order to prepare the new generation for the digital future. This is achieved by having an overview of current applications of the VR in the Middle East top Universities, followed by the application in the UAEU, Architectural engineering Department, Design Studios. The findings of this research can be of great use to the Academic of Engineering College in UAEU but also the industrial sector in UAE.

Keywords: Virtual Reality · Augmented Reality · Middle East

1 Introduction

In recent years, more research focused on technological advancements. With the hit of the COVID-19 pandemic in 2019, many firms announced multiple projects that are directed towards Virtual Reality (VR) and Augmented Reality (AR). Meta (2020), for instance

A. Marcus et al. (Eds.): HCII 2023, LNCS 14033, pp. 98–110, 2023.
https://doi.org/10.1007/978-3-031-35708-4_7

announced the transformation from Facebook to Meta, implying the shift towards a virtual world, where users are given the opportunity to interact and live a digital life via their avatars. To better understand the different terms, it is important to identify what a real environment is. A real environment is that which is limited to laws of physics, where objects can be sensed as they exist (Ardiny and Khanmirza 2018). A virtual world, on the other hand, only exists via the aid of computers or technological advancements, thus allowing for more flexibility in abiding by the rules of physics, including time, gravity, etc. (Ardiny and Khanmirza 2018; Bartle 2004). Ardiny and Khanmirza (2008) refer to anything between the two worlds as Reality-Virtuality (RV) continuum. This includes Virtual Reality (VR) and Augmented Reality (AR) with all their kinds and variations.

Schnabel et al. (2007) and Ardiny and Khanmirza (2018) refer to different kinds of VR and AR, depending on their relation to reality. Starting with Real Reality, Types of environments start gradually deviating away from the physical world to move to Amplified reality, Augmented Reality, Mediated Reality, Augmented Virtuality, Virtualized Reality, and Virtual Reality.

For simplicity's sake, this research focuses on the more general categorization adopted by Ardiny and Khanmirza (2018), where all the precise types are summarized under three general terms: Augmented Reality, Mixed Reality, and Virtual Reality. The following section will aim to define each of the three terms.

Augmented Reality (AR)

AR can be defined as the environment where computer-generated information (virtual content) is integrated within and linked to the real world (Ardiny and Khanmirza 2018). This is done via cameras, microphones, Global Positioning Systems (GPS), and haptic devices and sensors (Ardiny and Khanmirza 2018; Aalkhalidi et al. 2022). The production of AR environments requires the following steps: Sensors collect all real-world data, which is then analyzed. Data is then added from different information sources. Finally, the resultant information is displayed as digital elements (Ardiny and Khanmirza 2018).

The tools required for users to see the AR content, special glasses need to be worn. Those are equipped with cameras, microphone, and Inertial Measurement Unit (IMU) to indicate position, velocity and orientation (Ardiny and Khanmirza 2018). This allows users to experience the real environment with digital, computer-generated objects appearing simultaneously through the glasses.

Virtual Reality (VR)

Invented in 1968 by Evan Sutherland, VR started as a head mounted display (Champion 2018; Aalkhalidi et al. 2022). VR is distinguished from AR by its dependence on the artificial virtual environment, where users can control virtual elements via the aid of GPS, haptic and auditory devices, etc. (Ardiny and Khanmirza 2018; Mustafa and Hutton 2001; Aalkhalidi et al. 2022). Due to its ability to allow sensory feedback, the VR environment can be described as immersive and interactive (Ahmed, et al. 2022).

In order for users to enter the VR world, users need to use devices, such as a Head-mounted display (HMD), to enter a space with back-projected stereo projection screens, such as CAVE (an Automatic Virtual Environment). Alternatively, users can use Desktop displays (Ardiny and Khanmirza 2018).

HDMs are boxes worn on the head, that include displays in front of each eye with a wide 110-degree field of View (FOV), at least (Ahmed, et al. 2022). To display content, a smart phone -often equipped with software development kit (SDK)- is placed into the back of the lenses (Ardiny and Khanmirza 2018).

As opposed to HDMs, displays, such as CAVE, offers users the chance to experience the virtual environment through a display that covers the walls, ceiling, and floors of a room, thus freeing users from potential dizziness and eye fatigue associated with HMDs. Nonetheless, users experience VR via displays still need to use joysticks or specialized gloves to interact with the virtual elements on the display (Ardiny and Khanmirza 2018).

A third way to experience VR environments is via the use of desktop. Although cheaper and more accessible, users do not get fully immersed in the environment. This is because users watch a screen, potentially a computer monitor, and use devices such as a computer mouse to interact with the virtual content (Ardiny and Khanmirza 2018).

Regardless of the tools used, it is always crucial to consider price, quality of display and experience, as well as user friendliness, when choosing the means of working with VR and AR content (Ardiny and Khanmirza 2018).

Mixed Reality (MR)

Similar to AR, MR is an environment that combines the physical with the virtual world. With MR, however, users are provided with a more interactive experience, where vision, graphics processing, display technologies, input methods, and cloud computing contribute to the environment, allowing users to move and interact with virtual objects within the environment.

VR and AR in Academia

In Academia, the use of VR has been widely experimented. Previous studies show that VR offers an immersive and interactive experience, where students can learn with more interest and engagement, in a cost-effective manner that simulates real situations, which reflects on student performance in courses (Holly et al. 2021; Ahmed 2020, Slavova and Mu 2018). Wang et al. (2018), for instance, conducted a study that involved VR to allow design students to experience and communicate non-existing spaces, while Birt et al. (2017), used it to explore ways of understanding complex lighting theories.

In Architecture, Engineering and Construction (AEC), VR technology was used to tackle crucial considerations during the project's design phase. For example, to reduce energy performance gap, Niu et al. (2016) explored the use of Building Information Modeling (BIM) and VR to predict user behavior in spaces before their construction. To do that, desktop VR was used to expose potential users to different light-switch layouts in a typical residence in Hong Kong. Behavior was monitored and recorded to achieve optimal design that minimizes lighting energy consumption in the space.

Heydarian et al. (2015) used VR to conduct a comparative study, where participants were exposed to different lighting conditions (simulated by VR) and were requested to perform certain tasks related to reading and object identification. Significant results indicate that IVE can simulate close-to-reality environments, in order to measure effect of different environmental situations on user performance in certain activities.

2 Methodology

This research analyzes the VR application in Middle east with focus on UAE and UAEU University design courses. The methodology follows the below points:

– Literature review on current application of VR and AR in universities in Middle East.
– Current application of VR and AR in UAE Universities.
– Application of VR in design Courses in AE, COE, UAEU.

2.1 Literature Review on Current Application of VR and AR in Universities in Middle East

Rund Özgen et al. (2021) conducted a comparative study that targeted 20 first-year undergraduate students in the Interior Architecture and Architecture majors, at Bilkent University in Turkey. The study aimed to assess the use of VR-based vs. paper-based education of basic design, through equal grouping of participants, where each group is made of a mixture of both genders. The study prompted participants to conduct design-related tasks in a studio environment. The group working with VR-based applications, used Google Blocks software, and Oculus Rift DK2 as the HDM hardware. The paper-based approach group used conventional problem-solving media and craft material. Questionnaires targeting participants and an effectiveness test was conducted to evaluate the outcomes produced by each group. Results showed lack of significant difference in ease of application between the VR-based group and the paper-based group. On the other hand, significant difference was found in terms of enjoyment and intention of use. Authors also suggested that the use of VR enhances cognitive thinking of basic design education, visual design perception and support basic design solution development.

In Iraq, Salah et al. (2018) conducted a study that involved the use of remote laboratories in Science and Engineering education. The study formed a collaboration among four universities, including Duhok University, Zakho University, and Duhok Polytechnic University, all located in Kurdistan, Iraq, and Oklahoma State University, in the United States of America. Remote hosts and modules (learning units) of experiments allowed students to run experiments from different locations, via the Internet. This resulted in Virtual Reality Based Learning Environments (VRBLE), where teaching avatars help students in their learning journey. Researchers found the Remote Virtual Lab (VRL) to be beneficial to students as well as to teachers to develop their qualifications and skills, especially in situations that induce limitations in resources and equipment in labs. However, authors noted that although this technology offered good support to hand-on lab experiments, it will not permanently replace the need for physical hands-on lab experiments.

Various studies echoed the significant benefits associated with the use of use of different virtual environments in education. Those include reduced commuting cost, safety considerations, better understanding of the construction and building techniques, and foreseeing clashes and potential errors at the design phase, and better preparation to the future professional practice.

2.2 Current Application of VR and AR in UAE Universities

In the United Arab Emirates (UAE), universities were also involved in AR, and VR application studies. Aalkhalidi et al. (2022) surveyed 53 Interior Design students in Sharjah University, to measure students' general knowledge of VR, AR, and MR, and understand challenges faced by institutions in implanting these technologies. Results show that despite positive feedback to the proposed experiment, challenges including facilities, skilled instructors, course availability, budget, and technological awareness remain an existing challenge.

These results were echoed by Ahmed (2020), where a study explored the use of AR-enabled BIM models in online construction engineering courses offered to bachelor students in the Architectural Engineering program in the UAEU. The one-year-long study sampled male and female students in the Advanced Building Construction Systems course. Classes were gender segregated. In the study, AR-enabled BIM tools were used to build models mimicking site visits. Hardware included HoloLens 2 AR headset, while software included Autodesk Revit (BIM software), VisualLive and Remote Assist (AR applications). Instructor-student communication was conducted via online, video-audio conferencing tool (Microsoft teams). Data collection included questionnaires targeting male and female students and instructors, thus assessing potentials and challenges faced. Results show that significant benefits in using such advanced methods in education, thereby bridging the gap between the theoretical and practical aspects faced by many students upon their graduation, enhancing their employability. Further, the study highlights the benefits of the use of advanced technology in educating young engineers, by reducing the pressing needs of commuting between emirates to attend classes physically, to visit physical construction sites.

In yet another study, Abouelkhir et al. (2022) explored the use of 4-dimensional Building Information Models (BIM) and VR in training construction management undergraduate students in the United Arab Emirates University (UAEU), in the UAE. The study aimed to assess the effectiveness of VR simulation on students understanding of the construction process. Results show that students found it easy to navigate VR environments, with minimum training, resulting in a more favorable learning experience, and better understanding of the subject matter, when compared to traditional 2D drawings and documents.

2.3 Application of VR in Design Courses in AE, COE, UAEU

Virtual reality (VR) and augmented reality (AR) are technologies being used recently at universities in the middle east. Lab applications are performed to assist in modeling buildings and structures in several disciplines, including but not limited to Architecture, Civil-Mechanical-Electrical Engineering, and others. Virtual reality (VR) and augmented reality (AR) provide a variety of functions in each of these fields. But the larger goal is to help students navigate the challenging world of construction while they study. In addition, encouraging students to propose new ideas in designing innovative and creative patterns in their building enhanced their motivation to try and apply and don't give up until they reach what they are looking for.

As a tool for architects, engineers, and designers, virtual reality (VR) technology is useful at every step of a project's development, from initial planning to final completion. As a result, the use of VR in the built environment is poised to usher in a new era in which design is made available to and useful for everyone.

Teaching in UAEU revolves around helping students develop their individual abilities and learning styles, which allows them to prepare for the future and the field of work and provides a curriculum that includes all their needs to build advanced ideas in architecture in terms of materials, form, structure, and sustainable regulations. Students in United Arab Emirates university, after designing and building their concepts, students can check and evaluate their work using an advanced program in the architecture field through a Virtual Reality or Augmented Reality program that enables them to see their work as a real model through converting their BIM model in the VR headset.

Students were engaged through several activities which focuses on participatory and productivity while teaching them as follows:

- **First Phase:** The aim of this phase is to let the student check their projects (Concept Phase) and select the best one based on the shape of the model.
- **Phase Two:** The aim is for each student to Assess and analyze their BIM models through Virtual Reality in terms of structure, furniture, materials, etc.

Application of AR in Design 01: ARHC 320, Fall 2022. As part of the course improvement and the call of the UAEU University as the University of the future, a VR session was integrated in the class. The Design Studio 1 class was conducted in the VR lab, instead of the usual classroom. The class had 7 students of different levels of preparation. This call was conducted few weeks before their final submission of the project of Sustainable House Design. Each student identified different errors through the VR model. The model was quite developed and there was still time until the submission, therefore this class helped the students identify and correct the errors (Figs. 1, 2, 3, 4, 5 and 6).

ADD Space between the structure and the Curtain wall   Slab Is higher than the stairs

Fig. 1. VR application on the design of student 01.

Fig. 2. VR application on the design of student 02.

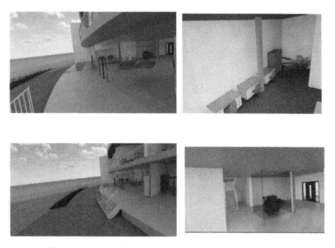

Fig. 3. VR application on the design of student 03.

Application of the VR in Design 02_Arch 335. Besides the usual architectural conceptual Solution generation and selection, Arch 335 Intermediate Building Design Studio focuses on the integration of building systems especially construction and architecture systems. Accordingly, the VR technology has been applied in the conceptual phase to select between alternatives where each student was asked to wear the VR headset and to navigate his/her conceptual design alternatives in a 'virtual' scale 1:1. This enabled the student to have an early sense about the design form and spatial relationships. Hence, this besides the applied early energy performance estimation for each conceptual design alternative, helped the student to apply the engineering design process more appropriately in this design phase. Figures 7 shows the assigned Teaching Assistant while helping students in the VR utilization in their design process at the VR Lab.

Fig. 4. VR application on the design of the student 04.

Fig. 5. VR application on the design of the student 05

Toward the end of the project and after the students have developed their schematic designs, they were guided to utilize the VR technique again but this time to check the appropriate integration of the building construction and structure systems as shown in some examples in Fig. 9. In this last phase, all errors are clearly exposed to students and their possible solutions are discussed with the course instructors to investigate possible viable solutions and apply them on the BIM model of the building schematic designs. Figure 9 illustrates some examples of this process (Fig. 8).

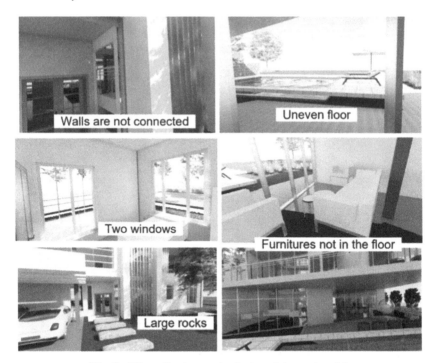

Fig. 6. VR application on the design of the student 06.

Fig. 7. A Teaching Assistant helping students in the VR utilization in the design process at the VR Lab.

Application of VR in AE Student Society Events: Another application of the VR is the Architectural Engineering Student Society Event held in October 2022. This was a very good opportunity for all students of different design studios to participate in the event and see their project progress with possible errors to modify. PhD students from The VR Lab assisted in the process and helped students understand how the VR process worked (Figs. 10, 11).

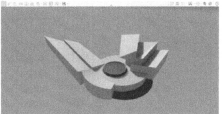

Fig. 8. Conceptual phase: Two conceptual design alternatives for the same project in Arch335 design studio.

Fig. 9. Examples of the building systems integration errors as disclosed via VR technique.

3 Results

Based on the above analysis through the different sections of the methodology, it is shown that VR is being used and adapted in various disciplines in academia in the Middle East. UAE has a large application where this technology is available in almost all universities where there are Engineering studies involved. Particularly in UAEU the VR has great value into assisting students of various studios.

The main feedback received in Design studio 1 is: errors in the stair's connections to the slabs, Different levels of windows, Walls not closed properly. Slabs not connected properly, sizes of furniture's out of scale and so on.

Meanwhile in Design Studio 2 the main use of the VR is selecting one of the two design options and structural errors from the students.

Fig. 10. VR application for the AE Student Society Event, October 2022, part 1.

Fig. 11. VR application for the AE Student Society Event, October 2022, part 2.

4   Conclusions and Discussion

Virtual Reality (VR) and Augmented Reality (AR) technology has been increasingly used in various disciplines in academia, particularly in engineering studies. The integration of VR technology in architectural design education is seen as a valuable tool in assisting students in their design process. In particular, the use of VR technology in Design Studio 1 at the UAEU University showed significant benefits in identifying and correcting design errors before the final submission of projects. This allowed students to have an early sense of the design form and spatial relationships and to apply the engineering design process more appropriately in the conceptual phase.

Furthermore, the use of VR in Design Studio 2 also helped students in selecting one of the two design options and correcting structural errors.

Based on the analysis of the use of VR technology in the architectural design education at UAEU University, it is evident that VR technology has a place in the educational context, especially in the case of architectural simulation. The use of VR technology helped students to identify and correct design errors, to select design options and to understand the VR process. The main feedback received from students was related to design and structural errors, which were corrected with the help of VR technology.

In conclusion, while VR and AR technology may not be particularly effective in education in general (as a replacement of physical classroom, see meta avatars), in the case of architectural simulation, we show that AR/VR has significant benefits. This is in line with what is known about the benefits of use of VR/AR technology in professional training and highlights the importance of incorporating VR technology in architectural design education.

References

Aalkhalidi, A.S., Izani, M., Razak, A.A.: Emerging technology (AR, VR and MR) in interior design program in the UAE: challenges and solutions. In: 2022 Engineering and Technology for Sustainable Architectural and Interior Design Environments (ETSAIDE), pp. 1–5. IEEE, June 2022

Abouelkhir, N., Tariq, M., Sami, M.: Exploring project planning in immersive environments in construction management education (2022)

Ahmed, K.G.: Augmented reality in remote learning: a proposed transformative approach for building construction education. In: 2020 Sixth International Conference on e-Learning (econf), pp. 115–120. IEEE, December 2020

Ahmed, K.G., Megahed, M., Al-Zaabi, F., Al-Sheebani, A., Al-Nuaimi, M.: Virtual reality as a student's learning and self-assessment tool in building construction education a proposed process. In: Virtual and Augmented Reality for Architecture and Design, pp. 179–201. CRC Press, Boca Raton (2022)

Ardiny, H., Khanmirza, E.: The role of AR and VR technologies in education developments: opportunities and challenges. In: 2018 6th RSI International Conference on Robotics and Mechatronics (IcRoM), pp. 482–487. IEEE, October 2018

Bartle, R.A.: Designing virtual worlds. New Riders (2004)

Birt, J.R., Manyuru, P., Nelson, J.: Using virtual and augmented reality to study architectural lighting. In: Partridge, H., Davis, K., Thomas, J. (eds.) Me, Us, IT! Proceedings ASCILITE2017: 34th International Conference on Innovation, Practice and Research in the Use of Educational Technologies in Tertiary Education, pp. 17–21 (2017). http://2017conference.ascilite.org/wp-content/uploads/2017/11/Concise-BIRT.pdf

Champion, E. (ed.): The Phenomenology of Real and Virtual Places. Routledge, New York (2019)

Heydarian, A., Carneiro, J.P., Gerber, D., Becerik-Gerber, B., Hayes, T., Wood, W.: Immersive virtual environments versus physical built environments: a benchmarking study for building design and user-built environment explorations. Autom. Constr. **54**, 116–126 (2015)

Holly, M., Pirker, J., Resch, S., Brettschuh, S., Gütl, C.: Designing VR experiences-expectations for teaching and learning in VR. Educ. Technol. Soc. **24**(2), 107–119 (2021)

Meta: Introducing Meta: A Social Technology Company (2020). https://about.fb.com/news/2021/10/facebook-company-is-now-meta/

Mustafa, M.M., Hutton, J.: Direct positioning and orientation systems: how do they work? What is the attainable accuracy. In: Proceedings, The American Society of Photogrammetry and Remote Sensing Annual Meeting, St. Louis, MO, USA, pp. 23–27, April 2001

Niu, S., Pan, W., Zhao, Y.: A virtual reality integrated design approach to improving occupancy information integrity for closing the building energy performance gap. Sustain. Cities Soc. **27**, 275–286 (2016). https://doi.org/10.1016/j.scs.2016.03.010

Özgen, D.S., Afacan, Y., Sürer, E.: Usability of virtual reality for basic design education: a comparative study with paper-based design. Int. J. Technol. Des. Educ. **31**(2), 357–377 (2019). https://doi.org/10.1007/s10798-019-09554-0

Salah, R.M., Cecil, J., Atrushi, D.: Collaborative remote laboratories for serving sciences and engineering education in Iraq: REXNet project. In: 2018 International Conference on Advanced Science and Engineering (ICOASE), pp. 134–139. IEEE, October 2018

Schnabel, M.A., Wang, X., Seichter, H., Kvan, T.: From virtuality to reality and back (2007)

Slavova, Y., Mu, M.: A comparative study of the learning outcomes and experience of VR in education. In: 2018 IEEE Conference on Virtual Reality and 3D User Interfaces (VR), pp. 685–686. IEEE, March 2018

Wang, P., Wu, P., Wang, J., Chi, H.-L., Wang, X.: A critical review of the use of virtual reality in construction engineering education and training. Int. J. Environ. Res. Public Health **15** (2018). https://doi.org/10.3390/ijerph15061204

Study on the Tangible User Interface Jigsaw Puzzle for Curing ADHD/ADD Children

Qian Lai[1]([⊠]), Chun Yu[2], Yuanchun Shi[3], and Yingqing Xu[2]

[1] Liuzhou Institute of Technology, Liuzhou 545616, China
lai_qian@163.com
[2] Tsinghua University, Beijing 100084, China
[3] Qinghai University, Xining 810016, China

Abstract. Neural feedback therapy and sensory integration training are effective means to treat attention deficit disorder (ADD)/attention deficit hyperactivity disorder (ADHD). The study on neural feedback therapy and sensory integration training adapted to family environment has long been the bottleneck in the practicalization of family treatment scheme. In light of this problem, we integrate BCI and TUI technique and propose the prototype of TUI jigsaw puzzle, E-Jigsaw, to treat ADD/ADHD children. E-Jigsaw consists of an interaction with the users that conform to neural feedback mechanism. Its TUI feature can help train the hand-eye coordination, precision manipulation, sensory integration ability and attention level. The design is based on the psychological feature of the patients, and thus prevents the psychological resistance from children. E-Jigsaw is an extension of the current mode of neural feedback therapy and sensory integration training, and overcomes the respective limitation. E-Jigsaw proposed in this article improves the user experience for ADD/ADHD children.

Keywords: Brain-Computer Interface · Tangible-User Interface · Neurofeedback

1 Introduction

Attention has always been regarded as an important mental factor in human activities. This is especially true for children who need to concentrate on their studies for a long time. Whether children have high quality of attention or not can affect their study performance because decentralization will lead to poor discipline of students at school, which will affect the overall effectiveness of students, their interaction with peers, which will lead to interpersonal tension.

It is common to see Attention Deficit Disorder (ADD) or Attention-deficit hyperactivity disorder (ADHD) in school-age children. Although behaviors of children with attention deficit disorder will be gradually improved with age, there are still nearly 20% of them who will suffer from that disease till their adulthood. What is worse, these children tend to have conduct disorder, poor social integration and other problems.

Helping children with ADD/ADHD to improve their quality of attention will ensure their sound growth and development and have wide social significance. Since the term

© The Author(s), under exclusive license to Springer Nature Switzerland AG 2023
A. Marcus et al. (Eds.): HCII 2023, LNCS 14033, pp. 111–119, 2023.
https://doi.org/10.1007/978-3-031-35708-4_8

"attention deficit disorder" was proposed, people from neuroscience, psychology and education have always focused on targeted treatment solutions. The mainstream therapy is still dominated by drug therapy, but it has a lot of side effects. Neurofeedback therapy and sensory integration therapy based on brain computer interface have provided safe and effective treatment means, but they have great limitations, long treatment cycle and slow effect. What is worse, they can only be completed in the hospital, which is time-consuming and laborious.

This paper analyzes the existing treatment programs for attention-deficit children and conducts related user surveys. What is more, E-Jigsaw, a physical jigsaw prototype for attention-deficit children is also put forward based on related researches on neurofeedback therapy, sensory integration training and physical user interface. This is a beneficial exploration of the family-oriented treatment scheme.

2   Related Work

Studies have shown that the incidence rate of ADD/ADHD in school-age children is 3%–5% while that of domestic statistics is about 3%–10%, with the male to female ratio of 4:1[1]. What is the pathogenesis for ADD/ADHD has not been made clear till now. It is generally believed that ADD/ADHD is the result of the comprehensive influence of multiple factors. The mainstream therapy is still dominated by drug therapy, but it has a lot of side effects.

Neurofeedback therapy is a treatment technique used for psychological, psychiatric treatment and rehabilitation which emerged after the 1960s. With the aid of EG collector, such as brain-computer interface, it collects EEG physiological signals into the system and then processes the signals and selectively feeds them back to users in a visual way so that users can perceive changes of their brain and nervous system. In this way, users can perceive the previously invisible changes in their physical conditions and learn to control corresponding behaviors and adjust their physical and mental states independently so as to finally treat some of their diseases.

Studies of Lubar et al. [2] show that human beings can enhance the amplitude of brainwaves in the frequency range of 12–15 Hz by learning and doing corresponding operational trainings. The regulation of 12–15 Hz brainwave can enhance functions of the patient's nervous system, so it is the main theoretical basis for neurofeedback treatment of ADD/ADHD. EEG neurofeedback treatment can help people perceive EEG electrical signals by BCI equipment and reward behaviors that can trigger the continuous increase of the amplitude of EEG SMR band (12–15 Hz) while punish behaviors of inhibiting SMR band. In this way, it can strengthen the subject's ability to spontaneously generate SMR brainwaves and enable them to gain better self-control ability and attention level [3].

Researches of Nash and Ali Reza show that EEG neurofeedback therapy has obvious effects in treating children with ADD/ADHD and can reduce medication. [4, 5].

TUI (Tangible User Interface) was first proposed by Hiroshi Ishii of MIT Media Laboratory in the conference of CHI 1997 [6]. In essence, TUI can implant digital information into physical entities. A typical TUI device needs to satisfy two features: 1. Physical entities can output digital information. 2. The state of physical entities also represents some digital information.

Because of two features of TUI, people can directly manipulate the digital world by using skills they learned in life and referring to the experience they accumulated so as to finally realize the integration of the virtual and real world. Researches done by Montessori [7] show that when touching physical toys, children are highly focused and show great interest in them. When playing with physical objects, children are immersed in the whole interaction process, which will help them a lot in improving their attention.

Therefore, we should expand TUI to the field of education and design children's toys and teaching aids which can conform to children's psychology digitalization. What is shown below is representative operations: Puchi Planet [8] designed for children hospitalized for a long time, Digital MiMs [9] which can help children to learn abstract concepts and Towards Utopia [10] which can help primary school students learn geography knowledge.

Sensory integration training is another therapy that helps ADHD children to improve their attention. Ayres took the lead in putting forward the concept of sensory integration [11]. It refers to the process in which the nervous system reorganizes and comprehensively processes the information of various sensory organs and then gives appropriate feedback. The process that a person fails to effectively integrate multiple senses triggered by the same event is called as sensory integration disorder. Clinical cases show that children with ADD/ADHD often have sensory integration problems. Ayres believes that our human brains can be shaped. Only by giving targeted training and stimulating the brain with different sensory information such as hearing, vision, touch, sense of balance and spatial perception, which can promote the development of nerve cells in the brain again, can patients recover their sensory integration ability.

Commonly used sensory integration training methods include balance seesawing board, cylinder, massage ball, slide, balance table, jumping bed, skateboard, jigsaw puzzle, building blocks, etc.

Researches done by CHEN Huali [12], et al., show that after sensory integration training, children with ADD/ADHD have improved a lot in terms of attention concentration, motor coordination, emotional stability and academic performance. The longer time, the better effects will be achieved. However, people should insist on that for a long time.

In fact, EEG neurofeedback training and sensory integration training also have the same effect on normal people. A large number of controlled experiments also show that normal people will also improve their attention performance after EEG neurofeedback training and sensory integration training.

3 Existing Problems

When EEG neurofeedback theory or sensory integration training is used, if people want to achieve significant results, they should insist on doing that for at least three months and some should do that for six months to a year or longer. In addition, both of these two treatment methods should be done in hospitals, so they are relatively limited and need to be guided by professionals. For families with children with ADD/ADHD, this is not only a protracted war which cost time and money. What is more, many families find it hard to afford the expensive treatment cost.

In real treatment process, many parents will let their children give up the treatment because of inconvenience, high cost or short-term efficacy. If they can finish their treatment at home, there will be no need for the children and their parents to rush back and forth between the hospital and home. This is easy to operate, can save time, labor and money and enhance parent-child relationship. Children's behaviors can be constantly affected by family affection which can help them grow up healthily and become more popular. Therefore, it is urgent to design effective treatment suitable for family settings. In order to solve this problem, the new treatment scheme should meet two requirements: 1) effectiveness and 2) compatibility with home environment.

The effectiveness of neurofeedback therapy should be guaranteed by the quality of brain-computer interface equipment. Although brain-computer interface devices in hospitals have good physical performance, most of them collect brainwaves in the form of wired headcaps. They have poor portability and utility and bad user experience, so they can not be used at home. In recent years, with the rapid development of information technology and biomedicine, more and more people have focused on the research of brain-computer interface equipment. After "Neurosky", an American company, developed a portable BCI device, many companies designed a number of games which can meet EEG neurofeedback principle with the aid of the device. In this way, users can learn about the state of their brain at home through a BCI device, which can improve their attention and cognitive ability.

With the aid of BCI technology, a device which can treat the disease of children with ADD / ADHD can be well designed. In addition, the development of TUI also provides a reliable technical support for the realization of digital physical toys and the improvement of sensory integration and attention of child patients.

4   Prototype Design of E-Jigsaw

Based on current research situations at present, this paper proposes an information interaction product—E-Jigsaw, which integrates BCI and TUI technology. It's a TUI jigsaw puzzle based on a brain-computer interface.

E-Jigsaw system is designed by the existing BCI technology, with which, people can know whether users can concentrate on the interaction process. Besides, feedback treatment can be done according to the principle of neurofeedback. This can make patients improve their attention and realize the homalization of neurofeedback treatment. At the same time, with the aid of TUI technology, it is designed as a physical jigsaw puzzle. Children can improve their graphic perception ability and limb activity ability when they play the game. This can well meet psychological characteristics of children and make them more willing to participate in the games. In addition, the system simplifies the treatment process and makes the treatment program more available so that it can be done at home.

4.1 Function Design

Main functions of "E-Jigsaw" can be set according to the jigsaw toy and their major functions are as follows:

1. *Shattering function:* Shatter complete pictures into a bunch of relatively disordered blocks and synchronize them to the four modules as shown in Fig. 1(a).
2. *Jigsaw function:* With touch interaction and physical splicing operation, users can splice messy and disordered blocks into complete pictures.
3. *Comparison of original pictures:* A complete original picture is provided for the reference of users.
4. *Completion tips:* When the puzzle is finished, completion tips will be given.
5. *Image replacement:* There are many built-in multiple jigsaw puzzles and pictures can be randomly changed according to users' commands.

In order to realize BCI neurofeedback technology, the following functions are added to E-Jigsaw:

6. *Real-time monitoring of attention status:* It can monitor changes of concentration value returned by BCI and connect them with the transparency of the puzzle pictures. That is to say, the higher the attention, the clearer the picture will be; the less the attention, the more transparent the pictures will be. Users can detect changes in their attention based on changes in the transparency of the images and continuously improve their attention by consciously adjusting themselves.
7. *Encouragement tips:* Related tips will be given according to user status. When user's attention is found to drop to a certain threshold value, they will be encouraged so that users can pay attention to the task interaction process again.
8. *Performance evaluation:* Scores will be given according to user performance and the time to complete the task.

When puzzle tasks are designed, in order to make the interaction more intuitive, corresponding TUI interaction modes need to be designed. This is also the difficulty in the design and implementation of E-Jigsaw system. Four modules with intelligent perception function are used in this paper to form a complete jigsaw puzzle. When playing games, users should complete the puzzle on a single intelligent module and integrate these four intelligent modules into a complete puzzle, as shown in Fig. 1(b).

Therefore, modules should be able to perceive whether they are matching modules and should synchronize their states to the server through wireless network so as to realize multi-screen interaction and synchronization.

4.2 Interactive Process Design

When the system is started, the system will detect EEG signals of users and, which is the value of the user's attention state provided by the system's BCI device (Concentration: original EEG data will be processed by DSP of BCI device. It is roughly equivalent to amplitude in the 12–15 Hz band). The system will then correlate the value of concentration with the transparency of the puzzle picture. The higher the concentration, the clearer the picture will be. In this way, users can directly perceive the state of attention visually.

During the interaction, users should try their best to keep the picture clear so that they can complete the jigsaw smoothly. After users finish the jigsaw well, the system will give them applause and will also give them corresponding prompt when they are not highly focused. According to the principle of neurofeedback, ADD/ADHD patients can improve their attention during this interaction.

E-Jigsaw system can constantly monitor users' attention according to concentration values provided by the BCI. If the concentration value returned by the BCI during the interaction process is too low (the threshold is 30% of the maximum value), the system will give an encouraging tone of "hold on a little longer, come on!" to remind users to gain attention again. If the concentration value is consistently above the threshold, the system will give no prompt. Awards will be given until users finish the final task. System interaction flows of users in their process of puzzle are shown in Fig. 2.

E-Jigsaw system is a TUI system with four physically independent intelligent modules. When playing games, users should not only finish the puzzle on single intelligent modules but should assemble the four intelligent modules into a complete puzzle.

5   Design of E-Jigsaw System

5.1   System Introduction

E-jigsaw system consists of BCI device, central control terminal and 4 independent intelligent modules, which are shown in Fig. 3.

BCI interface is a Mindwave mobile brain-computer interface (Fig. 4) of NeuroSky company. It can monitor electrical signals of the wearer in real time and use algorithms to identify mindfulness, meditation and blinking.

The central control terminal (as shown in Fig. 5) can receive and process signals transmitted from BCI, synchronize them according to the status of four independent intelligent modules. It can also display the whole picture.

The independent intelligent module (as shown in Fig. 6) is divided into two parts: one is the external state sensor (as shown in Fig. 7). It is composed of the singlechip Arduino Nano, four magnetic induction switches, four magnetic strips and a HC-06 Bluetooth serial communication module. With the aid of the magnetic sensor, external state sensor can sense whether there is a magnetic field in the neighboring region and send relevant signals to the outside. The other part is an Android smart tablet.

It has two main functions: 1. It can process users' interaction with the puzzle on the touch screen to realize the operation of virtual puzzle; 2) It can receive signals from the external sensor and process it in real time to constantly judge whether there is a corresponding module nearby to use.

5.2   Central Control Terminal

There are many built-in pictures in the central control terminal and users only need to choose one. After that, they can divide them into a number of different small picture blocks according to corresponding difficulties and synchronizes them to four independent intelligent modules. At that time, if BCI sends concentration data, the system will read them and give notice to all modules to change the transparency of its pictures. If the value is less than the specified threshold 30 (30% of the maximum value in this system), the system will send an encouraging prompt tone to smart modules that users are using so that users can pay attention to the tasks again. Then, the central control terminal will read the status data uploaded by each module from the buffer (including whether puzzles on the module are completed and in which direction the module is linked) and combine all state information together to judge whether the puzzle is completed. If so, it will calculate the total score.

The system correlates the transparency of the images with the concentration values to make the attention state visible. The users must stay focused and keep the picture clear enough so that they can finish the task well. This design can well meet the principle of neurofeedback. In order to facilitate the operation, the alpha value (0–255) of the image shall have the following relationship with the Attention value (0–100):

$$\text{alpha} = \left\lfloor Attention \times \frac{255}{100} \right\rfloor$$

When the Attention value is greater than 30, only the alpha value of pictures changes with the Attention value. In this way, it can reduce the interference to users. The Attention value smaller than 30 means that the system detects that the user's attention is seriously distracted and that users can not complete tasks successfully. At that time, the system will issue an "encouraging prompt" to help users refocus on the puzzle task again.

Therefore, the central control terminal mainly sends two kinds of control information to each module: first: the calculated alpha value of the picture; second: whether it is necessary to trigger the prompt to require each module to upload the status data, which is also the encoded information, including module ID, whether the puzzle has been completed and the state of the magnetic induction switch in each direction.

It is easy to prove that the state data is unique when the tasks are completed. In this way, the central control terminal can judge whether users have completed the whole jigsaw puzzle according to the ask completion state data.

5.3 Independent Intelligent Module

Each individual smart module is composed of an external status sensor and an Android smart tablet. It has four main functions. First, it can generate a virtual puzzle on the flat screen, process user information in the interaction process and mark the state when users complete the puzzle.

Second, it can receive real-time data sent from the external status sensor of this module. Third, it can encode the two functions above in accordance with the above coding rules and upload them to the central control terminal. Fourth, it will receive the control of the central control terminal, adjust the alpha value of images and trigger the "encouraging sound". What the independent intelligent module establishes is a TCP connection with the central control terminal. It can be used for reliable transmission and the synchronization of pictures and signals. It is relatively easy to deal with the interactive process of virtual puzzle, which will not be stated here.

Among external state sensors, four magnetic induction switches are distributed in the upper, lower, left and right directions. Arduino Nano can capture the status of magnetic induction switch in four directions in real time and send the status data to the plate in this module after the data are encoded. After the client program in the tablet captures the data, they will be coded according to the ID of the module and the completion situation of the puzzle and will be uploaded to the central control terminal.

At the same time, the control program in the module can periodically take out control commands issued by the central control terminal from the buffer, decode them and change them to alpha values of pictures, decide whether to trigger the encouraging sound and then carry out the corresponding operations.

6 User Testing

This is a standard test intended for children. Therefore, 30 volunteers (aged 6–12 years old, 16 males and 14 females) were selected to take part in a subjective test of system usage experience. How to use the system was explained to them first of all before the test was started (Fig. 8).

During the test, the testees should complete a puzzle task of medium difficulty (the whole picture is broken up into 9 × 4 pictures. That is to say, the whole picture is divided into 36 pieces which are randomly broken up by the system and synchronized to 4 independent intelligent modules) with no time limit.

After completing the tasks, testees should finish an overall satisfaction scale and score three key factors affecting their experience with the E-Jigsaw system (improved degree of attention, interestingness and usability to evaluate whether the subjective use experience of the system can meet predetermined design objectives. The results are shown in Table 1.The table shows the subjective evaluation of users on the improvement of concentration, the interestingness, usability and their overall user satisfaction of the system. More than 70% of users hold that their attention improved a lot in the usage process compared with common situations; 75% of users think that the system is interesting while 60% of users hold that the system is easy-to-use. 75% of users are satisfied with the system. The results show that users are satisfied with the overall situation of the system. The results show that the E-Jigsaw system can help improve user concentration and that it is easy and interesting to use. In general, it can meet the design requirements.

7 Conclusion

This paper researches related situations of "family therapy equipment for attention-deficit children based on BCI and TUI technology" and design a set of physical jigsaw toy E-Jigsaw for attention-deficit children. E-Jigsaw, based on the principle of neurofeedback therapy, uses a BCI interface to connect users' attention with the transparency of the image and map the result to the interactive process of intelligent jigsaw puzzle. Therefore, it is a set of therapeutic equipment suitable to be used at home. Those with attention deficits can treat their disease with this prototype. It saves time and energy for patients and their families to travel back and forth between their homes and the hospital. At the same time, this prototype combines the jigsaw puzzles with TUI technology, which provide an atmosphere in which patients can operate in physical environment. It can enhance sensory integration ability, graphic perception ability and fine manipulation ability of children patients and conform to psychological characteristics of children. In this way, this prototype makes the treatment program more interesting.

User tests show that the equipment can improve users' attention and that its interesting presentation forms can make users more interested in the interaction. Therefore, it is concluded that E-Jigsaw will help attention-deficit children receive treatment better.

References

1. Li, H., Yu, X., Jiang, F., Fu, Q.: Study on the incidence of attention deficit hyperactivity disorder in children with high level of blood lead. Lab. Med. **10**, 734–736 (2009). (in Chinese)
2. Lubar, J.F., Shouse, M.N.: EEG and behavioral changes in a hyperkinetic child concurrent with training of the sensorimotor rhythm (SMR): a preliminary report. Biofeedback Self Regul. **1**(3), 293–306 (1976)
3. Lubar, J.: Discourse on the development of EEG diagnostics and biofeedback for attention-deficit/hyperactivity disorders. Biofeedback Self Regul. **16**(3), 201–225 (1991)
4. Nash, J.K.: Treatment of attention deficit hyperactivity disorder with neurotherapy. Clin. EEG (Electroencephalogr.) **31**(1), 30–37 (2000)
5. Bakhshayesh, A.R., Hänsch, S., Wyschkon, A., Rezai, M.J., Esser, G.: Neurofeedback in ADHD: a single-blind randomized controlled trial. Eur. Child Adolesc. Psychiatry **20**(9), 481–491 (2011)
6. Ishii, H., Ullmer, B.: Tangible bits: towards seamless interfaces between people, bits and atoms. In: Proceedings of Conference on Human Factors in Computing Systems (CHI 1997), pp. 234–241. ACM, Atlanta, March 1997
7. Montessori, M.: The Montessori Method: Scientific Pedagogy as Applied to Child Education in "The Children's Houses" with Additions and Revisions by the Author. Frederick A. Stokes Company (1912)
8. Akabane, S., et al.: Puchi Planet: a tangible interface design for hospitalized children. In: Proceedings of CHI Extended Abstracts, pp. 1345–1350 (2011)
9. Zuckerman, O., Arida, S., Resnick, M.: Extending tangible interfaces for education: digital montessori-inspired manipulatives. In: Proceedings of CHI, pp. 859–868 (2005)
10. Antle, A.N., Wise, A.F., Nielsen, K.: Towards Utopia: designing tangibles for learning. In: Proceedings of the 10th International Conference on Interaction Design and Children (IDC 2011). ACM, New York (2011)
11. Wang, C.: Risk factors of ADHD children with different degree sensory integration dysfunction and curative effects of sensory integration training. Master dissertation. Southeast University, Nanjing (2005)
12. Chen, H., Li, Q., Yan, Y., Yuan, Y., Chen, J.: Application of sensory integration to the treatment of ADHD children. Nanfang J. Nurs. **02**, 17–18 (2003)

VPlaytime: Face-to-Face Recess in Virtual Reality Classrooms

Xin Li, DanDan Yu, Min Wang, and WenJing Li[✉]

Art and Design Academy, Beijing City University, Beijing, China
2660712945@qq.com

Abstract. Class break space is a potentially promising informal learning environment for both integrating formal and informal learning using Virtual Reality and supporting student self-regulated learning in art and design higher education contexts. The purpose of this paper is to (a) review research that support this claim, (b) conceptualize the connection breaking time, Virtual Reality, and self-regulated learning, and (c) provide a informal learning framework for using Virtual Reality to create between class that support student self-regulated learning. Implications a natural transition for connecting formal and informal learning for future research in this area are provided.

Keywords: Virtual Reality · Informal learning · Inter-class breaks · Learning framework · Art and design

1 Introduction

The term 'informal learning' refers to all learning resulting from activities undertaken by individuals in their own time. In essence, informal learning (IL) starts at birth and continues throughout an individual's life as a natural by-product of their activity. IL can be both intentional and unintentional and is unstructured in terms of objectives, time investment, and support. Related statistics show that 70–80% of human knowledge is acquired through informal learning channels; accordingly, informal learning has gradually become the main manner in which people learn and improve [1]. Informal learning can take place in public cultural activity spaces such as museums, libraries, and businesses, as well as occurring in individuals' practices, such as observing others' verbal expressions, imitating actions, and communicating with experienced people. Notably, all of these examples constitute IL. Regarding the learning of academic knowledge in universities, such learning has already expanded beyond the walls of the classroom and school; as a result, the acquisition of non-professional knowledge, social practical experience, or implicit knowledge closely related to the professional field deeply permeates all corners of society, such as network course learning during leisure time, online communication during class breaks, and practical learning during holidays.

2 Research Context and Concepts

This project focuses on the positive role of virtual reality in university extracurricular activities. To enrich university students' extracurricular activities, the current status of university students' extracurricular activities was researched and a survey was conducted. The current status of university students' extracurricular activities was obtained by analyzing the survey data. Based on the issues identified, a framework for solving problems is proposed. From this, university students can fully and reasonably make use of their spare time for activities that are beneficial to their physical and mental health and also improve their learning efficiency.

This survey was conducted online. The survey respondents were undergraduate and graduate students majoring in the arts at Beijing City University. A total of 48 questionnaire surveys were distributed.

2.1 Informal Learning Situation

Under the influence of a lifelong learning philosophy, the ways in which people acquire knowledge are increasingly diversified. Against this backdrop, informal learning has become an increasingly widespread, important mode of learning. It should be pointed out that informal learning is also prevalent in school education, although it typically focuses on formal learning, especially in higher education institutions. The learning environment and requirements in universities are relatively relaxed, in that students have less contact time and have to undertake a greater degree of self-study. The learning of university students also differs from learning in the previous stages of education, emphasizing their initiative, diversity and creativity, highlighting the importance and potential of informal learning. At the same time, the way university students learn has undergone a major shift: formal learning is the main focus in primary and secondary education, whilst higher education values formal and informal learning equally, with informal learning sometimes being preferred [2]. "Learning on demand is quickly becoming a type of lifestyle in modern society (McLoughlin & Lee, 2007). Learners constantly seek information to address problems at work or school, or even just to satisfy their curiosity. To do so, they take advantage of digital and networked technologies to both seek and share information. Thus, learners should not be considered passive consumers of information; rather, they are active co-producers of content. Additionally, learning the context of social media has become highly self-motivated, autonomous, and informal, constituting an integral part of the college experience" [3].

It should also be highlighted that informal learning is diverse and reflects the learning context in which it takes place: it can be in daily life or extracurricular activities, in the real or virtual worlds. Therefore, college students' informal learning is derived from and driven by their own interests and needs to be initiated by themselves, through self-guidance or social interactions of a non-teaching nature, to obtain new knowledge.

2.2 The Impact of Extracurricular Activities on Learning

The activities carried out between classes are typically used for rest, relaxation, and relief from the tense and focused classroom atmosphere. The key aim of such activities is to meet the physical and psychological needs of students, promoting better adjustment of their physical functions and revitalizing their learning efficiency for the next lesson.

Researchers have found that the time individuals spend sitting has significantly increased globally in recent decades, making it increasingly important to combat the negative health consequences of prolonged sitting. This is especially true in universities, where students spend an increasing amount of time sitting. Taking breaks from sitting during class by leaving one's seat and interacting with classmates can help increase feelings of closeness and improve class cohesion, thereby fostering a sense of unity and cooperation.

2.3 Learning the Behavioral Characteristics of Art and Design Major Students During Breaks

The results of the survey carried out in this paper show that, at present, art and design university students' activities during breaks consist of using electronic products, such as phones, for internet browsing, entertainment, and communication, going to the bathroom, taking a nap, chatting, viewing the exhibitions lining the hallways, simple physical activities, and buying snacks at the supermarket. From the survey data statistics (Fig. 1) on university students' inter-class activities, it can be seen that most students engage in activities in the supermarket and the corridor. It should be noted that students are not going to the supermarket to make a purchase, but rather to exercise and move around. Similarly, walking in the corridor is mainly undertaken for physical activity purposes and to look at work exhibitions, though such works are not replaced very often. Therefore, the survey results show that students' activities during class breaks are relatively simple and limited to rotating their waist and stretching their arms, without any scientific activity guidance. Slowly, they have joined the ranks of those who keep their heads down.

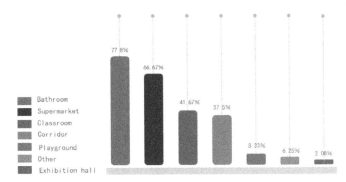

Fig. 1. The situation of the investigation on university students' extracurricular activities during breaks.

According to the survey results of the inter-class activities shown in Fig. 2, the way in which students engage with each other during class breaks has shifted from face-to-face to text-based chat through mobile phone applications like WeChat, even when they are physically located in the same classroom. The lack of verbal communication, body language, and gestures has precipitated a decline in oral communication skills and increased the distance in relationships between classmates (despite being in close physical proximity to each other).

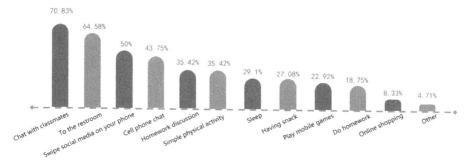

Fig. 2. The situation of the investigation on university students' extracurricular activities during breaks.

2.4 The Relationship Between Breaks, Virtual Reality, and Informal Learning

Jay Cross argues that the knowledge and skills people acquire at work are acquired through informal learning, such as conversations, observations, and trial and error. Contrastingly, formal learning from experience and interaction only accounts for 5–20% of all learning. It ought to be stressed that acquiring and absorbing knowledge through social interaction of a non-instructional nature in informal learning can facilitate the transformation of classroom knowledge. The application of virtual reality breaks, used in conjunction with informal learning, disrupts the constraints of time and space traditional learning is subject to. Virtual reality breaks provide an opportunity for students to engage in discussion with classmates, teachers, and out-of-school educators and students in an informal learning environment at any time. The difference between virtual reality breaks and actual breaks is shown in Fig. 3.

	R-Playtime	V-Playtime
Degree of freedom	Low	High
Location	Limited	Optional
Form	Reality	Virtual
Content	Single	Rich
Interact	Natural	Human-machine

Fig. 3. Comparison chart between virtual reality breaks and actual breaks.

3   Informal Learning Framework in Virtual Reality

Liao Shouqin and Song Quansong (2010) discussed the definition of network informal learning, which refers to the learning activities that take place through the personal learning environment of learners in network learning and the utilization of network information resources. To be precise, this can include self-directed learning, collaborative learning, and co-creation through network-based activities with the assistance of relevant information prompts and guidance from teachers [4].

In light of this goal, the present study was conducted based on the following questions:

1. How can the interaction between people and information and between people on the network be achieved?
2. How can effective and useful information be screened for on the internet to help learners achieve their learning objectives?
3. How can a positive atmosphere for online learning be created to effectively attract and maintain the interest of learners?
4. How can it be ensured that learning activities carried out in the online environment are effective and can help learners acquire the necessary knowledge and skills?
5. How can a personal learning environment be distinguished from a public learning environment in the network?

Guided by the above questions, the present study investigates the model of informal learning in virtual reality environments during class. Specifically, this model utilizes virtual reality technology to simulate after-class learning behaviors, providing learners with a broader range of learning resources and a more flexible learning environment, thereby enabling remote collaborative and co-creative learning. The model enhances learning participation and efficiency by making learning more interesting and natural. This paper analyzes the virtual reality inter-class informal learning model from four levels: (1) Intention; (2) Scope; (3) Interaction; (4) Situation (see Fig. 4).

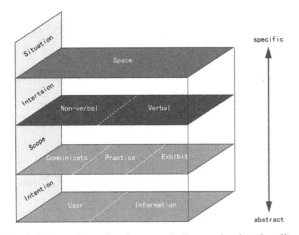

Fig. 4. Informal learning framework diagram in virtual reality.

3.1 Intention Layer

In the intention layer, it is necessary to consider the target user and the type of information in question. Determining the target user allows interaction style and informal learning scenarios to be established based on factors such as the user's age, behavioral characteristics, and psychological characteristics. This in turn enables a more effective and accurate learning content and method selection by determining the type of information, leading to the creation of interesting and effective virtual learning breaks in informal settings.

3.2 Scope Layer

In the content layer, the user's communication content, learning and practice content, and presentation content can be determined. Users can communicate, practice, and present in different scenarios to enrich their in-class activities. Regardless of whether it is in a real or virtual space, people have the same information content and social interaction needs. As the internet has become the dominant virtual platform integrated into people's real lives, this need has naturally been transferred to virtual reality. Therefore, different communication spaces can be created in the virtual space to provide communication opportunities for users and learning content. In the learning module, students were given the freedom to select social media tools to create personal and distributed learning spaces to facilitate individual and collaborative learning tasks in a VR environment. The presentation module satisfies the most important academic presentation function in the school corridor. Digital presentation is not only more convenient to update, but also capable of delivering personalized information to the user. Users can unconsciously learn through activities such as communication, practice, and presentation, deepening their understanding of the matters at hand. Virtual reality has more potential and development space, and socializing in virtual reality will be more convenient, much to the benefit of informal learning activities in virtual spaces.

3.3 Interaction Layer

In the interaction layer, the key consideration is the way in which people interact in virtual space, that is, their social presence. "Conveying the user's actions in the virtual environment (VE) enables others to understand the social context and properly interact with both the user and the VE itself. Consequently, a cornerstone challenge in designing an enjoyable and engaging social VR experience is supporting social presence. Social presence pertains to the ability to feel others present with you in a VE" [5]. "A greater presence in the VE allows for the formation of closer emotional responses and reactions that are comparable to those experienced in the real world" [6]. Moreover, full-body user representation has been found to significantly enhance social presence in immersive environments. Smith et al. conducted a user study to evaluate full-body avatars' impact social presence better than partial ones, the results of which showed that embodied VR setting resulted in significantly higher social presence scores than the non-embodied VR scores. Hence, it can be concluded that full-body user representation significantly enhanced social presence in immersive environments.

With regard to the interaction behaviors of the virtual avatar, they can be divided into verbal and non-verbal types. Language-based interactions include text and voice. These two forms are the users' habit of language communication, which can be used for problem discussions and communication in learning. Moreover, non-verbal interaction methods supplement the real "face-to-face" interaction experience. This allows users to see the actions, movements, and even facial expressions of others through the virtual image rendered by a computer, thereby replicating the real "face-to-face" interaction experience. "Non-verbal interaction" refers to the non-verbal cues people use to convey their intentions (such as waving when greeting). It supports interactive presentation and can include gazing, facial expressions, gestures, and sensory feedback for physical communicative actions. Roth et al. [7] conducted a user study to evaluate the effect of augmenting nonverbal cues in the VE on social presence. They concluded that perceiving eye contact significantly increased the user's social presence in the VE, such that gaze tracking can be used to refine the expression of social communication. Jun et al. found that the synchronicity of facial expression between the avatar and the user significantly affects presence [8], with participants preferring body and hand gestures using the keyboard and mouse during VE interactions [9]. Thus, the impact of facial expressions on social presence is a prime research opportunity.

3.4 Situation Layer

Informal learning occurs at informal learning times in informal learning places. To provide students who participate in the learning process with a sense of constraint different from traditional learning in the informal learning process, it is necessary to create a free and relaxed learning environment and advocate for easy and harmonious interpersonal relationships. English (2000) believes that informal learning and incidental learning can create a situation in which individuals can engage in mental dialogue [10]. Marsick and Watkins argued that informal learning is experiential, highly situational, loosely structured, and mainly initiated, supervised, and controlled by the learner [11]. Accordingly, the situational layer is the topmost composite environment in the informal learning framework, which refers to the context in which inter-class activities occur in VR: examples include virtual classrooms, virtual hallways, virtual cafes, virtual meeting rooms, and virtual supermarkets. Different situational spaces provide different communication opportunities, functions, and information, with students freely shuttling and switching between different scenes.

The framework for informal learning in inter-class in VR environments includes the intention layer, scope layer, interaction layer, and situational layer. To successfully build a virtual reality informal learning environment, each level needs to define the corresponding content. Doing so allows students to engage in different informal learning activities in virtual inter-class periods, providing space and time for them to both rest and socialize.

The informal learning situation is not sequenced beforehand, with the process preceded by the interaction of the participants in the activity. In the inter-class phase, learners can engage in various situational transitions through VR, observe and discuss different locations, create different informal learning spaces, and establish a relaxed inter-class environment.

4   Informal Learning Framework in Virtual Reality

The virtual reality inter-class framework project designs and provides virtual reality inter-class V-PlayTime for university students majoring in art and design. The design specifically addresses the phenomenon of single student activities during inter-class periods in universities, fully utilizing VR technology to create virtual spaces replicating cafes, classrooms, and hallways. In such spaces, students can participate in various learning activities that are beneficial for inter-class breaks. This design provides convenience for art and design students during class time, saves costs, presents otherwise hard-to-observe or experience things in a virtual manner, enhances class time experience, and improves informal learning efficiency, the effect of which is to promote professional learning cognitive development and make learning resources more diverse and class activities more enriched.

4.1   Virtual Café

Informal learning time goes beyond the classroom in many ways and is freely arranged in light of students' individual habits and preferences, such as taking place in informal learning spaces like restaurants, coffee shops and bookstores. Researchers have found that café spaces are often present in the teaching spaces of colleges specializing in art and design. Students use this space to carry out design research, project coordination, and topic discussion. Therefore, the design of the virtual "café" in this project (Fig. 5) is intended to provide students with a comfortable learning and open social interaction space. In this virtual "café", students can chat with classmates, discuss topics, read books, and complete research assignments. This offers a space in which students can complete their learning tasks in a relaxed environment. At the same time, the virtual classrooms provide space for students to relax and engage in entertainment activities such as "making coffee" and "song playback". This creates a flexible, dynamic, and situational leisure space that can be customized to suit individual needs. Students can also have a real latte by their side while chatting in the virtual space, to mirror what they are doing in the virtual space.

4.2   Virtual Classroom

VPlayTime's design of the "Virtual Classroom" (Fig. 6) provides students with a social space to communicate and engage in collaborative learning. The virtual classroom also enables the creation of different discussion groups. During break times, students can gather in small groups through discussion rooms, with the information discussed within each group only visible to the group members. Each person can freely enter and exit each group, participate in discussions, and engage in lively dialogues and brainstorming conversations during the breaks. At the same time, students can alter different virtual images through movement-based games, allowing them to undertake simple physical activity during class breaks and spark their interest in physical activity.

Fig. 5. "Virtual Café" Design Chart

Fig. 6. "Virtual Clssroom" Design Chart

4.3 Virtual Hallway

During the research, it was found that most students preferred to linger in the corridor during breaks, both to relieve tension from class and engage in more intimate conversations with classmates. Therefore, the design of VPlayTime's "Virtual Hallway" (Fig. 7) allows students to take a walk and relax during breaks through interactive guidance, while also viewing the design works and design information displayed on both sides of the "Virtual Hallway". The environment of the "Virtual Hallway" can be freely set and explored alone or with company. Of course, students are also allowed to comment on or collect the exhibits while visiting. These provisions attract students to view the exhibition multiple times, whilst also facilitating their interaction, communication, and evaluation.

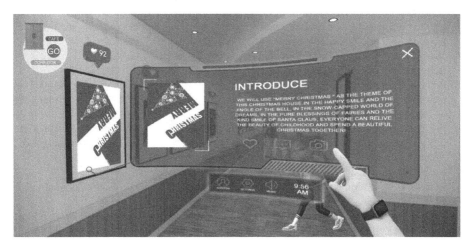

Fig. 7. "Virtual Hallway" Design Chart

5 Conclusion

In this paper, we studied the basic elements of informal learning in VR experiences. We present a four-levels informal learning model from analyzing the literature and research data. Our analysis shows that scenario and interaction mode are essential for VR informal learning, and nonverbal interaction are under-explored in the current literature due to their technical difficulty and cost. Additionally, Activity Type is the most considered design aspect in informal learning solutions.

Although the four levels cover various target and application areas, the focus on different user and application areas may vary in our selected scenario. For instance, scope layer focus primarily on Collaboration, Activity Type, such as extracurricular discussion. To enhance social presence, current research focuses on nonverbal interaction, particularly gaze and gestures. However, creating an interesting and effective informal learning VR space still requires further research and prototyping testing iterations. We believe that our work will guide designers in creating informal learning VR platforms that cater for all levels of user. Finally, we envision that our work will aid researchers to build engaging informal learning VR experiences.

References

1. Hou, Y.: Research on Informal Learning of College Students Based on Web 2.0 Environment. Guangxi Normal University (2008)
2. Li, Z., Wu, B.: Research on the construction of informal learning environment model combining virtual and real. China Educ. Informatization **03**, 86–89 (2015)

3. Hao, X.: Three-Dimensional Model Simplification Technology in Virtual Reality. Xi'an:Xidian University (2007)
4. Wu, X.: A preliminary study on the application of virtual reality technology in information interaction. Des. Art Res. **11**(06), 133–137 (2021)
5. Gao, L.: Application of VR virtual reality technology in the field of education and teaching. Electron. Technol. Softw. Eng. **09**, 53–54 (2020)
6. Marsick, V., Watkins, K.: Informal and Incidental Learning in the Work Place, pp. 25–34. Roledge, New York (1990)
7. Bourdin, P., Sanahuja, J.M.T., Moya, C.C., Haggard, P., Slater, M.: Persuading people in a remote destination to sing by beaming there. In: Proceedings of the 19th ACM Symposium on Virtual Reality Software and Technology, pp. 123–132. ACM (2013)
8. Jun, J., Jung, M., Kim, S.-Y., Kim, K.K.: FullBody ownership illusion can change our emotion. In: Proceedings of the 2018 CHI Conference on Human Factors in Computing Systems, p. 601. ACM (2018)
9. Rozzino, F.T., Bergamasco, M.: Evaluating the impact (2015)
10. English, L.M.: Spiritual dimensions of informal learning. New Dir. Adult Continuing **85**, 29–38 (2000)
11. Smith, H.J., Neff, M.: Communication behavior in embodied virtual reality. In: Proceedings of the 2018 CHI Conference on Human Factors in Computing Systems, p. 289. ACM (2018)
12. Schreurs, B., De Laat, M.: The network awareness tool: a web 2.0 tool to visualise informal learning in organisations. Manuscript submitted for publication (2013)

Transdisciplinary Teaching and Learning in Summer Camp by Service Design

Manhai Li[✉], Lianyu Huang, and Yingxuan Li

Chongqing University of Posts and Telecommunications, Chongqing 400065, China
limh@cqupt.edu.cn

Abstract. The work aims to propose the transdisciplinary teaching and learning in summer camp by service design, and try to find a way out of the dilemma. There are two main problems in the dilemma, the first one is valuing traveling more than delivering knowledge, the second one is the lack of interaction between trainer and trainee, and the third one is results float to the surface. In order to cultivate a group of outstanding talents with innovative entrepreneurial ability, cross-border integration ability, and humanities and arts literacy who can keep pace up with the times and solve social problems in the new era, some service design tools and methods such as service blueprint, co-creation and service design thinking are introduced and applied, including making trainees be more involved in learning through co-creation, and making trainers be easier guide to solve problems pertinently with the help of service blueprint. Finally, two design turns of transdisciplinary teaching and learning were illustrated through the exploration and practice in summer camp by service design, the one is paying more attention on enabling than traveling around, the other one is focusing on more coaching than delivering skills.

Keywords: Interdisciplinary · Teaching · Learning · Service Design · Education

1 Background

In terms of policy support, in June 2021, the State Council promulgated the Outline of the National Science Literacy Action Plan (2021–2035), which encouraged and support the establishment of scientific education and inspection bases in various industries and departments to improve scientific services capabilities. Through the implementation of "Opinions on Promoting Study Travel of Primary and Secondary School Students" (hereinafter referred to as "Opinions") initially issued in 2016, more than 20 provinces such as Tianjin, Shandong and Anhui have successively issued opinions or measures on study travel of primary and secondary schools. [1].Taking Chongqing's policy as an example, in recent years, it has issued the *Implementation Plan for the Construction of the Experimental Zone of Social Practice Education and Study Travel for Primary and Secondary Schools in Qianjiang District, Management Measures for Social Practice Education and Study Travel for Primary and Secondary Schools in Qianjiang District (for trial implementation), Implementation Opinions on Further Deepening the Pilot*

A. Marcus et al. (Eds.): HCII 2023, LNCS 14033, pp. 131–141, 2023.
https://doi.org/10.1007/978-3-031-35708-4_10

Work of Study Travel for Primary and Secondary School Students in Dadukou District, and the *Education Working Committee of Yuzhong District on Further Strengthening and Promoting Study Travel for Primary and Secondary Schools.*

"Implementation Opinions on Further Strengthening and Promoting Study Travel in Primary and Secondary Schools" incorporates study travel into school education and teaching plans, requires planning from the aspects of "natural ecology, history and culture, revolutionary traditions, artificial intelligence, and artistic public welfare", and carefully selecting study places at district and school level. In the external market side, Ctrip released the "2022 Summer Tour Report", which shows that the study tour experience has become the main force of customized summer tours. The total number of tourist orders in July was 50% higher than that in June. The average daily price for a single person in product orders for summer travel in July–August was around 790 yuan, a 20% increase from last year's average daily price for a single person. From a supply-side perspective, study travel products grew by more than 650% over the summer of 2021, and the search volume for study products grew more than two times over the same period last year. The report also shows that in 2021, the products of B&B with learning functions increased by more than 450% year-on-year the search volume increased by more than 3 times year-on-year. New professions such as study tour tutors began to rise, and study tour majors began to be offered in higher education high schools. China's research travel has entered a stage of rapid development. Although the policy and the market are good, there are also some problems, such as paying more attention to travel than knowledge, lacking interactive content and superficial result. (see Fig. 1).

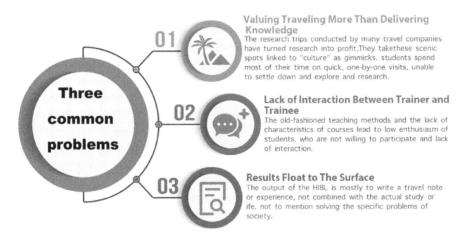

Fig. 1. Three common problems in the summer camp.

1.1 Valuing Traveling More Than Delivering Knowledge

The research trips conducted by many travel companies have turned research into profit. They just add some museums, art galleries and other elements to the tourist attractions, and think that they have achieved the purpose of studying and traveling. They take these scenic spots linked to "culture" as gimmicks and increase fees. In fact, students spend most of their time on quick, one-by-one visits, unable to settle down and explore and research. For example, students can pick their own tea on the hills of the scenic spot. Although they can experience the tea making process by themselves, the time is short. Essentially, it is mainly traditional tourism. This leads to learning becoming a tasteless tourism, but learning is more important in learning. At present, the state has issued a series of research and education plans, and all relevant departments across the country actively hold various forms of research and education travel activities. Some places have explored practical and experiential curriculum design schemes with regional characteristics in curriculum development. However, at present, China's study tours are still in the exploration and development stage, due to the various aspects of society for study tours ideological understanding is not yet in place, for the "travel" and "learning" balance problem, not only plagued by the relevant administrative departments and education departments, but also many students and parents are in a wait-and-see situation. Therefore, how to balance the "learning" and "doing" of study tour is crucial.

1.2 Lack of Interaction Between Trainer and Trainee

Most research institutes have forcibly moved their professional skills courses to tourist attractions. Many courses are highly homogeneous, without interdisciplinary teaching, and can be applied to other similar research fields. The old-fashioned teaching methods and the lack of characteristics of courses lead to low enthusiasm of students, who are not willing to participate and lack of interaction. For example, in the course of aesthetic education of ancient poetry during the Hands-on Inquiry Based Learning (HIBL), although students can experience and learn in the national tourist resort with beautiful environment, it is still the traditional cramming teaching method that makes students' low participation willing.

1.3 Results Float to the Surface

The output of the HIBL is mostly to write a travel note or experience, not combined with the actual study or life, not to mention solving the specific problems of society. For example, through the study of karst landforms, students are guided to think independently about global climate change and other issues, and then put forward reasonable suggestions according to the knowledge of biology, geography, science, and technology. Instead of simply visiting and introducing the karst landscapes, the final result of the research is to hand in a diary. The output of the learning process is simply writing a travel note or experience, which will only waste the learning experience and fail to achieve the purpose of learning.

2 Analyzing

Inquiry learning is research-based learning, also called inquiry learning. Research trip is an out-of-school activity combining research study and travel experience, an innovative form of education that connects school education and out-of-school education, an important content of quality education teaching, and an effective way to educate people through comprehensive practice. According to the Opinions on Promoting HIBL for Primary and Secondary School Students and the Curriculum Standards of HIBL developed by the Chinese Society of Education [2], the new concepts and methods of service design are adopted to solve the issues that contains valuing traveling more than knowledge, the content is lack of interaction, and the results are superficial.

2.1 Solving the Problem of Valuing Traveling More Than Knowledge by Service Design Thinking

Service design is a way of thinking and design method [3]. *Service Science: Fundamentals, Challenges and Future Development (2010)*, written by Bernd Stauss et al. (2010) in Germany, argues that service design is a value-creating activity, which provides solutions to problems and establishes interactive relationships between service providers and consumers [4]. Service design thinking makes this interaction smoother, avoiding the imbalance between supply and demand between service providers (research institutions) and consumers (students) in the process of interaction. This problem specifically refers to the fact that in order to deal with the peak experience and final experience of students well and make the experience overall pleasant [5], so as to achieve a good return rate, research institutions put the focus of the whole HIBL process on tourism while ignoring the critical purpose of students' study, which leads to the imbalance relationship between supply and demand.

The concept of service from the perspective of service science emphasizes the interdisciplinary nature and inter-disciplinary research methods of service science. Service design thinking is a kind of interdisciplinary method which combines different methods and tools of different disciplines. Through the interdisciplinary nature and inter-disciplinary research methods of service design, it can solve the problem of unequal supply and demand relationship, which means valuing traveling more than knowledge. The design idea advocates people-oriented, starting from users' basic needs, and considering users' needs, environmental conditions, and constraints in the whole design process, so as to create better service. Based on the thinking mode of service design, taking students as the main body of study, we should optimize the teaching courses from the perspective of students, optimize the students' learning and life itinerary, and solve the problem of travel rather than study.

2.2 Optimizing Content to Increase Teaching Interaction by Service Blueprint

The service blueprint is based on the flow chart of the service system, which accurately describes the service system in a visual manner. Shostack put forward a simple service blueprint similar to the flowchart in 1984, and stressed the importance of information visualization in service design [7].

The process of establishing the service blueprint can be divided into four stages: (1) Defining the object from the customer's point of view and showing the service process in the form of flow chart; (2) describing the customer's contact behavior with the front desk service personnel and the back office service personnel; (3) linking customer behavior and service personnel behavior with corresponding support functions; (4) Showing customer behavior by visual content, including what they see, hear, feel and think. The service blueprint is usually designed into four parts, which are user behavior, front desk contact service personnel behavior, background contact service personnel behavior and service support process from top to bottom [8].

In class, students are compared to "customers", and "customer journey map" is understood as "learning experience journey" [9]. The blueprint of service is to tell teachers the pain points of students in each learning stage and what they want at this stage from the perspective of students, with charts and stories. With the help of blueprints, the process of learning and traveling and their experiences, the roles of students and teachers, and the teaching situation are constantly described. Using tangible evidence to visually demonstrate learning outcomes. This visualization technology may help teachers to understand the pain points of students' learning, improve their academic performance and make students enjoy it.

2.3 Value Co-creation Solves the Problem of Results Floating on the Surface

In the teaching process, the result of solving problems together through the classroom value is superficial. Foreign scholars Vargo et al. proposed the value co-creation theory based on S-Dlogic [10]. The basic assumption of value co-creation is that customers will always be the co-creators of value, and experience and perception are important determinants of value. [11].Vargo and Lusch defined co-creation as the dynamic interaction and participation between customers and their suppliers at each stage of creating value. In this stage, customers are more actively involved in the dialogue and interaction with employees. In this sense, customers are the co-creators of value throughout the whole process, and value is established through the interaction between customers and the cooperation between the customer and the company. The service design system establishes a service design model based on value co-creation with relevant stakeholders, so that relevant roles participate in the creation process [12]. This will help service designers to deeply grasp the pain points, obtain the important contact points of service design, improve the service design system, and enable stakeholders to get a satisfactory activity experience through value co-creation. The core goal of value co-creation and service design is to create an "experience" service around "user-centered" to achieve a win-win goal [13].

From the perspective of value co-creation, the traditional view of value creation holds that value is created by the summer camp of the service providers, and it is passed on to students through communication. Students are not the creators of value, but the users of value. The environment has changed, and the role of students has also changed. Students are not passive buyers anymore, but active participants. Contributing their knowledge and skills to create a better experience. All these show that value comes not only from the camp of service providers, but also from the participation of students, that is, from the design of services and the co-creation of stakeholders. Research should be a student-centered and inductive learning process. Students can actively ask questions, investigate, and learn based on their original concepts in a learning environment composed of teachers and students. It is a practical form of learning that connects school education, social education, and family education. Research-based learning inherits and develops

China's educational philosophy and humanistic spirit of "studying in thousands of books and walking in Wan Li", and integrates the advanced concept, method, and models of international "research-based learning", thus becoming a new content and new way of quality-oriented education.

3 Case

In response to the above problems from the perspective of service design, this case through the "Pea Seedling summer camp" as an example of service design thinking and service blueprint, the value of co-creation of three aspects to build a kind of research and learning system. (see Fig. 2).

Fig. 2. Three aspects of exploration and practice

3.1 Integrating Interdisciplinary Courses Through Service Design Thinking

Service Design Thinking integrates interdisciplinary courses, solves the problem of valuing traveling more than knowledge, achieves a high level of ambition, and enhances practical skills. Through the integration of interdisciplinary courses, service design thinking stimulates innovative learning methods and forms a creative learning style aimed at developing students' design thinking skills [14]. Research-based learning emphasizes the cross-border knowledge, the diversification of situations, the generation of problems, critical construction, and the drive of innovation, and requires the integration, practicality, and activity of the curriculum, which embodies the essential demand of the curriculum to return to life, society, and nature. The concept of service thinking fits well with the design of interdisciplinary courses.

In 2022, the Ministry of Education issued "Compulsory Education Curriculum Program and Curriculum Standards (2022 Edition)", which provided new principles and ways for the in-depth implementation of "double reduction policy" [15], and proposed that "at least 10% of class hours will be used in each course to design interdisciplinary thematic learning". Through interdisciplinary thematic activities [16], the cultivation value and adaptability, ability, creativity value of the curriculum will be highlighted to meet the requirements. Service thinking is integrated with interdisciplinary courses to solve the problem of paying attention to practice but neglecting learning. Through interdisciplinary course, we can break the closed and isolated nature of subject teaching, overcome the fragmentation of knowledge learning, implement interdisciplinary integrated teaching, realize multi-dimensional, systematic, and creative application of students' knowledge to solve practical problems, meet students' diverse needs, and achieve the purpose of having a higher vision and improving practical skills. This makes the integration of service design and interdisciplinary course the main trend in research and study.

Fig. 3. The participants were coached by the instructor to assemble a robot that could be used for environmental testing in the field

True interdisciplinary subject learning requires extracting more perspectives of interdisciplinary course study from real situations, and then integrating them into a brand-new curriculum. For example, around the topic of water, we can study the physical and chemical properties of water, as well as the production and life. The relationship between water (animals, plants, microbes);And the system of water and earth (atmosphere, ecology, geology, climate, soil, heat);Water resources research (fresh water, sewage treatment, irrigation, purification, pollution, reuse); Management of water resources (dams, water source protection, power generation, water diversion, modern agriculture, rainwater collection); Interaction with water society and economy (values, cities, sports, beliefs, water governance, navigation, transportation, canals, origins, belt and road initiative, national boundaries, immigration, war); Coexistence with water culture (art, language, customs, music, tea ceremony, celebrations, poetry, photography).The interdisciplinary course of "Pea Seedling Summer Camp" introduces the concepts of sustainable design and green design through interdisciplinary integration, and was committed to solving complex problems in the real world and realizing knowledge transfer through the three steps of "problem orientation-theory-practice". Take the robotics programming course as an example. First, the instructor uses a variety of interactive methods to guide students to raise real-world issues such as aging, environmental pollution, and the gap between rich and poor. For example, if a student is concerned about the ecological environment, the instructor will help him or her analyze whether an underwater robot for testing water quality or planes for testing air quality are better solution. Then instruct the teacher to determine the theoretical points involved in the problem, such as the components of the robot and the basic principles of sensors. Then, the teacher will lead the student to choose the required components and join hands in assembling and debugging the robot. Finally, the tutor will accompany the students to the scenic spot to test the robot, collect real data, help the students solve specific problems and consolidate their theoretical knowledge through practice (see Fig. 3). Service design thinking integration of interdisciplinary courses, to solve the problem of low-level, shallow interdisciplinary integration, improve students' ability to use multidisciplinary knowledge to observe, analyze and solve problems in an integrated manner, forming an integrated, complete, and open problem-solving ability based on the development needs of students We seek to achieve a balance of learning and travel, high intention and enhance practical skills.

3.2 Service Blueprint Throughout the Teaching Context – Mentors Pointing Out and Developing Awareness

By introducing the blueprint of service into the whole teaching situation, the problem of lack of interactivity in the content is solved, and the goal of cultivating the problem consciousness of famous teachers is achieved. The construction of the teaching environment is planned through service blueprint, which is an important tool for service design. In the teaching activities of the "Pea Seedling Summer Camp", first of all, the "Pea Seedling Summer Camp" presents students' whole learning and life in pea seedling in the form of a flow chart from the perspective of students, carefully analyzes the contact points between the students and the instructors during the teaching process, links the behaviors of the students and the instructors with the corresponding support functions, and shows students' behaviors with visual content, including what they see, hear and hear. This includes what they see, hear, and feel physically, as well as what they think in their minds. The problem of lack of interaction in the teaching environment has been solved. By using this tool, we can present the logical relationship between courses and their order more completely. At the same time, the service design emphasizes that there should be interaction between the participants and the content, rather than just allowing participants to receive it and then be taught in a fill-in-the-blank way.

Fig. 4. Participants receiving on-site guidance from Zhang Jianguo, (President of the Creative Institute of the Chinese Academy of Calligraphers and Painters), in a beautiful scenic environment.

The teaching context of the "Pea Seedling Summer Camp" extends from the classroom to the art gallery, and then to the green mountains and green hills, in the form of blueprint of service, which meets the needs of "learning" and "doing". The combination of learning and travel motivates students and develops their awareness of problems. Through the concrete, intuitive and perceivable service design system of the service blueprint, the purpose of mastering the teacher's point of view and cultivating the problem consciousness can be achieved. Teachers from Chongqing University of Posts and Telecommunications, Chongqing University, Sichuan Fine Arts Institute, and other institutions of higher learning, and together with artists from the Bo Xiang Art Museum, are engaged in teaching. Teachers participate in the whole project, and master's teachers promote teaching, and fully capturing the social demand for interdisciplinary integration (see Fig. 4).

For example, the camp is combined with the BDS World Youth Street Dance Contest, the China Original Music Incubation Base, Children's Art Theater, Chongqing Youth Painting and Calligraphy Contest and other projects.

3.3 Value Co-creation – Mutual Respect, Equal Co-creation, Everyone is a Designer

"Pea Seedling Summer Camp" introduces the value of co-creation to solve the results floating on the surface, to achieve mutual respect and equal co-creation. Everyone is a designer. Participants in the learning process are the co-creators of value, and learning value is created and established by the learning institutions and students through interaction. Pea Seedling Summer Camp has narrowed the distance of physical space, allowing individuals to interact with each other, and individuals and space to establish a meaningful connection with each other, so that students and stakeholders in research institutions can have a good memory of the research process.

Fig. 5. Participants and instructors create food, drink, and fun together, feeling the equal love and mutual respect between teachers, students, and peers

The value of the classroom is not defined by the teacher, but by the student-teacher co-creation of the student as the main body. STEAM Summer Camp for Pea Seedlings advocates the educational concept of "technology" and "humanities and arts", and adopts the teaching method of "indoor teaching" and "outdoor practice". I hope every student can have a good memory of the learning process. For example, the summer camp pursues fresh, ecological, healthy, and balanced dishes and cooking methods in the daily meals provided for teachers and students, so as to ensure that they get diversified nutrition and rich energy. Therefore, a large central kitchen has been specially prepared in the summer camp base, which not only meets the cooking needs of all teachers and students, but also integrates labor education into life, thus bringing the distance between teachers and participants closer. All the ingredients were purchased from the local market in the early hours of the morning according to the menu jointly developed by the tutor and students the night before. Meanwhile, flat management and teaching methods are adopted in the camp. Teachers and students sit at the same table, share delicious food and daily life at the table, and feel equal love, understanding and respect. The distance between tutors and students is not only conducive to tutors' in-depth understanding of students' pain points and access to important contact points for service design, but also conducive to arranging teaching according to students' different personality characteristics and foundation. It also allows students to get a satisfactory activity experience through value co-creation (see Fig. 5).

4 Conclusion

The government's support and a large number of market demand make research and learning hot, but there is also a general problem that tourism is valued over knowledge, and interactive content is lacking. However, the results was superficial. The research should aim at cultivating high-quality and highly educated talents who keep pace with the times, and from the perspective of service design, through service design thinking, service blueprint and value co-creation, solve the common problems of research institutions, such as paying more attention to travel than knowledge, lack of interactive content, and superficial results.

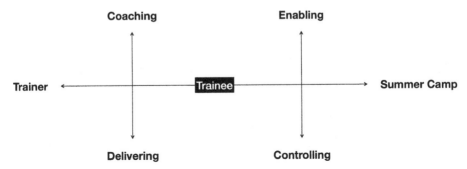

Fig. 6. Two design turns of transdisciplinary teaching and learning

The "Pea Seedling Summer Camp" introduces new ideas and methods of service design, focusing on the values and development trends of nurturing people, with literacy as the core, situation as the field, problems as the key link and technology as the wings.

Two design turns of transdisciplinary teaching and learning were illustrated through the exploration and practice in summer camp by service design, the one is paying more attention on enabling than traveling around, the other one is focusing on more coaching than delivering skills (see Fig. 6).

Acknowledgements. This work was supported by Doctoral startup fund and talent introduction fund project of Chongqing University of Posts and Telecommunications – Research on the cost and benefit distribution of big data productization (K2020–201) and Chongqing educational science planning project – Research on the talent training system of "social theme" in Colleges and Universities (2020-GX-284) and Research Center for network social development of Chongqing University of Posts and Telecommunications – Research on the cost of network big data production (2020SKJD06).

References

1. Li, J.: A Review on Research of Study Tour in China in the Past Five Years **31**(06), 13–19 (2017). https://doi.org/10.16398/j.cnki.jbjieissn1008-228x.2017.06.003
2. Zhang, Z.: The aesthetic education implication and path analysis of research travel in primary and secondary schools. China Art **2022**(S1), 66–69. Ding, X., Du, J.: The primary principle of service design: from user-centeredtostakeholder-centered. Decorate **2020**(03), 62–65. https://doi.org/10.16272/j.cnki.cn11-1392/j.2020.03.019
3. IBM University Cooperation Department University Relations: IBM GCG. IBM "Service Science (SSME) discipline construction" University Cooperation Project [EB/OL]. (2008-07-22) [2019-04-30]. https://www.doc88.com/p57432647427.html
4. Zeng, J.: Research on Product Interactive Design Method Under Sewice Design. Tianjin Academy of Fine Arts (2022). https://doi.org/10.27361/d.cnki.gtmsy.2022.000014
5. Hu, F., Li, W.: Definition of "service design." Packaging Eng. **40**(10), 37–51 (2019). https://doi.org/10.19554/j.cnki.1001-3563.2019.10.008
6. Wei, W., Wu, C.: Comparison of user experience map, customer journey mapand service blueprint. Packaging Eng. **40**(14), 217223 (2019). https://doi.org/10.19554/j.cnki.1001-3563.2019.14.036
7. Wang, Z.: Research and practice of service design based on blue-printand design experience. Packaging Eng. **36**(12), 4144+53 (2015). https://doi.org/10.19554/j.cnki.1001-3563.2015.12.011
8. He, S.: Application of service design thought in the teaching of design introduction. J. Nanjing Acad. Arts (Fine Arts Des.) **03**, 107–109 (2016)
9. Spohrer, J., Magliopp, B., et al.: Steps toward a science of service systems. Computer **40**(1), 71–77 (2007)
10. Zeng, J.: Research on the Influence of Nonmaterial Factors in the Involvement of Customers' Value Cocreation and Service Pricing. Northeast University (2017). https://doi.org/10.27007/d.cnki.gdbeu.2017.000927
11. Luo, S., Wang, S., Zhang, D., Fang, C.: Health service design strategy based on value co-creation. Creativity Des. (03), 5–11 (2022)
12. Peng, C., et al.: Research on value co-creation new business model of import cross-border E-commerce platform ecosystem. Secur. Commun. Netw. **2022**, 14 p. (2022). Article ID 8726075. https://doi.org/10.1155/2022/8726075
13. Wang, M., Zeng, F.: Service design thinking stimulates design innovation learning. Art Panorama **05**, 160 (2016)
14. Ministry of Education: Circular of the Ministry of Education on Printing and Distributing the Curriculum Scheme and Curriculum Standards for Compulsory Education (2022 Edition) [OL]. http: //www.gov.cn/zhengce/zhengceku/202204/21/content_5686535.htm
15. Wang, Z., Teng, J., Lei, M., Liao, C.: Opportunities and strategies for the implementation of "double reduction" empowered by STEAM inclusive education empowerment. Mod. Educ. Technol. **32**(08), 43–49 (2022)

Chinese Character Learning and Platform Tool Development for Junior Primary School Student Based on Orthographic Awareness

Zhen Liu[1](✉) and Ziyu Lin[2]

[1] School of Design, South China University of Technology, Guangzhou 510006, China
1192826732@qq.com
[2] Devision of Arts, Shenzhen University, Shenzhen 518060, China

Abstract. Chinese is the most spoken language in the world, and Chinese characters are the written symbol system of the Chinese language. As junior primary school students aged six to eight years old learning Chinese characters, they need to understand Chinese characters, learn to write and compose Chinese characters, and achieve certain reading skills in a relatively short period of time. In the actual learning process, junior primary school students face a variety of problems in learning Chinese characters, from their own factors to teaching methods and family environment. The need to learn Chinese characters well facing many challenges. Therefore, this study aims to understand the basic learning theory of Chinese characters and the characteristics of Chinese character learning for low school-age children, to explore the connection between Chinese character orthography awareness and children's Chinese character learning, to explore the possibility of combining Chinese character learning and digital technology, to design a mobile platform for Chinese character learning for the students, to promote the optimization and improvement of Chinese character education in the first school year, and to promote the improvement of Chinese character skills for the students aged six to eight. The study adopts a bibliometric approach, in which all the collected literature are from the China National Knowledge Infrastructure (CNKI) China Knowledge Database, and analyzed using keyword clustering via Citespace software to obtain the corresponding network. The analysis has obtained the current research hotspots and research trends, as well as relationships for Chinese character learning and tool platform development for the junior primary school student based on orthographic awareness.

Keywords: Orthographic Awareness · Meta-consciousness · Primary School · Junior Students · Chinese Character Learning · Cognitive Deficits · Learning Platform

1 Introduction

The age of six to eight is the developmental stage when children move from verbal expression to literacy and writing, and the learning goal for children at this stage is to master 3, 000 commonly used Chinese characters, as required by the Language Curriculum Standards for Full--Time Compulsory Education [1]. However, for junior primary school students who are just learning to read and write. They have not yet mastered the learning method, have a weak sense of independent learning, often needing parental accompaniment when learning Chinese characters, and their literacy efficiency is low and misspellings are common. 3,000-word literacy goal is a considerable burden for children at this stage. In the first grade of primary school, there is still a large proportion of students who are not able to take the initiative to learn Chinese characters, and there is also a significant proportion of students who do not have the habit of learning Chinese characters after school [2]. In addition, there are still many problems in the current literacy classroom. The current problems are manifested in the emphasis on the quantity of words rather than the quality of words, the teaching of Chinese characters staying on the surface of Chinese characters, and the outdated teaching methods [2].

In order to investigate how teaching Chinese characters can promote the learning outcomes of Chinese characters for junior primary school students, an understanding of the basic learning theories of Chinese characters is needed. Chinese characters are scripts with an internal hierarchical structure and can be broken down into components or strokes [3]. In addition, Chinese character components have a key role in the development of Chinese character cognition, and orthographic awareness including the awareness of the rules for combining Chinese character components [4]. Therefore, understanding the basic framework of orthographic awareness is helpful in exploring the design of Chinese character instruction for the junior primary school students.

A script is a symbol for recording language. Orthography is the rule used by each script to regulate the writing and use of the script [5]. Each language system has its own specific orthographic theory. A Chinese character is a character with an internal hierarchical structure, and a character can be divided into components or strokes, which are units of composition composed of strokes with the function of forming a Chinese character and strokes, which are the smallest writing units that form the standard form of a Chinese character, and strokes and components are combined to form a complete Chinese character through orthographic rules [3]. In Chinese characters, the strokes are oriented in a certain way, and the way the strokes and components are combined is not random, but has a certain regularity in its position and arrangement [6]. Therefore, orthographic awareness of Chinese characters can be divided into awareness of the structure of the character, awareness of the function of the components, and awareness of the position of the parts [6]. Chinese characters can also be divided into single character and combined characters according to the way the components are combined and matched [7]. More than 80% of modern orthographic characters are combined characters [8]. A uncomposed character is one that is made up of strokes as a direct unit, and there is no way to split the character into parts. A combined character is made up of parts that follow a certain structure type, and can be subdivided into two, three, or more pieces according to the number of combinations [7]. Depending on the position of the components, the two-block characters include left and right, upper and lower, and inner and outer structures [7]. Although strokes are the basic constituent units of Chinese characters, people tend to treat Chinese character parts as the basic units of Chinese characters in learning [9]. This is associated with the pronunciation and semantics of Chinese characters that are often influenced by their parts, and memorizing the semantics and phonology of a part can help learners to learn a large number of similar Chinese characters. However, not all parts have pronunciation and semantic features, so the parts can be classified into three main categories according to pronunciation and semantics: with pronunciation and semantics, with pronunciation without semantics/with semantics without pronunciation, and without semantics without pronunciation [10].

In addition, orthographic awareness, as a basic theory of Chinese character learning, requires finding appropriate methods and tools to convey these theories to junior primary school students. In the current teaching environment, teachers are mainly relied upon to talk about the basic rules of Chinese characters in the classroom and convey this concept through group activities, such as working together to draw the characters in the air with the students' fingers. However, the students are almost mechanized to this model, and such teaching may seem like a high level of student engagement, in which this mechanized memorization of Chinese characters is actually not conducive to their comprehension [2]. It is difficult for children to feel the meaning and help that orthographic awareness brings. To address these teaching pain points, exploring new technological tools to assist teaching could be a way.

In current rapidly evolving digital age environment, information technology brings unlimited possibilities for changes in teaching and education. And being in this special period of global epidemic, years of traditional teaching turning into online education in a short period of time also adds challenges to learning and mastering of Chinese characters for the junior primary school students. These issues can contribute to the exploration and development of Chinese character teaching in the first school year and help research on Chinese character learning and home education for the junior primary school students. As such, the purpose of this paper is to understand the basic learning theories of Chinese characters and the characteristics of Chinese character learning for the junior primary school students (aged six to eight), to explore the connection between Chinese character orthographic awareness and Chinese character learning, and to explore the possibility of integrating Chinese character learning and digital technology.

2   Method

In order to investigate the relationship between orthographic awareness and Chinese character learning for junior primary school students, and the feasibility of designing a mobile platform for children's Chinese character learning, this paper uses bibliometric method and data from the China National Knowledge Infrastructure (CNKI) China knowledge database. The search topics have been identified as "orthography, education," "orthography, children, learning," "orthography, tools," and "orthography, platform". And the obtained literature have been imported into Citespace software sequentially to generate keyword co-occurrence network for analysis.

3   Result

3.1   Orthography—Education (Year 2005 to 2021)

In the co-occurrence network of orthography and education, keywords with more than 2 co-occurrences were screened as shown in Table 1.

Table 1. Orthography and education literature high frequency co-occurrence keywords.

Count	Centrality	Year	Keywords
4	0.00	2011	Preschoolers
3	0.00	2005	Orthography
2	0.00	2011	Word Awareness
2	0.00	2014	Dyslexia
2	0.00	2018	Reading
2	0.00	2012	Eye-tracking
2	0.00	2011	Phonological awareness

The results of high-frequency co-occurring keywords reveal that orthography education has been a research hotspot in the last decade focusing on preschoolers, with articles about preschoolers first appearing in year 2011 and four related papers discussing it within a decade. The relationship between orthography and word awareness, and even dyslexia, has been explored in recent years. There have also been discussions of orthography education and reading, eye tracking, and phonological awareness. The discussion of word awareness under orthographic education first appeared in year 2011 and has been mentioned in a total of two papers until year 2021, while the discussion related to dyslexia appeared in year 2014 and appeared twice in total until year 2021.

A keyword clustering analysis has been conducted based on the keyword co-occurrence study to obtain a clustered view of the orthographic education field, as shown in Fig. 1.

Fig. 1. Cluster analysis of orthography and education keywords Citespace software.

As shown in Fig. 1, the 12 sets of keyword clusters obtained are Second grade, Textual attention, Elementary school students, Chinese characters, Visual language, Context, Dyslexia, Structure, Pictogram method of literacy, Theory of Second Language Acquisition, and Complementary teaching method. The Second grade includes integrated literacy, writing skills, and orthography. The Textual attention contains a study of children's word awareness and reading. Junior primary school students are key players in orthographic education, and their learning goals are the focus of educational research. The research directions include teaching methods, Chinese character structure, and the study of children's word vision and related pathologies. In addition, previous studies have shown that orthographic awareness is an important part of children's cognitive mechanisms, and if the junior primary school students lack orthographic awareness, it can lead to deficits in cognitive development [11]. Many children have reading difficulties at an early age, and if they are provided with targeted intervention and instruction, the symptoms of reading difficulties can be effectively alleviated.

The development of orthographic awareness in children includes many aspects: shape rules (drawings and scribbles), spatial arrangement rules (spaces and non-squares), knowledge of primary parts (with letters, with numbers, and with shapes), and awareness of orthography (mirror images, misplaced parts, false words, and part errors) [11]. The development of these aspects is not simultaneous and has a certain order of sequence, which is also closely related to the development of the physical brain [12]. In a study on the relationship between orthographic awareness and family reading in junior primary school students, it was found that the higher the quality of parent-child reading and the better the family reading environment, the higher the level of picture recognition and doodling of young children, which promotes the improvement of orthographic awareness [11].

There is a correlation between the development of orthographic awareness and dyslexia in children [13]. Dyslexia is generally divided into two major categories: congenital acquired dyslexia and acquired developmental dyslexia [14]. Acquired brain damage or disease caused by reading difficulties is called acquired dyslexia; while developmental dyslexia generally refers to individuals who do not differ from other individuals in terms of intelligence, motivation to learn, life environment and educational resources, as well as no obvious sexual impairment in vision, hearing, or neurological system, but they are unable to reach the appropriate reading level at the appropriate age and have generalized difficulties in reading [14].

A competency component assessment model has been developed for children with dyslexia, which suggests that students' literacy skills are influenced by an association with cognitive, psychological, and ecological components [15]. The cognitive component is literacy and comprehension, which focuses on the development of orthographic awareness, while the psychological component involves the child's motivation and interest in learning, and the ecological component includes the home environment, parental involvement and classroom environment, peers, and so on [15]. Therefore, the orthographic awareness teaching method is one aspect that affects children with dyslexia, and the design process needs to be aware of the influence of the other two components.

In literacy teaching, characteristics of Chinese characters, psychological features, and the use of technology has been identified as the three major categories of literacy teaching [16]. The literacy methods from psychological characteristics include word puzzle literacy and rapid cycle literacy, while computer-assisted instruction and multimedia are considered in the use of technology [16]. The three approaches have been integrated to design an effective instructional program: component-based meaningful literacy (pictographic literacy) to help learners to achieve memory associations, and the use of multisensory memory methods and computer-assisted instruction to increase student-teacher interaction [15]. These results indicate that orthographic awareness interventions were effective in promoting dyslexic students' Chinese character recognition skills.

Therefore, in orthography and Chinese character education, there is a need to consider how orthographic awareness can be acquired through effective training methods and to focus on children with dyslexia who are closely associated with orthographic awareness. Training children in orthographic awareness at an early age can reduce their cognitive deficits in this area. Attention also needs to be paid to the family education and home environment of the junior primary school students. A good parent-child reading process and a combination of instructional methods can work together to influence students' literacy skills.

3.2 Orthography—Children—Learning (Year 1996 to 2021)

In the co-occurrence network of orthography, children, and learning, keywords with more than 2 co-occurrences have been screened as shown in Table 2.

The results of the high-frequency co-occurrence keywords, sorted by frequency of occurrence, show that phonological awareness appeared a total of eight times since year 2007, which indicates that phonological awareness is closely related to children's learning of Chinese characters. Reading ability has been mentioned for the first time in 2008 and appeared six times. Rapid naming and dyslexia have been discussed from year 2010 and appeared four times.

As shown in Fig. 2, keyword clustering analysis has been performed based on the keyword co-occurrence results to obtain clustered views of orthography, children, and learning domains, of which five groups of keyword clusters have been obtained namely rapid naming, Chinese, cognitive resources, reading ability, and reading.

Both phonology and morphemes are present in two keyword groups, i.e., cognitive resources and rapid naming, and exploring phonological and morphemic related information can help to understand the content of Chinese character learning. In the professional domain, meta-linguistic awareness (phonological awareness, morpheme awareness, and orthographic awareness) and rapid naming are important criteria for considering Chinese character learning [17]. Phonological awareness refers to the recognition and use of the phonological system in language, while morpheme awareness refers to the perception and use of the smallest units of meaning in language [18]. Rapid naming mainly examines children's ability to quickly communicate the phonology of familiar symbols [19], in which the main content is to enable children to master the pronunciation of the same type of Chinese characters through the recognized parts. Interestingly, the phonological awareness and orthographic awareness play an important role in Chinese character dictation for children in the lower grades, but rapid naming has no significant effect on the

Table 2. Orthography and children, learning literature high frequency co-occurring keywords.

Count	Centrality	Year	Keywords
8	0.00	2007	Phonological awareness
6	0.00	2008	Reading ability
4	0.00	2010	Rapid Naming
4	0.00	2010	Dyslexia
2	0.00	2012	Learning Disabilities
2	0.00	2001	Chinese
2	0.00	2011	Reading Instruction
2	0.00	2014	Cognitive processing
2	0.00	2018	Chinese Characters
2	0.00	2019	Components
2	0.00	2005	Bilingual
2	0.00	1996	Reading
2	0.00	2013	Pa
2	0.00	2006	Reading Instruction
2	0.00	2010	Cognitive deficits
2	0.00	2018	Intervention
2	0.00	2009	Elementary school students

Fig. 2. Orthography, clustering view of children and learning domains Citespace software.

lower grades, and phonological awareness plays an important role in Chinese character dictation throughout the primary grades [18].

In addition to helping learners recognize characters accurately, Chinese character instruction should also strengthen fluency training in order to achieve improvement in reading ability [20]. Moreover, mastering orthographic processing skills, phonological processing, and morphemes in the initial stages of reading learning is a necessary part of reading development for beginning readers [20].

In terms of learning orthographic awareness, early learners can start with the basic structure of stroke parts, train their understanding of the structure of Chinese character parts, learn the common positions of the parts and try to construct Chinese characters, and learn to learn by example [21].

Since the paraphernalia of Chinese characters are closely related to the semantics and phonology of Chinese characters, understanding the vocal and morphological paraphernalia can improve children's understanding of Chinese characters [22]. It is important to explain the semantic, grammatical, and pragmatic aspects of Chinese characters and to help children understand the phonemic aspects, which also reinforces the use of morphemes in Chinese characters through word formation [22].

In addition, phonological awareness deficits, orthographic awareness deficits, rapid naming deficits, and morpheme awareness deficits are responsible for dyslexia in Chinese children [23, 24]. In terms of cognitive abilities, deficits in verbal memory, attention, and comprehension also contribute to dyslexia symptoms in Chinese children [23, 24]. Related cognitive training has a multisensory approach by using different senses such as sight, hearing, and touch, to create a good literacy atmosphere for literacy learning through a variety of teaching formats, which assists children to remember the related Chinese characters [25].

Therefore, three aspects need to be considered for the learning of Chinese characters for junior primary school students: 1) the learning of Chinese characters with orthographic awareness, 2) the development of Chinese character phonology, morphology, and rapid naming skills, and 3) the simultaneous development of cognitive aspects such as attention.

3.3 Orthography—Tools (Year 1996 to 2021)

Keyword clustering analysis has been performed based on keyword co-occurrence to obtain clustered views on the orthographic and instrumental domains, as shown in Fig. 3, which suggests that interventions for dyslexia is a research hotspot in orthographic and tool domains.

Fig. 3. Cluster view of orthographic and tool domains Citespace software.

Computer-assisted instruction is the most important component in special education teaching, for which the tools are now not limited to computers, but emerging mobile terminals have made the teaching format more enriched [16]. In addition to using emerging information technology, functional interactive picture books has been designed for orthography and literacy to increase children's interest and literacy [26]. Additionally, word images have been incorporated into the books for the use of anthropomorphic character images to gain children's recognition [26]. Further, nursery rhymes and songs are also turned into the stories of the picture books. Therefore, when designing with existing tools, the daily life and living environment for junior primary school students should be considered [26].

3.4   Orthography—Platform

Keyword clustering analysis based on keyword co-occurrence studies can reveal the exploration of Chinese character educational games in the research field, as shown in Fig. 4.

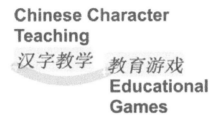

Fig. 4. Cluster view of orthography and platform Citespace software.

From the practical point of view on teaching Chinese as a foreign language, integrated immersion theory and game-based learning mode can be used to design a Chinese character education game on an intelligent mobile platform to assist in teaching Chinese characters to foreigners [27]. The main content of this game has two parts, of which one part is representative Chinese characters that are easy to read and write wrongly, and another part is Chinese Proficiency Test level words, which is believed to enable users to determine the correctness of Chinese characters through orthographic awareness [27]. In addition, teaching Chinese characters by components is the consensus of the academic community, as well as the fact that writing needs to rely on adequate recognition of Chinese characters [27]. Moreover, teaching Chinese characters can be conducted through handwriting recognition technology and an interactive approach that can effectively compensate for learning Chinese characters by rote [28]. Furthermore, the advantage of learning Chinese characters in the form of a game is that it can mobilize students' memory patterns for teaching Chinese characters in a holistic way, while learning and entertaining at the same time [27]. It is also designed with the learning cycle in mind, so that students can be motivated enough to persist in learning through a reasonable input-output design [27]. Although these activities cannot replace normal teaching activities, they can increase students' interest in learning.

Therefore, when designing a mobile platform for Chinese character learning using orthography, it is necessary to consider the age characteristics of the users and the content of Chinese character learning, find the Chinese characters that are more likely to be misspelling and misremembered by the junior primary school students, and target them to help the students to improve their Chinese character memory. It is also necessary to consider the learning cycle and help the students to output relevant knowledge and solve their problems through reasonable content input. And, it is possible to think about the students' writing exercises and related handwriting.

The design feasibility of recognition technology can be considered to make up for the one-way output on platform teaching content and increase the active output of the junior primary school students through the current mature digital technology.

4   Discussion and Conclusion

The current research hotspots and research trends have been obtained that getting orthographic awareness teaching with junior primary school students is a research hotspot in recent years as indicated in the results of Table 1 and Fig. 1, from which teaching methods, kanji structure, family environment factors, and related symptoms have been generated. In terms of children's learning, the children's meta-awareness is an important criterion for determining whether children have mastered Chinese characters, which has been a recent research direction. Orthographic awareness, phonological phonemes, and rapid naming are fundamental factors in children's learning of Chinese characters, as well as other cognitive abilities and upbringing that can affect children's learning of Chinese characters in the early school years. In addition, the link between the acquisition of meta-awareness and dyslexia and the related interventions have been mentioned in both the learning and instrumental literature – orthographic awareness in the junior primary school students can reduce the occurrence of dyslexia, adding social significance to this design theme. The use of new and emerging technologies to enrich teaching methods and design for the students' recognition can reduce their feelings of boredom. In the literature related to orthography and platforms, educational games are important with mobile platforms and digital technologies that are portable, and in line with the trend and educational direction of today's times. Further, the results of orthography and tools (platforms) indicate that there are not many designs related to applying abovementioned theories to children's Chinese character learning tools and platforms compared to the well-established theoretical literature, making it difficult for parents to find suitable Chinese character learning aids at present resulting in constant trial and error in educating their children's learning on Chinese character. Therefore, based on the results of the study, the design goal could be set as an orthography-aware Chinese character learning platform for the junior primary school students associating with emerging digital technologies. In terms of design, based on existing theories and problems, five aspects need to be considered: 1) The parents and children of the same age of the students are also the users of the platform. The accompanying learning style not only meets the psychological needs of the students, but also enhances family relationships and creates a good learning atmosphere in the family; 2) Associating meta-awareness with rapid naming, the students cogitate these basic contents enable them to learn Chinese characters from the perspective of parts, with the training contents of phonetic phonology, so that the shape, sound, and meaning of Chinese characters can be unified and incorporated relevant cognitive training, from the underlying logic, to design training contents that meet the needs of them; 3) Considering the psychological characteristics of the students, through appropriate training methods to obtain their psychological recognition, reduce distraction in learning, and make the training content that is live, exciting, and interesting, for which the related tools and aids need to be close to the living environment of the students and align to their habits of use; 4) The learning cycle of the learning platform should be designed to reduce one-way content output through input content and output methods to create interactive learning, improve the students' learning gains and interest in learning, and enable them to persist in their learning; and 5) Integrating the emerging digital technology such as AR, to make Chinese character learning follow is the trend with conforming to the users' habits of the current information and digital era.

References

1. Language Curriculum Standards Development Group: Language Curriculum Standards for Full-time Compulsory Education (Revised Draft of the Experimental Version). Beijing Normal University Press, Beijing (2012)
2. Liu, H.O.: A Study on the Difficulties of Literacy Teaching in Lower Elementary School. CHN: Ningbo University, Ningbo (2020)
3. Gong, Y.L.: A Study on the Influence of Chinese Character Structure on Elementary and Middle School Students' Recognition Of Character Shapes Under the Condition of Speed Display. CHN: Hunan Sports Vocational College, Changsha (2011)
4. Qian, Y., Zhao, J., Bi, H.Y.: The development of orthographic awareness in Chinese preschoolers. J. Psychol. **45**, 60–69 (2013)
5. Ding, G.S., Peng, D.L., Taft. M.: The Processing of Chinese Inverse-Order Words - the Role of Lexemes in Word Processing. CHN: Beijing Normal University, AUS: University of New South Wales, Beijing (2004)
6. Wu, X.L.: REP Research on Orthographic Processing for Chinese Character Recognition. CHN: Hunan Normal University, Changsha (2009)
7. Yang, R.L.: General Theory of Modern Chinese Characters. Great Wall Press, Beijing (2000)
8. Zhang, L.D.: A study on the relationship between orthographic awareness, reading ability and Chinese character writing ability. CHN: Shenzhen University, Shenzhen, Shenzhen (2020)
9. Chan, L.: Children Learn to Read and Write Chinese Analytically. University of London, London (1996)
10. Zhou, L., Peng. G., Zheng, H.Y.: Sub-lexical phonological and semantic processing of semantic radicals: a primed naming study, Reading and Writing (2013)
11. Zhu, Q.: A Study on the Development of Orthographic Awareness and the Family Reading Environment in Primary and Secondary School Children. CHN: Tianjin Normal University, Tianjin (2019)
12. Yan, G.L., Liu, N.N.: A study on the development of preschool children's word awareness. Tianjin Normal University, Tianjin, CHN (2012)
13. Liu, W.L., Liu, X.P., Zhang, J.Q.: A preliminary exploration of subtypes of developmental dyslexia in Chinese. J. Psychol. **38**, 681–693 (2006)
14. Bai, L.R.: A study on the origin, definition and deficits of dyslexia. Contemp. Linguist. **15**, 466–479 (2013)

15. Lin, J.Y.: Study on the Characteristics of Orthographic Awareness and Intervention for Chinese Dyslexic Elementary School Students. CHN: Southwestern University, Chongqing (2021)

16. Dai, R.X.: Teaching and Learning Chinese Characters. Shandong Education Press, Jinan (1999)

17. Pan, J., Shu, C., Liu, H.Y., Zhang, Y.P., Zhang, H.Y., Li, H.: What is in the naming? A 5-year longitudinal study of early rapid naming and phonological sensitivity in relation to subsequent reading skills in both native Chinese and English as a second language. J. Educ. Psychol. **103**, 897–908 (2011)

18. Li, L.P., Wu, X.C., Xiong, C.Y., Cheng, Y.H., Ruan, S.F.: The effects of meta-linguistic awareness and rapid naming on elementary school students' Chinese character dictation. Psychol. Dev. Educ. **32**, 698–705 (2016)

19. Li, H., Rao, X.Y., Dong, Q., Zhu, J., Wu, X.C.: Phonological awareness, phonological awareness and rapid naming in children's speech development. Psychol. Dev. Educ. **27**, 158–163 (2011)

20. Hao, M.L., Zhou, S.N.: A study on the factors affecting Chinese reading accuracy and fluency of Chinese beginners. World Chin. Lang. Teach. **33**, 548–562 (2019)

21. Li, H., Hua, S., Chang, C., Liu, H.Y., Peng, H.: Chinese children's character recognition: Visuo-orthographic, phonological processing and morphological skills. J. Res. Reading **5**, 287–307 (2012)

22. Shen, D.D.: The Effects of Phonological Awareness and Orthographic Awareness on the Reading Ability of Children with Developmental Dyslexia in Chinese. CHN: Nanjing Normal University, Nanjing (2017)

23. Li, Q.W.: Cognitive process basis of phonological and orthographic deficits in Chinese developmental dyslexia. CHN: East China Normal University, Shanghai (2010)

24. Lin, M., Liu, J.X.: A Study on the Cognitive Characteristics of Chinese Developmental Dyslexic Children. CHN: Xiamen University, Xiamen (2014)

25. Chen, M.T.: Using multisensory teaching to improve the literacy efficiency of children with literacy disorders. Mod. Spec. Educ. **13**, 58–59 (2018)

26. Wen, Q.Y.: Research on the Design of Interactive Picture Books Based on the Function of Literacy Preparation in the Early Elementary School Interface. CHN: Guangdong University of Technology, Guangzhou (2015)

27. Xu, C.H.: Software Design of Chinese Character Education Game Based on Intelligent Mobile Platform. CHN: Guangdong University, Guangzhou (2013)

28. Wu, Y.C.: Handwritten Chinese character recognition and literacy teaching. World Chin. Lang. Teach. **2**, 21–26 (1999)

Pair-Teamwork Effect on First Semester IT Students to Achieve Collaborative Learning Through Social Relations

Jan P. Nees[(✉)] [ID] and XiaoLei Bi[(✉)] [ID]

Erhvervsakademi Midtvest, Gl. Landevej 2, 7400 Herning, Denmark
{jpn,xbi}@eamv.dk

Abstract. This research aims to investigate the impact of pair-programing and teamwork and whether they will have positive effects on IT students' social skills. Our hypothesis is the usage of Pair Programming (or Pair Teamwork) and shuffling the groups within the first semester will create a better social relation inside the classroom and better collaborative environments. This can introduce a better class dynamic, where "knowledge skills" (Eng. professional knowledge) will be shared and a better social environment to be created, resulting in an increase in satisfaction and motivation among IT-students, where we had access to two classes (DMU – Eng. Computer Science AP course, MMD – Eng. Multimedia designer AP course). During our research, we designed a survey that was distributed four times, during the period of three months. The result is combined into an excel sheet and measured with the average. We get an overview of the general population's response. The research design was in two stages, where the first part was to measure their response to pair-programming (PP) teamwork, with shuffling, and the second part was to test the effect of converting to Mob Programming (MP) groups. The result of these four surveys indicated that during the PP, the motivation and knowledge sharing started to decrease with time, however, when changing to MP there was a renewed motivational effect which started to increase motivation for their study. However, this is mainly true for the class of DMU, the other class of MMD had a slower response to the change of going from PP to MP. During the research, we also see Tuckman's model of stages of group development in action, which is more profound with the DMU class than with the MMD class.

Keywords: Pair Programming · Mob Programming · Group teamwork · Cooperative and Cooperative learning

1 Introduction

Our observation about IT students is that they often form groups at the beginning of the first weeks of the first semester, resulting in them staying in the same group during the whole education (our academy provides DMU courses for 2.5 years and MMD courses for 2 years). Knowledge in these small groups is often not shared between other groups, which makes the small groups very exclusive. Our interviews with the companies where the students make their internship (in their last semester and their exam projects) are more and more willing to take students in pairs. The industry is setting more requirements for education institutes that graduates and students need to have soft skills to collaborate and communicate with each other.

This is supported by Bernd Schulz's research paper, which points out that "Employers as well as educators frequently complain about a lack in soft skills among graduates from tertiary education institutions. Predominantly missed are communication skills" [1]. We experience that the students come from different technical backgrounds before they enter the first-semester programming courses, some students have already learned programming in high school/at work/home while some have no experience in programming. Programming which is considered the most difficult and time-consuming subject of study could be a root cause of the students choosing to stop/quit their studies. Our academy offers both DMU and MMD as 2 ½ and 2 years courses. Both IT education is facing the problem that students lacking social skills, especially after the corona period. Those who come directly from high school are used to sitting at home using online teaching, which is causing a problem when they are entering a new studying environment and meeting a group of people. Different factors are causing a high dropout rate during the first semester for IT students. We are invited to research how we can improve this situation. Another challenge is that we experience that the students come from different technical backgrounds before they enter the first semester of IT courses, some students have already learned programming in high school/at work/home while others have absolutely no experience in programming. Programming course is considered the most time-consuming and difficult for most students during the first semester. Traditionally, students prefer to solve the problem and program along, which is not helping their social and interaction skills. Our solution is we would like to see if introducing pair programming combined with shuffling, the knowledge transfer will happen in a classroom setup and result in better social environments and thereby share knowledge across groups. There could be an added benefit to reducing the drop-out rate, which normally is around 33% for first-year computer science students [2]. We have 62 IT students in this research (31 DMU students and 31 MMD students) as they start their 1st semester in EAMV 2022 on 1st September when we planned our experiment. We choose to research pair programming and used it as the main learning setup. Pair programming (PP) which originates from eXtreme Programming lets two programmers sit together, one as the driver, and another one as the navigator, and work collaboratively to complete programming tasks. Pair programming appears to be a simple, straightforward concept. Two programmers work side-by-side at one computer, continuously collaborating on the same design, algorithm, code, and test [3].

Our PP setup is to assign random groups where two students are paired in a classroom and complete a programming task. They need to use the PP as a software development technique in which two programmers work together on the same PC. They typically switch their roles after around 30 min. The roles are, one of the programmers, the driver, has control of the keyboard/mouse and actively implements the program. The other programmer, the observer, continuously observes the work of the driver to identify tactical (syntactic, spelling, etc.) defects, and also thinks strategically about the direction of the work [4].

We find there is a high tendency of those who are relatively experienced in programming tends to not have a motivation to collaborate in the pair work [4]. After researching and reviewing pair programming, we also discover there could be disadvantages/downsides of using Pair Programming because *"Experienced programmers are very reluctant to program with another person. Some say their code is "personal," or that another person would only slow them down."* [5].

We experienced and observed from our previous teaching experience that some students who are very good at programming prefer to work alone. Our solution is to shuffle the pairs more often in the three-month project period, which increase the possibility that the students can meet different type of partners. We also decided to research other software development methods to increase the more social interaction. We found Mob programming (MP) is another novel software development practice which is featured in *"Two people or more (the whole team) sit at the same computer and collaborate on the same code at the same time. With mob programming, the collaboration is extended to everyone on the team, while still using a single computer for writing the code and inputting it into the code base."* [6].

MP is very similar to PP. With mob programming, the collaboration is extended to everyone on the team, while still using a single computer for writing the code and inputting it into the code base [6]. MP might be a better approach/method in our study, because the student's attendance in the classroom variates during the 1st semester, during the high season of influenza, we normally have 5–8 students taking sick leaves per week. Setting up the students into a larger study group and working in MP can minimize the problem that they cannot find their normally assigned pairs.

However, we are also aware of the disadvantage of MP. During the project time, they could prefer not to meet in the classroom room but do their tasks in their own home space and cooperatively complete the task given, students preference for working at home could be an obstacle to promoting the concept of MP. The chances that they work collaboratively in the same physical learning space are reduced, introducing a side effect that they prefer to divide their tasks, work cooperatively, and communicate less often. This is not an ideal situation if our focus is on soft and social/soft skills. Research from cooperative and collaborative learning suggests that collaborative working together involves a higher level of learning and awareness than cooperation. (self-translation from Danish [7]. We would also prefer students to do more face-to-face collaboration work instead of virtual. This is also supported by research findings that students in face-to-face collaboration will perform better [8]. It becomes one of the recommendations when we introduce students to pair/teamwork. After investigating how to conduct PP and MP, and how these methods can be used theoretically. We will continue to the next stage to find out who made similar work related to our research.

2   Related Work

In the next step, we find other research about PP in other Danish business academy (Danish: Erhvervsakademi) IT related education. One similar study we found is focused on measuring the PP effect on code quality and participants programming self-confidence level [9]. Other research paper is concentrated on PP code ownership and coding standards [10]. Those papers provide good ideas of how to integrate PP into daily teaching, however, they have not been able to provide us with the methodology for how to measure the effect of PP/MP and the social soft skills of the students.

Furthermore, we found research on how to implement PP to make students socialize, however the experiment is made in primary schools [11].

Compared to other research and study, our contribution is to combine Pair-Programming (Pair-Teamwork), with shuffling of the groups, to increase social skills and knowledge sharing in small groups first. Then later in the project period, they are given the choice to make their own MP groups, and we will measure the effect in survey. Our hypothesis is that by starting with Pair-teamwork, and late change to larger groups, which they will choose themselves, will increase satisfaction with social contribution and knowledge sharing in the classroom.

The reason that we want to start with PP first instead of MP is, most students starting the IT education having introverted personalities. Putting them into small groups of two is better than introducing them in larger groups in the beginning.

Another technical consideration is the students just start their education in our academy, in programming intro courses, we introduce Scratch (https://scratch.mit.edu/) as the first tool of learning programing for both DMU and MMD students.

The reason for using scratch is that it is a good introduction tool for beginner programmers [12]. For the time being, scratch is a good platform to transdisciplinary teaching and learning. IT can build a learning community and game/play based learning for both MMD and DMU studies. Later, we use Visual Studio Code (VS Code) as the programming editor for both MMD and DMU students.

3 Framework

To carry out this study, it was designed and developed 4 x projects for both MMD and DMU studies. Each project varies around 14 days from the study start. The research period was one semester (2022), starting on 30th august ends 30th November. At the end of each project, the students are asked to fill in a survey questionnaire which indicates whether they agreed or not with the statement of their professional knowledge and social learning experience. The whole experiment and pairing of groups are made randomly during the research period. To get an in-depth understanding of the students' internal understanding of their experience with pair-teamwork, we decided to use Likerts 7-scale point instead of 5-points [13]. More depth in the survey will help the let the students reflect more carefully about their choice, thereby also setting them into a mindset of their deliberations. This is supported by the research done by [14].

Projects during the semester on the two different courses can be seen in the tables (Table 1 and Table 2). As can be seen, DMU and MMD have different projects each, this is due to that they have study goals, however, the common factor is that they share is the same programming teacher.

We decided to print out this anonymous survey and give it to each student and collect the data after each assigned project is finished. The students are getting the same questions and fill out the same form during the study. Those questions' details are described in Table 3 below. As can be seen in the above two tables. During the first stage, from week 36 to week 40, students were required to work in pair teams (PP) and then

Table 1. DMU Project list

Project	Content	Type of team design
P1 week 36	Scratch- make your Online Game	Pair-teamwork
P2 week 40	Java- build a terminal Game and Simple Calculator	Pair-teamwork
P3 week 44	Pizza Shop System UML diagram	Teamwork
P4 week 46	Little airport's Database in Karup	Teamwork

Table 2. MMD Project list

Project	Content	Type of team design
P1 week 36	Scratch- make your Online Game	Pair-teamwork
P2 week 40	HTML-make a movie with closed captions	Pair-teamwork
P3 week 44	CSS Zen Garden -style your online garden with Zen style that you like	Teamwork
P4 week 46	Modern Kitchen build in Bootstrap	Teamwork

later from week 44 to week 46 given the option of choosing their own 3–4 person groups (MP). The results of the two-stage approach to student groups in weeks 36 to 46 might show that both pairing and self-selected groups can have a positive impact on student performance and satisfaction. By allowing students to work in both environments, they can experience the benefits and challenges of both approaches, allowing them to make informed decisions about their future group work. This flexible approach can help to create a more inclusive and diverse learning environment, as well as promote independent thinking and teamwork skills. Overall, the two-stage approach provides a balanced and effective solution for student group work.

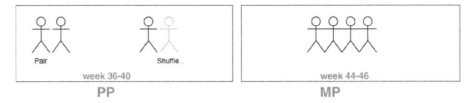

Fig. 1. Research design

As can be seen in Fig. 1, during our research we have two stages, first is where the students start with Pair-teamwork combined with shuffling, and the second is in weeks 44 to 46 they now can arrange their team-groups of 3–4 students. The results of this research design will be analyzed to understand its impact on the students and their social outcomes. The analysis will provide valuable insights into the effectiveness of the different methods of teamwork and their impact on student engagement and collaboration. Overall, the research design provided a framework for analyzing the impact of teamwork on student collaboration and offered valuable insights for future research and educational practices.

Table 3. List of Questions in the survey

Q	Content	Type of Question
Q1	Is programming interesting and challenging	General
Q2	How good you can collaborate with others	General
Q3	How well you are studying programming	Knowledge-Skills
Q4	How much you feel others ahead of you in the studying	Knowledge-Skills
Q5	How do you feel your Pair /team worker contribute in the collaboration	Knowledge-Skills
Q6	I contribute positively to the class knowledge and learning community	Knowledge-Skills
Q7	How much you are helping your classmate	Social
Q8	How much feel you and your pair/team worker help you	Social
Q9	How much do you feel that you are willing to come school and work as a team in the same physical room	Social
Q10	How much time you use in your spare time to communicate with one or more of your team/pair	Social
Q11	I contribute positively to the social environment in the class	Social

We are aware that the fact that we collect survey for ourselves might be not the best practice because of the participatory bias, which respondents are more likely to prefer a technological artifact they believe to be developed by the interviewer [15].

4   Analysis of How the Students Responded to Pair-Teamwork

Pair teamwork can be a beneficial way for students to learn and collaborate within the classroom. It can help with problem-solving, communication, and accountability. It also allows students to learn from their peers and gain different perspectives on the task at hand. Additionally, working in pairs can also increase motivation and engagement, leading to better learning outcomes. It allows students to practice and develop their teamwork skills, which are valuable in both academic and professional settings. Overall, the positive experience of working in pairs can contribute to a more enjoyable and effective learning environment. The following is a dissection of our survey conducted to see if the above is seen in our experiment.

As can be seen from the above Fig. 2, regarding Q1 the respondents fall from Week 36 to Week 40 in both classes. The question is about how exciting and challenging the course is. This should be noted that in Week 36 they had just met the teachers and the

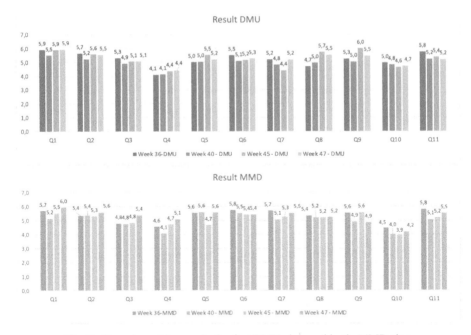

Fig. 2. Overview of the results for first DMU class and lastly MMD class

school, and a certain level of excitement is to be expected from this time. However, during the weeks with pair-team working the result seems to be that both classes are falling in excitement. This could be an indicator that pair teamwork is failing. In week 44 indicated by the grey column in Fig. 2, we saw a positive increase, this is where they have gone away from pair-teamwork over to Group-teamwork (MP) instead. This could be a result of working with various partners, until now that they are finally at a stage where they feel they produce work. Meaning, using the model by Bruce Tuckman from 1965 (Forming, Storming, Norming, Performing), we are probably seeing this from the result. Each time we shuffled the student, they were in a new Forming and Storming stage, but probably never had the time to go to Norming and Performing. However, when we then asked them to form groups after week 40, they now had gotten through the stage of Forming and Storming with many different students and now know whom they would work together with. So, in the process of going to mob teamwork, we made the student go through the first two stages with many in their class. So now when they started working on the next project, they probably felt that they were finally starting to Perform and deliver quality work. This is supported by Q2, where from the DMU class, the drop from week 36 to week 40 is clearly there. As well as it increases as they go over to Group-teamwork. However, for the MMD class the drop is not to be found.

This could indicate that these students enjoy working with others, and the nondevelopment in Q2 (see Fig. 3) is due to their nature as softer students, who enjoy working together with building something creative. The DMU students are more critical thinking of nature, and their courses are designed to develop programmers with a fixed mindset

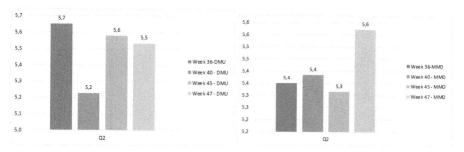

Fig. 3. Q2 for first DMU and lastly MMD class

for design patterns. As both classes go over to Group-work, they start to enjoy working as a team and this improves their overall satisfaction in Q1 and Q2.

The Q3 to Q6 was meant to investigate their knowledge skills, the data here is hard to compare DMU with MMD. Q5 (see Fig. 4) is the most interesting since it evaluates pair teamwork. Looking at Fig. 4 we can see that DMU started slightly lower to the idea of pair teamwork and did not increase over the period. However, after altering to group teamwork, DMU increased in motivation. The opposite is true for MMD class, which decreased significantly, but then increased during the next project period.

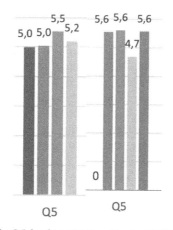

Fig. 4. Q5 for first DMU and lastly MMD class

The Q9 and Q10 (see Fig. 5) are interesting because here DMU and MMD classes are responding similarly to the survey about social skills. Q9 also correlate to Q1 and Q2 statement that in the beginning students were active and engaged in the course, but as the pair-team started to shuffle, they never reached the performing stage and probably started to feel a drain under each shuffle. However, when they started group-work indicated by the grey bar, a clear motivation increase happened, where they feel that now their team is starting to perform and as they started to work together over time this initial boost faded. This might be an alignment with Tuckman's model of group development, which states that a team goes through stages of forming, storming, norming, and performing, where there may be fluctuations in motivation and performance during the process of team formation and development.

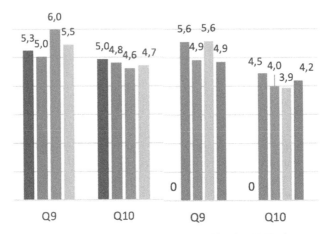

Fig. 5. Q9 and Q10 for first DMU and lastly MMD class

They are performing and have set internal rules and are following them more tacit (*Polanyi, Michael. 1958. Personal Knowledge: Towards a Post-Critical Philosophy. Chicago: University of Chicago Press. ISBN 0-226-67288-3.*). The drop in the last survey is therefore likely a natural indicator of this. They are motivated in a tacit manner without externalizing, why they are working well together.

Tacit knowledge refers to knowledge that is learned through personal experience and cannot be easily transferred or codified. According to Michael Polanyi's concept of personal knowledge [16], individuals tend to rely on tacit knowledge in their daily practices, which are shaped by internalized rules and norms that guide their actions. The drop in the survey may indicate a shift towards more reliance on tacit knowledge and internal motivation, which can contribute to effective collaboration within a group. This shift towards relying on tacit knowledge and internal motivation may lead to a more efficient and cohesive working environment, as individuals can work together harmoniously without being overly influenced by external pressures or distractions.

Their social interaction after lessons is rated by Q10, as can be seen, DMU is more socially active compared to MMD class, and over time both drop, this compared with Q9 is probably due to that teams are now internalizing by working together and sharing knowledge. However, as can be noticed in Q11 both classes are starting to contribute to the overall welfare of the whole class, which is returning to a level seen when they started the course. Most though for MMD, DMU has found it more difficult to increase overall social interaction with the whole class environment. If we look at the social skills of MMD class, they seem to be more inclined to dislike changes in team dynamics, which is indicated by the below figure (see Fig. 6).

For the MMD class, there seems to be a trend downwards over time, but as they start to enjoy group work this trend is broken and returning to near starting level, or a bit over starting level excitement. Q9 week 45 is an outliner from the rest of the trend. It

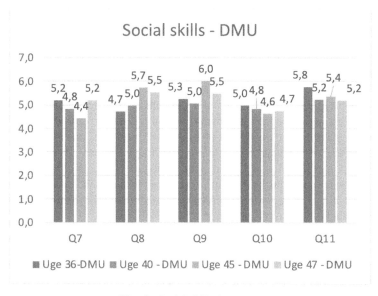

Fig. 6. Social skills for DMU

appears that there is a trend of decreasing excitement for the MMD class, but this trend is broken when the students start to enjoy group work. The excitement level then returns to near the starting level or slightly above it. However, there is an exception in week 45, where the excitement level is an outlier compared to the rest of the trend. it is unclear why this is the case, and it would be beneficial to investigate the reason for this outlier to understand the dynamics of the class better.

In conclusion, the results of the survey suggest that pair teamwork can be a challenging experience for students. The drop in excitement and motivation in the DMU class during the weeks with pair teamwork could indicate that students were struggling to form effective working relationships with their partners, as seen through the drop in Week 36 and Week 40. However, the switch to group teamwork (MP) led to an increase in motivation and overall satisfaction, which is supported by the results of Q5, Q7, Q8 and Q9. The results of these questions align with the stages of group development theory by Bruce Tuckman, where a team goes through forming, storming, norming, and performing stages. The shift towards relying on tacit knowledge and internal motivation during group work may lead to a more efficient and cohesive working environment. However, it's important to note that the results of Q3 to Q6 were difficult to compare between the DMU and MMD classes and further research is needed to gain a clearer understanding of the impact of pair and group teamwork on knowledge skills. The students' perceptions of pair teamwork vs group teamwork vary between the two classes. The DMU class was seen to have a decrease in motivation and satisfaction when using pair teamwork, but an increase after switching to group teamwork. The MMD class showed the opposite pattern. The shift towards relying on tacit knowledge and internal motivation during group teamwork may contribute to a more efficient and cohesive working environment.

The results suggest that Tuckman's model of group development may have played a role in the changes in motivation and satisfaction.

5 Conclusion

The development of this project is still an ongoing phase. We are planning to implement more MP projects in the second semester, so we can continue to measure the effect. The results suggest that the shift towards group-teamwork may have contributed to improved satisfaction and a more efficient and cohesive working environment, as students were able to develop internal rules and norms that guided their actions. The results suggest that while pair-teamwork has its benefits, it may not always be the best approach for all students and classes. It is important to consider the nature of the students and the course when determining the most effective method of collaboration.

Our research indicates that starting with Pair-teamwork, can benefit in staging several storming phases, and shuffling the students, they go through Tuckman's model of; forming, storming, and norming, but never reaching performing. However, in week 45 we hypothesized that now they had gone through the first stage and making their own groups would increase satisfaction and we do find support this during our surveys.

6 Future Work

We will continue our research in semester 2023 for both MMD and DMU students where they facilitate self their study groups. At the same time, there will be minimal pedagogist intervention. By the end of semester, we will make a final survey and we can see more Pair programming/teamwork's effects for the first-year IT students.

References

1. Schulz, B.: The importance of soft skills: education beyond academic knowledge. J. Lang. Commun. (2008)
2. Bennedsen, J., Caspersen, M.E.: Failure rates in introductory programming: 12 years later. ACM Inroads **10**(2), 30–36 (2019). https://doi.org/10.1145/3324888
3. Williams, L., Kessler, R.: Pair Programming Illuminated. Pearson Education, Boston (2003)
4. Williams, L.: Integrating pair programming into a software development process. In: 14th Conference on Software Engineering Education and Training, pp. 27–36, 19–20 Feb 2001
5. Cockburn, A., Williams, L.: The Costs and Benefits of Pair Programming, XPSardinia.PDF (2000)
6. Zuill, W.: Mob Programming: A Whole Team Approach. Agile2014 Conference Experience Reports, p. 11
7. Bang, J.: Samarbejde - kooperation eller kollaboration? Tidsskrift for Universiteternes Efter- og Videreuddannelse (UNEV) **3**(5),(2005). https://doi.org/10.7146/unev.v3i5.4953
8. Tutty, J.I., Klein, J.D.: Computer-mediated instruction: a comparison of online and face-to-face collaboration. Educ. Technol. Res. Develop. **56**(2), 101–124 (2008). https://doi.org/10.1007/s11423-007-9050-9
9. Lind, R.: Pair programmings indflydelse på vurdering af self-efficacy inden for programmering blandt semitekniske fagprofiler. https://www.eaviden.dk/. 30 juni 2022

10. Skov, T.H.K.: Personal Extreme Programming- agil metode for single udvikler, EAViden, 28 Nov 2018
11. Zhong, B., Wang, Q., Chen, J.: The impact of social factors on pair programming in a primary school. Comput. Hum. Behav. **64**, 423–431 (2016). https://doi.org/10.1016/j.chb.2016.07.017
12. Demir, Ö., Seferoglu, S.S.: A comparison of solo and pair programming in terms of flow experience, coding quality, and coding achievement. J. Educ. Comput. Res. **58**(8), 1448–1466 (2020). https://doi.org/10.1177/0735633120949788
13. Likert, R.: A technique for the measurement of attitudes. Arch. Psychol. 55 (1932)
14. Finstad, K.: Response interpolation and scale sensitivity: evidence against 5-point scales. J. Usabil. Stud. **5**, 104–110 (2010)
15. Dell, N., Vaidyanathan, V., Medhi, I., Cutrell, E., Thies, W.: Yours is better!": participant response bias in HCI. In: CHI 2012: Proceedings of the SIGCHI Conference on Human Factors in Computing Systems, pp. 1321–1330 (2012)
16. Polanyi, M.: Knowing and Being: Essays by Michael Polanyi. University of Chicago Press (1969) (2(5), 99–110 (2016))

Potential Attempt to Treat Attention Deficit/Hyperactivity Disorder (ADHD) Children with Engineering Education Games

Zhiya Tan, Zhen Liu[✉], and Shiqi Gong[✉]

School of Design, South China University of Technology, Guangzhou 510006, People's Republic of China

liuzjames@scut.edu.cn, 201930091063@mail.scut.edu.cn

Abstract. Over the past two decades, interventions for children and adolescents with Attention Deficit/Hyperactivity Disorder (ADHD) have greatly increased, especially gamification interventions, which have become a focus of research. However, gamified intervention therapy is still in the research and development stage, and few ADHD treatment games have been widely promoted. In the context of new engineering education development, games have been shown to have educational potential, primarily to increase learner engagement and motivation. Although ADHD treatment games and engineering education (EE) games are two different research hotspots, they may have the same characteristics to prove that engineering education games can be directly used in intervention therapy for ADHD children. Therefore, the objective of this paper is to explore the correlation between treatment games and engineering education games for ADHD children and to explore the potential of EE games as a direct intervention for children with ADHD. This paper utilizes the bibliometric research method that draws upon the Web of Science database as a source of literature, to perform a keyword co-occurrence analysis using VOSviewer visualization software, determines important research structures, and themes, and qualitatively reviews the literature to reveal deeper insights. Subsequently, this paper employs augmented reality (AR) EE Game for experiments, and electroencephalography (EEG) to explore the potential of EE Game as a gamification intervention for ADHD children.

Keywords: Attention Deficit/Hyperactivity Disorder (ADHD) · Gamification Intervention · Engineering Education · Gamified · Augmented Reality (AR) · Electroencephalography (EEG) · VOSviewer

1 Introduction

Attention Deficit/Hyperactivity Disorder (ADHD) is a behavioral disorder characterized by symptoms of inattention, impulsivity, and/or hyperactivity, affecting various aspects of behavior and performance in academic and home settings [1]. The most recent meta-analysis estimates the prevalence of ADHD in children to be 3.4% (95% CI 2.6–4.5) in the general population [2]. And In the United States, the prevalence of ADHD diagnosis

A. Marcus et al. (Eds.): HCII 2023, LNCS 14033, pp. 166–184, 2023.
https://doi.org/10.1007/978-3-031-35708-4_13

among children aged 2 to 17 years was estimated to be 9.4% in 2016, with 2.4% of children aged 2 to 5 years having received a diagnosis [3]. Along with medication, individuals with ADHD may require specialized interventions to assist in developing personal and behavioral skills for improved social interaction [4]. In the past two decades, the prevalence of ADHD in children has increased [5], and research on treatments is also growing rapidly. Serious games (SGs) have been used as gamified interventions to sustain the attention of individuals with ADHD and enhance their motivation and engagement [4], which indicates that gamified intervention is a promising non-medical treatment alternative for individuals with ADHD.

The widespread adoption of computer-assisted learning (CAL) has seen a significant rise globally in recent years due to its demonstrated effectiveness in enhancing learning outcomes for both adults and children [4]. Although playing games as a vehicle for learning is not a new concept [6], the topic of CAL has recently become a focus of experimental research [7]. SGs can be a new kind of CAL educational game by integrating gaming with learning, which is primarily focused on education rather than entertainment [8]. Several studies have investigated the use of SGs, such as health-related behavior change [9], and psychotherapeutic gaming interventions [10]. The latter designed a game prototype called "ATHYNOS" integrating AR with SGs to create a new approach for enhancing cognitive and behavioral patterns in individuals with ADHD, which has revealed a noteworthy enhancement in managing time, social skills, and concentration [11]. In addition, SGs offer an engaging and accessible online learning environment, keeping children with ADHD motivated to train and develop strategies to manage impairments that affect their daily life [12].

Engineering education (EE) equips the next generation with the knowledge, skills, and mindset required to tackle complex problems, increase productivity, and attain excellence, setting them on the path to becoming successful engineers [13]. Engineering graduates are expected to possess unique abilities, distinct from those in humanities or social sciences [13]. The concept of "Engineering Education 5.0" has been recently proposed by Diaz Lantada et al. who stress that enjoyable learning produces enhanced results, especially when resorting to "learning through play" strategies [14]. Several studies have designed SGs in different disciplines, such as industrial engineering education [15], and software engineering education [16]. In addition, a large number of engineering education games have been developed and put into use. For example Swift Playgrounds (One tool for learning to program, practicing computational thinking through Programming) [17] and Poly Bridge [18] (By building a bridge simulator, the player's creativity as an engineer can be brought into play).

Since SGs have been applied in both ADHD gamification treatment and engineering education games, the relationship between ADHD gamification treatment and engineering education games is unclear. Hence, this paper aims to explore the correlation between treatment games and engineering education games for ADHD children and to investigate intervention games that can be directly used and promoted for ADHD patients.

2 Method

2.1 Bibliometric Method

As shown in Fig. 1, a bibliometric method involving five stages has been adopted to obtain related studies from the Web of Science Core Collection (WoSCC) database and then imports them into VOSviewer for keyword visualization analysis, in which the first group of search keywords is "Attention Deficit/Hyperactivity Disorder (ADHD)" AND "Gamified" from the core collection of WoSCC, the second group of search topic is "Engineering Education (EE)" AND "Gamified", and then keyword co-occurrence has been conducted.

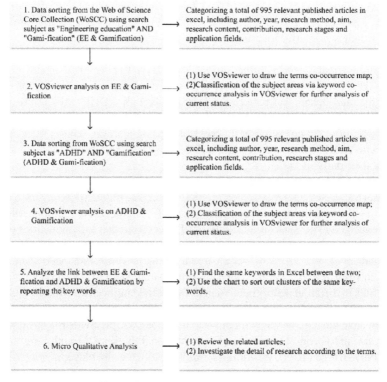

Fig. 1. Flow of the bibliometric analysis.

2.2   Experiment

In this study, two children with Attention Deficit/Hyperactivity Disorder (ADHD) aged 6–12 years were randomly selected, and their brain electrical activity characteristics were analyzed by EPOC X wireless wearable device during experimental tasks [19]. The Interest (VAL), Focus (FOC), and Engagement (ENG) scores in the Equipment Performance Metrics section were used as the final primary analysis data.

The scores of VAL, FOC, and ENG correspond to the level of interest, focus, and engagement of the subjects, respectively [20].

Subjects. A total of two children with ADHD, aged 6–12 years, who were diagnosed according to CIE-10 or DSM-5 criteria by a multidisciplinary team participated in the study. None of the children had intellectual disabilities, and each child's guardian received written informed consent and cooperated with the experiment.

Experimental Arrangement. This study lasted a total of seven days and was divided into three phases: Pretest, EE Game-Therapy Part, and Postest, with a time allocation ratio of 1:5:1, as shown in Fig. 2.

Fig. 2. Experimental steps.

3   Results

3.1   "Engineering Education (EE)" and "Gamified"

In terms of searching a topic on "Engineering education" and "Gamified" screening and relevant keyword screening, a total of 996 articles meet the criteria, which have been imported into the VOSviewer (version 1.6.18) software.to extract important terms and construct a visual network of keyword co-occurrence by setting the minimum number of occurrences of keywords to 10 and manually screening for useless keywords, 145 keywords have met the threshold to perform network visualization.

In network visualization, different color regions represent different clusters. As shown in Fig. 3, the 145 keywords were divided into six color-coded clusters by VOSviewer. Cluster 1 is related to EE game design for disciplines such as mathematics, civil engineering, and computer science. Cluster 2 is associated with technologies, such as computers, video games, robots, virtual reality (VR), and augmented reality (AR).

Cluster 3 is focused on the devices, with its mobile device, smartphone, and digital medium. Cluster 4 mainly includes game design and software, as well as game elements, gamification strategy, digital games, and teaching software engineering. Cluster 5 is aimed at the classroom, for its exam, efficacy, and student perception. Cluster 6 is about a simulation game.

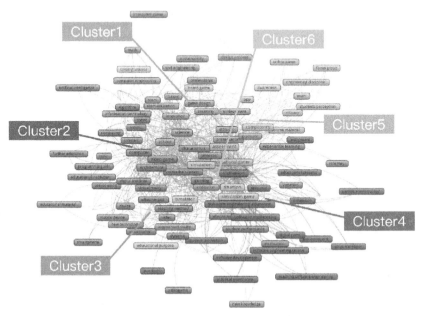

Fig. 3. Keyword network visualization of "Engineering education (EE)" & "Gamified" via VOSviewer.

3.2 "Attention Deficit/Hyperactivity Disorder (ADHD)" and "Gamified"

In terms of searching a topic on "ADHD" and "Gamified" screening and relevant keyword screening, a total of 506 articles meet the criteria. By setting the minimum number of occurrences of keywords to 3 and manually screening for useless keywords, 135 keywords have met the threshold, as shown in Fig. 4.

All terms are divided into five different types of clusters. Cluster 1 studies related to electroencephalography (EEG), including EEG tests and Brain Computer Interface (BCI) games in ADHD patients. Cluster 2 is mainly related to new technologies in ADHD gamification, such as VR, AR, and digital games. Cluster 3 focuses on patient behavior. Cluster 4 is related to the use of digital media and mobile devices. Cluster 5 is about effect testing.

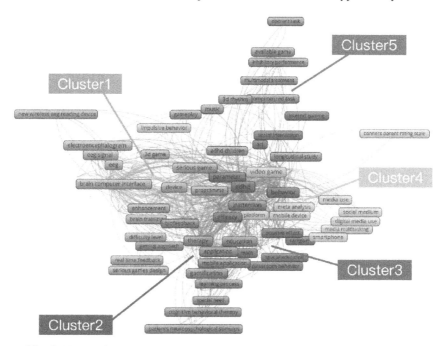

Fig. 4. Keyword network visualization of "ADHD" & "Gamified" via VOSviewer.

3.3 "Attention Deficit/Hyperactivity Disorder (ADHD) Gamified" and "Engineering Education (EE) Gamified"

Excel has been used to sort out the keywords generated by VOSviewer based on the search topic "EE" & "Gamified" and "ADHD" & "Gamified", and find the 27 repeated keywords between the two, as shown in Fig. 5, in which the results are quite clear in the form of a Sankey diagram.

As shown in Fig. 5, the left side shows the distribution of 27 keywords in six clusters of "EE & Gamified" and their occurrence times, while the right side shows the distribution of 27 keywords in five clusters of "ADHD & Gamified" and their occurrence times. The same keywords are connected by lines in order to show the relationship between the two fields by setting clusters with three or more of the same keywords to be strongly associated, of which four pairs of clusters are strongly associated, such as EE game design examples and technology in ADHD gamification; technology in EE gamification and technology in ADHD gamification; device in EE gamification and The use of digital media and devices in ADHD gamification; and classroom in EE game and ADHD patient behavior. As shown in Fig. 6, indicating that "EE & Gamified" and "ADHD & Gamified" are:

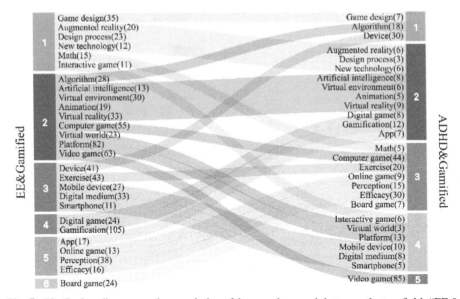

Fig. 5. The Sankey diagram on the correlation of the same keywords between the two fields "EE & Gamified" and "ADHD & Gamified".

EE&Gamified

1 EE game design examples	2 Technology	3 Device	5 Classroom
Augmented reality Design process New technology	Artificial intelligence Virtual environment Animation Virtual reality	Mobile device Digital medium Smartphone	Online game Perception Efficacy
2 Technology	2 Technology	4 The use of digital media and devices	3 ADHD patient behavior

ADHD&Gamified

Fig. 6. Associated clusters and the keywords between "EE & Gamified" and "ADHD & Gamified".

Figure 6 shows the similarities between the two:

- Both try to use new technology in games;
- Both conduct research based on mobile devices and digital media;
- Both are designed for children's perceptions; and
- Both have been proven to be useful in their respective fields.

As well as the difference between the two:

- EE game cases have been found in many subject areas, while ADHD gamification treatment cases are not as many as in the EE field; and
- EE games are mostly designed for classroom behaviors, while ADHD treatment games are designed for the needs of ADHD patients.

3.4   Micro Qualitative Analysis

In order to further investigate whether there is a certain relationship between "Engineering Education (EE) & Gamified" and "Attention Deficit/Hyperactivity Disorder (ADHD) & Gamified", this paper takes "Augmented reality (AR)" in the first pair of clustering, "Artificial intelligence (AI)" in the second pair of clustering, "Mobile device" and "Smartphone" in the third pair of clustering, and "Efficacy" in the fourth pair of clustering (Fig. 5) as an example for analysis.

"Augmented Reality (AR)"

"Augmented Reality" in "EE Game Design Example" (EE & Gamified). In the field of EE, the use of AR simplifies the comprehension of complex physical concepts by breaking them down into manageable stages, resulting in a deeper and more diverse understanding [21]. There have been examples of EE games designed for various disciplines, and the feasibility and effectiveness of the games including:

- *Skill Training for Engineers.* AR virtual lab can construct complex system research models integrating role-playing games, exercise games, situational games, and blitz play, which guides engineers from the layout planning phase to the prototyping of the final product [2].Skill Training for Engineers.
- *Interaction in Class.* In class, children prefer the idea of hands-on training and learning through experience [22]. For example, the smart classroom can be expanded using the Internet of Things (IoT), mobile, and internet technologies, as well as AR, to offer game-based learning experiences for students through interactive engagements [23]. In addition, AR 3D geometry learning software has been developed based on 2D images from textbooks, which indicates that the use of AR in this learning setting is effective in terms of student learning gain [24]. Additionally, in the field of biology, a gamified and story-based app has been created as a means of leveraging technology to engage students and enhance their participation in the course, thus improving the teaching and learning process [25]. There are studies of EE games in various disciplines, such as mathematics, civil engineering, computer science, climatology, and architecture [26–30].
- *Outside of the Classroom. EE games are not only used in the classroom but also outside the classroom, where engineering knowledge can be transmitted using EE games.* An AR card game focused on renewable energy has been developed for children to learn about these topics in a fun and interactive way. The game's design encourages users, particularly children, to gain a sense of accomplishment and enjoyment from understanding renewable energy after school [31].

"Augmented Reality" in "Technology" (Attention Deficit/Hyperactivity Disorder (ADHD) & Gamified). Many children with ADHD experience low engagement during traditional therapy [32]. Consequently, there is a requirement for incorporating more interactive elements with visual components in computer-based therapy programs to improve engagement and overall therapy experience for children with ADHD [10]. Gamification therapy is a type of Cognitive Behavioral Therapy (CBT) that uses various psychosocial interventions to promote mental health improvement in patients. This therapy involves patients participating in multiple sessions with specialized therapists [33].

In the treatment of ADHD, therapy sessions can be structured to gradually increase in difficulty, helping patients expand their cognitive abilities and overcome behavioral limitations [34]. The use of advanced and immersive technologies, such as AR and VR, in therapy, underscores the significance of utilizing cutting-edge and engaging technologies in therapy [34]. A study examining the usefulness of using VR for rehabilitation suggests that immersive VR with cognitive training is effective for attention enhancement [35].

There are some innovative AR game designs for ADHD treatment. The BRAVO project strives to create an immersive therapeutic gaming environment, utilizing cutting-edge Information and Communications Technology (ICT) systems, to mend the relationship between young patients and therapy [36]. By utilizing wearable technology and augmented reality devices, new customized therapy methods can be implemented that adapt dynamically to the patient's evolution and assist therapists in managing the rehabilitation program [36]. Interestingly, the creators of Gremlins in My Mirror, another game, argue for the need to design an inclusive learning environment that not only takes into account the needs of the ADHD community but also benefits all students [37].

Relationship. As discussed in the above sections, one of the reasons for using AR technology in EE games is that the new technology can arouse children's interest and increase learning motivation through integration with the form of games. In the treatment of ADHD, the addition of AR technology can also make patients cooperate. AR has the effect of increasing participant motivation in both. ADHD therapy should concentrate on three essential components: acquiring self-discipline, establishing and maintaining relationships with others, and fostering a positive sense of self-worth [38]. This does not contradict the content of EE games, as such the EE games can be directly used in the treatment of ADHD.

"Artificial Intelligence (AI)".
"Artificial Intelligence" in "Technology" (Engineering Education (EE) & Gamified).
The area of artificial and computational intelligence in gaming has experienced significant growth and numerous successful outcomes since it emerged as a distinct research field approximately a decade ago [39]. Instructing Artificial Intelligence (AI) or multi-agent systems is a demanding task due to the intricacies of the algorithms that are effective in highly dynamic and complex environments [40]. An educational software tool that facilitates the teaching of AI techniques has been created based on the "Bubble Breaker" puzzle game, which is a captivating game featuring an M x M matrix of colored bubbles [41]. Likewise, a serious game can be utilized to instruct and showcase the optimization of production through the use of AI techniques [42].

In addition to direct AI education, some studies integrate AI into other disciplines. Aspects of Artificial Intelligence have been incorporated into introductory computing courses to deepen the understanding of computational thinking, enabling the development of skills for collaborative problem-solving, including abstract thinking, logical reasoning, critical analysis, and analytical thinking [43]. AI is also playing a role in microelectronics, robotics, and other fields [44, 45]. At the same time, AI has a place in the digital transformation of engineering education [46].

"Artificial Intelligence" in "Technology" (Attention Deficit/Hyperactivity Disorder (ADHD) & Gamified). Artificial Intelligence plays a role in numerous processes in contemporary life, such as e-health and psychological treatments. AI has been combined with a robotic assistant to assist children in correcting negative behaviors stemming from disorders. AI algorithms process information and make real-time decisions to help children maintain their focus while completing homework [47]. Similarly, A patient-centered interaction project of Pepper humanoid robotic has been developed, which can capture children's emotions in real time and use AI to process data [48]. In addition, a wearable device "Empowered Brain" has been used, which is an augmented reality (AR) and AI-based social-emotional communication to exercise patient's attention [49]. The effective integration of AI and augmented reality (AR) has strengthened the collaboration between technology services and mental health professionals, and timely feedback from both patients/clients and physicians has helped to improve the application of digital gaming in mental health [50].

Relationship. Although EE and ADHD both use AI, their methods and effects are different. AI is often presented as educational content in EE games, while in ADHD treatment, it is often used as a data processing tool to analyze the patient's condition. However, in EE gamification and ADHD gamification treatment, AI is integrated with robots. In ADHD, AI is more associated with AR, VR, and wearable devices.

"Mobile device" and "Smartphone".

"Mobile Device" and "Smartphone" in "Device" (Engineering Education (EE) & Gamified). In a world where students are increasingly and digitally connected to powerful devices, especially mobile, engineering education needs to evolve to create new modes of engagement and educational approaches [51, 52], which are broadly fallen into two categories:

- *Specific Applications. They are committed to making use of the convenience of mobile devices for EE games in achieving better educational effects.* They include areas such as mechanical engineering, spatial ability, diet health, and network information security [53–56].
- *Mechanism Exploration.* They are committed to exploring how SGs can be used to increase student engagement and motivation. Mapping teaching elements to game elements while maintaining a balance between fun and game can improve player engagement [51]. Additionally, a web service for social and gamified education learning, Kathe Kahoot Platform, is beneficial to improve the participation and enthusiasm of students in class [57].

"Mobile Device" and "Smartphone" in "The Use of Digital Media and Devices" (ADHD & Gamified). With the development of the Internet and mobile technology, non-invasive treatment for children with ADHD has shown a great help [58]. Behavioral intervention games and serious games based on mobile devices facilitate the treatment of

ADHD [59]. Some studies are trying to integrate mobile devices with personal computers, which could be appealing to children with ADHD, allowing children to be immersed in games [60].

Relationship. Several health mobile apps adapted from other mobile apps have been developed by added screening, monitoring, and support during the treatment of children with ADHD [59], which indicates that developing and validating EE games may require only a small amount of modification to generate significant utilization value in gamification treatment programs for children with ADHD.

"Efficacy"

"Efficacy" in "Classroom" (Engineering Education (EE) & Gamified). There is a significant demand for empirical studies on the understanding of the impacts and efficacy of gamification [61]. In a design project, students' engagement with learning activities can be evaluated through a survey utilizing an adapted version of the Longitudinal Assessment of Engineering Self-Efficacy (LAESE) instrument and a second technology self-efficacy tool [62]. And the learning performance of students in the gamified condition has significantly improved [63].

"Efficacy" in "ADHD Patient Behavior" (ADHD & Gamified). Since ADHD efficacy evaluation is associated with the medical field, the methods used are more rigorous and professional. Double-blind experiments are common [64], and are accepted by medicine as an objective scientific methodology [65]. Most studies on ADHD efficacy set the control group, and use scales such as the ADHD Rating Scale, the Young Internet Addiction Scale, the Beck Depression Inventory, the Clinical Global Impression-Severity Scale, and the Behavioral Inhibition and Activation Scales to measure the effectiveness of the intervention [66]–[69].

Relationship. The efficacy experiments of EE games are not as complex and rigorous as those of ADHD gamification, nor have formed a system. However, most of the experiments are evaluated by scales and interviews. The ADHD experiment is more convincing in exploring effectiveness.

4   Ongoing Experiment

To explore the effect of Engineering Education (EE) Games in the treatment of Attention Deficit/Hyperactivity Disorder (ADHD) by gamification intervention, this study designed a set of experiments. After several days of experience in advance, Arloon Plants was selected as an experimental game because it was highly praised by both parents and children and stood out from many EE Games. EEG has been used as the main technical means to test the experimental effect, which can systematically examine human cerebral cortex activity. With the development of EEG information processing and visualization, EEG can be used to rapidly and objectively display scalp electrical signals, resulting in more objective and reliable results than questionnaires [70].

EEG has been widely adopted as a more objective diagnostic tool for ADHD in children, with Theta/Beta Power Ratio (TBR) being the most significant measurement for distinguishing between normal and ADHD children [71]. The TBR has demonstrated a sensitivity of 86% and a specificity of 98% in classifying ADHD status [71].

Although EEG technology has been widely applied in the field of ADHD diagnosis, traditional EEG equipment is still very expensive and complicated for non-professionals to use. In most cases, it is necessary to carry out tedious calculations on the data in Matlab to obtain useful information from EEG [72–76]. To reduce the cost and complexity of the experiment, EPOC X head-mounted device has been used in this experiment to provide an economical and convenient alternative with good signal quality for unlimited EEG signal acquisition. EPOC X is a new generation of products released by EMOTIV in recent years, which leads to its rare appearance in the EEG field [19]. However, many studies have analyzed the performance of the EEG information acquisition system of its previous generation product EPOC+ [77, 78], which show that EPOC+ devices have an overall lower signal-to-noise ratio (SNR) and are more robust than medical-grade systems, but with difficulties in correcting the placement of electrodes [79]. Since the previous generation of EPOC+ has been widely recognized in the EEG field, this also ensures the credibility of the EPOC X device.

4.1 Result

After five days of EE game therapy, as shown in the left side of Fig. 7, the Interest (VAL), Focus (FOC), and Engagement (ENG) in the reading process of the two children have been improved to varying degrees, and the fluctuation degree has also been significantly reduced, which indicates that EE game-therapy can indeed improve the focus, interest, and engagement of ADHD children with stable emotional traits.

By recording the VAL, FOC, and ENG data of 10 games over five days, as shown on the right side of Fig. 7, the following phenomena have been suggested:

- The results of average values of VAL, FOC, and ENG indicate that children are more interested, focused, and engaged in the process of EE-game than reading.
- The results of VAL and FOC show a stable state in the experiment for five consecutive days, whilst ENG performs a significant decline in the following two days, which means that children may be bored with EE Game.
- From the perspective of data fluctuation, the experimental results of the last two days were significantly larger than those of the first three days, indicating to some extent that the children had some mental fluctuation to this EE Game after playing it for a long time.

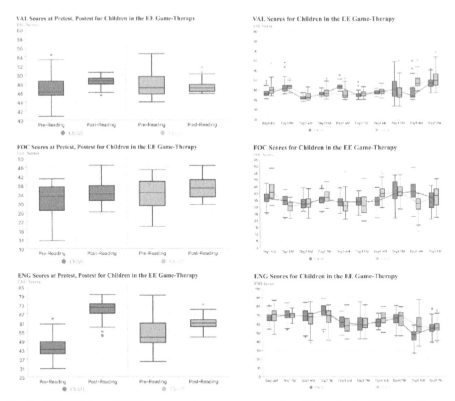

Fig. 7. VAL, FOC, and ENG scores at the pretest, postest for children in the EE Game-Therapy, and children in the EE Game-Therapy.

5 Discussion and Conclusion

In this paper, bibliometrics has been used to explore the relationship between the gamification of Engineering Education (EE) and Attention Deficit/Hyperactivity Disorder (ADHD) gamification treatment. The main contribution and novelty of this paper are as follows:

- It is the first to combine EE Game with Gamified intervention treatment for ADHD children in a cross-field. It is also found that the field "EE" & "Gamified" can be divided into six categories and the field "ADHD" & "Gamified" have five categories. In these categories, four pairs of strongly associated clusters and the keywords that connect them have been identified by comparison of the Sankey diagram.
- Through micro-qualitative analysis, several possible links between EE games and ADHD gamification intervention have been revealed, which provided theoretical feasibility for subsequent implementation.
- EEG experiments have been conducted to verify the conjecture that some existing EE games can be directly used in ADHD gamification treatment.

- The experiments in this paper proved the positive effect of EE Games on gamification intervention for ADHD children to a certain extent.

However, there are still many limitations in this study:

- Attempts to find a relationship between two domains based mainly on the relevance of keywords may lead to one-sided results.
- Although they have similarities, they are designed for different purposes: one is for children's education, and the other is for patients' treatment. Therefore, directly using EE games as therapeutic games will have certain treatment limitations, and EE games need to be redesigned according to the needs of both.
- The existing cognitive behavioral therapy (CBT) is a customized treatment. If EE games are used directly, the treatment process will not be personalized enough. Therefore, EE games may be used as a family daily treatment in the treatment scene of ADHD
- The papers analyzed using VOSviewer are relatively limited and all sources are from the Web of Science.
- In the experimental part, due to the small number of overall samples and short experimental time, it is not enough to draw quantitative conclusions. In addition, only one game has been tested, making it difficult to verify the universality of the EE Game's efficacy.

However, there is an unexpected finding in this study. Three days after the game test, the VAL, FOC, and ENG of the two ADHD children all fluctuated to a certain extent, which means that although the EE Game participated in the test had a certain effect on the treatment of ADHD children, which has not been fully adapting to the quality of ADHD children. There is still room for improvement.

Based on the current reality, if the ready-made EE Game can be put into the treatment of ADHD children, it will greatly save the cost of doctors and parents, although it is not perfect. This potential feasibility also means that exploring AHDH gamification therapy may not need to develop a treatment game from scratch, but to improve and redesign based on the existing EE Game instead, which will greatly reduce research time and cost. Subsequent experiments will increase the number of samples, experimental time, and types of games, and conduct statistical analysis on the data to ensure the validity of the conclusion and reduce the error caused by irrelevant variables. In addition, games with good efficacy will be redesigned and more suitable for the characteristics of ADHD children.

Acknowledgements. This research was funded by "2022 Constructing Project of Teaching Quality and Teaching Reform Project for Undergraduate Universities in Guangdong Province" Higher Education Teaching Reform Project (project No. 386), 'Innovation and practice of teaching methods for information and interaction design in the context of new liberal arts' (project grant number x2sj-C9233001).

References

1. Faraone, S.V., Sergeant, J., Gillberg, C., Biederman, J.: The worldwide prevalence of ADHD: is it an American condition? World Psych. **2**, 104–113 (2003)

2. Polanczyk, G.V., Salum, G.A., Sugaya, L.S., Caye, A., Rohde, L.A.: Annual research review: a meta-analysis of the worldwide prevalence of mental disorders in children and adolescents. J. Child Psychol. Psych. **56**, 345–365 (2015). https://doi.org/10.1111/jcpp.12381

3. Danielson, M.L., Bitsko, R.H., Ghandour, R.M., Holbrook, J.R., Kogan, M.D., Blumberg, S.J.: Prevalence of parent-reported ADHD diagnosis and associated treatment among U.S. Children and Adolescents, 2016. J. Clin. Child Adolescent Psycho. **47**, 199–212 (2018). https://doi.org/10.1080/15374416.2017.1417860

4. Alabdulakareem, E., Jamjoom, M.: Computer-assisted learning for improving ADHD individuals' executive functions through gamified interventions: a review. Entertain. Comput. **33**, 100341 (2020). https://doi.org/10.1016/j.entcom.2020.100341

5. News, A.B.C.: ADHD rates in kids have increased over the past 20 years, a new study says. https://abcnews.go.com/Health/adhd-rates-kids-increased-past-20-years-study/story?id=57526368. Accessed 22 July 2022

6. Annetta, L.A., Minogue, J., Holmes, S.Y., Cheng, M.-T.: Investigating the impact of video games on high school students' engagement and learning about genetics. Comput. Educ. **53**, 74–85 (2009). https://doi.org/10.1016/j.compedu.2008.12.020

7. Girard, C., Ecalle, J., Magnan, A.: Serious games as new educational tools: how effective are they? A meta-analysis of recent studies. J. Comput. Assist. Learn. **29**, 207–219 (2013). https://doi.org/10.1111/j.1365-2729.2012.00489.x

8. Miller, L.M., Chang, C.-I., Wang, S., Beier, M.E., Klisch, Y.: Learning and motivational impacts of a multimedia science game. Comput. Educ. **57**, 1425–1433 (2011). https://doi.org/10.1016/j.compedu.2011.01.016

9. Baranowski, T., Buday, R., Thompson, D.I., Baranowski, J.: Playing for real: video games and stories for health-related behavior change. Am. J. Prev. Med. **34**, 74–82.e10 (2008). https://doi.org/10.1016/j.amepre.2007.09.027

10. Avila-Pesantez, D., Rivera, L.A., Vaca-Cardenas, L., Aguayo, S., Zuñiga, L.: Towards the improvement of ADHD children through augmented reality serious games: preliminary results. In: 2018 IEEE Global Engineering Education Conference (EDUCON), pp. 843–848 (2018). https://doi.org/10.1109/EDUCON.2018.8363318

11. D Avila-Pesantez, M Vaca-Cardenas, L M Avila, L Vaca-Cardenas: conceptual model for serious games design: case study of children with attention deficit hyperactivity disorder. KEG. **3** (2018). https://doi.org/10.18502/keg.v3i9.3646

12. Bul, K.C., et al.: Behavioral outcome effects of serious gaming as an adjunct to treatment for children with attention-deficit/hyperactivity disorder: a randomized controlled trial. J. Med. Internet Res. **18**, e5173 (2016). https://doi.org/10.2196/jmir.5173

13. Zhuang, T., Xu, X.: 'New engineering education' in chinese higher education: prospects and challenges. Tuning J. High. Educ. **6**, 69–109 (2018). https://doi.org/10.18543/tjhe-6(1)-2018pp69-109

14. Diaz Lantada, A.: Engineering education 5.0: continuously evolving engineering education. Int. J. Eng. Educ. **36**, 1814–1832 (2020)

15. Despeisse, M.: Games and simulations in industrial engineering education: a review of the cognitive and affective learning outcomes. In: 2018 Winter Simulation Conference (WSC), pp. 4046–4057 (2018). https://doi.org/10.1109/WSC.2018.8632285

16. Mccallum, S., Mishra, D., Nowostawski, M.: Enhancing software engineering education with game design and development. Int. J. Eng. Educ. **34**, 471–481 (2018)

17. Cheng, G.-M., Chen, C.-P.: Processing analysis of swift playgrounds in a children's computational thinking course to learn programming. Computers **10**, 68 (2021). https://doi.org/10.3390/computers10050068

18. Poly Bridge 2 | Home. https://www.polybridge2.com/. Accessed 4 Aug 2022

19. EMOTIV | Brain Data Measuring Hardware and Software Solutions. https://www.emotiv.com/. Accessed 6 Aug 2022

20. Performance Metrics. https://emotiv.gitbook.io/emotivpro-v3/data-streams/performance-met rics. Accessed 31 July 2022
21. Almenara, J., Osuna, J.: Los escenarios tecnológicos en Realidad Aumentada (RA): posibil-idades educativas en estudios universitarios. Aula Abierta. **47**, 327–336 (2018). https://doi.org/10.17811/rifie.47.3.2018.327-336
22. Karvinen, K., Karvinen, T.: IoT Rapid Prototyping Laboratory Setup. Int. J. Eng. Educ. **34**, 263–272 (2018)
23. Petrovic, L., Stojanovic, D., Mitrovic, S., Barac, D., Bogdanovic, Z.: Designing an extended smart classroom: an approach to game-based learning for IoT. Comput. Appl. Eng. Educ. **30**, 117–132 (2022). https://doi.org/10.1002/cae.22446
24. Cazzolla, A., Lanzilotti, R., Roselli, T., Rossano, V.: Augmented reality to support education in Industry 4.0. In: 2019 18th International Conference on Information Technology Based Higher Education and Training (2019). IEEE, New York (2019)
25. Ibarra-Herrera, C.C., Carrizosa, A., Yunes-Rojas, J.A., Mata-Gómez, M.A.: Design of an app based on gamification and storytelling as a tool for biology courses. Int. J. Interact. Design Manufac. **13**(4), 1271–1282 (2019). https://doi.org/10.1007/s12008-019-00600-8
26. Seebauer, S., Berger, M., Kettl, K.-H., Moser, M.: Green Gang vs. Captain Carbon Integration of automated data collection and ecological footprint feedback in a smartphone-based social game for carbon saving. In: 2013 5th International Conference on Games and Virtual Worlds for Serious Applications (vs-Games). IEEE, New York (2013)
27. Seebauer, S.: Measuring climate change knowledge in a social media game with a purpose. In: 2013 5th International Conference on Games and Virtual Worlds for Serious Applications (vs-Games). IEEE, New York (2013)
28. Ribeiro, C., Antunes, T., Monteiro, M., Pereira, J.: Serious games in formal medical education: an experimental study. In: 2013 5th International Conference on Games and Virtual Worlds for Serious Applications (vs-Games). IEEE, New York (2013)
29. Burgos, V., Guevara, C., Espinosa, L.: Electric circuit simulator applying augmented reality and gamification. In: Russo, D., Ahram, T., Karwowski, W., Di Bucchianico, G., Taiar, R. (eds.) IHSI 2021. AISC, vol. 1322, pp. 657–662. Springer, Cham (2021). https://doi.org/10.1007/978-3-030-68017-6_97
30. Alanne, K.: An overview of game-based learning in building services engineering education. Eur. J. Eng. Educ. **41**, 204–219 (2016). https://doi.org/10.1080/03043797.2015.1056097
31. Salahuddin, M., Kristanda, M.B.: Development of gameplay design for renewable energy learning based on augmented reality. In: 2019 IEEE R10 Humanitarian Technology Conference (R10-HTC)(47129), pp. 244–247 (2019). https://doi.org/10.1109/R10-HTC47129.2019.9042487
32. Bussing, R., Koro-Ljungberg, M., Noguchi, K., Mason, D., Mayerson, G., Garvan, C.W.: Willingness to use ADHD treatments: a mixed methods study of perceptions by adolescents, parents, health professionals, and teachers. Soc. Sci. Med. **74**, 92–100 (2012). https://doi.org/10.1016/j.socscimed.2011.10.009
33. Antshel, K.M., Olszewski, A.K.: Cognitive behavioral therapy for adolescents with ADHD. Child Adolesc. Psychiatr. Clin. N. Am. **23**, 825–842 (2014). https://doi.org/10.1016/j.chc.2014.05.001
34. Alqithami, S.: Modeling an AR serious game to increase attention of ADHD patients. In: Chan, W.K., et al. (eds.) 2020 IEEE 44th Annual Computers, Software, and Applications Conference (compact 2020), pp. 1379–1384. IEEE, New York (2020). https://doi.org/10.1109/COMPSAC48688.2020.00-63
35. Cho, B.-H., et al.: The effect of virtual reality cognitive training for attention enhancement. Cyberpsychol. Behav. **5**, 129–137 (2002). https://doi.org/10.1089/109493102753770516

36. Barba, M.C., et al.: BRAVO: a gaming environment for the treatment of ADHD. In: De Paolis, L.T., Bourdot, P. (eds.) AVR 2019. LNCS, vol. 11613, pp. 394–407. Springer, Cham (2019). https://doi.org/10.1007/978-3-030-25965-5_30

37. Tobar-Munoz, H., Baldiris, S., Fabregat, R.: Gremlins in my mirror: an inclusive AR-enriched videogame for logical math skills learning. In: 2014 14th IEEE International Conference on Advanced Learning Technologies (ICT), pp. 576–578. IEEE, New York (2014). https://doi.org/10.1109/ICALT.2014.168

38. Shapiro, L.: ADHD: il mio libro di esercizi: Attività per sviluppare la fiducia in se stessi, le abilità sociali e l'autocontrollo. Edizioni Centro Studi Erickson (2015)

39. Yannakakis, G.N., Togelius, J.: A panorama of artificial and computational intelligence in games. IEEE Trans. Comput. Intell. AI Games 7, 317–335 (2015). https://doi.org/10.1109/TCIAIG.2014.2339221

40. Timm, I.J., Bogon, T., Lattner, A.D., Schumann, R.: Teaching distributed artificial intelligence with RoboRally. In: Bergmann, R., Lindemann, G., Kirn, S., Pěchouček, M. (eds.) MATES 2008. LNCS (LNAI), vol. 5244, pp. 171–182. Springer, Heidelberg (2008). https://doi.org/10.1007/978-3-540-87805-6_16

41. Salcedo-Sanz, S., Jiménez-Fernández, S., Matías-Román, J.M., Portilla-Figueras, J.A.: An educational software tool to teach hyper-heuristics to engineering students based on the bubble breaker puzzle. Comput. Appl. Eng. Educ. 23, 277–285 (2015). https://doi.org/10.1002/cae.21597

42. Syberfeldt, A., Syberfeldt, S.: A serious game for understanding artificial intelligence in production optimization. In: Proceedings of the 2010 IEEE Conference on Computational Intelligence and Games, pp. 443–449 (2010). https://doi.org/10.1109/ITW.2010.5593321

43. Silapachote, P., Srisuphab, A.: Teaching and learning computational thinking through solving problems in Artificial Intelligence: on designing introductory engineering and computing courses. In: 2016 IEEE International Conference on Teaching, Assessment, and Learning for Engineering (TALE), pp. 50–54 (2016). https://doi.org/10.1109/TALE.2016.7851769

44. Mielke, M., Grünewald, A., Brück, R.: Motivating students through problem-based learning and chip-fabrication in a microelectronics design laboratory. In: 2016 IEEE Global Engineering Education Conference (EDUCON), pp. 163–170 (2016). https://doi.org/10.1109/EDUCON.2016.7474548

45. de Lemos, M.A., Liberado, E.V.: Industrial robotics applied to education. In: Proceedings of 2011 International Conference on Computer Science and Network Technology, pp. 2843–2846 (2011). https://doi.org/10.1109/ICCSNT.2011.6182556

46. Aleksandrov, A.A., Tsvetkov, Y.B., Zhileykin, M.M.: Engineering education: key features of the digital transformation. ITM Web Conf. 35, 01001 (2020). https://doi.org/10.1051/itmconf/20203501001

47. Berrezueta-Guzman, J., Pau, I., Martín-Ruiz, M.-L., Máximo-Bocanegra, N.: Assessment of a robotic assistant for supporting homework activities of children with ADHD. IEEE Access 9, 93450–93465 (2021). https://doi.org/10.1109/ACCESS.2021.3093233

48. Amato, F., Di Gregorio, M., Monaco, C., Sebillo, M., Tortora, G., Vitiello, G.: Socially assistive robotics combined with artificial intelligence for ADHD. In: 2021 IEEE 18th Annual Consumer Communications & Networking Conference (CCNC), pp. 1–6 (2021). https://doi.org/10.1109/CCNC49032.2021.9369633

49. Keshav, N.U., Vogt-Lowell, K., Vahabzadeh, A., Sahin, N.T.: Digital attention-related augmented-reality game: significant correlation between student game performance and validated clinical measures of attention-deficit/hyperactivity disorder (ADHD). Children 6, 72 (2019). https://doi.org/10.3390/children6060072

50. Vajawat, B., Varshney, P., Banerjee, D.: Digital gaming interventions in psychiatry: evidence, applications, and challenges. Psychiatry Res. 295, 113585 (2021). https://doi.org/10.1016/j.psychres.2020.113585

51. Callaghan, M., Savin-Baden, M., McShane, N., Eguíluz, A.G.: mapping learning and game mechanics for serious games analysis in engineering education. IEEE Trans. Emerg. Top. Comput. **5**, 77–83 (2017). https://doi.org/10.1109/TETC.2015.2504241

52. Johri, A., Teo, H.J., Lo, J., Dufour, M., Schram, A.: Millennial engineers: digital media and information ecology of engineering students. Comput. Hum. Behav. **33**, 286–301 (2014). https://doi.org/10.1016/j.chb.2013.01.048

53. Wilke, A., Magenheim, J.: Requirements analysis for the design of workplace-integrated learning scenarios with mobile devices: Mapping the territory for learning in industry 4.0. In: 2017 IEEE Global Engineering Education Conference (EDUCON), pp. 476–485 (2017). https://doi.org/10.1109/EDUCON.2017.7942890

54. Martin-Dorta, N., Sanchez-Berriel, I., Bravo, M., Hernandez, J., Saorin, J.L., Contero, M.: Virtual blocks: a serious game for spatial ability improvement on mobile devices. Multimedia Tools Appl. **73**(3), 1575–1595 (2013). https://doi.org/10.1007/s11042-013-1652-0

55. Gonçalves, F., Carvalho, V., Matos, D., Soares, F.: Development of a serious game to fight childhood obesity: "Barty." In: 2020 IEEE Global Engineering Education Conference (EDUCON), pp. 1641–1646 (2020). https://doi.org/10.1109/EDUCON45650.2020.9125408

56. Salazar, M., Gaviria, J., Laorden, C., Bringas, P.G.: Enhancing cybersecurity learning through an augmented reality-based serious game. In: 2013 IEEE Global Engineering Education Conference (EDUCON), pp. 602–607 (2013). https://doi.org/10.1109/EduCon.2013.6530167

57. Criollo-C, S., Luján-Mora, S.: Encouraging student motivation through gamification in engineering education. In: Auer, M.E., Tsiatsos, T. (eds.) IMCL 2018. AISC, vol. 909, pp. 204–211. Springer, Cham (2019). https://doi.org/10.1007/978-3-030-11434-3_24

58. Guía, E. de la, Lozano, M., Penichet, V.: Stimulating Capabilities: A Proposal for Learning and Stimulation in Children with ADHD. https://www.semanticscholar.org/paper/Stimulating-Capabilities%3A-A-Proposal-for-Learning-Gu%C3%ADa-Lozano/cb5cdb7561815db1ddd65d0425053b9e46d320a6. Accessed 8 Feb 2023

59. Rodriguez-Perez, N., Caballero-Gil, P., Rivero-Garcia, A., Toledo-Castro, J.: A secure mHealth application for attention deficit and hyperactivity disorder. Expert Syst. **37**, e12431 (2020). https://doi.org/10.1111/exsy.12431

60. Alves, R.M.B., Silva, M., Schmitz, E., Alencar, A.: Mobile devices and systems in ADHD treatment. In: WEBSITE (2020). https://doi.org/10.5220/0010148201410146

61. Barbosa Monteiro, R.H., de Almeida Souza, M.R., Bezerra Oliveira, S.R., dos Santos Portela, C., de Cristo Lobato, C.E.: The diversity of gamification evaluation in the software engineering education and industry: trends, comparisons and gaps. In: 2021 IEEE/ACM 43rd International Conference on Software Engineering: Software Engineering Education and Training (ICSE-SEET), pp. 154–164 (2021). https://doi.org/10.1109/ICSE-SEET52601.2021.00025

62. Ranalli, J., Ritzko, J.: Assessing the impact of video game-based design projects in a first-year engineering design course. In: 2013 IEEE Frontiers in Education Conference (FIE), pp. 530–534 (2013). https://doi.org/10.1109/FIE.2013.6684880

63. Ortiz-Rojas, M., Chiluiza, K., Valcke, M.: Gamification through leaderboards: an empirical study in engineering education. Comput. Appl. Eng. Educ. **27**, 777–788 (2019). https://doi.org/10.1002/cae.12116

64. Bikic, A., Christensen, T.Ø., Leckman, J.F., Bilenberg, N., Dalsgaard, S.: A double-blind randomized pilot trial comparing computerized cognitive exercises to Tetris in adolescents with attention-deficit/hyperactivity disorder. Nord. J. Psychiatry. **71**, 455–464 (2017). https://doi.org/10.1080/08039488.2017.1328070

65. Kaptchuk, T.J.: The double-blind, randomized, placebo-controlled trial: gold standard or golden calf? J. Clin. Epidemiol. **54**, 541–549 (2001). https://doi.org/10.1016/S0895-4356(00)00347-4

66. Bemanalizadeh, M., Yazdi, M., Yaghini, O., Kelishadi, R.: A meta-analysis on the effect of telemedicine on the management of attention deficit and hyperactivity disorder in children and adolescents. J. Telemed. Telecare. 1357633X211045186 (2021). https://doi.org/10.1177/1357633X211045186

67. Rodrigo-Yanguas, M., et al.: A virtual reality serious videogame versus online chess augmentation in patients with attention deficit hyperactivity disorder: a randomized clinical trial. Games Health J. **10**, 283–292 (2021). https://doi.org/10.1089/g4h.2021.0073

68. Estrada-Plana, V., Esquerda, M., Mangues, R., March-Llanes, J., Moya-Higueras, J.: A pilot study of the efficacy of a cognitive training based on board games in children with attention-deficit/hyperactivity disorder: a randomized controlled trial. Games Health J. **8**, 265–274 (2019). https://doi.org/10.1089/g4h.2018.0051

69. Goodwin, A., et al.: Erratum to Attention training for infants at familial risk of ADHD (INTERSTAARS): study protocol for a randomized controlled trial. Trials **18**, 419 (2017). https://doi.org/10.1186/s13063-017-2167-1

70. Loo, S.K., Makeig, S.: Clinical utility of EEG in attention-deficit/hyperactivity disorder: a research update. Neurotherapeutics **9**, 569–587 (2012). https://doi.org/10.1007/s13311-012-0131-z

71. Arns, M., Conners, C.K., Kraemer, H.C.: A decade of EEG theta/beta ratio research in ADHD: a meta-analysis. J Atten Disord. **17**, 374–383 (2013). https://doi.org/10.1177/1087054712460087

72. Ahmadi, M., et al.: Cortical source analysis of resting state EEG data in children with attention deficit hyperactivity disorder. Clin. Neurophysiol. **131**, 2115–2130 (2020). https://doi.org/10.1016/j.clinph.2020.05.028

73. Arns, M., Heinrich, H., Strehl, U.: Evaluation of neurofeedback in ADHD: the long and winding road. Biol. Psychol. **95**, 108–115 (2014). https://doi.org/10.1016/j.biopsycho.2013.11.013

74. Miranda, P., Cox, C.D., Alexander, M., Danev, S., Lakey, J.R.T.: In quest of pathognomonic/endophenotypic markers of attention deficit hyperactivity disorder (ADHD): potential of EEG-based frequency analysis and erps to better detect, prevent and manage ADHD. Med Devices (Auckl). **13**, 115–137 (2020). https://doi.org/10.2147/MDER.S241205

75. Brown, C.R., Clarke, A.R., Barry, R.J., McCarthy, R., Selikowitz, M., Magee, C.: Event-related potentials in attention-deficit/hyperactivity disorder of the predominantly inattentive type: an investigation of EEG-defined subtypes. Int. J. Psychophysiol. **58**, 94–107 (2005). https://doi.org/10.1016/j.ijpsycho.2005.03.012

76. Van Doren, J., et al.: Theta/beta neurofeedback in children with ADHD: feasibility of a short-term setting and plasticity effects. Int. J. Psychophysiol. **112**, 80–88 (2017). https://doi.org/10.1016/j.ijpsycho.2016.11.004

77. Implementation of SSVEP Based BCI with Emotiv EPOC. https://www.webofscience.com/wos/alldb/full-record/INSPEC:12947371. Accessed 30 July 2022

78. Benitez, D.S., Toscano, S., Silva, A.: On the use of the Emotiv EPOC neuroheadset as a low-cost alternative for EEG signal acquisition. In: 2016 IEEE Colombian Conference on Communications and Computing (COLCOM), pp. 1–6. IEEE, Cartagena, Colombia (2016). https://doi.org/10.1109/ColComCon.2016.7516380

79. Duvinage, M., Castermans, T., Petieau, M., Hoellinger, T., Cheron, G., Dutoit, T.: Performance of the Emotiv Epoc headset for P300-based applications. Biomed. Eng. Online. **12**, 56 (2013). https://doi.org/10.1186/1475-925X-12-56

Playable Modeling: Interactive Learning Process in Science and Art

Qi Tan[✉]

Central Academy of Fine Arts, No. 8 Hua Jia Di Nan Jie, Beijing 100102, China
tanqi@cafa.edu.cn

Abstract. Models are simplified and idealized representations of everyday reality or imaginary truth. Scientists use all range of models to assume, analyze, simulate, as well as artists use them to imitate, imagine, query. No matter what the usage of models are, modeling would be a desirable working process and interactive media to interconnect and even interconvert in between science and art. Some models invented by the professionals but encouraging common people to manipulate and interact with them, they are mainly used for learning purposes. This paper will interpret the principles of several common playable models, such as Tangram and building blocks, and a new invented versatile model, Tangram Blocks, in order to analyze essential activity of interactive modeling process in these playable models, then use these models and their modeling methods to play with uncertainties and possibilities for future learning. This paper also will explore different formulas and approaches of modeling that can help people understanding science knowledge or art thoughts, especially in the museum and gallery context as an interesting, playful, interactive visiting experience. The playable modeling as a creative learning process could open participatory opportunities and led interactive co-operation for the scientists, artists and general public. It helps us to communicate and understand each other, then to stimulate imagination and variable future possibilities.

Keywords: Playable Models · Modeling Learning · Tangram Blocks · Museum Participatory Experience

1 Introduction: Modeling and Its Playable Possibilities

In science studies and artistic creations, even philosophy thinking, modeling is a fundamental methodology to simplify and analyze complex systems, in order to master the essences of things. On the one hand, models are abstracted from reality but beyond the real world, it functionalizes as bird's-eye view or the extracted quintessence. On the other hand, models have their fictional and suppositive nature that indicate uncertainties and unreality.

The development of science and technology as well as the division of social classes, it makes us living in a specialized world that's being sliced finer and finer. People are hardly to understand each other and common senses are difficult to reach. In other words, we can't see the wood for the trees. The harm of this subdivision tendency specially embodies in the learning process which is an essential living skill of human beings. When scientific terminologies and contemporary art concepts are too obscure and unreachable to the general population, it stops us from interesting and approaching deeper knowledge and understanding in science and art. To resolve this learning crisis, could models, especially the interactive ones which allow people to play with, be useful to enhance intellectual curiosity? This paper would like to explore and discuss the possibilities of playable modeling as a powerful learning method and process for fostering and improving deeper understanding of complex issues. If this public engagement through interactive modeling could be established, it may in turn positively influence science and art development.

2   Modeling, a Creative Methodology in Science and Art

Modeling is widely used in most of scientific field to approximate represent real-world objects and phenomena in a logical and objective way, as well as arts and humanities consider modeling as props to "prescribe imaginings" and "generate fictional truths" [1]. The creativity of modeling builds on its suppositive nature, it is more like an ever-changing process rather than a given answer. Conceptual models help us to transfer complex nature phenomena into useable and apprehensible mental models, even we do not completely understand a complex system, we still can manipulate it through models. The scientists and designers' work is how to provide appropriate conceptual models for the people, for more complex system, models are more important. Some models are the result of researches, some are presented as an ongoing process that can be manipulating by the users. Modeling that can be engaged by most of people is full of adventures, serendipities and uncertainties, which is similar to create an artwork. How modeling works and processes creatively will be demonstrated in the following sections.

2.1   The Principal, Process and Purpose of Modeling

Every model for different subjects and purposes has its own formulation. However, there are some general principals within models. Models can be considered as outline and skeleton of things and phenomena; they omit the details and nonsignificant aspects. The modeling process could sort order in six stages as described below.

Observation. The modeling process starts from observation that looks at an object or event in both holistic and detailed ways, both objective and subjective aspects. If we can observe a phenomenon from reasonably wide areas as much as possible, the model we made will be more precise and representative. Anatomy and sampling in the science provide modeling details and data, observational drawing and sketching in the art give modeling materials to shape and generalize.

Simplify. After observation, we may recognize the complexity of real things and phenomena, too many of details and branches stop us to clarify the true features and core. Therefore, simplify is the very important juncture during the modeling process. For example, in data science, a model is a certain type of algorithm to analysis and summarizing huge amount of data, then to present them in a simple and clear diagram or chart.

People don't need to read all the data in the background, they can find the information they need directly from graphs of the models.

Abstraction. Simplifying and abstracting are commonly considered as an integrative process in the modeling. The creating process of Piet Mondrian's pure abstract painting could visualize how abstraction works. His use of vertical and horizontal lines to structure his painting, these lines are transferred from the real landscape drawing from step to step. In every step, his arrangement is reducing some contents of original observation drawing, until there are no clearly discernible concretes.

Visualization. After abstraction, the result will be presented as a model, which is a general shape object or a graphics.

Variation. The last two phases may not happen in every modeling process. Only the models allowed adjusting and manipulating can be varied. By repeatedly using a conceptual or fundamental model, more practical models can be derived from it.

Creation. Especially in art, some versatile models can create multiple usage, such as human skeleton model in 3D modeling.

2.2 Modeling Types Allow Participating

Not all the models could be allowed people to manipulate them, some models are fixed by their creator as formulas, for example, the Pythagorean theorem; but some other models need people to involve, to change and to verify, such as Atoms and Molecules or Domino, the chain of conduction.

Modeling Atoms and Molecules. As atoms and molecules, can't be observed by naked eye, it is hard to describe their forms only by pain text and illustration. Thus, scientists had invented different types of models to represent molecular structures. Because of the variability of atoms and molecules, most of models are changeable, especially when the models are used as teaching aids.

There are 3 common molecular models: ball and spoke models, space-filling models and crystal lattice models [2]. Two of them have open structures, and the other one has designed both re-useable and permanent. Students could recognize how atoms bond together through composing ball and spoke models; and they can notice the size and shape of the whole molecule through adjusting the space-filling models; and then their teacher can demonstrate the spatial relationship of atoms by using the crystallographic models.

Developing and using models is an important practice at the middle and high school level, it helps students to understand more and more abstract contents of science. In this phase of learning, when the scale of physics and chemistry contents is much smaller or bigger than which we can directly see or touch or experience, modeling will be the most intuitional way to understand these topics.

Dominos: Chain and Relationship. Dominos is originally appeared as a family of tile-based games; but then people extend its cumulative effect to explain some chain reactions, literally as series of mechanical collisions and metaphorically as causal linkages and relationships within systems. Thus, dominos can be considered as a kind of playable models, using it and it variants can easily visualize the cause, effect and variate of an event or a phenomenon.

In the TV series "Genius by Stephen Hawking", the volunteers make an experiment with a domino installation called Machine of Life to demonstrate how the life comes from. Sustained by the correct input of energy and installing order, the machine transfers an impulse from one place to another. Each installation part moves following the laws of physics and together they keep the impulse moving as a chain effect.

3   Modeling as Learning Process

As a fundamental learning process, modeling help humans to understand the world and human beings from childhood to adulthood. Learning through modeling is not only suitable for the early childhood education, but also important for the advanced study continuing in our lifetime. There are mainly two kinds of modeling learning. One is to imitate models, such as people's activities or behaviors, it also called observational learning; the other is to form models, whatever it is physical or virtual model, conceptual or practical model.

3.1   Modeling Learning as a Social Behaviour

Modeling is mentioned in Albert Bandura's social learning theory as an interaction in between environmental and cognitive factors influencing human learning and behavior [3]. During the modeling, especially playable modeling process, children are observing, modelling, and imitating the behaviors, attitudes, and emotional reactions of each other. They are not only learning the knowledges through manipulating the models, but also learning how to communicate and socialize with others.

3.2   Set Model Learning as a Game

Learning as playing, there are a lot of participative models that set as toys and games. Puzzles, such as Tangram, an ancient Chinese puzzle, help people to understand the relationship in between shapes and colors, entirety and portion through placing. Building blocks, such as LEGO, in wooden or plastic materials set as toy modules to let people cognizing 3D shapes, extending their space perception and training their manipulative abilities through building. These puzzles and building blocks can be considered as playable learning media for children and students, their variable forms and extensions also can be advanced used in business strategies, art installation, scientist analysis and architecture or furniture design as prototypes or study tools for professionals and researchers.

Props and Toys. Props, are usually seen in the film and TV to simulate real world scenes, but they are also used as teaching models, for example, assembled plastic heart and head on the anatomy class. For the young children, toys can act as models to let children learning through playing. When we are toddlers, toys are simple-shaped and colourful, which help us to cognize the basic shapes and colours.

Recreational Mathematics. Recreational mathematics is mathematics hidden in the amateur activities, such as Sudoku and puzzles. It is not necessary to know the formulas and theorems; children or untrained adults can solve some maths problems by simply playing the games. So, it may can inspire them to seek for further learning about mathematics. Sometimes, professionals also use puzzles, Rubik cubes and other forms of play as basic models to deduce and predict.

Block Play. In our childhood, when we are playing the building blocks, we are having fun and we don't realize there is a process of learning involved in the playing. This open-ended and no-rules play is called Block Play; it was recommended by Friedrich Froebel in the early 1800s as an early learning strategy using wooden blocks play to help with child development [4]. To construct the blocks, normally made by wood or plastic, young children need to apply a range of abilities, such as mind-hand coordination, modeling ability, imagination and communication skill.

The physical movement and motor coordination abilities also can be trained through block play. Carrying, lifting, stacking and adjusting, these constructive actions involve both gross motor skill and fine motor skill, especially precise finger movements. We are always playing building blocks with our fellows, it is a common social event that happens at our early age. So, language skill, communication skill and cooperative skill can also be developed.

4   Tangram Blocks: A Possible Versatile Model

Puzzles game and building blocks could be regarded as serial playable developmental models. They are invented by scientists, artists or designers for amusement or knowledge popularization purpose. Although these kinds of modeling games normally carried out as children's toy and endeavour for amateurs, actually, they are not as simple as that and they have more potentials. Deep ideas that are hidden in puzzles and building games, such as mathematics, cognitive science, logic, configuration management and communication. Various forms of play allow people to explore and understand these deep ideas in a voluntary and active way.

Therefore, there would be some possibilities to create and formulate a versatile model and its gamified modeling process which can suit for most of learning and usage scenarios. Extracting modeling methods and rules from Tangram and snowflake building blocks, next content will assume a new puzzle building game named "Tangram Blocks" that can be a tryout of playable model combining geometry, construction and fractals.

4.1   Tangram, the Chinese Wisdom in Puzzle Game

Tangram (Chinese: 七巧板; 'seven boards of skill') is a seven-pieces dissection puzzle originate from China, its history can be traced back to at least the first century BC. Scientific historian and biochemist, Dr. Joseph Needham, mentioned in the serial book "Science and Civilisation in China" that the Tangram is "one of the oldest oriental entertainment" [5]. Seven flat polygons, named *tans*, which can put together to form more than 1600 shapes, such as triangle, parallelogram, irregular polygon and all kind of figures, animals, architecture etc. The design and playing method are finalized around the Mind Dynasty (later 18th century) and then spread to American and Europe by trading ships in the same period.

Though Tangram's design is minimalism, it had created over 6500 different tangram problems, and the current number is ever-growing. Tangram is the best example of playable modeling for creative learning in both mathematics, shape recognition and art. Following, we will try to explain how Tangram as a playable model enlighten variable interactive learning process to achieve different educational aims.

Geometric Learning. The in-and-out complementary principle, established by Liu Hui [6], the third-century famous Chinese mathematician, is the main mathematics theory behind Tangram, when a 2D or 3D geometric figure to be divided to several parts and then to be displaced to the other positions, its total area or volume is invariant. Tangram could be considered as a square (sides 1, area 1) divided to 7 polygons, including 5 isosceles right triangles, 2 small ones (hypotenuse $\frac{1}{2}$, sides $\frac{\sqrt{2}}{4}$, area $\frac{1}{16}$), 1 medium one (hypotenuse $\frac{\sqrt{2}}{2}$, sides $\frac{1}{2}$, area $\frac{1}{8}$), and 2 large ones (hypotenuse 1, sides $\frac{\sqrt{2}}{2}$, area $\frac{1}{4}$); 1 square (sides $\frac{\sqrt{2}}{4}$, area $\frac{1}{8}$) and 1 parallelogram (sides of $\frac{1}{2}$ and $\frac{\sqrt{2}}{4}$, height of $\frac{1}{4}$, area $\frac{1}{8}$) (see Fig. 1). All 7 tangram figures can satisfy particular geometric properties, such as convex polygons. Using Euclidean isometries, tangram usually apply to form dissections of prescribed polygons in the mathematics classroom. According to student's level, teachers will ask them to arrange different prescribed polygons, for example, triangle, quadrangle, pentagon and hexagon. Students will learn geometric knowledge about the Pythagorean theorem (the *Gou-Gu* theorem in China), the in-and-out complementary principle, calculating perimeter and area through the dissection of different polygons.

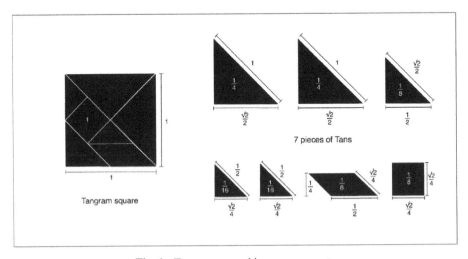

Fig. 1. Tangram set and its measurement.

Tangram is widely used in the senior class of kindergarten and junior class of primary school to teach children of basic geometry. Tangram playing helps the young age students to stay focus and motivated thinking during the course learning. Rather than only listen to the teacher, students can hands-on composing the geometric figures and explore different solutions to geometric questions through numbers of trying. Under the instructions of teacher, the learning process using tangram could be set as individual activity or group work. Firstly, teacher can ask students to observe the relationship in between seven tans and try to piece together. For example, the 2 small isosceles right triangles can form the 1 middle triangle, or the 1 square, or the 1 parallelogram, then the 2 small triangles and the 1 middle triangle can form the 1 big triangle. Secondly, students can be divided to the groups, teacher can give each group an outline of a common convex polygon, such as triangle, square, rhomboid or trapezoid, let students to construct with all seven tans without overlap. If this challenge is easily solved out, teacher can upgrade the challenge to arrange pentagons and hexagons. According to Wang and Hsiung's research paper "A Theorem on the Tangram" [7], using all seven tans, there only exists 13 convex tangram configurations up to isometry. Thus, the convex tangram configurations of tangram are not too complex above the understanding of primary school students. Because of its simple and intuitional, tangram is a perfect playable model for basic geometric learning.

For the senior students in the primary school, tangram could help them to calculate perimeter and area of both convex polygons and concave polygons using the in-and-out complementary principle. If a complex polygon can be formed by tangram, students can dissect the complex polygon into tans, then recomposed the tans into a simpler sharp for calculating. There may exist more than one solution to the question, so playing with tangram could motivate students to find out different approaches as more as possible.

Training of Shape Recognition and Configuration. The common playing method of the tangram is to replicate patterns with given outline or silhouette using all seven tans without overlap. Gestalt principles are involved in the gameplay, for example, proximity, similarity, closure and figure-ground relationship, so, playing tangram is a training to strengthen our perceptivity and coordinate our mind and hand.

The accessary puzzle book of tangram normally put outlines/silhouettes of patterns in the front of a page and the schematic patterns to show how they are formed by tangram in the back. Therefore, we can play the tangram with the puzzle book in 3 degree of difficulties:

- Level 1: To configure the pattern according to the schematic pattern on the puzzle book. This easiest way is mostly for the young children aged 3–5, it helps them to cognize shapes and colours. Each piece could be considered as an abstracted part of a figure, such as a cat ear, a dog feet or a human face, arranging these seven tans can carry out different shapes of one figure. The learning process through this play is from abstract parts to configure the figural whole, then the parents or the teacher can guide the young children to link the tangram figures with the daily things.
- Level 2: To replicate patterns according to their outlines or silhouettes. This way of play requests the skill to dissect the figure into parts, it needs more imagination and numbers of try. Tangram can form more than 1600 patterns, there are many possible try-outs for the players. The pattern numbers vary from 100 to 1000 on the puzzle

book, which are aliened by difficulties of recognition and configuration. From front to back, the patterns are from simple to complex, from figurative to abstract, and could be divided into catalogues, including animals, humans, architecture and objects. The richness and various of tangram configuration makes it suitable for all range of age groups, and perfectly act as a family game.

- Level 3: To recognize tangram paradoxes. In the thousands of composed tangram patterns, some are paradoxes that two or more patterns look similar but have detailed difference. For example, the famous two-monk paradox [8] (see Fig. 2). Presents as two similar shapes, one has a longer body and the other one has one more foot. The subtly differences of two monk figures need the players to distinguish from the outline/silhouette, then use different composing to form two monks. Playing with third level of difficulties, the players could learn how to coordinate with higher visual acuity and multiple problem-solving thinking.

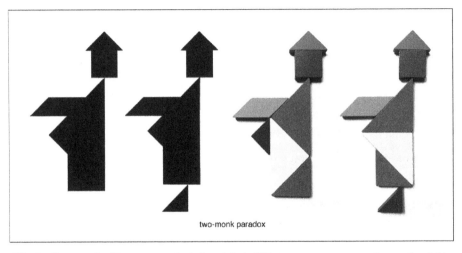

two-monk paradox

Fig. 2. Two-monk silhouettes on the left and their different tangram composing on the right.

Learning of Abstract Art and Story Telling. Tangram itself has inherent beauty of its composition with colored geometric pieces. Set of tangram in square somehow looks like a Mondrian's abstract painting. Mentioned in previous section, Mondrian created his paintings from the abstraction of nature; therefore, the tangram pieces could be excellent models to create abstract artwork. No matter you are child or adult, it can simply use tans as moulds to create a sketch of abstract painting by drawing the outline along the edge of tangram piece and tiling full of the paper or the canvas, then colours could be filled in different tangram triangles and squares to form a latticed abstract painting. Alternatively, to paint colour on the surface of tans, it can be used as stamps that allow children to imprint on different surfaces.

Visualized story telling also can be taught by playing tangram. Teacher can arrange students to use multiple tangram sets to compose figures, houses, animals and landscapes in the story. Then each student can move his/her protagonist around according to the plots, dubbed of dialogues can be finished in the same time. Setting up camera and lighting equipment, students even can make a stop motion animation with tangram composed scenes and figures. It will be a good interactive collaboration for the students to enhance their organizing and communicating abilities.

Art creations have no clear rules and regular process, the variability of tangram configurations gives the players endless possibilities to imagine, to create and to develop.

4.2 Snowflake Building Blocks, the Interlocking Blocks to Form Everything

Block play has been mentioned in the foregoing section of this paper as a gamified model learning process for training spatial skills, it is the earliest touch of modeling in our childhood. There are different types of building blocks, their functions and gameplays are not the same. For example, some are plastic-moulding building blocks, like Lego® bricks and Mega Bloks®, with concavo-convex dots on the surface connected each other by their dots, they can form solid and immobile structure; some are wooden building blocks having thick side surface, they are cubes, triangle blocks, rectangular blocks, arch blocks and semi-circular blocks that pile up to form constructions, but sometime the structures constituted by wooden blocks aren't well-knit and easy to push over.

Besides these common 3D block types, there are some other types of block play using 2D pieces to compose 3D structure. How could these 2D pieces link together and stand up to allow the 3D modeling? There are 3 common designs of the building piece that can achieve the goal:

- Magnet. 2D piece with magnet inside can attract each other to make up 3D space. The magnetic piece is easy to stick together, and hard to pull down, so, it is not easy to control the 3D shape.
- Tenon-and-mortise joint. Making the 2D piece edge tenon and mortise, thus, two pieces can conjunct together with their edges. Sometimes, it is a bit difficult to align all the tenons and mortises when more than two pieces to conjunct together.
- Grooves on the edge. Typically, the 2D piece in this type is in a snowflake shape, which is a rounded plastic piece with 8 grooves on the edge and a hole in the middle. Snowflake shape allows the 2D pieces joint each other from 8 directions, giving a lot of spatial developing potentials.

From variation and creativity aspect, snowflake building blocks is the most flexible and user-friendly design using 2D pieces to make 3D modeling. Because the snowflake pieces are quite small compared to other building blocks, it needs so many pieces to construct a 3D object. Playing with snowflake pieces has more challenge to the players, they need more patience to construct and more envision to imagine the final result.

4.3 Tangram Blocks, Gamified Model Combining Tangram and Snowflake Building Blocks

As tangram is very popular in both east and west for many years, variable game inspired by tangram have been invented and designed, some of them try to add a dimension on the tangram. For example, a 3D block game called "Pangram" using 7 volumes to form a cube, it develops polygons of tangram to polyhedrons by adding a height of $\frac{\sqrt{2}}{4}$ to each side of tans. The gameplay of Pangram is similar to wooden building blocks. Because the 3D shapes are directly pulled up from 2D shapes, there are total 7 slopes on the blocks. When the blocks stacked more than two layers, the slopes are easily slipping that make the 3D structure unstable and limit the configuring possibilities. Thus, to turn tangram into 3D in this way has its natural shortcomings.

Therefore, if we would like to apply tangram to 3D modeling, the better way is to use original 2D pieces to form 3D models. The main difficulty of this method is how to make a stable 3D structure. Discussed in the previous Sect. 3.2, the optimal solution is to cut grooves on the edges of a plate, then interlock each piece to form 3D structures.

The Design of Tangram Blocks. Inspiring from the design and its playing method of tangram and snowflake building blocks, there is a potential versatile model could be invented to accomplish both 2D puzzle play and 3D block play. The new designed playing model named Tangram Blocks, which make use of the original 7 tans and cutting grooves on their edges, then turning 2D tangram into 3D building blocks.

In order to balance weight and enlarge interlock area, the cutting grooves are better to be in the middle or to be symmetrized on the panel. The position and length of the grooves are the key points for the design of Tangram Blocks. For the 5 isosceles right triangles, 1 groove is cut in the middle of hypotenuse, groove reached the barycentre of the triangle, its length is $\frac{1}{4}$ of side length and its width as the thickness of the piece. While, it is to cut 2 grooves in the middle of the both long sides of the parallelogram and 4 grooves in the middle of each side of square, each groove's length and width equal to the small triangle's groove size. Because the large triangles have bigger area, they may have two symmetric grooves, as the same size as the middle triangle's groove, on the two sides to allow more interlocking modes and to support their own weight in the later constructing. (see Fig. 3).

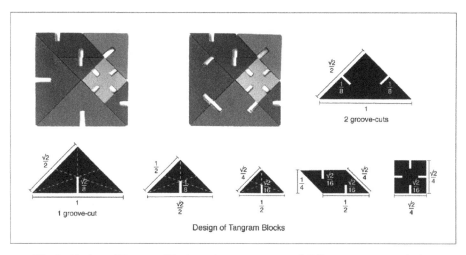

Fig. 3. Design of Tangram Blocks and two prototypes of different groove-cut design

The Gameplay of Tangram Blocks. Tangram Blocks is an evolutive Tangram that can be constructed in 3D space. It has all gameplay features that the tangram has, and that more gameplay only can be realized in 3D structures. For example:

- Geometric sculpture. The geometric shape of tan-pieces is convenient for making constructivism sculptures. Because of its abstract and minimal nature, this 3D format of modern art and design seems a bit hard to be understood by general public. Playing tangram blocks, people can be hands-on to compose the constructivism sculptures, to know how shapes and colours are related and jointed together three-dimensionally. During the constructing process, the players should look at the structure from different perspective, it is a different experience than playing tangram on a flat surface. (see Fig. 4 and Fig. 5)

- Tridimensional figure. In accordance with outline/silhouette on the puzzle book, tangram can form more than 1000 2D figures. However, to shape figures in 3D need higher spatial cognitive ability, as well as using 2D tan-pieces to form 3D shapes need to know how to balance weight and stand stable. Children, even adult would be benefit from playing Tangram Blocks as it is a thought-provoking figure modeling. (see Fig. 6 and Fig. 7)

- Shadow play. Sometimes, chaotic 3D objects can compose a whole clear shadow figure relying on certain kind of lighting and distance. Under the proper lighting, we can compose magic shadow plays with one or more sets of Tangram Blocks, we can change the model structure and position in order to form different shadow figures continuously. Thus, time has been involved in this creative playing, 2D is the shadow of 3D, and 3D is the shadow of 4D. Therefore, the players are not only playing a game, they are actually making a piece of art in time and space. (see Fig. 8)

Fig. 4. Geometric sculpture made by tangram blocks.

Fig. 5. Geometric sculpture can be looked from different perspectives.

As a 3D block play, playing with multiple sets of Tangram Blocks will have more fun, and the Tangram Blocks also has more room for interaction and collaboration than the Tangram. It is a full interactive process in between players and blocks, player and player. If creativity has no limit, the gameplay of Tangram Blocks could be expanded further, and it may even be considered as a playable development model that we will discuss in next section.

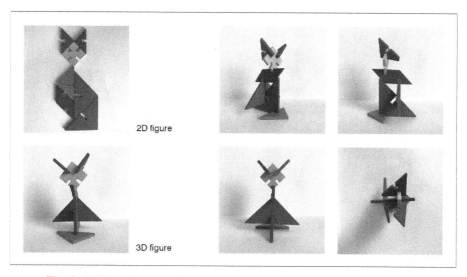

Fig. 6. A 2D cat figure can be transferred into 3D figure using tangram blocks.

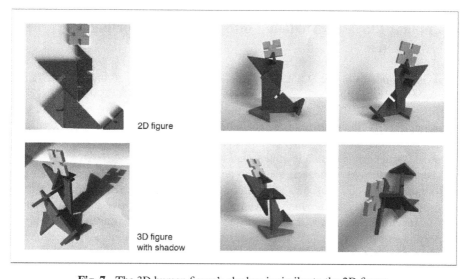

Fig. 7. The 3D human figure's shadow is similar to the 2D figure.

Fig. 8. Three sets of tangram blocks in different lightings and positions compose various shadow plays.

5 Implant Playable Modeling into Museum Participatory Experience

Today, museum does not only function as a place to collect antiques and cultural relics, but also as a creative and exchange venue. Quoted by sociologists Daniel Aaron Silver and Terry Nichols Clark, "Amenities" are the syntagmatic and unique scenes that give us meaningful city life, participatory experience and emotional resonance [9]. As a kind of amenities, museums and galleries now more focus on people's visiting experience and process rather than the static objects and collections.

Therefore, playable modeling seems to be an excellent new presented formats and interesting activities for museums and galleries to explore and enrich visitors' exchange and communication. Transferring passive watch to hands-on positive activity, modeling bring us together to engage with the ideas and disciplines shaping our lives, not only in science and art but also in fields such as politics, literature, environmental protection and economics. Paola Antonelli, senior curator of design at MoMA, suggests "museums can become laboratories for rethinking society, places for showing not what already exists, but more important, what is yet to exist" [10].

Playable modeling can address an interactive museum user experience by promoting enjoyment in science museums and enhancing participatory experience in art museums and galleries.

An interactive art installation Domino Effect presented by Ingrid Ingrid in the 9th 'Luminothérapie' event in downtown Montreal. 120 giant dominos with LED lights and sensors inside had distributed across six stations. When people pushed over the domino piece, the light color of domino is changing and fair-sounding music is following by the kinetic potential of tumbling dominos. Domino as a playable model inspired the artists to enhance interactive experience in between people and artwork, and among each other.

"It's rare that people can really play with art installations like our dominos that you can manipulate with your hands. That's what drove us to come up with the idea of using dominos," says the studio's creative director, Geneviève Levasseur [11].

6 Conclusion: The Development Prospect and Future of Playable Modeling in Learning Science and Art

Playable modeling will be an evolvable active learning methodology in the nearly future, this paper already provides some evidences to prove its feasibility and possibilities. Tangram Blocks, the new versatile gamified model, will be developed as both a physical model and a mixed reality game. It could be developed as a good example and realizable model of playable modeling in learning science and art.

Play, its concept, however, is much more than an activity related to the games, it can be a learning process involving spontaneous and joyful interaction. When we learning by playing, we can motivate our self-enhancement drive and creativity. It is a real freedom to understand the world by our hands-on modeling process. Playable modeling, an adventure to observe, to act, to explore, to discover orders and meanings in a brand-new world.

References

1. Dunne, A., Raby, F.: Speculative Everything: Design, Fiction, and Social Dreaming, pp. 117–122. The MIT Press, London, UK (2013)
2. Whipple Museum webpage. Types of Molecular Models. https://www.whipplemuseum.cam. ac.uk/explore-whipple-collections/models/modelling-chemistry/types-molecular-models. Accessed 22 Feb 2023
3. McLeod, S.A.: Bandura - social learning theory. Simply Psychology. www.simplypsycho logy.org/bandura.html. Accessed 21 Jan 2023
4. Main, P.: Block play: a teacher's guide, https://www.structural-learning.com/post/block-play-a-teachers-guide. Accessed 20 Feb 2023
5. Tangram puzzles page. https://tabularaisa.com/tangram-puzzles. Accessed 20 Feb 2023
6. Pohl, S.S., Richter, C.: The complete characterization of tangram pentagons. Beitr. Algebra Geom. **62**(1), 121–135 (2020). https://doi.org/10.1007/s13366-020-00528-1
7. Tian, X.: The art and mathematics of tangrams. In: Bridges 2012: Mathematics, Music, Art, Architecture, Culture. https://archive.bridgesmathart.org/2012/bridges2012-553.pdf. Accessed 20 Feb 2023
8. Margherita, B.: Tangram Paradox. From MathWorld—A Wolfram Web Resource, created by Eric W. Weisstein. https://mathworld.wolfram.com/TangramParadox.html
9. Silver, D.A., Clark, T.N.: Scenescapes: How Qualities of Place Shape Social Life. Illustrated Edition, pp. 12–17. The University of Chicago, Chicago, US (2016)
10. Dunne, A., Raby, F.: Speculative Everything: Design, Fiction, and Social Dreaming, p. 154. The MIT Press, London, UK (2013)
11. Cousineau, M.: Domino Effect, a New Interactive Art Installation Brightens up Winter in Montreal. https://www.signify.com/en-us/blog/archive/spotlight/domino-effect. Accessed 22 Feb 2023

A Study on the Effect of Teaching Effectiveness of Online Courses and the Number of Bullet Screen

Gengyi Wang[✉], Wenda Tian, and Qianhang Qin

Guangxi Normal University, Guilin 541000, China
353965085@qq.com

Abstract. Compared with offline courses, the interaction between teachers and students, and between students and students in online courses is relatively simple and mainly realized through bullet screen. The presence of bullet screen can help guide students to participate in classroom interactions and enhance the attractiveness of the course, but also brings problems such as the increase in the perceived difficulty of knowledge points and the increase in the cognitive load of course knowledge points. In order to optimize the learning effect of online courses and promote the effective development of online courses, this paper focuses on the influence of the number of bullet screen on the teaching effect of online courses through an experimental design. In the experiment, the number of bullet screen was divided into 4 levels: online videos with no bullet screen, online videos with about 33% bullet screen, Online videos with about 66% bullet screen, Online videos with about 100% bullet screen. After the subjects watched online instructional videos with different bullet screen number levels in groups, the answer scores of different groups of subjects were analyzed. Following the experiment, this paper interviewed the subjects to understand their main concerns, self-assessed concentration level, concentration duration, and overall experience of online video watching while watching online courses. Finally, this paper draws the following conclusions: (1) The teaching effect of the online course with about 33% of bullet screen is excellent, learners get good scores and learn with low cognitive load and reasonable sight distribution. (2) The effect of video teaching without bullet screen is also not so bad, learners get good learning experience, but the time for learners to continue to focus on learning is shorter, so online teaching videos with no bullet screen are suitable for shorter online courses. (3) Online videos with about 66% bullet screen as well as online videos with about 100% bullet screen are less suitable for online teaching, and learners will have a greater cognitive load pressure and poorer learning results.

Keywords: teaching effectiveness · online course · number · bullet screen

1 Introduction

In recent years, influenced by the normalization of the epidemic, a large number of offline courses need to be transformed into online teaching. Along with the significant increase in social demand for online courses, the number of both catechism platforms and online courses are growing upward at a very fast rate, online teaching has become another important way of teaching besides traditional offline teaching. In online courses, students usually need to watch the teacher's recorded teaching videos, and when they want to communicate and interact, they send messages to the teacher and other students watching the videos by sending bullet screen, and other viewers can also reply to the previous bullet screen by sending bullet screen. Thus, the final online course will often consist of a combination of videos from the instructor and bullet screen from the viewers. In the above context, it is important to investigate the influence of the number of bullet screen on the teaching effectiveness of online courses, which can help promote the effective development of online courses and provide theoretical references for optimizing the teaching effectiveness of the corresponding online courses, as the original purpose of conducting online courses is to deliver the corresponding knowledge to learners in need.

2   Analysis of Offline Teaching and Online Teaching Characteristics

Traditional offline teaching usually takes place in classrooms, where teachers present course knowledge to students through blackboard-writing and PowerPoint projections, etc. This teaching mode has the following characteristics:

1. Since the teacher and students are in the same relatively confined and concentrated space, the teacher's presence can better supervise the students and motivate them to stay focused during the course so that they can digest the course knowledge more efficiently.
2. The teaching methods of offline courses are more flexible. In addition to the traditional lecture method, teachers can also carry out interactive teaching, or divide students into small groups and use the peer teaching method to let students help each other to complete the transfer of knowledge.
3. Communication between teachers and students is easier and faster, when students have questions in the course, they can ask them immediately, and teachers can quickly answer them accordingly.

Compared with offline courses, online courses require teachers to upload corresponding teaching videos to the Internet, and learners can choose corresponding courses for online learning according to their own needs. This learning mode can make more flexible use of fragmented time, and in addition to the learners' school courses, they can also access other schools' open course resources, so that they can learn almost any knowledge they are interested in without leaving home. These are the advantages of online courses, but there are also certain problems in teaching online courses:

1. Due to the lack of teacher's supervision, learners' learning effectiveness depends largely on their personal self-awareness level, and they are more likely to desert and wander off.
2. The communication between teachers and students, and between learners and peers is mainly through bullet screen, and the bullet screen left in the video will have an

impact on the rest of the learners, thus affecting the teaching effect of the online course.

To sum up, bullet screen, as an important part of online courses, assume the important role of mutual communication between teachers and students as well as the communication between learners. When the number of bullet screen reaches a certain level, the leftover bullet screen may have further influence on the teaching effect of online courses, and the relationship between the number of bullet screen and the teaching effectiveness of online courses needs to be studied.

3   Relevant Research

Along with the popularity of online teaching videos, some domestic and foreign scholars have conducted studies on the correlation between bullet screen, video watching experience and learning effects. Hongyan Xu found that interactive teaching through bullet screen facilitated collaborative learning and deep learning and enhanced students' course stickiness [1]. Rui Yang et al. considered bullet screen as an instant, convenient and efficient interactive tool, and based on this, designed a software for analyzing bullet screen and producing corresponding analysis results of teaching performance [2]. Soussan Djamasbi et al. found that the viewing experience of bullet screen videos was superior to traditional online non-bullet-screen videos, and that bullet screen enhance viewers' attention to the video content [3]. Zhizheng Zhang et al. used hierarchical analysis to explore the interaction behavior of young bullet screen users and found that videos with bullet screen provided a more engaging viewing experience [4]. Wang Xue et al. explored the effect of bullet screen on learners' learning effects through an eye-movement experiment and found that those who paid attention to both bullet screen and video content could obtain better learning effects, while negative emotions of learning would be significantly higher for learners who paid attention to bullet screen only and video content only, and the perceived difficulty of knowledge points would be higher for those who paid attention to video content [5]. Liu Chen et al. found that the location and playback method of bullet screen significantly affects the efficiency of viewers' information extraction, and bullet screen that are at the bottom of the video and scrolling can get more attention [6]. Qinjie Lin found that bullet screen have a facilitating effect on video learning, that bullet screen related to the learning video can facilitate learning, and that the speed and position of bullet screen have an impact on the learning effect [7]. Ruishan Li found that college students had positive attitudes toward bullet screen videos, and bullet screen videos would have different effects on learners with different cognitive styles when teaching, with field-dependent learners having higher learning engagement and learning satisfaction than independent learners, and field-dependent learners having lower cognitive load, while independent learners tended not to watch or post bullet screen [8]. Aiping Qian found that bullet screen related to video content can enhance learners' learning satisfaction, but can bring greater cognitive load [9].

A synthesis of the above-mentioned literature studies on bullet screen, video viewing experience and teaching effectiveness reveals that:

1. Bullet screen helps to enhance the attractiveness of online courses to students, thus leading them to actively participate in classroom interactions and obtain better learning results, but the existence of bullet screen also brings certain negative effects, such as an increase in the perceived difficulty of knowledge points and an increase in the cognitive load on course knowledge points.
2. The relationship between the number of bullet screen and the teaching effect of online courses is not sufficiently explored in the current study. As the initiators of bullet screen are mostly learners themselves, the content of bullet screen is diverse, including both course-related and non-knowledge-related bullet screen, and the time for learners to pay attention to and understand the content of the teaching video itself is compressed while acquiring and understanding a large amount of bullet screen information, which results in an increase in the cognitive load of learners and a possible decrease in the learning effect.

Therefore, at a time when online courses are becoming increasingly important, this study will focus on exploring the connection between the number of bullet screen and the teaching effectiveness of online courses, and provide corresponding theoretical references and improvement suggestions for optimizing the teaching effectiveness of online courses.

4   Experimental Design

In order to fully explore the relationship between the number of bullet screen and the teaching effect of online courses, and to restore the class experience of online courses as realistically as possible, the length of the teaching video is set to 10 min, which is in line with the current length division of most online catechism platforms for a small section of course knowledge. In the selection of video content, the instructional content that all subjects had no prior knowledge of was chosen as the video genre to exclude the influence of some students on the experimental results due to their prior mastery of understanding the corresponding knowledge points. On the basis of the above, the online teaching videos are equipped with interactive bullet screen and the number of bullet screen is divided into four levels, namely, video with no bullet screen at all, video with about 33% number of bullet screen, video with about 66% number of bullet screen and video with about 100% number of bullet screen, with part of the bullet screen content related to the teaching content and part not related to the teaching content, simulating the bullet screen viewing experience of learners when they actually browse the online courses. The final experimental teaching videos and the distribution of bullet screen volume are shown in Fig. 1.

The experimental subjects were randomly divided into 4 groups of 15 subjects each, with a total of 60 subjects, of whom 27 were male and 33 were female, with a male to female ratio of nearly 1:1. The subjects in each group had no a priori knowledge of the content taught in the video, and one learner in each group was randomly selected to track the eye movement trajectory to provide a more detailed reference basis for the

Fig. 1. Differential settings for the amount of bullet **screen**

subsequent analysis of the experimental results. After the 4 groups of subjects watched the videos with different amounts of bullet screen, they would enter the post-lesson test session, which was designed with 10 questions, all of which were based on the content taught in the videos. After the test was completed, the subjects were interviewed and asked about the learning experience of this online instruction.

5   Experimental Results and Conclusions

5.1   Analysis of Correct Response Rate

Table 1 shows that the observed value of the test statistic for the chi-square test is 1.402 and the probability p- is 0.252. If the significance level α is 0.05, as the probability p- is greater than the significance level, the overall variance of the groups' responses is considered not significantly different and the prerequisite requirements for ANOVA are met.

Table 1. Results of chi-square test with different number of pop-ups

Accuracy of answers			
Levene's statistic	df1	df2	sig
1.402	3	56	.252

Table 2 shows the results of the one-way ANOVA for the effect of the number of bullet screen level on the answer scores, and it can be found that the observed value of the F-statistic is 109.67, which corresponds to a probability p- value of approximately 0. If the significance level α is 0.05, since the probability p- is smaller than the significance level α, it can be considered that different of the number of bullet screen level has a significant effect on the answer results of the subjects.

Table 2. One-way ANOVA results of the number of bullet screen and answer scores

Accuracy of answers

	Sum of squares	df	Mean of squares	F	sig
Intergroup	28280.000	3	9426.667	109.673	.000
Within the group	4813.333	56	85.952		
sum	33093.333	59			

Table 3. Basic descriptive statistics and 95% confidence interval descriptions of responses at different levels of the number of bullet screen

Description

Accuracy of answers

	N	Mean	Standard deviation	Standard gap	95% confidence interval of mean value		Min value	Max value
					Lower limit	Upper limit		
no bullet screen	15	85.3333	7.43223	1.91899	81.2175	89.4492	70.00	100.00
videos with about 33% bullet screen	15	84.6667	10.60099	2.73716	78.7960	90.5373	70.00	100.00
videos with about 66% bullet screen	15	58.6667	11.25463	2.90593	52.4341	64.8993	40.00	80.00
videos with 100% bullet screen	15	32.6667	7.03732	1.81703	28.7695	36.5638	20.00	40.00
Total	60	65.3333	23.68341	3.05752	59.2153	71.4514	20.00	100.00

In order to further determine the effect of different levels of the number of bullet screen on the answer results and to determine the most suitable number of bullet screen for online learning, the paper further subjected the answer results of each group of subjects to multiple comparison tests. Table 3 provides a basic description of the subjects' answers at different levels of the number of bullet screen, and it can be found that there are 15 observations at each of the four levels of the number of bullet screen. The average scores of the subjects who watched no bullet screen videos and videos with about 33% number of bullet screen were higher, reaching 85.33 and 84.67, while those who watched videos with about 33% or 100% number of bullet screen had less favorable results, scoring 58.67 and 32.67 on average. This result is visually evident in Fig. 2.

Means Plots

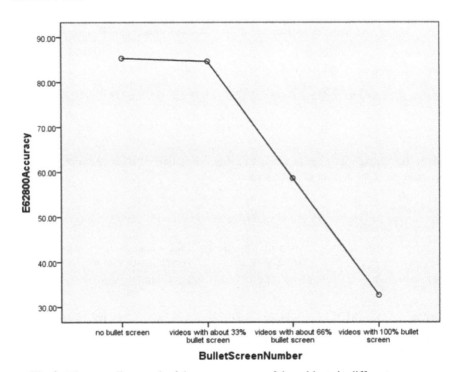

Fig. 2. The mean line graph of the answer scores of the subjects in different groups

In this paper, two methods, Tukey and LSD, were used to conduct multiple comparison tests on the answer results of watching videos with different number of bullet screen levels, and the final results are shown in Table 4. It can be found that, no matter which method was used, there was no significant difference between the answer of subjects who watched videos without bullet screen and those who watched videos with about 33% number of bullet screen levels (probability p-values of 0.997 and 0.845), and the results of the two groups of subjects' answers were quite similar. The results of the subjects who watched videos with about 66% number of bullet screen were significantly different from the other three groups (probability p-value close to 0), and the same situation existed in the group of subjects who watched videos with 100% number of bullet screen (probability p-value close to 0). Based on the results of the above data analysis, if the appropriate number of video bullet screen is chosen from the perspective of obtaining better online instructional results, videos without bullet screen or with about 33% number of bullet screen can be considered.

Table 5 shows the similarity subsets classified by both S-N-K and Tukey methods. It can be seen that the results of the subsets obtained from the two methods divided in the table are consistent, at a significance level α of 0.05, firstly viewing the results of the S-N-K method, the instructional videos with 33% bullet screen count level and the videos without bullet screen are divided into group 3 with mean values of 84.6667 and 85.3333 respectively, which are significantly different from the group mean values of the other two groups of instructional videos with pop-up count level, being in the Tukey method, the videos with 33% bullet screen count level and the videos without bullet screen were still divided into one group with a similar probability of 0.997, which is greater than 0.05. This result also indicates that the study effectiveness of the 33% and no pop-ups videos is very similar.

5.2 Analysis of Subject Interviews

The interview focused on the following four dimensions: the main object of attention, self-assessed concentration level, duration of concentration and overall experience of online video viewing at different levels of number of bullet screen. The final interview results for each group of subjects are as follows.

(1) When the bullet screen completely filled the online instructional video, the subjects' eyes arc casily attracted by the bullet screen scrolling all over the screen, and the course content subtitles are basically ignored, while the content of the bullet screen is not necessarily related to the course content, and the thinking and understanding of the content of the bullet screen easily distract the subjects' attention, resulting in poor absorption of the course content. The overall online course experience is not good and there is a greater cognitive load pressure in the face of the full screen of bullet screen.

(2) When the bullet screen occupied about 66% of the space of the online instructional video content, the subjects basically reported that they could balance the time spent on watching the bullet screen and the course content to a certain extent, and they could maintain a certain degree of concentration during the lesson, but it was difficult to maintain concentration for a long time. This is mainly because the bullet screen still occupy a large screen space, and the uncertainty of the bullet screen content and the continuous scrolling of the bullet screen may interfere with the subjects from time to time, and the overall learning experience of the course is not great, there is still a large cognitive load pressure.

(3) When the bullet screen occupied about 33% of the space of the online instructional video content, the subjects could easily handle and balance the relationship between the scrolling bullet screen and the static video content subtitles. Since the number of bullet screen was small, even if the dynamic bullet screen could attract the subjects at first or the content of the bullet screen was not related to the course content, the subjects still had enough time to return to the understanding of the course content, so the subjects could basically stay focused for a long time during the lesson. The

Table 4. Multiple comparison test of the number of bullet screen

Multiple comparison

Dependent variable: Accuracy of answers

method	(I) BulletScreenNumber	(J) BulletScreenNumber	Mean difference (I-J)	Standard gap	Sig	95% confidence interval of mean value	
						Lower limit	Lower limit
Tukey HSD	no bullet screen	videos with about 33% bullet screen	.66667	3.38531	.997	−8.2973	9.6306
		videos with about 66% bullet screen	26.66667*	3.38531	.000	17.7027	35.6306
		videos with 100% bullet screen	52.66667*	3.38531	.000	43.7027	61.6306
	videos with about 33% bullet screen	no bullet screen	−.66667	3.38531	.997	−9.6306	8.2973
		videos with about 66% bullet screen	26.00000*	3.38531	.000	17.0361	34.9639
		videos with 100% bullet screen	52.00000*	3.38531	.000	43.0361	60.9639
	videos with about 66% bullet screen	no bullet screen	−26.66667*	3.38531	.000	−35.6306	−17.7027
		videos with about 33% bullet screen	−26.00000*	3.38531	.000	−34.9639	−17.0361
		videos with 100% bullet screen	26.00000*	3.38531	.000	17.0361	34.9639
	videos with 100% bullet screen	no bullet screen	−52.66667*	3.38531	.000	−61.6306	−43.7027
		videos with about 33% bullet screen	−52.00000*	3.38531	.000	−60.9639	−43.0361
		videos with about 66% bullet screen	−26.00000*	3.38531	.000	−34.9639	−17.0361
LSD	no bullet screen	videos with about 33% bullet screen	.66667	3.38531	.845	−6.1149	7.4483
		videos with about 66% bullet screen	26.66667*	3.38531	.000	19.8851	33.4483
		videos with 100% bullet screen	52.66667*	3.38531	.000	45.8851	59.4483
	videos with about 33% bullet screen	no bullet screen	−.66667	3.38531	–	–	6.1149
		videos with about 66% bullet screen	26.00000*	3.38531	.000	19.2184	32.7816
		videos with 100% bullet screen	52.00000*	3.38531	.000	45.2184	58.7816
	videos with about 66% bullet screen	no bullet screen	−26.66667*	3.38531	.000	−33.4483	−19.8851
		videos with about 33% bullet screen	−26.00000*	3.38531	.000	−32.7816	−19.2184
		videos with 100% bullet screen	26.00000*	3.38531	.000	19.2184	32.7816
	videos with 100% bullet screen	no bullet screen	−52.66667*	3.38531	.000	−59.4483	−45.8851
		videos with about 33% bullet screen	−52.00000*	3.38531	.000	−58.7816	−45.2184

(continued)

Table 4. (*continued*)

Multiple comparison							
Dependent variable: Accuracy of answers							
method	(I) BulletScreenNumber	(J) BulletScreenNumber	Mean difference (I-J)	Standard gap	Sig	95% confidence interval of mean value	
						Lower limit	Lower limit
		videos with about 66% bullet screen	−26.00000*	3.38531	.000	−32.7816	−19.2184

*. The significance level for the difference in means is 0.05

Table 5. Subset of similarity for multiple comparison tests

Accuracy of answers					
Bullet Screen Number		N	Subset of alpha = 0.05		
			1	2	3
Student-Newman-Keulsa	videos with 100% bullet screen	15	32.6667		
	videos with about 66% bullet screen	15		58.6667	
	videos with about 33% bullet screen	15			84.6667
	no bullet screen	15			85.3333
	Sig		1.000	1.000	.845
Tukey HSDa	videos with 100% bullet screen	15	32.6667		
	videos with about 66% bullet screen	15		58.6667	
	videos with about 33% bullet screen	15			84.6667
	no bullet screen	15			85.3333
	Sig		1.000	1.000	.997

Group means in similar subsets will be displayed

a. A reconciled mean sample size = 15.000 will be used

overall feedback from the subjects was that they had excellent learning experience and low cognitive load pressure.

(4) When the instructional video was provided without interactive bullet screen, the subjects' main focus was on the subtitles of the video content, and after understanding the subtitles, they still had a lot of time left for thinking and remembering, and their concentration level in the class was good. However, compared to the groups that

watched the videos with bullet screen, some subjects were prone to desertion and drifting off because the entire online course lacked dynamic elements and only the content of the subtitles changed statically, the duration of concentration in the class was relatively more affected by their self-monitoring level. Despite the small number of problems, the group that watched the videos without bullet screen still had a good overall viewing experience of the online course, and the cognitive load pressure was maintained at a low level.

5.3 Experimental Conclusions

The comprehensive correct rate of online course content knowledge quiz and subjects' interviews show that the learning effect of online course with about 33% number of bullet screen volume is excellent, learners learn with small cognitive load and have a reasonable distribution of vision when watching instructional videos. They can better understand the content of the scrolling pop-ups and the video subtitles at the same time and maintain their concentration level for a long time. Online course with about 33% number of bullet screen are suitable for online course teaching.

The learning effect of video without bullet screen is also quite well and the learning experience is good, but it is relatively suitable for short online courses, that is, in a short time, learners can get a good learning effect, if the video length is lengthened, it is difficult to maintain the concentration level of learners for a long time with a single video content subtitle, and the learning effect will drop accordingly.

The videos video with 66% as well as 100% number of bullet screen are not suitable for online teaching. Faced with a large number of scrolling bullet screen, learners will have a greater cognitive load and their attention will be easily attracted by bullet screen that are not related to the course content, resulting in a poor learning effect. Online videos with these levels of number of bullet screen are more suitable for amusement and entertainment, and the viewers of these videos do not take learning as the first purpose, and the fact that part of the video content is ignored does not prevent the video itself from bringing entertainment and amusement to the viewers.

6 Summary and Prospect

Online courses are usually composed of teaching videos filmed and uploaded by teachers as well as interactive bullet screen. As an important part of online courses, bullet screen is closely related to the learning experience and actual effect of online courses for learners. In this context, this paper simulates the actual online teaching situation, divides the level of number of bullet screen of teaching videos into four levels: 0%, 33%, 66% and 100%, explores the relationship between the number of bullet screen and the learning effect of online courses through experiments, and provides a theoretical reference for the guarantee of online teaching effect and the management of bullet screen by online course platforms. This study still has some room for improvement in the experimental design due to personal knowledge and conditions. In future studies, the hierarchy of the number of pop-ups could be more detailed, expand the number of subjects and try to establish a mathematical relationship between the number of pop-ups and the teaching effect of online courses.

Support Project. Education Teaching Reform Project of Guangxi Normal University.
Project Name: Study on Optimization of Interactive Interface Design Course under the Background of New Liberal Arts Construction.
Project No: 2021JGA33.

References

1. Xu, H.: Research on the influence of online bullet screen interactive teaching on high school students' art learning investment. In: 2021 4th International Conference on Education Technology Management, pp. 131–135 (2021)
2. Yang, R., Zhou, C., Huang, M., et al.: Design of an interactive classroom with bullet screen function in university teaching. In: 2021 9th International Conference on Information and Education Technology (ICIET), pp. 47–51. IEEE (2021)
3. Djamasbi, S., Hall-Phillips, A., Liu, Z., et al.: social viewing, bullet screen, & user experience: a first look (2019)
4. Zhang, Z., Zhang, L., Li, Y.: The analysis of influence factors of user experience in bullet screen. In: Ahram, T., Falcão, C. (eds.) AHFE 2020. AISC, vol. 1217, pp. 272–278. Springer, Cham (2020). https://doi.org/10.1007/978-3-030-51828-8_36
5. Wang, X., Zhang, L., Wang, R., et al.: Study on learners' eye-movement behavior patterns and its mechanism of action in pop-up teaching videos. J. Dist. Educ. **40**(5), 10 (2022)
6. Chen, L., Chen, S., Cai, H., et al.: The influence of science pop-up setting method on information extraction efficiency. J. Xiamen Inst. Technol. **28**(4), 7 (2020)
7. Lin, Q.: Study on the learning effect of pop-up videos and its influencing factors. Fujian Normal University (2017)
8. Li, R.: Research on the effect of pop-ups on learners with different cognitive styles in online video teaching. Southwest University (2020)
9. Qian, A.: The impact of pop-ups on learners in online instructional videos. Huazhong Normal University (2017)

Research on Undergraduate Classroom Teaching Quality Assurance System Based on Student Experience

Qiong Yang[✉]

Academic Affairs Office, South China University of Technology, Guangzhou 510006, China
jwqyang@scut.edu.cn

Abstract. Teaching quality is the lifeline of college education and teaching. At present, undergraduate classroom teaching evaluation experience and learning achievements is unclear. Hence, with reference to the four stages of PDCA ("Plan", "Do", "Check", and "Action") cycle, this paper explores and constructs an undergraduate classroom teaching quality assurance system with continuous improvement function based on student experience. Focusing on four basic teaching links, namely, teaching preparation, teaching implementation, teaching evaluation, and teaching feedback, this proposed undergraduate classroom teaching quality assurance system is expected to integrate "teacher's teaching" and "student's learning" in the midst of contradictions, enabling classroom teaching assurance to play a more important role in improving the quality of classroom teaching and talent cultivation.

Keywords: Student Experience · Teaching Quality · Talent Cultivation

1 Introduction

At present, the higher education is from elite education to popular education. It is necessary to build high-level and high-quality higher education, and promoting the quality revolution of higher education will be the theme of the era leading the comprehensive, long-term and full development of higher education in the future. High-level and high-quality higher education requires that all colleges and universities must comprehensively rectify the order of education and teaching, strictly manage the teaching process of undergraduate education, strengthen the management of classroom teaching, carefully find out the outstanding problems and weak links in classroom construction and management, strictly manage and grasp the teaching order, formulate rectification measures, implement the responsibility to people, set up strict rules, strengthen the construction of classroom teaching, and improve the quality of classroom teaching.

Classroom teaching is the main battlefield of talent training in colleges and universities, and the main channel of education and teaching reform [1]. The quality of classroom teaching is the key to guarantee the quality of talent cultivation. The establishment of classroom teaching quality assurance system with continuous improvement function based on student experience is an effective way to continuously improve the quality of classroom teaching [2]. At present, countries have successively issued national standards for the quality of higher education teaching, and put forward a series of requirements for college classroom teaching norms, classroom teaching effects, and classroom teaching quality assurance [3]. The national standards of teaching quality in higher education point out the direction for the reform of the concept and method of classroom teaching evaluation in colleges and universities, and provide ideas for the establishment of a sound classroom teaching quality assurance system in colleges and universities [4]. Therefore, while respecting the diversified development needs of colleges and universities, further strengthening the concept of continuous improvement and exploring the construction of a comprehensive and scientific classroom teaching quality assurance system in colleges and universities have become a research hotspot. Colleges and universities are also paying more and more attention to the quality assurance mechanism and quality culture construction [5].

2 Problems in the Evaluation System of Undergraduate Classroom Teaching Quality

There are still some outstanding problems in the classroom quality assurance system in colleges and universities. For example, the classroom quality assurance system is mainly based on general standards, the quality objectives and standards are highly similar, and the lack of quality assurance standards that reflect the characteristics of the specialty and curriculum itself [6]. The quality assurance system for evaluating students' experience is not sound enough, and the evaluation subject and evaluation form of classroom teaching quality assurance are simplistic and scientific [7]. The classroom teaching quality management has not formed an effective closed loop, which emphasizes feedback, neglects rectification, and neglects tracking [8]. The long-term improvement mechanism of quality assurance with continuous improvement function has not been effectively established, and the links of quality assurance have not been effectively connected [9]. The monitoring data of classroom teaching quality is lack of information and intelligent management and utilization, effective use of modern information technology to process data, and exploration, mining and analysis of deep problems in teaching are not enough, and quality management decision-making is lack of data support [10].

Therefore, we must re-examine the current situation of the construction of the classroom teaching quality assurance system, analyze the factors affecting the classroom teaching quality in colleges and universities, and explore to build a classroom teaching quality assurance system based on students' experience, which is "all-round, whole-process, closed-loop and continuous improvement", so as to continuously improve the of classroom teaching, and provide strong support for the high-quality operation of undergraduate teaching.

3 Construction of Undergraduate Classroom Teaching Quality Assurance System Based on Student Experience

In view of the above problems, this paper which applied TQM theory (Total Quality Management) try to build an effective closed-loop classroom teaching quality assurance system based on the principles of objectivity, comprehensiveness, characteristic and scientific nature, and explore to optimize the college classroom teaching quality assurance system based on student experience. This proposed undergraduate classroom teaching quality assurance system is expected to realize the whole-process and dynamic quality monitoring and assurance of the whole classroom teaching.

With reference to the four stages of PDCA ("Plan", "Do (Execute)", "Check" and "Action (Process)") cycle [11], this paper explored and constructed an undergraduate classroom teaching quality evaluation system with continuous improvement function based on student experience in the construction of classroom teaching quality assurance system. Centering on four basic teaching links, namely teaching preparation, teaching implementation, teaching evaluation and teaching feedback, this proposed undergraduate classroom teaching quality assurance system is expected to build a "all-round, whole-process, closed-loop and continuous improvement" classroom teaching quality assurance system, including quality objectives and standards, quality assurance activities, quality analysis and evaluation, quality feedback and improvement, and quality support assurance (as shown in Fig. 1). Based on the dynamic management of classroom teaching quality, this paper has realized the continuous improvement of teaching quality and ensured the spiral rise of classroom teaching quality in the process of paying attention to students' experience.

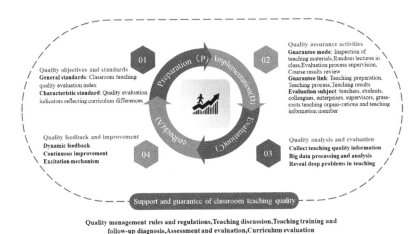

Fig. 1. Classroom teaching quality assurance system of "all-round, whole-process, closed-loop and continuous improvement".

3.1 Quality Objectives and Standards

Construct a classroom teaching quality assurance system with general quality, characteristic quality objectives and standards from multi-levels [12]. The combination of general quality indicators and characteristic quality indicators will jointly build classroom indicators to ensure quality objectives and standards, so that the objectives and contents of the curriculum can not only reflect the generality of school talent training and professional talent training personality, but also reflect the needs of social industries.

3.2 Quality Assurance Activities

This proposal introduces multiple evaluation subjects such as teachers, students, colleagues, enterprises, supervisors, grass-roots teaching organizations and teaching information members [13]. The quality assurance activities of classroom teaching focus on teaching links, such as teaching evaluation, teaching reform projects, teaching training, teaching discussion, teaching diagnosis, assessment and evaluation, excellent teaching selection, teacher honor, etc. These quality assurance activities will play a role in the framework of the school classroom teaching quality assurance system and form a joint force for quality development [14].

3.3 Quality Analysis and Evaluation

The teaching quality information data of each link can be collected and stored through the classroom teaching quality management database [15]. Pay attention to the update and maintenance of teaching quality information, use big data mining technology to do a good job in the comprehensive evaluation and analysis of teaching quality, and strengthen the depth of guarantee and the effectiveness of information application on the basis of the effective use and analysis of quality information and the formation of text materials from quality information.

3.4 Quality Feedback and Improvement

Obtain quality improvement information and suggestions through analysis and evaluation and various ways, and feed them back to departments and teachers in a timely, accurate and efficient manner [16]. Relevant departments establish a linkage mechanism based on problem analysis and solution according to the feedback information, develop rectification plans, and ensure that continuous improvement work is implemented through accountability or incentives [17]. Feedback of teaching quality information focuses on the effectiveness of feedback, and the improvement of teaching focuses on the effectiveness of problem improvement [18].

3.5 Quality Support and Assurance

Innovate the training methods of teachers' teaching ability, attach importance to the improvement and training of teachers' teaching methods and teaching skills, and improve teachers' awareness of high teaching standards and teaching quality in classroom teaching [19].

4 Optimization of Undergraduate Classroom Teaching Quality Assurance System Based on Student Experience

4.1 Construct an Effective Closed-loop of Classroom Teaching Quality Assurance to Strengthen the Breadth and Depth of Assurance

TQM theory advocates the quality assurance system of "all-staff, all-process and all-factor". Most of the existing classroom teaching quality assurance focuses on the classroom teaching process, but not much on teachers' pre-class preparation and post-class improvement. Explore and expand the content of classroom quality assurance, and incorporate the following aspects into the classroom teaching quality assurance system, such as teaching materials, teaching material selection, teacher preparation, assessment methods, reflecting cutting-edge scientific research theories and achievements, answering questions and coaching, assessment methods, etc. This optimization realizes the effective closed-loop of all factors, and extends the quality assurance work to the whole process of talent training [20].

4.2 Establish Classroom Quality Construction Objectives and Standards Combining General Standards and Characteristic Standards

Scientific and reasonable classroom quality objectives and standards play a positive guiding role to stimulate teachers' spontaneity and autonomy in improving classroom teaching quality. Courses of different nature and types often have great differences, and it is difficult to measure all classroom teaching with the same quality evaluation standard. On the basis of strengthening the theoretical research of classroom teaching quality standards, new curriculum quality objectives and standards have been established to improve the refinement and pertinence of quality standards. It includes general standards and characteristic standards, considering the characteristics of specialty and curriculum.

Firstly, improving the relevant management system of classroom teaching quality assurance, the result is to standardize teachers' teaching behavior and improve teaching evaluation methods. Secondly, teachers are invited to formulate classroom quality standards and effective measures for its implementation to further clarify the connotation, responsibilities and specific responsibilities of the quality objectives and standards in each link of classroom teaching. These characteristic quality standard indicators of targeted, characteristic and differentiated classroom quality assurance will further strengthen teachers' subjective awareness and execution of quality assurance. Thirdly, teachers gain the autonomy and independence of quality assurance by participating in the formulation of quality standards, and then truly feel the process of participating in quality assurance.

4.3 Develop Quality Assurance Activities Combining the Process and Result of Multi-agent Evaluation

To improve the evaluation subject of classroom teaching, the new teaching evaluation needs the joint participation of multiple evaluation subjects such as teachers, students, colleagues, enterprises, supervisors, grass-roots teaching organizations and teaching information members. Classroom quality assurance activities should be diversified and have both process evaluation and result evaluation. To guide the evaluation subject to establish a correct evaluation consciousness is conducive to better promote the steady improvement of school classroom teaching quality, and promote the virtuous circle development between teachers and students, rather than accountability [21].

For different evaluation subjects, different evaluation methods are adopted to carry out quality assurance activities. Teachers' self-evaluation makes quality assurance become a part of teachers' classroom teaching activities, transforming classroom teaching quality assurance from work tasks into teachers' conscious actions and endogenous teaching reform motivation. In the self-evaluation, teachers gradually establish a systematic view of talent cultivation and an overall view of quality, deeply understand the position and role of the courses they undertake in the achievement of educational objectives and the overall training system, and effectively perform their first responsibility in the main position of teaching and educating people in the classroom. Students' evaluation of teaching can enable students to participate in the process of teaching and control their own learning, and integrate "teacher's teaching" and "student's learning" in the midst of contradictions [22]. At the same time, in order to improve students' sense of responsibility and interest in teaching evaluation, this proposed creates an evaluation method that students can easily understand and enjoy by streamlining the evaluation content and optimizing the evaluation approach, so that students can truly play the role of ownership in the evaluation of classroom teaching quality [23]. The evaluation of teaching by grass-roots teaching organizations focuses on giving full play to the role of grass-roots teaching organizations in curriculum supply and curriculum quality [24]. Grass-roots teaching organizations can effectively evaluate whether the teaching preparation is scientific and reasonable, in terms of curriculum objectives, teaching materials, teaching material selection, assessment methods, etc. Colleagues' evaluation of teaching constructs a professional perspective to evaluate the teaching process of colleague teachers. Colleagues' evaluation represents the strength of academic community and profession. Colleagues' evaluation is not only the communication and exchange at the professional teaching level, but also the process of mutual cooperation and knowledge exchange among professional teachers [25]. Enterprise expert evaluation of teaching can promote the close integration of professional theoretical knowledge and enterprise production practice, and bring the talent needs of industry enterprises into classroom teaching. This proposal integrates classroom theoretical teaching and practice, tests the knowledge learned in practice, and promotes the integration of industry and education and school-enterprise cooperation. The supervisor's evaluation of teaching aims to grasp the key links of classroom teaching, highlight the supervision and management and give play to the function of diagnosis and guidance [26]. The supervisor's evaluation of teaching focuses on the courses with great differences in students' evaluation, teachers' self-evaluation and colleagues' evaluation to avoid evaluation distortion. The evaluation of teaching by teaching information member helps to collect students' opinions and suggestions on the whole process of classroom teaching, and feed them back to teachers in time. Teachers can adjust teaching content and teaching methods in a short time to improve teaching quality.

4.4 Analysis, Feedback and Continuous Improvement of Quality Management Information

Firstly, establish a classroom teaching quality information management database to ensure that classroom teaching quality monitoring covers the whole process of classroom teaching. It is necessary to carry out regular monitoring of daily teaching activities, and implement effective quality monitoring and tracking by establishing the classroom teaching quality file of each teacher to ensure effective closed-loop and continuous improvement of classroom teaching quality. Secondly, the research and application of classroom teaching quality information based on big data mining technology is the key to the comprehensive evaluation and analysis of classroom teaching quality. Using classroom teaching quality information can effectively excavate the deep problems of classroom teaching and analyze the main problems in classroom teaching. This proposed is expected to provide guidance for schools to further improve the quality of classroom teaching, and provide reference for the development of talent training programs and classroom quality objectives and standards.

4.5 Establish Effective Classroom Teaching Quality Assurance and Incentive Mechanism

First, establish and improve the multi-level quality assurance management system. The quality assurance system can ensure that the daily management system and mechanism of classroom teaching have a practical and effective top-level design, and form an effective closed-loop with evaluation, feedback, improvement and supervision. Secondly, teachers are encouraged to boldly carry out the reform of teaching methods and teaching means. This measure gives teachers the subjectivity in teaching and the initiative in class, and promotes the curriculum construction and curriculum teaching reform by taking the curriculum evaluation as the starting point. Finally, teaching incentive mechanism is an effective way to encourage teachers to participate in teaching. Through the establishment of demonstration classes, first-class classes, teaching competitions, teacher honor system and other activities, teachers are mobilized and encouraged to participate in classroom teaching and improve teaching quality from the material and spiritual levels [27].

5 Key Problems to Be Solved by Undergraduate Classroom Teaching Quality Evaluation System Based on Student Experience

5.1 Differentiated Quality Objectives and Standards

In terms of quality objectives and standards, based on the concept of continuous improvement, add dynamic and flexible characteristic quality indicators with teachers' participation to reflect the differentiated evaluation of courses, and give professional and teachers certain autonomy. Particularly, we should develop characteristic quality evaluation indicators for enterprise classrooms, strengthen the close combination of theoretical knowledge and production practice, and integrate industry standards into curriculum objectives and content.

5.2 Comprehensive Quality Assurance Activities

In terms of quality assurance activities, introduce multiple evaluation subjects such as colleagues, enterprises, grass-roots teaching organizations and teaching informants to enrich the evaluation of quality assurance activities, strengthen the quality monitoring of teaching preparation and teaching results, and ensure that classroom teaching quality monitoring covers the whole process of classroom teaching.

5.3 Effective Quality Assessment and Continuous Improvement

In terms of quality assessment and continuous improvement, quality assessment and comprehensive analysis are carried out based on the combination of quantitative indicators and specific classroom scenes. The evaluation analysis reflects both the static results of classroom teaching activities and the dynamic continuous improvement.

6 Conclusion

The quality of classroom teaching is a process of continuous improvement, improvement and development. This paper proposes to build a classroom teaching quality assurance system based on students' experience, which is "all-around, whole-process, closed-loop, and continuous improvement". This proposed undergraduate classroom teaching quality evaluation system is expected to focus on promoting the implementation and effective operation of classroom teaching, enabling classroom teaching evaluation to play a more important role in improving the quality of classroom teaching and talent cultivation.

Acknowledgements. This research was funded by Department of Education of Guangdong Province, grant number j2jw-C9223037.

References

1. Jones, R.: The student experience of undergraduate students: towards a conceptual framework. J. Furth. High. Educ. **42**(8), 1040–1054 (2018)
2. Zheng, C.: Exploration on the construction of dynamic management mechanism about classroom teaching quality. Sci. Educ. Article Collects **26**(1), 67–70 (2021)
3. Xin, S.: An analysis of the development and characteristics of Holland's mode of guaranteeing the teaching quality of higher education. J. Higher Educ. Manag. **6**(4), 53–58 (2012)
4. Limin, Y., Aixiang, C., Zhuqing, J.: An investigation and analysis of the instructional development of the young teachers in local universities. J. Educ. Sci. Hunan Normal Univ. **16**(1), 82–89 (2017)
5. Junyang, S.: Educational Supervision. Beijing Normal University Press, Beijing (2015)
6. Zhipeng, W., Xiaojie, Y., Xuefang, X.: The research on teaching quality monitoring system of university curriculum under the background of "first-class curriculum." J. Suzhou Educ. Inst. **23**(5), 38–41 (2020)
7. Zhou, M.: Exploration on the mode of "Teachers-students Two Subjects" in the evaluation of classroom teaching in colleges and universities. Jiangsu Sci. Technol. Inf. **16**(1), 63–65 (2019)

8. Dunrong, B., Fan, M.: On student evaluation of teaching and improvement of the teaching quality assurance system in HEIs. J. Higher Educ. **28**(12), 77–83 (2007)
9. Qiliang, Y.: Evaluation for teaching or teaching for evaluation. Educ. Res. **7**(3), 98–103 (2012)
10. Jianyong, Z.: A study of the construction of the student-centered course evaluation system. J. Zhejiang Univ. Technol. (Soc. Sci.) **10**(1), 67–70 (2011)
11. Bertalanffy, L.V.: General system theory: foundations, development, applications. IEEE Trans. Syst. Man Cybern. SMC-**4**(6), 592 (1993)
12. Jin, C., Zhiqiang, T., Dinghong, W.: The establishment of teaching quality monitoring system in secondary institutes of local colleges and universities. Mod. Educ. Sci. **69**(5), 69–73 (2017)
13. Jingjing, X., Weiyi, W.: The operating mechanism of faculty development in Leiden university in the Netherlands. Higher Educ. Dev. Eval. **37**(2), 56–66 (2021)
14. Hui, S.: Research on good course dimension innovation and teaching quality monitoring mechanism construction in the context of big data. Wirel. Int. Technol. **7**(3), 127–129 (2021)
15. Zhentian, L., Qiang, L.: How online teaching can help college classroom revolution: understanding large-scale online teaching under epidemic situation. J. East China Normal Univ. **7**(2), 31–41 (2020)
16. Herazo, J.D., Davin, K.J.: L2 dynamic assessment: an activity theory perspective. Mod. Lang. J. **103**(2), 443–458 (2019)
17. Andujar, A.: Mobile-mediated dynamic assessment: a new perspective for second language development. ReCALL **32**(2), 178–194 (2020)
18. Rico, C.: Constructing learning in translation technology. Interpreter Trans. Trainer **11**(1), 79–95 (2017)
19. Xuzhi, L., Jia, L.: Teaching evaluation methods in Chinese universities and the path reconstruction. Shanghai J. Educ. Eval. **5**(2), 69–74 (2021)
20. Qiaoying, Z.: Examines based on the achievement guidance classroom instruction changes studies. J. Xingtai Polytech. College **36**(3), 8–11 (2019)
21. Prosser, M., Trigwell, K.: Understanding Learning and Teaching: The Experience in Higher Education. Open University Press, Buckingham (1999)
22. Jianfang, Z.: Research and practice of "Student-Centered" internal teaching quality assurance system in colleges and universities. Heilongjiang Res. Higher Educ. **301**(5), 138–141 (2019)
23. Lijun, G.: To the evaluation for teaching: on the teaching evaluation system in local colleges and universities. J. Higher Educ. **37**(6), 68–73 (2016)
24. Lijun, G., Guiyou, J.: The institutionalization plight of peer review in college teaching - an analysis from the perspective of new institutionalism. J. Educ. Sci. Hunan Normal Univ. **18**(3), 100–104 (2019)
25. Shijian, C., Hong, Z.: The connotation of faculty teaching development and its practice path. J. Higher Educ. **37**(8), 35–39 (2016)
26. Shuimei, Y., Hongyu, D., Ning, H.: Improvement of online teaching supervision ability under the background of first-class undergraduate course construction. J. Chengdu Normal Univ. **37**(10), 88–93 (2021)
27. Zefang, D., Xiaohui, W.: Common characteristics of first-class foreign universities' undergraduate education and inspirations-based on their experiences in cultivating outstanding talents. J. Nat. Acad. Educ. Adm. **83**(7), 83–89 (2014)

Research on the Application of Interaction Design in the Digital Education of Traditional Crafts

Hai'ou Yang[✉]

Guangxi Normal University, Guilin 541004, China
19514936@qq.com

Abstract. This paper takes the "The Virtual Simulation Experimental Teaching System of Guangxi Zhuang Traditional Wooden Implements" of the Design Institute of Guangxi Normal University of China as the research object to carry out the application research of interaction design in traditional craft digital education.The paper studies the three main functions of interaction design in the digital education of traditional crafts, and the three functions are in-depth relationship.First,interaction design promotes the achievement of virtual simulation teaching goals for traditional crafts. Firstly, it clarifies the users and their characteristics in the digital education of traditional crafts, analyzes the three main goals of users in the digital education of traditional crafts, and points out the differences of users' goals and motivations in the traditional crafts virtual simulation teaching and the traditional crafts learning in reality, which leads to the uniqueness of the interaction design of the digital education products the of traditional crafts. Then the paper analyzes the traditional craft production activity of Guangxi Zhuang traditional wooden implements, and summarizes the user's behavior, action, operation and interaction needs in digital education products, and then constructs the interaction design framework. Secondly, interaction design improves the usability of traditional process virtual simulation teaching, summarizes the methods to improve usability, such as anticipating the mistakes that students will make and correct the mistakes, predicting user needs to achieve user potential needs, omitting repetitive actions, the simplest tools, and prefabricated design. Thirdly, interaction design enhances user experience. From the perspective of sensory experience, interactive experience and emotional experience, this paper analyzes how the national cultural characteristics of traditional crafts and the characteristics of various crafts provides a unique user experience design method for the experience of digital education of traditional crafts.

Keyword: Interaction Design · Traditional Craft · Digital Education · Virtual Simulation · Application

1 Introduction

In all countries of the world, traditional crafts are the integration of traditional creation systems and conceptual systems of each country. The essence of traditional crafts is the art of life, covering all aspects of clothing, food, housing and transportation; The rich shapes, materials, techniques and cultural images in traditional crafts are a huge resource treasure house of traditional culture. The education of traditional crafts for schools and the public is of great significance for the maintenance of folk customs and the identification and inheritance of culture [1].

At the same time, traditional crafts is an important part of design education.Traditional crafts are the cultural foundation and creative source of contemporary design around the world. In the design education, we should strengthen the study of traditional modeling, skills and creation ideas by offering traditional craft education courses that are in line with the school's reality and local characteristics, and deeply understand the traditional cultural spirit of our nation. Through the study of traditional crafts, we can truly grasp the people's demands for life, culture and aesthetics, and form a design with vitality and broad application space [2]. The education of traditional crafts is not only the inheritance of skills, but also the identification and inheritance of culture.

Traditional crafts are the product of history and the product of the lower level of social productivity development, reflecting the production and life style of the historical era. Traditional crafts use traditional materials, such as wood, bamboo, mud, stone, copper, etc., and use traditional techniques to make various implements through people's hands [2]. With the development of modern machine mass production technology and intelligent production technology, nowadays people mainly use industrial products made of industrial materials in daily life. Yanagi once said: "The fundamental difference between the hand and the machine is that the hand is always connected with the heart, while the machine is not intentional" [3]. However, despite its warmth and refinement, traditional handicrafts no longer represent the main trend of social development. In today's society, it declines and even gradually disappears. For example, the Japanese government promulgated the "Traditional Craft Industry Revitalization Plan" in 1974; In March 2017, the Ministry of Culture, the Ministry of Industry and Information Technology and the Ministry of Finance of China jointly formulated the Revitalization Plan of Chinese Traditional Crafts to promote the inheritance and revitalization of Chinese traditional crafts [2]; Among them, popular education and professional education of traditional crafts are effective ways. However, there are many problems in the process of implementing traditional craft education. For example, how traditional crafts learners practice and experience traditional crafts. As mentioned above, traditional crafts need protection and development in today's society and are not common in daily life.it is the most common way to practice and learn traditional crafts at places where traditional crafts gather (such as museums, folk museums, traditional craft training institutions, Intangible Cultural Heritage Workshop, etc.) However, due to the short learning time and the lack of in-depth learning, there is little effect on the practical learning of traditional crafts.

2 Digital Education of Traditional Crafts

With the development and application of digital technology, the digitization of traditional crafts has become a new and more effective method and way for traditional crafts education. Simple ones, such as traditional crafts in the form of text, pictures, videos and web pages, for the purpose of preservation, display and education [4]. The disadvantage of this digital way is that it can only be watched, not interactive experience. Virtual simulation is a more effective, interactive, immersive experience. It uses 3D simulation, 2D animation and mathematical modeling technology and component development technology, and uses Unity 3D, 3D Studio Max, Visual Studio and other development tools to build a 360-degree virtual scene, to achieve the best interactive experience of free viewing and free control [5]. In the field of traditional culture, there is a growing tendency to use digital forms for display and education. The advantage of digitization is that it can better protect precious cultural relics that are easily damaged and can display traditional culture on a wider scale; it is also a new form of innovation of traditional culture.

Digital teaching of traditional crafts, especially virtual simulation technology, can not only improve the interactive operation experience of traditional craft teaching, but also have more advantages. During the epidemic prevention and control period, it is suitable for online teaching. It can effectively reduce the high cost caused by the purchase and loss of equipment and materials in the real traditional crafts practice teaching. At the same time, digital teaching is not affected by the place and region, and it spreads more widely. Teachers and students only need a computer to carry out teaching and learning, which can enable students to repeatedly learn and practice at any time on mobile devices such as computers or mobile tablets. Learning is more flexible and education benefits are broader.

However, there are obvious differences between virtual and reality. Virtual is an advanced human-computer interface that can simulate the behavior of seeing, hearing and touching in reality. Reality is the existence of the upper layer, and virtual is the existence of the lower layer. The virtual relies on a certain simulation system (hardware and software) as the reality of the upper layer [6]. For example, there is a difference between the information of reality and the information of virtual existence. The information of reality, as the upper existence, is larger than that of virtual existence. Virtual reality, as a subset of the amount of information in reality, is the relationship between the included part and the whole; Another example is the lack of background and head up information display in reality, which is more inclined to gradually explore, fuzzy feedback, and reflect information and conditions through indirect hidden attributes (for example, when assembling objects, there is no display of what to assemble next, and the saw cutting wood is an indirect physical examination, which is determined by feeling and experience),while virtual is a deterministic by numerical display of background and header information; Another example is that in reality, people complete their behaviors and tasks through human body organs and minds, with the help of real tools, in the face of real objects, while virtual is that people complete their behaviors and tasks by controlling the mouse, keyboard and some sensing devices, such as hand axis, VR glasses, etc., through controlling the buttons, sliders and other control parts of the interface.

There is such a big difference between virtual and reality, so how the virtual simulation system can help teachers and students achieve the teaching and learning objectives of traditional crafts, rather than lead to the inability to complete tasks and behaviors; improving the usability of the virtual simulation system in the teaching process, rather than making teachers and students feel stupid and unable to operate the virtual system; enhancing the sense of experience, rather than being busy, becomes the key to the success of the virtual simulation system. The theory and method of interaction design may be the effective way [7]. The following is the research on the application of interaction design in traditional craft digital education, taking the "Virtual Experimental Teaching System of Guangxi Zhuang Traditional Wooden Implements" of the Design Institute of Guangxi Normal University of China as the research object.

3 Interaction Design Promotes the Achievement of Virtual Simulation Teaching Goals for Traditional Crafts

3.1 Define the User of Interaction Design

The core of interaction design is behavior design, and behavior is the behavior of human. Therefore, It is primary to define the users of the virtual simulation system. In the virtual simulation experiment teaching system of Guangxi Zhuang traditional wooden implements, the main users are teachers and students of design major in colleges and universities. However, as a digital product with open network, its users are far more than university personnel. Anyone who is interested in Guangxi Zhuang traditional wooden implements and wants to know about them may become a secondary user of the product. Finally, it also includes some stakeholders, such as system management and maintenance personnel, system developers, etc.

3.2 Analyze Behavioral Goals and Motivations

There must be some kind of goals and motivation behind the user's behavior. The ultimate purpose of interaction design is not to complete a series of tasks and behaviors of users, but to achieve users' goals, so that digital products can improve user's satisfaction. User's goal is the key to design interactive behavior [8]. When we set goals, we should first meet the goals of the main users - the teachers and students of design majors in university and then try to meet the needs of secondary users.

The key is to distinguish the differences in user goals and motivations between the virtual simulation teaching of traditional crafts and the learning of traditional crafts in reality [9]. Take the "virtual simulation experiment teaching system of Guangxi Zhuang traditional wooden implements" as an example the main users are teachers and students majoring in design. For teaching, the teaching goal does not need to be like a special craft apprentice, to really master the various skills of wooden implements [9]; For teachers and students majoring in design, the goal is:

First. Focus on experience education and thinking training: the goal is to be able to understand the manufacturing process of Guangxi Zhuang traditional wooden implements, complete the basic processing and assembly skills, and understand the working principle and creation wisdom of some Guangxi Zhuang traditional wooden implements.

Second. To stimulate students 'interest in learning, to guide students to have interest and motivation to try the real woodworking skills.

Third. A transition allows learners, especially those who are afraid of mechanical processing, to become familiar with woodworking operations through virtual experiments and become less afraid of woodworking, and then carry out physical operations.

3.3 Behavior and Needs Analysis

The realization of the goal requires the user to perform a series of tasks. Donald Norman believes that activities are composed of tasks, tasks are composed of behaviors, and behaviors are composed of operations. Users have many needs in a series of actions to complete tasks. The interaction designer needs to meet the user's behavior and needs in completing the task [8].

In the Zhuang area of Guangxi, people carry out the activity of making wooden implements, which is usually composed of tasks such as size design, wood selection, tool selection, parts processing and assembly. Each task contains a series of actions. The practice in reality is that the carpenter truly completes the action, and the virtual simulation system is through the digital method, through the three-dimensional software to reproduce all the scenes, tools, equipment, etc. while the virtual simulation system reproduces all the scenes, tools, equipment, etc. that appear in the process of making wooden tools and implements through the digital method, and creates the interface and operation control of user's various actions through software programming and interaction design, and the user completes the action in the interface. When setting the action and operation, it is necessary to pay attention to the difference between the traditional craft teaching goal and the master craft goal. The teaching goal mainly lies in experience and thinking [10]. The following is an analysis of the behavior and needs of "the Virtual Experimental Teaching System of Guangxi Zhuang Traditional Wooden Implements":

Analyze the Behavior and Needs of Size Design. The teaching goal of size design: the purpose of artificial objects is to be used and operated by people, and the parameters of human body are an important source of the size of artificial creation. In the teaching of size design, the size design of traditional implement is mainly carried out by measuring human body parameters. The characteristics of body shape parameters of Guangxi Zhuang people are the important basis for Guangxi Zhuang wooden implements. In teaching, the parameters of different parts of the human body should be measured as the reference for the functional size of the implement according to the contact between the wooden implement and different parts of the human body, and the specific meaning and measurement range of the implement corresponding to different parts of the human body should be clear when measuring the human body parameters (Table 1).

Analyze the Behavior and Needs of Wood Selection. The teaching goal of wood selection: material is the foundation of creation, and different materials determine the function, structure and shape of the appliance. When designing and making implement, the appropriate wood shall be selected according to the use function, load bearing, environmental impact, etc., combined with the density, hardness, anti-corrosion and other properties of different wood. Students need to understand the characteristics of wood and master the thinking of selecting wood. According to the analysis, wood selection is more suitable for teachers and students to choose teaching and learning in the form of text and pictures (Table 2).

Analyze the Behavior and Needs of Tools Selection. The teaching goal of tools selection: the distinctive feature of traditional craft is handmade, and the tools used for handmade are the basis of traditional craft. After thousands of years of development and evolution, Guangxi Zhuang people have invented and mastered a large number of

Table 1. Analyze the behavior and needs of size design

Action	Operation	Interactive needs
Determine the size measurement of the human body model	Choose male and female, choose height, choose sitting posture	1. The interface for selecting the gender, height and posture of the human model;
Use measuring tools to measure the size of human body parts	Determine the human body parts, measuring the starting point to the end of the size	2. The human body model display; 3. The measurement space can rotate 720°, Zoom Out、 Zoom In and translation;
Get body size data	Read data, record data	4. Measuring tools with "point-to-point" measurement and accurate reading; 5. Record human body parameters

Table 2. Analyze the behavior and needs of wood selection

Action	Operation	Interactive needs
Choose wood	Select the appropriate wood from the wood library of Guangxi Zhuang nationality commonly used	1. A material warehouse for storing different timbers, which is easy to select and view; 2. Display the characteristics of wood in the form of text, pictures and 3D models
Understanding Wood Properties	View the wood properties, like tree type, wood grain, density, Anti-corrosion	

ingenious wooden tools. Different woodworking tools have their unique functions and modeling processing ability. In teaching, appropriate wooden tools should be selected according to the requirements of material hardness and the modeling requirements, and the processing technology of each tool should be mastered (Table 3).

The tools are also selected in the form of text and animation, and in the form of database for teachers and students to choose teaching and learning.

Table 3. Analyze the behavior and needs of tools selection

Action	Operation	Interactive needs
Choose traditional woodworking tools	Select the appropriate tools from the traditional woodworking tool library	1. The tool library for storing different tools is easy to select and view
Understand traditional tool features	View the function, structure and usage of various tools	2. Explain the characteristics of tools with words and pictures 3. Display the appearance and structure of woodworking tools in the form of 3D models 4. Animation shows the processing method of woodworking tools

Analyze the Behavior and Needs of Parts Processing of Traditional Wooden Implement. Teaching objectives of parts processing: due to the different shapes and structures of different parts on different wooden implements, the processing process and tools used will be different, so this part adopts the form of concrete cases and virtual simulation interactive operation for teaching. In the teaching, it is required to select the appropriate processing tools according to the shape and structure of wooden components, and master the processing methods and processes of each tool. Let's take the long coaming of the fire bucket stool which is a traditional daily implement of Guangxi Zhuang as an example to analyze (Table 4).

Table 4. Analyze the behavior and needs of parts processing

Action	Operation	Interactive needs
Cut logs into squares	Select ink bucket - fix ink stick - snap line - select saw - cut	1. Processing operation interface, it can show the parts being processed in all directions
Cut the square timber thin	Select ink bucket - fix ink stick - snap line - select saw - cut	2. Display woodworking tool library, store common woodworking tools, which can be extracted at any time
Outer arc forming	Elect ink bucket - fix ink stick - snap line - select saw - cut-Select plane- shaping with plane	3. Processing flow prompt bar that can be referenced at any time
Inner arc forming	Select ink bucket - fix ink stick - snap line - select shovel - chisel - select inner circle planer - planer smooth	4. The final processing effect of the part is displayed in 3D mode, which can be rotated and zoomed in
Finish machining	Select ink bucket - fix ink stick - snap line - select saw - cut - select planer - planer forming - select drill - drill hole	

Analyze the Behavior and Needs of Assembly of Traditional Wooden Implement. The final part of the production of wooden implement is to assemble each component. Each wooden implement has a unique assembly sequence due to its unique structure and function. In the teaching, it is required to disassemble the whole wooden implement to understand the basic framework and the composition of each component. and it can be reassembled completely to Achieve the teaching goal of understanding traditional implement. Let's take the brocade machine of Guangxi Zhuang traditional wooden implements as an example to analyze the assembly action and operation of the implements (Table 5).

Table 5. Analyze the behavior and needs of assembly

Action	Operation	Interactive needs
Assembly of left foot pedal mechanism	Select lever I - place on crossbar I - select pull rope I - place on lever I - select pedal I - place on pull rope I	1. In order to meet the needs of students' self-study, it should have the function of automatic decomposition and assembly, which is convenient for students to observe and learn;
Assembly of right foot pedal mechanism	Select lever II - place on crossbar II - select pull rope II - place on lever II - select pedal II - place on pull rope II	2. In order to meet the needs of students' test requirement, it should have the function of manual assembly
Assembly of bamboo cage	Select the bamboo cage - place it on the front of lever II	3.Assembly operation platform occupying the main space, and can be rotated at 720° for viewing;
Assembly of jacquard system	Select Jacquard thread - place it on the bamboo cage - select bamboo needle - orderly pass through the Jacquard thread according to the pattern shape and fix it on the bamboo cage	4. Brocade machine parts library for students to choose when testing and assembling;
Assembly of plain system	Select the heald wire - wear to the rod - hang to the front of the lever by pulling the rope	5. The assembly process guidance is convenient for students to forget the assembly sequence when testing and learning
Assembly of seat plate	Select the seat plate-place on the bracket seat plate	

3.4 Interaction Design Framework

According to the above behavior and demand analysis, it provides the basis for the next frame design. The advantage of the design framework is that it can focus on the overall structure of the user interface and related behaviors at a high level to ensure the realization of user goals. The following is an example of the construction of the interactive framework of the virtual experimental teaching system of Guangxi Zhuang traditional wooden implements.After confirming the final interaction framework, the framework of digital product interface design is also established, and the low fidelity model can be used for the preliminary design of the interface. However, the final interface design needs to fully consider the ease of use and emotional experience of users using digital products (Fig. 1).

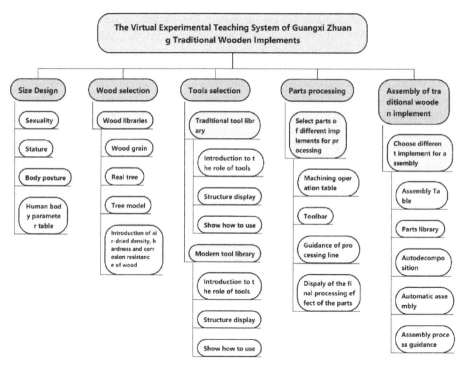

Fig. 1. The interaction design framework of "The virtual simulation experimental teaching system of Guangxi Zhuang traditional wooden implements"

4 Interaction Design Improves the Usability of Traditional Crafts Virtual Simulation Teaching

Good interaction design is not only satisfied with the successful completion of the user 's goal, but also to improve the user 's ease of use and good experience in the process of achieving the task, so that users feel easy to operate, improve efficiency and fun.The ease of use we discuss here does not refer to the ease of use of general digital products. For example, the browsing bar is pulled smoothly, the button click is responsive, the window pops up quickly, the mouse cursor is positioned accurately, and it is easy to find when returning to the previous page. We mainly focus on the special field of digital educational products of traditional crafts, and find some design strategies to improve the usability of teachers and students.Taking the Virtual Simulation Experimental Teaching System of Guangxi Zhuang Traditional Wooden Implements as an example, the design strategies to improve the usability of digital products are as follows:

4.1 Anticipate the Mistakes that Students will Make and Correct the Mistakes

The production of traditional wooden implements of the Zhuang nationality in Guangxi is a very complicated thing in reality, which is full of various operational behaviors and movements, and requires skilled craftsmen to complete it successfully. For the beginners of wooden implements, it is inevitable to forget the content and order of action. It is easy to make mistakes in the process of learning this skill. Unless there is an old craftsman nearby to guide you, there will be no one to help you predict the wrong behavior and correct the wrong. In the virtual simulation system, developers and designers can predict the mistakes that students will make, remind students through interactive design, correct mistakes in time, and make learning tasks proceed smoothly [4]. For example, in the process of parts processing, it is easy to happen for students to choose the wrong processing tool because of their lack of understanding and application of traditional processing tools; For example, when assembling wooden implements, students will easily forget the assembly sequence and choose the wrong parts due to the complex structure and various parts; in the interaction design, if the students choose the wrong processing tools or parts, the system will show red, accompanied by a short buzzer, reminding the user that the error needs to be corrected (Fig. 2).

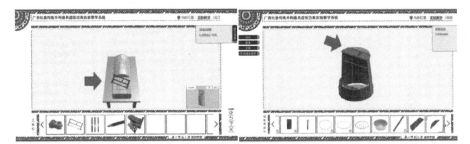

Fig. 2. If the students choose the wrong processing tools or parts, the system will show red, accompanied by a short buzzer, reminding the user that the error needs to be corrected

4.2 Anticipate the Needs of Teachers and Students

The greatest advantage of designers is empathy [8]. Through research methods such as user interviews, observation and personal experience of designers, we can find out the potential needs of users, and help users realize these needs in interactive design, which will greatly improve users' trust and experience of digital products.

For example, the processing and assembly process is complicated, and students easily forget the execution content and sequence of the action. At the development and design stage, we can add processing process and assembly process prompt bar windows to prompt students with short text descriptions. However, some students have strong learning ability and do not want to be prompted. In this way, the prompt window can be designed to expand or retract, which can effectively promote students' self-learning and facilitate students' self-test.

There are some hidden requirements in the teaching process of traditional crafts, which may need to be discovered several times. If the system can develop functions that teachers and students themselves are not aware of, it will greatly improve the usability of digital products. For example, we found that the difficulty of assembling wooden implements may lie in the variety of the same parts, which makes students confused during the assembly process. How to make students not confused, you can design the form of parts library. The same parts are presented in the form of groups, and have the counting function. If the student complete one piece of assembly, the same parts group minus one, so that the student can clearly know how many pieces are left (FIg. 3).

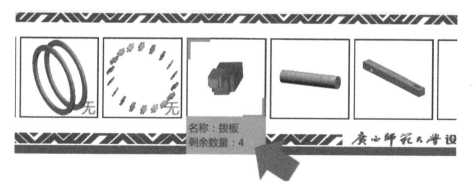

Fig. 3. The system automatically calculates the number of plates and there are four pieces left

4.3 Simplified Design Method

The task is only a means to achieve the result, and the goal is the ultimate goal. Usually, the fewer the tasks, the better, the simpler the operation, the better [8]. The processing and production of wooden implements in reality is very complicated. For apprentices in reality, it is necessary to master every detail of every link. However, for students majoring in design in colleges and universities, focusing on experience and thinking training, it is not necessary to limit them to too complicated details. as long as they summarize the main tasks and extract important behaviors.

Omitting the Repetitive Actions of the Traditional Craft Production. In the interactive behavior design of virtual simulation system, it is different from the traditional process production behavior in reality. For example, in reality, it is necessary to repeat the same actions continuously in order to master the manufacturing technology of wooden implements. For these repetitive processing behaviors, the omitted design method can be adopted in the virtual simulation system to allow the system to automatically complete repetitive tasks and actions, so as to reduce monotonous repetitive actions, ensure the smooth and continuous rhythm of teachers 'teaching and students' operation, and maintain continuous interest in learning (Fig. 4).

Taking the Simplest Tool Design. Norman put forward "Activity-Centered Design" (ACD), which emphasizes that we should understand and attach importance to activities first[8].He believes that understanding how people adapt to the tools at hand and the activities carried out using tools can better affect the design of tools. This principle is also applicable in digital traditional craft education. In the experiment of human body parameter measurement, one of the teaching purposes is to let students understand the specific meaning of human body parts, such as height, which is the distance from the bottom of the foot to the top of the head. The measuring tool can take the advantages of digitalization and adopt the "Point-To-Point" automatic reading tool design, that is, as long as you click once on the bottom of your foot and then on the top of your head, you can automatically recognize the precise height value of the human body (Fig. 5).

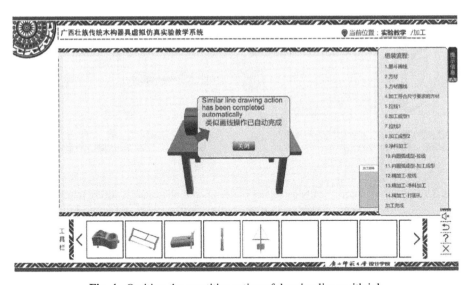

Fig. 4. Omiting the repetitive action of drawing lines with ink

Prefabricated Design. Just like prefabricated food, it is designed for young people who cannot cook and want to eat nutritious food. In traditional crafts, there are often some complex skills that require years of painstaking cultivation before they can be skilled for the inheritors of traditional crafts in reality, it is necessary to master these complex skills. However, for learners of digital education of traditional crafts, with the goal of experience and thinking training, they cannot quickly master complex traditional skills, but want to

Fig. 5. Adopting the "point-to-point" automatic reading tool design

experience and master thinking methods, so we can adopt prefabricated design methods. That is, semi-finished products are made in advance and can be completed as long as they are slightly processed in the later stage. prefabricated interactive design method has been adopted in the virtual simulation experiment teaching system of Guangxi Zhuang traditional wooden implements. For example, in the assembly task of the fire bucket stool, due to the complex structure of the fire bucket stool, there are more than 40 parts. If students assemble one part by one, it will be very difficult. Therefore, the developer has designed a transparent framework to complete the assembly. Students only need to find the correct parts and put them in the correct position according to the correct assembly sequence. Through this prefabricated transparent framework, students can not only quickly complete the assembly task of the fire bucket stool, but also master its structure and assembly method, achieving the goal of the entire traditional craft education (Fig. 6).

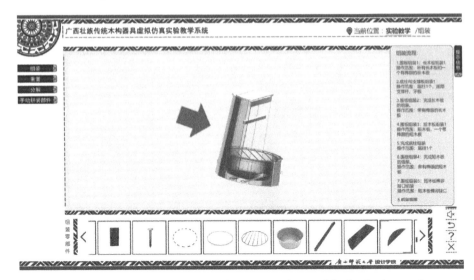

Fig. 6. The prefabricated design of transparent frame of the fire bucket stool

5   Interaction Design Enhances User Experience

User experience is the cognitive impression and response of people to the products, systems or services they use or expect to use, and it is a subjective feeling established by users in the process of using products. It is still not enough to realize the ease of use of digital products. Ease of use is a necessary condition to enhance the user experience. The realization of ease of use does not necessarily bring a good experience to users. Designers need to pay more attention to the user's experience and emotional experience. The following is an analysis of ways to enhance the experience of teachers and students in the special field of traditional craft digital education:

5.1   The Sensory Experience of Traditional Craft Digital Education Products

In digital products, people will make instinctive psychological and emotional reactions to visual and sensory aspects before deeply interacting with products. The user's instinctive reaction will make emotional judgments on whether the product is beautiful or ugly, good or bad, safe or dangerous. Traditional crafts have natural advantages in the extraction of experience elements. Because most of the traditional crafts have rich ethnic and regional characteristics, the ethnic and regional cultural elements behind the traditional crafts can be applied to the interface design of the digital education. In the virtual simulation experiment teaching system of Guangxi Zhuang traditional wooden implements, the application design of Zhuang culture is emphasized on the visual appearance, such as Guangxi Zhuang bronze drum, Zhuang brocade pattern, Zhuang dyed cloth blue and other visual elements, which are repeatedly used in the interface decoration and control key pattern of the virtual simulation system, so that the virtual simulation system has a unified Zhuang cultural characteristics as a whole; In terms of sound design, you can choose whether to play Zhuang background music to give learners an immersive Zhuang cultural atmosphere. At the same time, in the process of processing parts with some woodworking tools, some sound designs will also be used together, such as the sound of the planer cutting the wood particles in the process of smoothing the wood, the "thump" sound of the hammer in the process of tapping the shovel for hole processing, and so on (Fig. 7).

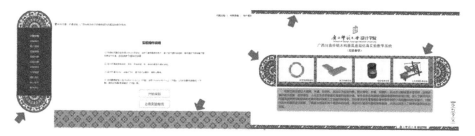

Fig. 7. The application of the culture elements of Guangxi Zhuang

5.2 Interactive Experience of Traditional Craft Digital Education Products

The digital product interface gives users the experience of the use process, emphasizing interactional characteristics. Not only set up regular online questions, class discussion forums, students and teachers, students and students can interact and discuss the problems encountered in the learning process, but also design more interesting interaction forms. For example, in the study of traditional wooden mortise and tenon structure, students can quickly grasp the design principle of mortise and tenon through detachable and assembled interactive mode. Another example is that in the principle display of traditional implements, users can click the mouse to drive the mechanical movement of the implements, such as the mouse click, the water wheel of the water hammer turns up (Figs. 8 and 9).

5.3 Emotional Experience of Traditional Craft Digital Education Products

It is difficult to master any traditional craft unless you are determined to learn it or are particularly interested in some craft. In reality, the manufacturing technology of Zhuang traditional wooden implements is a skill that needs years of learning to master. However, through the virtual experiment system, students can quickly get started and successfully complete the whole process of traditional crafts, so that users feel themselves very smart. It stimulates the interest of design students in learning, and guides students to have interest and courage to try real woodworking skills. This also achieved the original goal of digital education in traditional crafts. At the same time, for advanced technologies such as digitalization, and for art students who are relatively insensitive to technology, they may feel strange, boring and profound when they first contact with virtual simulation system. in terms of interface design, tool design, situation design, etc., It may be better to adopt a style that is familiar to students and looks simple, don't let students feel that the virtual experiment system is difficult to use and learn.

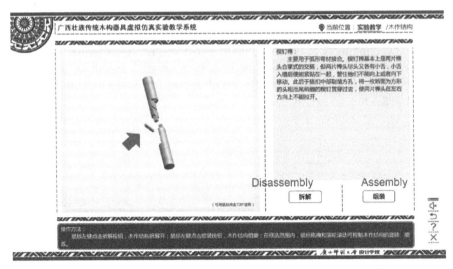

Fig. 8. The interactive mode of Chinese mortise and tenon structure that can be disassembled and assembled

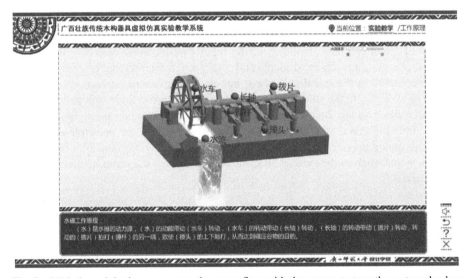

Fig. 9. Click the red dot button next to the water flow with the mouse to turn the water wheel up

6   Conclusion and Outlook

In the computer age, almost infinite behavior can be made through software programming, which has completely changed the form and nature of everything in the world [8]. In the field of traditional culture, there is also a growing tendency to use digital forms for display and education. Digitalization can display traditional culture in a wider range, and it is also a new form of innovation of traditional culture.

Traditional crafts are an important part of the traditional culture of all nationalities in the world. Digital display and education are bound to better inherit, innovate and disseminate the traditional crafts of all nationalities in the world. This paper takes the virtual simulation teaching of traditional wooden implements of Guangxi Zhuang in China as an example to analyze the digital education, highlighting the role of interaction design in digital education again, especially in the field of traditional crafts digital education. This paper explains the methods of user analysis and user goal analysis in traditional crafts digital education, analyzes in detail the methods of extracting and summarizing interaction behaviors, actions, operations and user needs from the actual traditional crafts production process, and constructs the interaction framework accordingly. This paper has repeatedly emphasized that due to the different goals of students learning traditional crafts in digital education and apprentices learning traditional crafts in reality, as well as the advantages of digital technology, design and thinking, it provides interactive design methods such as error prediction, demand prediction, and simplest design for the ease of use of digital education of traditional crafts. At the same time, combined with the national cultural characteristics of traditional crafts and the characteristics of various crafts themselves, it provides a unique emotional experience design method for the experience of digital education of traditional crafts.

Finally, the author wants to explain that the digital education of traditional crafts is not the end. As mentioned above, through the digital education of traditional crafts, the learners of traditional crafts have mastered the basic operation process and action points of traditional crafts, understood the thinking of traditional crafts, and then stimulated the public 's interest in traditional crafts. Then they are willing and dare to really contact and learn the traditional crafts production technology, and carry out innovative design, which is the real purpose of the inheritance and innovation of traditional crafts digital education.

Acknowledgement. This paper is the initial result of the scientific research project of Guangxi Humanities and Social Sciences Development Research Center in 2019, "Research on Woodworking Implements under the Background of New Countryside - Taking the Rural Areas of Northern Guangxi as an Example" (Project No.: XNC2019001). This paper is the initial result of the project" Research and Innovation Design Transformation Practice of Traditional Folk Implements in Nanling Corridor "(Project No.: GXKT202010) of the 2020 annual project of Guixue Research Institute, the key research base of humanities and social sciences in Guangxi colleges and universities. This paper is the initial result of the 2021 Guangxi University Young and Middle-aged Teachers 'Scientific Research Basic Ability Improvement Project "Research on the Creation Thought and Innovative Design of Traditional Folk Implements in Northern Guangxi "(Project No.: 2021KY0027); This paper is the initial result of the 2022 Guangxi Higher Education Undergraduate Teaching Reform Project" Exploration and Practice of National Traditional Implements Inheritance and Innovative Design Talents Training Based on Virtual Simulation Teaching Platform "(Project No.: 2022JGB124).

References

1. Pan, L.: Traditional craft is the treasure of design education. J. Chinese Art (Z1), 1 (2018). .(in Chinese)

2. Li, Y.: The contemporary and regional nature of traditional arts and crafts -- on the protection and development of traditional arts and crafts. J. Nanjing Arts Inst. (Art and Design Edition) (01), 5–9 (2008). (in Chinese)
3. Yanagi, translated by Zhang Lu, Japanese Crafts. Guangxi Normal University Press, Guilin (2006). 4
4. Akhmetshina, G.R.: Methods of actualisation of traditional arts and crafts as the bases of creative self-realisation of design students. J. Revista San Gregorio **25**, 87–93 (2018)
5. Chen, R., Ashutosh Sharma: Construction of complex environmental art design system based on 3D virtual simulation technology. J. Int. J. Syst. Assur. Eng. 1–8 (2021)
6. Guo, Ch.: Exploration and practice of virtual simulation technology in art teaching in colleges and universities. J. Educ. J. **4**(04) (2021)
7. Hong, E.: Providing a direction to interactive design education according to the changes in it environment -focusing on college education. J. Dig. Converg. **12**(4), 265–276 (2014)
8. Cooper. A.: Translated by Ni Weiguo, About Face 4:The Essentials of Interaction Design. Electronic Industry Press, Beijing (2015)
9. Rahmatina, R.F., Yulia, S.S., Dwi, S.P., Fauzan, A., Naila, F.: Interactive design of physics learning media: the role of teachers and students in a teaching innovation. J. Phys. **2309**(01) (2022)
10. Huang, Z.: Interactive design and management method of art teaching system in colleges and universities under the background of big data. J. Math. Probl. Eng. (2022)

Trends in Research Related to Product Design for Rural Teaching from 2012 to 2022: A Bibliometric and Knowledge Mapping Analysis

Xing Yuan[1,2,3], Yang Zhao[3(✉)], Yixin Xie[4], Liuyi Wu[2], and Tiantian Wang[2]

[1] Kyiv National University of Technologies and Design, Kyiv 01011, Ukraine
[2] School of Culture and Media, Hezhou University, Hezhou 542899, China
[3] The College of Design and Art, Shaanxi University of Science and Technology, Xi'an, Shaanxi 710021, China
515428420@qq.com
[4] School of Design, Guangxi Normal University, Guilin 541006, China

Abstract. Aim: To retrospect the global trends in and explore hotspots of Product design for rural teaching research. **Methods:** Therefore, a bibliometric analysis was conducted using the Web of Science Core Collection to examine the publication trends of Product Design for Rural Teaching in various academic journals. The data was analyzed using the VOSviewer version 1.6.14 software, generating an information map which incorporated keywords, journals, countries, international collaborations, authors, research hotspots, and the focus area of Product Design for Rural Teaching. **Results:** A thorough examination of the Web of Science Core Collection database revealed that there were a total of 211 publications in the realm of product design for rural education published between the years 2012 and 2022. The number of publications in 2012 was 10, while in 2022, it rose to 29, indicating a remarkable growth in the volume of research output in this area over the past decade. China emerged as the leading country in terms of publication numbers, followed by the United States and Brazil. **Conclusion:** Based on a review of the latest trends in Web of Science Core Collection data, it was found that the "Attitude", "Student", "Concern", and "Growth" are prominent themes in the field of rural education product development. The aim of rural education product design is to enhance teaching effectiveness and learning motivation through optimized and upgraded methods and instructional materials. These findings can provide valuable insights and guidance for education researchers and designers in improving the product design process in rural education.

Keywords: Product design for rural teaching · Ten-year trends · bibliometric analysis · VOSviewer

1   Introduction

"Product Design for Rural Education" encompasses the creation of educational materials and tools that are suitable for use in rural educational settings, including rural classrooms and teaching aids, as well as educational games for subjects such as parasitology [1]. The field of academic research in this area has explored various aspects of "rural teaching products," including the relationship between teaching and these products, the educational meaning they convey, and the balancing of traditional and modern teaching methods, all with the goal of promoting sustainable educational value [2].

Over the past decade, numerous research articles on the subject of Product Design for Rural Education have been published in various academic journals. This study employs bibliometric analysis and knowledge graph techniques to examine the trend of development in the field of Product Design for Rural Education, utilizing the Web of Science Core Collection database as the source of information. Bibliometric analysis, as a method of evaluating and quantifying relevant literature, uses mathematical and statistical methods to achieve its objectives [3]. This study aims to quantitatively measure the profiles, the most influential articles, and the clusters of keywords in the field of Product Design for Rural Education.

In order to comprehensively assess the state and trends of research in the area of product design for rural education between 2012 and 2022, this study employs VOSviewer, a scientifically robust econometric software, to visually analyze the Web of Science database search results. The analysis aims to identify key research topics within the field and provide a summary of the major research hotspots and trends. The findings of this analysis can serve as valuable references for future research in this area.

2   Materials and Methods

2.1   Data Source and Research Strategy

In this study, we conducted a search of the Web of Science Core Collection (https://www.webofscience.com/), a highly regarded academic database widely utilized for bibliometric and scholarly research.

The data collection process was carried out on February 8, 2023, using the search terms "Product design for rural teaching" and "Rural teaching product". The time frame for the data search was set between January 1, 2012, and December 31, 2022, and was limited to articles written in English. The retrieved data was stored in a tab-delimited file format, including the full record and cited references, to facilitate further analysis. The basic information extracted from each document included the author, keywords, title, abstract, and other relevant details.

2.2   Bibliometric and Visualized Analysis

VOSviewer version 1.6.14 (https://www.vosviewer.com/) is a free software tool developed by the Center for Science and Technology Studies (CWTS) for constructing and displaying bibliometric maps. These node-link diagrams can represent researchers, scientific journals, specific publications, or relevant terms and can be constructed based on co-authorship, co-citation, or co-occurrence relationships [4].

Based on a comprehensive analysis of the Web of Science Core Collection, a total of 211 peer-reviewed articles with complete research findings were identified. An econometric analysis and visualization metrics were performed to uncover the following insights: (1) The decade-long publishing trend; (2) The most influential academic institutions; (3) The leading authors in the field; (4) The top 10 highly published and cited countries; (5) The prominent source journals contributing to the research; (6) The highly co-occurring keywords in the research.

3   Results

3.1   Analysis of Annual Publication Volumes

Based on the analysis of data collected from the Web of Science Core Collection, the trend of published research articles related to "Product Design for Rural Teaching" has been examined over the period of 2012 to 2022. The results reveal an increasing trend in the number of published articles, with the count rising from 10 in 2012 to 29 in 2022 (see Fig. 1). The minimum number of articles was recorded in 2013, with a count of 9, while the highest number was observed in 2018, with 32 articles. These findings highlight the growing interest in this field of study and demonstrate a growing need for further research in the area of Product Design for Rural Teaching.

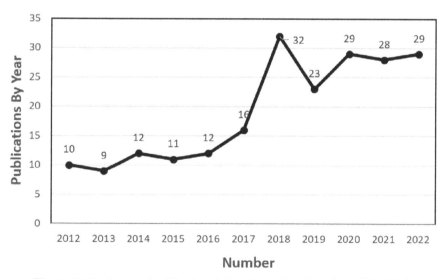

Fig. 1. Publication trends of Product design for rural teaching from 2010–2019.

3.2 Source Country Analysis

The country-by-country analysis indicates that 211 research documents have been produced by authors from 109 different countries and regions. The top 10 countries and regions with the largest number of contributing authors are detailed in Table 1, with China having the highest number of authors (43, 20.379%), followed by the United States (42, 19.905%) and Brazil (20, 9.479%).

Citations are widely recognized as a crucial metric for evaluating the academic impact of research. The analysis of citations reveals that the United States leads with the highest number of citations (1015 times cited), followed by China (750 times cited) and England (710 times cited).

The results of the inter-country collaboration analysis in the field of Product design for rural education demonstrate the extent of collaboration between nations with significant scientific strengths in this area. The criteria for inclusion were set as a minimum of 2 documents per country or region. Out of the 109 countries and regions that engaged in Product design for rural education research, 48 satisfied this requirement. The size of each node represents the impact of the corresponding country, while the distance and thickness of the connecting lines indicate the extent of their collaboration in the field of Product design for rural education. The United States and China emerged as the two nations with the highest degree of collaboration, partnering with countries such as Nigeria, the United Kingdom, Brazil, Germany, Australia, and Romania. This highlights that geographical distance does not impede cooperation between nations in this field (see Fig. 2).

Table 1. Top 10 countries/regions in Product design study for rural teaching, 2012–2022.

Rank	Country/region	Count (%)	Times Cited
1	China	43 (20.379%)	750
2	Usa	42 (19.905%)	1015
3	Brazil	20 (9.479%)	632
4	England	18 (8.531%)	710
5	Nigeria	18 (8.531%)	190
6	Australia	16 (7.583%)	545
7	India	15 (7.109%)	85
8	Spain	15 (7.109%)	490
9	Belgium	14 (6.635%)	606
10	Germany	43 (20.379%)	750

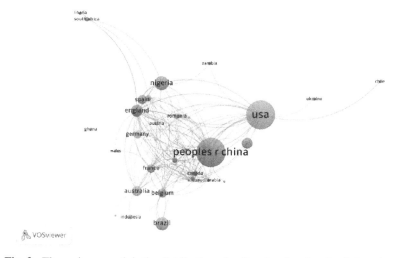

Fig. 2. The main research is the distribution of national and regional collaboration.

3.3 Organizational Analysis

An analysis of research institutions revealed that 211 authors were affiliated with 1271 institutions. The top 10 institutions were responsible for publishing a total of 49 articles, representing 23.222% of the total publications (Table 2).

The minimum requirement for the number of publications per institution was set at 2. Out of the 1271 institutions involved in research on product design for rural education, 359 institutions met this threshold (see Fig. 3). The size of each node represents the number of publications, while the connections between nodes indicate the intensity of collaboration.

Table 2. Top 10 organizations in Product design study for rural teaching, 2012–2022.

Rank	Organization	Country/region	Documents	Citations
1	Univ liege	Belgium	10	566
2	Univ Melbourne	Australia	6	440
3	Univ montpellier	France	6	549
4	Harvard univ	Usa	5	558
5	Monash univ	Australia	5	455
6	Shanghai ocean univ	China	5	13
7	Chinese Academy of Sciences	China	4	372
8	Univ edinburgh	England	4	98
9	Zhejiang univ	China	4	20
10	Duke univ	Usa	4	79

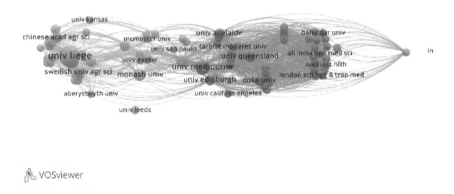

VOSviewer

Fig. 3. Collaboration network of research organizations in Product design for rural teaching.

3.4 Author and Study Co-authors Group Analysis

The analysis of authors revealed that Cremonese Edoardo, Marius Schmidt, Chen Nai-song, Li Song-lin, and Sandeep Chaudhary were highly productive authors, demonstrating their strong interest and impact in the field (Table 3).

The co-author analysis presented a visual representation of the distribution and collaboration within the field of product design for rural education. The size of each node corresponds to the number of publications by each author. The relationships between co-authors were illustrated through links, with stronger links indicating a higher degree of collaboration (see Fig. 4).

Table 3. Analysis of the top ten authors and co-cited authors from 2012–2022.

Rank	Co-cited author	Documents	Citations
1	Cremonese·Edoardo	3	512
2	Schmidt·marius	3	512
3	Chen nai-song	3	12
4	Li song-lin	3	12
5	Chaudhary·Sandeep	2	44
6	Abbastabar·Hedayat	2	44
7	Hu guo-qing	2	44
8	Li shan-shan	2	44
9	Ahmadi·keivan	2	44
10	Adabi·maryam	2	44

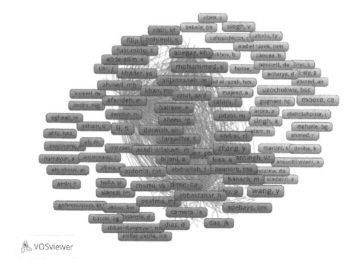

Fig. 4. Co-authorship network in Product design study for rural teaching.

3.5 Source Journal Distribution

The analysis of academic journals revealed that the majority of research on product design for rural education was published in the fields of education and sociology (Table 4). The United States, known for its strong cultural exports, and the United Kingdom, with its extensive experience in education, were identified as important contributors to the field. Additionally, Brazil, as a significant agricultural country, and countries such as Latvia, Switzerland, and Colombia also received significant attention in the research.

Table 4. Journals of significant in Product design study for rural teaching, 2012–2022.

Rank	Journal	Country
1	*ASIA PACIFIC JOURNAL OF EDUCATION*	England
2	*TEACHING SOCIOLOGY*	Usa
3	*RURAL ENVIRONMENT, EDUCATION, PERSONALITY. (REEP)*	Latvia
4	*SUSTAINABILITY*	Switzerland
5	*TEACHER EDUCATION AND SPECIAL EDUCATION*	Usa
6	*REVISTA CORPOICA-CIENCIA Y TECNOLOGIA AGROPECUARIA*	Colombia
7	*RESEARCH IN DANCE EDUCATION*	England
8	*CHILDHOOD AND PHILOSOPHY*	Brazil

3.6 Distribution of Keywords: Hotspots of Product Design for Rural Teaching

A product design was developed for the purpose of identifying hotspots in a rural teaching network through the analysis of co-occurring keywords. A minimum co-occurrence threshold of 4 was established, resulting in the identification of 489 keywords from a sample of 9919. Network analysis was employed to cluster the keywords based on similarities, leading to the formation of four main clusters represented by red, green, blue, and yellow (see Fig. 5). The top 10 keywords for each cluster are listed in Table 5.

Table 5. Co-occurrence analysis of keywords.

Cluster 1 (red)	Cluster 2(green)	Cluster 3 (blue)	Cluster 4 (yellow)
Conclusion	Student	Concern	Growth
Adolescent	School	Company	Nutrition
Age	Production	Expansion	Challenges
Attitude	China	Culture	Inclusion
Average	Rural school	Operation	Dataset
Trend	Educator	Association	First time
Care	Experience	Conception	Product
Ratio	Debate	Expectation	Design
Cause	Rural region	Consumer	Week
Predictor	Technology	Teaching	Tool

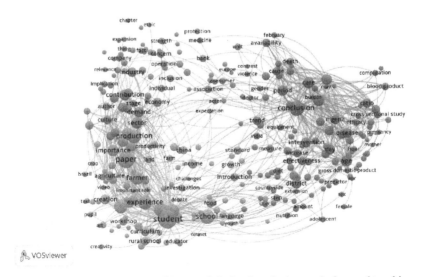

Fig. 5. Co-occurrence network of keywords in Product design study for rural teaching.

4 Discussion

The number of academic publications can serve as a valuable indicator to reflect the growth and development of a particular field. In the field of Product Design for Rural Teaching, a total of 211 articles were published between 2012 and 2022 (see Fig. 1). The increase in the number of annual publications during the period from 2012 to 2017 was relatively slow, but there was a noticeable increase in 2018, with 32 articles being published. Since 2018, the number of annual publications has remained above 20, which may be due to increased investment in education across various countries, particularly in China, where poverty alleviation in rural areas is considered a significant priority.

In terms of countries with the highest publication output, China stands out as the leading producer. Zhejiang University and the Chinese Academy of Sciences are notable institutions that have consistently contributed to the field of rural education innovation. Meanwhile, the United States and the United Kingdom also exert significant influence in the education sector, with a relatively high citation rate for their published articles (Table 2).

The analysis of co-authors and co-citations by authors can yield valuable information and offer researchers potential opportunities and information for collaboration. Based on the co-authorship analysis, it can be observed that China, the United States, Brazil, Nigeria, the United Kingdom, Belgium, Australia, and other countries have a high level of collaboration (see Fig. 2). This indicates that the research in the field of Product Design for Rural Teaching has a global reach, encompassing regions such as Asia, Africa, the Americas, Europe, and Australia, making it a widely recognized academic topic among the international community.

An analysis of the distribution of academic journals can shed light on the journals that concentrate on the field of Product Design for Rural Teaching (Table 4). For instance, some of the journals that have a focus on this field include the *Asia Pacific Journal of Education*, *Teaching Sociology*, *Sustainability*, *Teacher Education and Special Education*, among others. These journals have a strong interest in issues related to education.

The keyword co-occurrence analysis reveals the high-frequency keywords that are deemed as search topics and representative keywords in the field of Product Design for Rural Teaching. The analysis reveals that the keywords "Attitude", "Student", "Concern", and "Growth" are considered important topics within this field (Table 5). These keywords are further grouped into four clusters: Cluster 1 (in red) relates to "Attitude" and common keywords include "Adolescent", "Age", "Average", "Care", "Cause", and "Predictor"; Cluster 2 (in green) pertains to "Student" and the common keywords extracted include "School", "Production", "Rural school", "Educator", "Experience", "Rural region", and "Technology"; Cluster 3 (in blue) focuses on "Concern" and common keywords extracted include "Company", "Expansion", "Culture", "Operation", "Conception", "Expectation", and "Consumer"; Cluster 4 (in yellow) pertains to "Growth" and the common keywords extracted include "Nutrition", "Challenges", "Inclusion", "Dataset", "Design", "Tool", and "Week".

In this study, we utilized the VOSviewer scientometrics software to analyze the research literature in the field of "Product Design for Rural Teaching" present in the Web of Science Core Collection database. The data was mined from academic publications published between 2011 and 2022 to provide insights into the state of research in this field. Our analysis revealed key findings in the form of word maps, journal distributions, country collaborations, authorship patterns, and research hotspots, providing a roadmap for future research in the field of "Product Design for Rural Teaching."

It is important to note that the results of this analysis are subject to certain limitations. Firstly, our methodology may introduce limitations in the analysis. Additionally, language restrictions and potential language biases may have impacted the results. Furthermore, our study was limited to the Web of Science Core Collection database and did not include other search engines such as PubMed and Google Scholar or country-specific databases, which could have resulted in further limitations.

Acknowledgements. The authors acknowledge the contributions and support of the experts and team members in the writing process.

Foundations: Shaanxi University of Science & Technology and Kyiv National University of Technologies and Design jointly conduct a doctoral education program in design (program code: MOE61UA1A20212205N); the Project for Improving the Research Capabilities of Young and Middle-Aged Teachers in Guangxi Universities(China): "Genealogy Arrangement and Creative Product Design Research of Yao Ethnic Costume Art in the Gui-Dong Region" (Program Code: 2021KY0689); Guangxi Educational Science Planning Project(China): "Research on the Integration Path of 'Art Education + Political Education' Design Education Based on GUangxi's Intangible Cultural Heritage Resources" (Program Code: 2021C360); Guangxi Zhuang Autonomous Region College Students' Innovation and Entrepreneurship Training Plan: "Hezhou Intangible Cultural Heritage Research" (Program Code: S202211838095); Guangxi Zhuang Autonomous Region College Students' Innovation and Entrepreneurship Training Plan: "Digital Creative Design of Yao Ethnic Costume Art in the Gui-Dong Region" (Program Code: S202111838150); Guangxi Zhuang Autonomous Region National College Student Innovation and Entrepreneurship Training Plan "Design of Cultural and Tourism Products Based on the Traditional Ancestral Hall Architecture Art in Hezhou." (Program Code: 202111838003).

References

1. Mota, P.A., Garzedim, A.B., Quintaneiro, M.J., et al.: Initial teacher education and rural education: a game for teaching parasitology. Revista Brasileira de Educação do Campo. **06**, 1–27 (2021)
2. Cheng, A., Sinha, A., Shen, J., et al.: Opportunities for social innovation at the intersection of ICT education and rural supply chains. In: 2012 IEEE Global Humanitarian Technology Conference, pp. 328–335. IEEE (2012)
3. Zou, X., Yue, W.L., Vu, H.L.: Visualization and analysis of mapping knowledge domain of road safety studies. Accid Anal Prev **118**, 131–145 (2018)
4. Van Eck, N.J., Waltman, L.: Software survey: VOSviewer, a computer program for bibliometric mapping. Scientometrics **84**(2), 523–538 (2010)

A Study on the Fogg Behavior Model in Designing Educational Apps for Children

Youtian Zhou[✉], Qianhang Qin, Bo Tang, and Wenda Tian

School of Design, Guangxi Normal University, Guilin 541004, China
zhouyoyo@live.com

Abstract. This paper focuses on the design strategies for children's educational apps based on the Fogg Behavior Model. By analyzing motivation, ability, and prompts factors, combined with the rule of children's mental and cognitive development, the feasibility and design principles of the persuasive behavior model for changing children's behavior are derived. Through analyzing existing cases and applying persuasive principles, the design strategies and methods of the Fogg Behavior Model in children's educational apps are proposed. Based on theoretical research and case analysis, it is suggested that creating personified visual images and setting understandable and manipulable interactive methods can enhance user motivation. In addition, setting up age-appropriate activities, creating exploratory games, and adding physical teaching aids can improve user abilities. Finally, timely celebration, increasing live teaching, and establishing a fixed learning process can awaken trigger mechanisms. Furthermore, the application of the Fogg Behavior Model in children's educational apps can help promote children's active participation in learning, rather than forcing them to comply with external commands. The increasing penetration of mobile internet has led to a rise in the number of mobile terminals, and children's educational apps are expected to experience a development period in the future. The design strategies and methods proposed in this paper can contribute to the improvement of learning efficiency and the enjoyment of the learning process.

Keywords: Interaction Design · Fogg Behavior Model · Behavioral Design · Educational Applications · Children

1 Introduction

The proliferation of digital technology and the widespread adoption of smartphones and other connected devices have brought interaction design to the forefront of contemporary design. Designers tasked with creating digital interfaces for users must now consider not only the visual design of the product, but also the nature of users' interactions with it. This involves understanding users' navigation patterns, actions, and the motivations that drive them to use the product in question. To this end, designers have shifted their focus from traditional design concerns such as functionality, structure, and color to a greater emphasis on understanding and guiding user behavior. In particular, designers have begun to invest significant time in studying users and building psychological models to understand their behavior. This may involve conducting user research to collect data on how people use similar products, or conducting surveys to gain insight into users' attitudes and motivations. The study of user psychology by designers has thus shifted from an initial focus on understanding human behavior to a focus on guiding it [1]. This has culminated in the emergence of the discipline of behavioral design, which sees designers working to shape user behavior by designing digital interfaces that encourage specific patterns of use. A key concept in this approach to design is the Fogg Behavior Model. This paper will examine the Fogg Behavior Model in greater detail by focusing on the development of educational apps for children.

2   Fogg Behavior Model

BJ Fogg, the founder of the Behavior Design Lab at Stanford University, proposed the Fogg Behavior Model to understand human behavior [2]. This model comprises three elements that predict behavior: motivation, ability, and prompts (also called triggers) (see Fig. 1). This persuasive model is a tool that changes the behavior path by influencing the user's consciousness [3]. Motivation is the starting point for behavior. The stronger the motivation, the more likely the behavior will occur. Ability is the permission for behavior. The stronger the ability or the easier the behavior, the more likely the behavior will be completed. Prompts are the signal for behavior. Without prompts, no behavior will occur. According to Fogg, all three elements need to align correctly to influence someone's behavior. When a behavior does not occur, at least one of these three elements is missing. In other words, by analyzing the motivation, ability, and prompts in a specific behavior and applying them to app design, users can be guided by the product to complete the desired behavior.

Fig. 1. Fogg Behavior Model (Source: behaviormodel.org)

Since the proposal of the Fogg Behavior Model, it has been widely applied in various fields such as education, healthcare, and public health [4]. Persuading users to change their behavior mainly involves the following three aspects: (1) increasing the user's motivation to promote behavior; (2) increasing the user's ability to promote behavior. In actual design, changing the user's ability is difficult to achieve, so generally, reducing the requirement for ability is used to promote behavior; (3) selecting appropriate triggers to promote behavior. This article will focus on the above three aspects and explore the application strategies of the Fogg Behavior Model in the design of educational apps for children.

3   Definition and Current Status of Educational Apps for Children

3.1   Definition of Educational Apps for Children

According to the United Nations Convention on the Rights of the Child, children can be divided into four different stages: infancy (0–1 years old), toddlerhood (2–3 years old), early childhood (4–6 years old), and middle childhood (6–12 years old). Therefore, in this paper, children mainly refer to those under 12 years old. Educational apps for adults are mainly designed to learn a specific skill, while educational apps for children are designed to cultivate their language, movement, and cognitive abilities in accordance with their physiological and psychological development.

3.2   Current Status of Educational Apps for Children

In the past decade, as the number of modern electronic devices in households has increased, the proportion of children using electronic devices has also risen steadily. Relevant surveys have shown that more than half of preschool children have the habit of watching videos, playing games, and listening to stories on their phones or tablets [5]. Studies have found that combining children's education with electronic devices can stimulate their curiosity and encourage them to participate more actively in learning [6]. For example, to address children's short attention spans, apps can use dynamic visuals and interactive gestures to attract attention and extend concentration time. Apps can also broaden children's horizons by introducing high-quality audio and video content. Therefore, using educational apps as an enlightenment tool can help children expand their cognitive awareness, enrich their language expression, and learn behavioral norms while enjoying a pleasant learning experience.

4   The Relationship between Fogg Behavior Model and the Design of Educational Apps for Kids

4.1   The Relationship Between Motivation and the Design of Educational Apps for Kids

Motivation is a crucial factor in determining user behavior. Fogg Behavior Model posits that there are three key motivations - sensation, anticipation, and belonging - each with corresponding emotional dimensions of pleasure/pain, hope/fear, and acceptance/rejection. Fogg's "Motivation Wave" theory suggests that high levels of motivation lead to a willingness to undertake challenging tasks, while lower levels of motivation lead to a preference for easy tasks [7]. In the context of learning, adults may experience negative emotions during the process of acquiring new skills, but they are motivated by the expectation of improved quality of life after mastering the skill. In contrast, children may not fully comprehend the long-term benefits of learning and may only experience negative emotions associated with traditional learning methods. Consequently, they may develop a dislike for learning and discontinue the learning process. Therefore, when designing educational apps for kids, it is important to consider strategies that increase motivation in a manner that is easily understood by children, such that they become interested in the learning content and enjoy the learning experience. This can foster a strong motivation to engage in challenging tasks and persist in the learning process.

4.2 The Relationship Between Ability and the Design of Educational Apps for Kids

The meaning of ability refers to the range of behaviors that a user can perform within their personal capacity. When the required behavior exceeds a certain level of ability, the behavior becomes impossible to perform. There are three ways to increase ability: (1) training, (2) providing more skills, and (3) providing more resources to do the target behavior, as proposed by Fogg Behavior Model [1]. In the field of educational products, when there is a lack of products specifically designed for children, many parents rely on repetitive training to help their children complete certain learning tasks. For example, when learning English, parents may repeat the word "apple" to help their children remember the word. However, this method is based on adult cognitive logic and may not be effective for children.

Providing more skills involves reflecting on the apps' process and design, reducing the user's cognitive burden and usage difficulty. While adults often learn through reading and testing, children are more sensitive to color, music, and graphics than to words. In the design process, designers should consider children's cognitive level and aesthetic preferences, simplify interface information, remove unnecessary functions, use cartoonish icons, and gamify the usage process to lower information to a level that is easy for children to understand and operate, helping children enter the learning state more happily and actively.

Providing additional tools can be seen as providing physical tools to complete behavior or designing reward mechanisms. Parents often tell their children, "If you put the cup in the sink, you will get a candy," or "If you finish this book, you can go to play." The former can be seen as a reward mechanism, while the latter is a rule. In the design of children's educational products, designers need to focus on both rewards and rules. Rewards can encourage children to do something, while rules can help them form habits.

4.3 The Relationship Between Prompts and the Design of Educational Apps for Kids

Fogg revised the term "trigger" to "prompt" in 2017 and extended it to all words representing "trigger," including cue, trigger, call to action, and request, indicating that triggers are diverse and can be a button, such as a light switch, an explicit request, such as a red light meaning stop and green light meaning go, or a habit, such as taking a sip when seeing a straw [8]. Based on different motivations and abilities, there are three type of triggers: Sparks, Facilitator, and Sign. "Sparks" refers to the situation where users have the ability but lack motivation, and the triggering factor should associate motivation to induce user motivation and promote behavior. For example, if children do not want to get up on time, parents promise to reward them with one hour of playing on the slide after getting up, which increases their motivation and makes getting up more likely to occur. "Facilitator" refers to the situation where users have sufficient motivation but lack ability, and they need certain guidance or prompts to complete the behavior. For example, when children encounter toy levels that are difficult to understand, they often lose interest and stop playing, so parental guidance or assistance is needed. The last type, "Sign," refers to the situation where users have both motivation and ability, and behavior can be initiated directly, such as when children see a carousel and want to play. In the design of educational products for children, because children's cognitive ways of understanding the external world are different from those of adults, using empathy to deeply understand children's psychology and behavior and balancing the relationship between user motivation and ability can effectively improve the usability of the product.

5 Fogg Behavior Model in the Design Strategy of Children's Educational Apps

5.1 Enhancing User Motivation

Creating a Warm Visual Image. Motivation can be understood as attractiveness. For children, if a product can attract their attention like a carousel and make them want to play with it, they have the motivation. So how can children be interested in educational apps? Psychologist Harry Harlow confirmed in his famous monkey experiment that when faced with an iron mother who could provide milk and a warm light and a cloth mother who could not provide milk but was gentler, the newborn monkeys all chose to stay close to the cloth mother. The experiment shows that the establishment of a close relationship for children not only depends on the satisfaction of physiological needs (food, temperature) but also on the satisfaction of emotional needs (acceptance, love) [9]. Applying this to the product, children are more concerned about the emotional attributes (the warmth brought by the cloth mother) than the functional attributes of the product (providing milk and light). Children naturally crave a role like a mother or friend and hope to be treated gently and responded to in a timely manner. The coldness of the classroom and blackboard in adult educational products is like the iron mother in the experiment, which can provide functions but cannot make children feel warm and willing to approach. According to the Fogg Behavior Model, designers need to transform negative motivation brought by the product into positive motivation. The transformation of motivation can start with creating a visual image. A round and warm-colored cartoon image can be built in the visual image to give children a positive association with the image of "mother" or "little friend," making them feel "familiar" and "willing to be with it" when they come into contact with the product, bringing joy and motivation.

Jiliguala is an educational app dedicated to enlightenment for children aged 0–8. The product has created a cute parrot, which serves as a product navigator, course assistant, cartoon actor, and many other roles. The parrot introduces tasks at the beginning of each section, participates in interactive scenes of different games, and provides clear feedback in the familiar language of children, helping children to be guided into the learning state unconsciously (see Fig. 2).

Fig. 2. The image of a parrot created by Jiliguala app

Establishing Understandable and Controllable Interaction Methods. The interaction logic of children's products differs significantly from that of adult products. Icons that are commonplace for adults are unfamiliar to children. Moreover, children's fingers lack the agility and control of adults, making it difficult for them to perform operations such as double-clicking, swiping, and long-pressing. Therefore, children's products should use a user interface composed of clear icons and distinct colors to help children form correct associations and easily remember them. At the same time, ui elements must be larger than normal and provide sufficient click area to avoid inadvertent clicks. On the other hand, children have a curious nature. In design, we should take advantage of their desire to click on the screen unconsciously and guide them to operate and complete learning tasks through simple interactive actions such as tapping, pressing, and swiping, combined with interesting storylines. in the case shown in Fig. 3, the UKids Online app designed multiple games for word learning, including a rotating wheel that randomly generates clicks, and when a word is clicked, it pops up and emits a sound, and a parachute that opens and pops out a word and emits a sound when it lands. Random clicking conforms to children's habits of unconsciously clicking on the screen, and the popping of different screens attracts them to continue clicking on other areas to see what opens, thus completing the task of learning words unconsciously.

Fig. 3. The game interface design of Ukids Online APP

5.2 Improving User Abilities

Designing Curriculum Based on Children's Cognitive Development Characteristics. Improving user abilities can be understood as reducing the difficulty of product usage based on the user's abilities, so that the user's abilities match the product difficulty. The development of children's cognition is a gradual process, and children of different age groups have different developmental characteristics [10]. Therefore, products designed for 5-year-old children are generally difficult to meet the needs of 2-year-old children. When designing educational products for children, the target user age should be determined first, and the design should focus on the cognitive development characteristics and aesthetic preferences of children of that age as much as possible.

Taking KissABC as an example, which is a language learning app, its curriculum adopts age-appropriate teaching. Children aged 0–3 years do not have independent learning ability and should not use electronic products alone. They can enter the parent-child classroom, where parents can lead children to listen to nursery rhymes and do actions to establish a preliminary understanding of English. Children aged 3–6 years begin to have curiosity and exploratory desires, and can enter the basic classroom to learn simple words and sentences through short animation and interactive games. At the same time, considering that children aged 3–6 years are in the chaotic pre-school stage, their attention is prone to shift. In the design process, the learning content is divided into several short and easy-to-operate tasks. For example, in KissABC, children first watch a 5-min animation in section one, then play a 5-min interactive game in section two, and finally have a 15-min game-based conversation with a real English teacher in section three. In the 30-min course, children experience three short activities: watching animation, learning words, and speaking English, which helps them maintain attention and make the learning process more enjoyable.

Replacing Mechanical Repetition with Exploratory Games. As mentioned earlier, curiosity is a natural characteristic of children. After being exposed to electronic products, the strong curiosity of children will prompt them to explore and click the screen. In product design, this characteristic of children should be actively utilized, and mechanical repetition learning tasks should be transformed into rich and diverse interactive operations in the app to stimulate their desire for active exploration and dialogue. Taking the Jiliguala app as an example, to explain the two meanings of the word "Block," which are "Toy" and "Obstacle," the first round of introduction is done by the teacher's exaggerated language and actions. Then in Game 1, children users need to use their fingers to click on the blocks hidden behind the furniture to understand that "Block" means a Toy. In Game 2, children users also need to use their fingers to help the parrot driving the car to move away the obstacles, to understand that "Block" Means an obstacle. In the review stage, "Block" is placed in a picture book, and children can play the game of finding blocks and moving obstacles with their parents again following the story plot (See Fig. 4). This interesting and exploratory learning method is more attractive to children and can achieve the learning effect of memory and understanding through repeated games.

Provide Physical Teaching Tools Such as Picture Books and Flashcards. Introducing additional teaching tools can shorten the time that children spend on electronic devices

Fig. 4. The game interface design of Jiliguala APP

and also provide a variety of colorful and engaging materials that quickly capture their attention. Furthermore, depending on the method of use, these teaching tools can also enhance other aspects of children's abilities, such as fine motor skills and logical thinking. when providing additional teaching tools, it is important to consider the following three issues: (1) Matching the teaching tools with the learning content and progress of the app, (2) Ensuring that both the app and the teaching tools facilitate parental involvement and parent-child interaction, and (3) Providing a diverse range of teaching tools.

As an example, in the Jiliguala farm-themed English course, children first watch a nursery rhyme video on the app to establish their initial understanding of farm-related words such as "cow" and "duck". They then play jigsaw puzzles while listening to the nursery rhyme to further strengthen their cognitive abilities. In the third step, parents read picture books with their children to repeatedly reinforce the words "cow" and "duck" through the story. The fourth step involves consolidating vocabulary through playing flashcard games. After class, children can review and reinforce their memory of the words through playing connection games and using stickers. In this case, children only watch one video on the app, and the subsequent learning is achieved through the use of various teaching tools, including picture books, jigsaw puzzles, and flashcards.

Children lack the awareness to review actively, and the provision of teaching aids is also a way to help children review. In the above case, the last step is to use posters and stickers for review. The product has produced a poster based on the learning progress from Day 1 to Day 21, and the words learned each day are made into stickers. After completing each day's learning task, children can stick the corresponding sticker on the appropriate date. For example, if they learned "cow" on Day 1, they can stick the cow sticker on Day 1. For children, the act of sticking stickers is equivalent to "ending the learning task," which helps to gradually develop a conditioned reflex in children to "stick a sticker every day" or "complete the learning task every day." At the same time, hanging the poster at home can also help parents review with children through daily conversations.

5.3 Trigger Mechanism for Awakening

Timely Celebration of Cultivating Positive Emotional Feedback. Timely celebration refers to celebrating every small progress made. Most educational apps displays an "excellent" celebration interface after completing a learning task, which is a form of timely celebration. there are four ways to achieve timely celebration: (1) Maintaining positive encouragement, (2) Introducing peer competition, (3) Transforming into games, and (4) Linking to the real world.

Due to the tediousness of the learning process and poor learning outcomes, the probability of adult users experiencing negative emotions in the learning scenario is higher than in other scenarios. People naturally remember negative experiences more clearly than happy memories, and the existence of such negative emotions can greatly affect the user's enthusiasm for active learning. Therefore, in the learning scenario, it is more important to provide users with positive feedback to counteract the negative impact. Taking Know You app as an example, the system gives different feedback on the learning results page based on the user's different learning performance. Even if the performance is not good, the system still gives positive feedback to encourage users to continue learning.

Children are born needing and eager to establish connections with others and gain recognition, and their desire for recognition from teachers far outweighs that from parents. This is also the " belonging" motivation mentioned in the Fogg Behavior Model. Figure 5 shows the design made by Tencent QQ to solve the problem of primary school students submitting homework remotely during the epidemic. The design team found that the proportion of young students who submitted homework on time significantly decreased during remote learning. So how to solve this problem? The team found that students attach great importance to the avatar in the class group, so the team associated the design with the interactive icon in front of the user image to enhance students' enthusiasm for submitting homework. There are two types of interactive icons. One is becoming a junior model by submitting homework on time for three consecutive days and becoming a senior model for five consecutive days. The models can add trophies, stars, and small flowers in front of their avatars. In addition, the three students who submit their homework earliest each time can add a lightning icon, and the optional items include lightning, rockets, and tornadoes. The interactive icons make students who submit homework on time feel encouraged and feel "different from others." Other students will also strive to submit their homework on time to get the icons.

Fig. 5. The interactive icon design of QQ APP

The Sagomini app has swapped reward mechanisms with role-playing games. Child users can choose different dress-up elements to dress up cartoon characters after earning a certain amount of points (Fig. 6). Another example comes from the Plano Jingling app. This is an app designed to help children develop good eye care habits. The product has created a park, and in order for children to build it, they must complete eye care tasks. Every time a child completes an eye care task, such as doing eye exercises or looking into the distance for 30 min, they can successfully plant a small tree, a small animal, or build a leisure chair or swimming pool. The more goals the child completes, the richer the scene of the park becomes. In this way, the child's learning motivation is transformed into a game motivation, and driven by the motivation to build the park as quickly as possible, the child unknowingly completes the task.

Fig. 6. The game interface design of Sagomini APP

The third approach is to connect rewards to the real world. Parents often make agreements with their children, such as offering a piece of chocolate in exchange for helping with yard work or cleaning their own rooms. This kind of agreement can also be applied to the digital world, such as offering points for completing daily learning tasks on an app, which can then be exchanged for products that children enjoy in a virtual marketplace. The Jiliguala app has designed a complete "check-in reward" mechanism, where users can exchange gifts such as puzzles, pillows, and backpacks at different time nodes, such as 8 check-ins in 15 days, 16 check-ins in 30 days, and 45 check-ins in 90 days, with the value of the gift increasing as the number of check-ins increases. The "check-in reward" can also be more creative. As shown in Fig. 7, the app includes a DIY material kit, where parents and children can cut out candy jar and candy designs from paper, and children can add a candy to the jar for each task completed. The candy can be replaced with cookies, crayons, and other themed items. In another case, the product team designed a stack of blank checks, where children can negotiate with their parents for rewards, such as a "companion coupon" where the child can receive an unconditional day of playtime with their mother after completing a task, or an "apology coupon" where the child can show the coupon after making a mistake and the mother must unconditionally forgive them. These designs not only encourage children to complete learning tasks in a way that they enjoy, but also promote the establishment of a positive parent-child relationship.

Designing Curriculum Bas Introducing Live Teaching. The main difference between traditional teaching methods and app-based teaching is that teachers and students communicate through language and actions, and teachers can adjust the teaching pace based on students' responses. Live teaching can to some extent replicate the teaching effect of offline classrooms. The Jiliguala app has introduced live teaching into its courses,

Fig. 7. The DIY material kit

allowing children to see the teaching content, the teacher's vivid expressions, and their own reactions on the screen as shown in Fig. 8. Although the courses are recorded, the teacher leaves room for interaction during the teaching process. For example, after teaching a word, the teacher will pause for several seconds to wait for the child to read it aloud, and then give encouragement. This approach maximizes the replication of the rhythm of offline classrooms. Lingumi, an English learning app developed in the UK, uses exaggerated body language and animations to attract children's attention, while using directive language to guide them in interacting. In these cases, the app can simulate the atmosphere of traditional classrooms to a large extent, and the teacher becomes a force for initiating signals and guiding behaviors.

Fig. 8. The user interface design of Jiliguala APP

Initiating Learning Signals at Fixed Times and in Fixed Ways. The signal in the trigger mechanism can be seen as a type of conditioned reflex. The Little albert experiment demonstrated that conditioned reflexes can be established through repeated execution of the same behaviors and actions. In educational products, when a conditioned reflex is established, children will unconsciously do something in a certain situation. currently, many children's educational products unlock courses at set times, for example, unlocking a new course every day at 5 pm. this is not only to control children's use of electronic products but also to establish the conditioned reflex of "studying for 15 min every night". Using the same opening animation and music to start each learning session is also a way to establish a conditioned reflex. In the Children's show Peppa pig, children can hear peppa's snoring at the beginning of each Episode. This sound of the pig snoring is associated with "it's time to watch peppa", which makes children unconsciously enter a state of watching. similarly, children's educational products use fixed opening animations to trigger the signal of "it's time to start learning".

6   Conclusion

The paper proposes the use of the Fogg Behavior Model as a framework for designing educational apps for children. This model emphasizes the importance of motivation, ability, and prompts in influencing behavior. By incorporating these principles into app design, children can become more engaged and active learners, rather than passive recipients of information. The paper highlights several strategies for incorporating the Fogg Behavior Model into educational app design, including creating personified visual images and establishing understandable and controllable interaction methods to enhance user motivation, setting up graded courses, creating exploratory games, and incorporating physical teaching aids to improve user ability, and timely celebrations, increasing human teaching support, and a fixed learning process to trigger the mechanism to wake up learners. By taking into account the behaviors, emotions, and psychological characteristics of children, these strategies can encourage children to take a more active role in the learning process, rather than simply following commands from external sources. Ultimately, these strategies have the potential to improve learning efficiency and enjoyment for children.

Funding. This research was supported by 2021 Guangxi Normal University Innovation and Entrepreneurship Education Fund (No. CXCYSZ2021007), 2020 Project of Basic Ability Enhancement for Young and Middle-Aged Teachers in Guangxi Universities (no. 2020KY02049), 2013 Guangxi Humanities Society Science Development Research Center for Youth (no. QNZD13010).

References

1. Xiang-Yang, X.: Interaction design: from logic of things to logic of behaviors. Zhuang Shi **261**(01), 58–62 (2015)
2. Fogg, B.J.: A behavior model for persuasive design. In: Proceedings of the 4th International Conference on Persuasive Technology, p. 40. ACM (2009)
3. Wei, G., Fei, H.: Persuasion mechanism design and application research on mobile health promotion product. Zhuang Shi **281**(09), 68–69 (2016)
4. Oinas-Kukkonen, H., Harjumaa, M.: Persuasive systems design: key issues, process model, and system features. Commun. Assoc. Inf. Syst. **24**, 28 (2009)
5. Iresearch   Homepage.   http://www.iresearch.com.cn/Detail/rep-ort?id=2383&isfree=0. Accessed 30 Dec 2022
6. Zosh, J.M., Lytle, S.R., Golinkoff, R.M., Hirsh-Pasek, K.: Putting the education back in educational apps: how content and context interact to promote learning. In: Barr, R., Linebarger, D.N. (eds.) Media Exposure During Infancy and Early Childhood, pp. 259–282. Springer, Cham (2017). https://doi.org/10.1007/978-3-319-45102-2_17

7. Fogg Behavior Model Homepage. https://behaviormodel.org/motivation/. Accessed 30 Dec 2022
8. Fogg, B.J.: Tiny Habits: The Small Changes That Change Everything, 1st edn. Mariner Books, Boston (2019)
9. Damon, E.: Early social-emotional functioning and public health: the relationship between kindergarten social competence and future wellness. Am. J. Public Health **105**, 2283–2290 (2015)
10. Tong-Xiu, L., Mo, L., Zhe, C.: A review of overseas new researches on children's cognitive development and learning. Psychol. Sci. 735–739 (2006)

Teaching Design Practice of Statistics Course for Economics and Management Majors Based on Humanized Participation Mode Model Technology

Jixu Zhu[1], Xiaoshi Chen[1(✉)], and Zhichao Liu[2]

[1] Guangzhou City University of Technology, Guangzhou, China
601668750@qq.com
[2] South China University of Technology, Guangzhou City University of Technology, Guangzhou, China

Abstract. With the development of the Internet and the improvement of digitalization in various fields, the era of big data has come, and the systematization, integration and efficiency of big data processing have put forward new requirements for the teaching system of traditional "statistics" courses. Aiming at the problems of single teaching method, emphasis on theory, light on practice, unreasonable assessment contents and methods that generally exist in the traditional teaching of statistics course of economics and management, the BOPPPS teaching model is mainly introduced for teaching design to explore the application of humanized participation mode model technology in the teaching of statistics course of economics and management. Combined with years of educational practice and teaching research, we found that the BOPPPS teaching model better emphasizes students' all-round participatory learning, stimulates students' motivation and interest in learning, increases students' awareness of participation and becomes the real subject of learning.

Keywords: Human participation approach · BOPPPS model · Economics and management · Statistics

1 Introduction

On August 31, 2015, the State Council issued the "Outline of Action to Promote the Development of Big Data". The Outline points out that the convergence of information technology and economic and social integration has led to the rapid growth of data, data has become a national fundamental strategic resources, big data is increasingly important impact on global production, circulation, distribution, consumption activities and economic operation mechanism, social lifestyle and national governance capacity. At present, China has a certain foundation in the development and application of big data, with huge market advantages and development potential. Jobs related to big data require complex talents who can master mathematics, statistics, data analysis, machine learning and natural language processing [1]. In order to meet the current development requirements of the society, the teaching objectives of statistics courses in higher education should focus on improving the students' software operation ability and practical ability in the teaching of statistics courses [2].

The advent of the era of big data has put forward new requirements for the teaching of statistics courses in economics and management majors, and this teaching model combines the characteristics and teaching requirements of economics and management majors, incorporates the teaching technology of the humanized participation model - BOPPPS model, connects various teaching resources, and uses artificial intelligence, big data and other The teaching technology is integrated with the BOPPPS model, which is a humanized participation model. It solves the problems of single teaching method, emphasis on theory and practice, unreasonable assessment contents and methods, etc., which generally exist in the traditional teaching of statistics courses of economic and management majors [3]. The BOPPPS model constructs a specific teaching process, reflects the student-centered teaching concept, emphasizes stimulating students' learning initiative, and improves students' participation in learning, which is a more advanced teaching mode at present. Therefore, based on the theory of BOPPPS model, the teaching design of statistics course is of great significance to cultivate applied economic and management professionals.

2   Problems in Teaching Statistics in Economics and Management Majors

The authors used China Knowledge Network (CNKI) as the search platform, selected the general search database of CNKI as the sample source, and searched 95 research papers related to the teaching of statistics courses in economics and management, and found a total of 92 journal papers (80 academic journals and 11 special journals) and 1 conference paper in the field of teaching statistics courses in economics and management in China after eliminating invalid and duplicate literature. The literature is generally considered to be the most important. In these papers, it is generally believed that the following problems exist in the teaching of statistics courses for economics and management majors.

2.1   Single Teaching Method

At present, statistics teaching is basically a single classroom teaching. The teaching method is based on the traditional "indoctrination" lecture, in which the teacher himself sings a monologue on the podium without interaction with students [4]. With the traditional teaching method that teachers teach theoretical knowledge in the classroom and students passively receive knowledge, the course teaching does not run through the "student-centered" education concept, and it is difficult to mobilize students' initiative and enthusiasm for learning. Although the rapid development of the Internet has put forward new requirements for the education mode of universities, and more and more universities are gradually promoting the teaching and learning reform and innovation of the deep integration of information technology and education teaching, the teaching of statistics courses is still mainly offline lectures, without good use of MOOC and other teaching resources.

2.2   Emphasis on Theory, not on Practice

Statistics is a course that is somewhat theoretical, but at the same time has a strong application. The course mainly introduces various statistical analysis methods and instructs students to use statistical methods to analyze realistic data. The course involves a lot of knowledge content, and the class hours are usually 32 or 48 h, so the class hours are very limited, and the theoretical study still accounts for a large proportion of the class hours. The content of teaching generally focuses on theoretical knowledge, but less on actual socio-economic issues, or even does not pay attention to them, which dilutes the practical application ability of students. The theoretical teaching is detached from practice, resulting in students' high scores and low ability to apply relevant knowledge flexibly [5].

2.3   The Contents and Methods of Assessment Are not Reasonable

The book "Learning to Survive" published by UNESCO's International Commission on Educational Development says: "Theoretically, the purpose of examinations is firstly to measure past achievements and secondly to evaluate one's future abilities [6]." Many colleges and universities mainly adopt the assessment method of "final grade (70%) + usual grade (30%)" and focus on "result-oriented" evaluation, and pay more attention to the final exam results of students in this course. As the last step of teaching, examinations are the evaluation of teachers' teaching quality for a semester and an important means to measure students' learning effect. As a result, students just pursue the final grade scores and do not pay attention to the development of comprehensive qualities such as statistical and analytical thinking and statistical principles in the learning process, and neglect the cultivation of students' practical application ability [7].

The long-term existence of the above-mentioned teaching problems largely affects the teaching effect of statistics courses in economics and management majors, which is a core course in economics and management majors and is a practical and practice-oriented subject. In order to implement the student-centered teaching concept, stimulate students' learning potential, activate the classroom atmosphere and improve the teaching effect. We can introduce the BOPPPS model for the teaching design of statistics courses, which is an effective way to carry out the classroom organization of teaching design.

3   BOPPPS Teaching Model Overview

The BOPPPS model was introduced by Douglas Kerr at the University of British Columbia, Canada, in 1987. The BOPPPS model emphasizes "participatory" teaching methods, highlights the concept of student-centered teaching, breaks the traditional teacher's monolithic teaching model, and builds an equal and interactive teacher-student relationship. The BOPPPS model has been widely used in teacher training at all levels and in many countries around the world, especially in teaching frontline teachers some core skills of instructional design [8].

The BOPPPS model consists of six elements: Bridge-in, Objective, Pre-assessment, Participatory Learning, Post-assessment, and Summary [9]. As shown in Fig. 1.

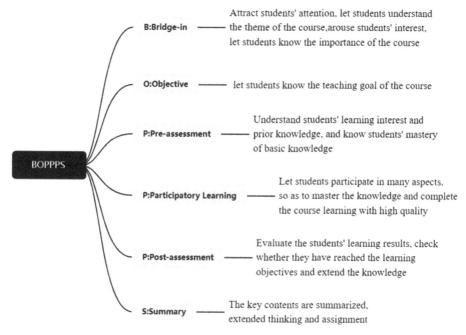

Fig. 1. BOPPPS model

The BOPPPS teaching model is a closed-loop feedback course design model that focuses on teaching interaction and reflection. The six elements are interlinked to form a kind of closed loop of teaching and learning, which organically constitutes the framework of classroom teaching. In the teaching process of statistics, the reasonable application of BOPPPS method is an effective way to optimize the teaching process. Through participatory learning, it can effectively focus learners' attention and enhance the learning effect.

4 Instructional Design Based on the BOPPPS Model

The following is an example of a very important chapter of the statistics course: "Correlation and Regression Analysis", and details the process of organizing and implementing six teaching sessions based on the BOPPPS teaching model. "Correlation and regression analysis is a statistical method for studying the interrelationship of transactions, determining their closeness, revealing specific forms and regularities of changes, and is an important tool for constructing economic models, structural analysis, policy evaluation, forecasting, and control [10]. This chapter is taught in 6 credit hours and each credit hour is 45 min long. The teaching implementation process of this chapter is shown in Fig. 2.

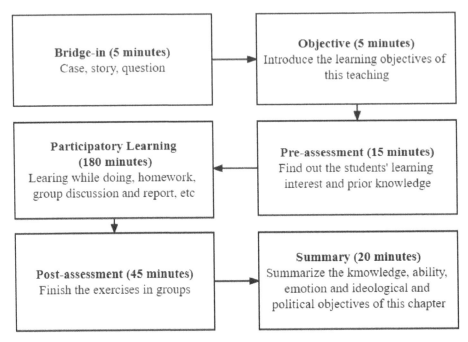

Fig. 2. Teaching and learning process

4.1 Bridge-In

The teacher introduces the subject to let students understand the importance of the content of the chapter, attracts their attention, arouses strong motivation to learn, and thus actively seeks ways and means to solve the problem and improve classroom learning. The teacher can then ask a question or case related to the topic of study, tell a story related to the topic, provide a fascinating introduction or an unusual fact. Care needs to be taken when designing the introduction section so that the introduction point has a strong logical relationship with the teaching knowledge and the teaching objectives. For example, introduce "correlation and regression analysis" with the causes of non-performing bank loans or the per capita consumption level in China, and thus introduce the concepts of correlation analysis, regression analysis, one-dimensional linear regression equation, and the dependence and constraints between various socio-economic phenomena.

4.2 Objective

Before classroom teaching, the teacher should clarify the teaching objectives of the chapter "Correlation and Regression Analysis", and then design the course teaching practice or practical training activities according to the teaching objectives to provide guidance for students' learning process. After setting the objectives, teachers can complete the teaching content of this class around the objectives set, and the appropriateness of the learning objectives directly affects the teaching effect of this chapter. Referring to the American psychologist Bloom's classification of educational objectives, the teaching objectives of this chapter are grouped into four areas, such as: knowledge, ability, emotion, and thinking objectives. Figure 3 below.

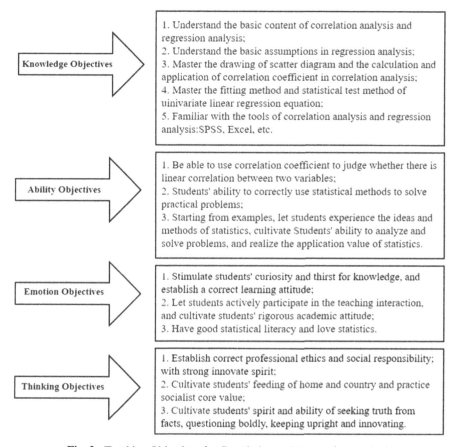

Fig. 3. Teaching Objectives for Correlation and Regression Analysis

4.3 Pre-assessment

A pre-test is a test administered prior to formal learning, through which students can express their need for review or clarification to the instructor. The purpose of the pre-test is to understand the student's interests and prior knowledge, to adjust the pace and depth of the follow-up, and to bring the objectives of the course into focus. It can be administered using questions, anonymous voting, open-ended questions, questionnaires, and quizzes in order to understand students' attention to the content of the chapter on correlation and regression analysis and their knowledge base.

4.4 Participatory Learning

This session is the main part of the classroom. Participatory teaching focuses on mobilizing students to actively participate in the classroom, taking students as the center, cultivating students' ability of independent thinking and independent learning, and is a collaborative and cooperative teaching method between teachers and students. It is a collaborative and cooperative teaching method. Teachers must adopt flexible and visual teaching methods to stimulate students' interest in learning, so that students at different levels can participate in the classroom learning. The chapter of "Correlation and Regression Analysis" has four areas of study: basic concepts of correlation analysis, linear regression analysis, non-linear regression analysis, and the application of SPSS/Excel in correlation and regression analysis. For the participatory learning phase of this class, instruction was organized as follows.

Firstly, the teacher introduces the learning content and course objectives of this chapter to the students, and then explains the characteristics, concepts and types of correlations, correlation coefficients, etc., in order to facilitate students' understanding of the theoretical knowledge.

Then, the teacher teaches linear regression analysis, so that students can understand how to analyze what kind of relationship exists between the quantities of phenomena and the closeness of the correlation, etc. After the theoretical knowledge is explained, each student is asked to complete a course assignment.

And then, the linear regression analysis leads to the nonlinear regression analysis, which follows the nonlinear regression model to correctly reflect the relationship between the phenomena.

Finally, the teacher explains and demonstrates through small cases, using the SPSS/Excel tool of correlation and regression analysis to study a certain phenomenon in society. After the teacher's explanation, students are required to complete the class assignment - in groups, based on the given information of ten stores, they are required to complete the following four problems: calculate the correlation coefficient between the average monthly sales per person and the profit rate, and determine the degree of correlation between the two; find the regression equation of the profit rate on the average monthly sales per person; calculate the estimated standard error; predict the profitability when the average monthly sales per person is $2,000. The teacher will observe the content and atmosphere of each group's discussion at any time during the analysis of the case to ensure that the discussion is not off-topic and effective. At the end of each group's report, the teacher will make comments and necessary additions to the group report and review the learning gains.

4.5 Post-assessment

The main purpose is to test whether students have mastered the chapter content, whether they have achieved the teaching objectives, and how effective the teaching is. In this section, we mainly work in groups to complete the chapter assignment - using correlation analysis and regression analysis to quantitatively analyze the per capita disposable income of Guangzhou residents and their savings and deposits, and send representatives from each group to present on stage. How well did the students master the chapter through their group work report and completion?

4.6 Summary

This session is mainly for students to summarize what they have learned in this chapter to deepen their impressions, starting with group discussion, each student elaborates on "what I have learned, what I have learned, what I still want to learn", and each group sends a representative to share on stage. Finally, the teacher will summarize and emphasize the key points and difficulties of the chapter, and then assign the homework to consolidate what the students have learned and strengthen the learning effect.

5   Teaching Effect

The authors selected a class of economics and management majors to conduct a questionnaire survey to conduct a study to compare and analyze whether there were differences in the teaching effects of the class before and after the adoption of the BOPPPS teaching model. The results were statistically analyzed by paired-sample t-test, and the returned questionnaires were quantitatively analyzed by SPSS16.0 statistical software, and the results are shown in Table 1.

Table 1. Paired sample test

Paired Samples Test

	Paired Difference					t	df	Sig (2-tailed)
	Mean	Std Deviation	Std Error Mean	95% Confidence Interval of the Difference				
				Lower	Upper			
Pair1 Boppps-Non Boppps	− 37868	1.12831	− 07900	− 22292	− 53444	4.794	203	− 000

From Table 1, since $P = 0 < 0.05$, the original hypothesis should be rejected, that is, there is a significant difference between the teaching effect before adopting the BOPPPS teaching model and after adopting the BOPPPS teaching model. It can be seen that the application of BOPPPS teaching model in the teaching of statistics course of economics and management majors is more likely to improve the teaching effect of this course.

6   Summary

The results of this study, compared with the results of existing literature studies, provide a more intuitive understanding of which teaching mode students prefer and the ultimate effectiveness of this teaching mode. This teaching mode improves the shortcomings of traditional teaching to a certain extent, and the teacher is able to adjust the content and schedule of the lesson in time to improve the teaching effect. However, it also has its shortcomings. If too many teaching activities are set in the classroom, students will be resistant to them and will not achieve the desired effect. Next, we will study how much interactive tasks are appropriate for different students, and how to design the activities for students in the classroom in a "precise" and "smart" way. In view of the problems in the teaching of statistics course of economic and management, the BOPPPS model is used for teaching design, which implements the "student-centered" education concept, highlights the main position of students in the classroom, can fully mobilize students' desire to learn and initiative, and through group discussion and cooperation, case studies, etc., can effectively improve the language expression, communication and teamwork skills.

References

1. Notice of the State Council on the issuance of an action plan to promote the development of big data. Bull. State Council People's Repub. China (26), 26–35 (2015)
2. Zhang, Y.: Research on teaching statistics courses in economics and management in the era of big data. Contemp. Educ. Pract. Teach. Res. (08), 52–53 (2018)
3. Liang, Q., Wang, Y.: Teaching reform of statistics course in economics and management majors--a case study of economics and management majors in Jingdezhen College of Ceramics. Chin. Foreign Entrep. (26), 210+212 (2013)
4. Qiu, T.: Teaching reform of statistics course in economics and management of independent colleges. Mod. Bus. Ind. **26**(09), 139–140 (2014)
5. Huang, T.C., Yang, P., Wang, J.: Teaching reform and reflection of statistics courses in under-graduate economics and management in private institutions. Singapore Management and Sports Science Institute, Singapore. In: Proceedings of 2015 2nd International Conference on Education and Education Research (EER 2015), p. 6. Singapore Management and Sports Science Institute, Society for the Application of Intelligent Information Technology, Singapore (2015)
6. UNESCO International Commission on Educational Development, Learning to Survive. Education Science Press, Shanghai People's Publishing House (2017)
7. Wang, X., Wu, Y., He, X., et al.: Problems and countermeasures of teaching statistics courses in economics and management based on questionnaire survey. Exam Wkly (39), 1–2 (2019). https://doi.org/10.3969/j.issn.1673-8918.2019.39.002
8. Cao, D.P., Yin, X.Y.: The Canadian BOPPPS teaching model and its inspiration for higher education reform. Lab. Res. Explor. **35**(02), 196–200+249 (2016)
9. Shi, J.: Research on the informative teaching design of statistics based on BOPPPS model–an example of business enterprise management major in an Industry and trade. J. Nanchang Norm. Coll. **40**(06), 74–76 (2019)
10. Xu, G.: Statistics, 2nd edn. Gezhi Publishing House, Shanghai People's Publishing House (2014)

Chatbots, Conversational Agents and Robots: Design and User Experience

Exploring Emotions in Avatar Design to Increase Adherence to Chatbot Technology

Bernardo Cortes[1], Júlia Teles[2,3] ⬤, and Emília Duarte[1,4(✉)] ⬤

[1] Universidade Europeia, IADE, Lisbon, Portugal
bernardocortes96@icloud.com,
emilia.duarte@universidadeeuropeia.pt
[2] Faculdade de Motricidade Humana, Universidade de Lisboa, Cruz Quebrada, Portugal
jteles@fmh.ulisboa.pt
[3] Centro Interdisciplinar de Performance Humana, CIPER, Cruz Quebrada, Portugal
[4] UNIDCOM/IADE, Unidade de Investigação em Design e Comunicação, Lisbon, Portugal

Abstract. A mock-up of a simulated e-commerce platform was used to evaluate the intentions to start the interaction with a chatbot during a system failure. The participants ($N = 60$) that volunteered to evaluate the platform's usability were not aware that the chatbot's design was the object of study. They were randomly assigned to one of the two experimental groups created based on the emotions expressed by the chatbots' avatars (e.g., sad vs. humoristic) and were asked to buy a certain product as quickly as possible, under the pretext of an upcoming promotion. The purchasing process was suddenly interrupted by a system crash followed by an error message. Participants had three options: repeat the process, ask the chatbot for help, or give up the purchase. The decision to interact (yes/no) with the chatbot was the main dependent variable. Affective response to the chatbot-avatar was assessed with the Affective Slider and User Experience (UX) of the platform with the Attrakdiff questionnaire. The results suggest that the presence of an avatar tends to increase the intention to interact with the chatbot and that the inclusion of emotional expression has a significantly positive impact on adherence to chatbot technology, with greater strength in the case of humoristic expression compared to sadness. However, these differences do not seem to have been enough to affect UX. Overall, considering the various results obtained, this study supports the use of avatars to initiate interaction with chatbots and points out advantages in the use of emotional design strategies, namely humour.

Keywords: Interaction Design · Emotional Design · UX · chatbot

1 Introduction

There has been a growing interest in chatbot technology [1]. A chatbot, also known as smart bot, interactive agent or digital assistant, is a software program with natural language capabilities, often based on artificial intelligence [2].

A. Marcus et al. (Eds.): HCII 2023, LNCS 14033, pp. 273–282, 2023.
https://doi.org/10.1007/978-3-031-35708-4_21

Chatbots are being used in many sectors, such as education, healthcare, business, and commerce, being a valuable solution for both businesses and users. The motivations for using this technology are diverse, ranging from increasing productivity, because multiple conversations can be established simultaneously, providing support and assistance at any time with low costs, to increased User Experience (UX), by offering quick responses in an attractive and innovative way [3] that meet the needs and expectations of users with increasingly fast-paced and hyper-connected lives.

However, paradoxically, despite chatbots are designed to mimic interactions between humans [4], most online consumers are reluctant in interacting with these systems and many of those who use them report some frustration in the experience, which greatly affects the success of this technology [5]. Some studies suggest that the lack of human-ization of chatbots [6], combined with their appearance [7] and personality [6], may explain the refraining of users, who seem to distrust these bots. Also, users seem to appreciate a balanced combination between productivity, entertainment and relational aspects, preferring chatbots with a friendly or empathic appearance [8], close to the idea of toy and/or a friend [3].

In this context, this study aims to contribute to the success of chatbots by finding design strategies that raise users' decision to initiate conversation with chatbots in e-commerce platforms. Failures will inevitably happen in such platforms, so designers must explicitly work towards such situations to minimise the negative impact on the UX. To increase the possibilities for users to interact with the chatbot, this study explores a combination of text and buttons with avatars in error pages, not only to facilitate the discovery of the chatbot but also to make it more friendly and thus more appealing to dialogue. Based on the assumption that users expect the chatbot to have a personality that is adjusted to the context of use, and that in the commercial domain it is acceptable for the chatbot to have a casual mood [9], we choose to investigate the potential of different emotional responses to error. For such, we selected humour and sadness. In this sense, this study sought to answer the questions: What impact does the use of avatars, to personalize the chatbot, have on the decision to interact with this technology? How does the emotional expression of an avatar affect the decision to interact with a chatbot?

2   Method

2.1   Participants

60 participants were recruited through advertisements in the researchers' personal social media pages and direct invitation by e-mail. All participants were Portuguese native speakers. Their demographics by experimental group are described in Table 1.

Familiarity with chatbots was assessed through a question with a 4-point scale, where 1 stood for "No experience, never heard of chatbots" and 4 for "Very experienced, I use chatbots regularly". The mode of familiarity level obtained in both groups was 3, meaning "Some experience, I sometimes use chatbots".

Table 1. Participants' demographics

Experimental groups	N	Gender		Age	
		Males	Females	Min-Max	Mean (SD)
Sad	30	17 (56.7%)	13 (43.3%)	20–62	34.93 (9.46)
Humoristic	30	16 (53.3%)	14 (46.7%)	20–65	37.57 (11.98)

2.2 Apparatus

Since the procedure was planned to be remote but with moderation, both participants and moderator had a computer with Internet access, microphone, speakers or headphones, camera, and real-time online meeting app (i.e., Zoom, Teams, Skype). Because the mock-up was not responsive, mobile devices, such as smartphones or tablets were not allowed.

2.3 Stimuli

A semi-functional mock-up of an e-commerce platform (see Fig. 2) was built on Figma® for the simulated task of purchasing electronic products. This mock-up follows a common flow for this type of platform (see Fig. 1), designed after a benchmark analysis.

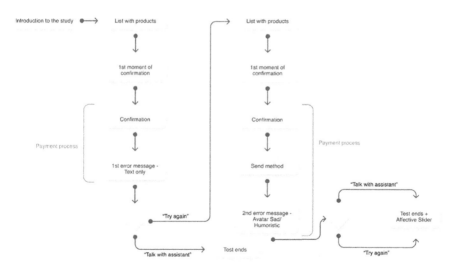

Fig. 1. Flow of the e-commerce platform mock-up.

Three error pages were created, one with text only (see Fig. 3) and two with avatars, representing the chatbot together with text message and buttons.

Fig. 2. Page of the e-commerce platform   **Fig. 3.** Error page text-only.

Cartoon-like avatars were created as they are suggested for humanising technology [10, 11]. For the same reason, rounded and anthropomorphic shapes, small stature and soft colours were preferred [12–14]. The avatars were inserted in error pages, seconded by a main text and a secondary text, together with action buttons.

To create the avatar's emotional states we resorted to Ekman's recommendations [15]. For sadness we worked mainly on the eyes, namely the angle of the eyebrows (see Fig. 4). For the humoristic counterpart (see Fig. 5) we worked on the emotion of surprise, exploring the idea of incongruity, unexpected or unusual, which are suggested as important in humour [16].

Fig. 4. Error page with sad avatar.   **Fig. 5.** Error page with humoristic avatar.

2.4 Affective Slider

To assess the affective responses to our designs, we applied the Affective Slider (AS) [17], which is a digital tool with two sliders, one for pleasure and the other for activation, based on the Self-Assessment Manikin (SAM) [18]. In this study, due to technical limitations that prevented us from implementing the slider, we resorted to a 9-point scale. Immediately after finishing interacting with the e-commerce platform and keeping in mind the error screen with the chatbot avatar, participants evaluated the affective response using the two AS dimensions.

2.5 Attrakdiff Questionnaire

After evaluating the affective response to the avatars, we wanted to assess if the User Experience (UX) with the platform was affected by the avatar design. For that we applied a translated to Portuguese language version of Attrakdiff questionnaire [19]. Attrakdiff is composed of a set of 28 pairs of antagonistic adjectives, grouped into four distinct groups: PQ (Pragmatic Quality), HQ-I (Hedonic Quality - Identity), HQ-S (Hedonic Quality - Stimulus) and ATT (Attractiveness).

2.6 Procedure

The participants were invited to evaluate the usability of an e-commerce platform. The evaluation of the chatbots was kept hidden until the end of the task. After responding to the invitation, a video chat was scheduled and run through a platform for online real-time meetings. The meeting started with a presentation of the study, followed by instructions on what to do next. There being no further questions, the informed consent was obtained, and the session began. Participants were randomly assigned to one of the two experimental groups created based on the emotions expressed by the chatbots' avatars (e.g., humoristic vs. sad). During the procedure the participants kept the screen sharing function active, the microphone and the computer camera on.

Participants were asked to buy a certain product as quickly as possible, under the pretext of an upcoming promotion. When entering the payment stage, a system crash followed by an error message interrupted the process. At that moment the screen displayed a text-only message and the action buttons. The chatbot was always available to provide help in recovering from the error. Participants had three options: repeat the process, ask the chatbot for help, or give up the purchase. The last two would result in the end of the experimental task. If they decided to repeat the operation, a new error message would appear again before the payment. However, on that occasion, the error message would be displayed accompanied by the image of an avatar, which could be humoristic or sad. Participants would have the same three options as before, but with the difference that any one of them would finish the task.

Having finished the task, they answered the AS questionnaire, followed by the Attrakdiff and, finally the demographic data. The procedure ended with a clarification of the real objectives of the study, followed by an acknowledgement of the contribution.

3 Results

3.1 Interaction with the Chatbot

The intention to interact with the chatbot was evaluated through the number of clicks on the action button labelled with "talk to the assistant", present in each error screen next to "Try again". Table 2 shows the number of interaction intentions in each error message.

Table 2. Number of interaction intentions with the chatbot when exposed to the error screen.

	1st error message	2nd error message
Sad (N = 30)	0	5
Humoristic (N = 30)	0	12

Two Chi-square tests of homogeneity, one for each error message, were run to assess if the decision to interact with the chatbot depend on the type of avatar (experimental condition). The results reveal no significant difference in the proportion of interactions with the chatbot between avatars in both error messages (1st error 1: sad *prop.* = 0.000, humoristic *prop.* = 0.000, no statistics are computed because interaction intention is a constant; 2nd error: sad *prop.* = 0.167, humoristic *prop.* = 0.400, $X^2(1, N = 60) = 4.022, p = 0.084$).

Subsequently, two paired-samples proportions McNemar tests were run, one for each avatar, to assess if there was a significant change in the decision to ask the chatbot for help from the first to the second error message. The results reveal that the proportion of interactions with the chatbot in 2nd error was higher than in 1st error in both conditions (sad: 2nd error *prop.* = 0.167, 1st error *prop.* = 0.000, $z = 2.236, p = 0.013$; humoristic: 2nd error *prop.* = 0.400, 1st error *prop.* = 0.000, $z = 3.464, p < 0.001$).

3.2 Affective Response

The affective response to the avatars was rated with the Affetive Slider, on a 9-point scale, where, for the pleasure dimension the far left indicated that the avatar made you feel unhappy, angry, dissatisfied, melancholic, hopeless, or bored and the far right indicated that the avatar made you feel happy, content, satisfied, or hopeful. For the activation dimension the far left indicates that the avatar made you feel relaxed, calm, slow, bored, sleepy, apathetic, and the far right indicates that the avatar made you feel stimulated, excited, frantic, agitated, awakened, or activated. Table 3 shows descriptive statistics of the responses to the Affective Slider per experimental condition.

Table 3. Descriptive statistics of responses to the Affective Slider per experimental condition

Experimental condition	Dimension	N	Min	Max	Median	IQR
Sad	Pleasure	30	2	9	5	3
	Activation	30	1	9	6	2
Humoristic	Pleasure	30	1	9	6	3
	Activation	30	1	8	5	3

To find whether the affective evaluation (AS) is different depending on the type of emotion expressed by the avatar, Mann-Whitney U tests were done to compare pleasure and activation distributions in the two experimental conditions. There was a significant difference in the AS pleasure distribution between sad (Mean rank = 25.4, Mdn = 5, IQR = 3) and humoristic (Mean rank = 35.6, Mdn = 6, IQR = 3) conditions ($U = 297.0$, $z = -2.202$, $p = 0.048$). There was not a significant difference in the AS activation distribution between sad (Mean rank = 34.2, Mdn = 6, IQR = 2) and humoristic (Mean rank = 26.8, Mdn = 5, IQR = 3) conditions ($U = 340.0$, $z = -1.662$, $p = 0.098$).

3.3 User Experience

The participants evaluated the UX of the prototype using the Attrakdiff. For this analysis we transformed the scale from 1 to 7 to a scale from -3 to 3, where zero served as the central/neutral point. Table 4 shows the descriptive statistics of scores obtained per each one of the four qualities assessed by this questionnaire and of the in Fig. 6 we can visually compare the results of both avatars.

Table 4. Descriptive statistics, Mean (SD), of Attrakdiff scores per quality and experimental condition

Experimental condition	PQ	HQ-I	HQ-S	ATT
Sad	1.13 (0.61)	0.85 (0.85)	0.22 (0.50)	1.28 (0.29)
Humoristic	1.36 (0.63)	0.64 (0.92)	0.69 (0.56)	1.30 (0.26)

To explore whether the UX evaluation is different depending on the type of emotion expressed by the avatar, four Independent Samples t-tests were conducted, one for each quality, to compare Attrakdiff scores in the two experimental conditions. There was a significant difference in the Attrakdiff HQ-S scores between sad (M = 4.16, SD = 0.86) and humoristic (M = 4.69, SD = 1.13) conditions ($t(58) = -2.202$, $p = 0.048$). There were not significant differences between the experimental conditions relatively to Attrakdiff HQ-I scores (sad: M = 4.80, SD = 0.78; humoristic: M = 4.65, SD = 0.91; $t(58) = 0.676$, $p = 0.501$), Attrakdiff PQ scores (sad: M = 5.10, SD = 0.57; humoristic: M = 5.30, SD = 0.77; $t(58) = -1.145$, $p = 0.257$) and Attrakdiff ATT scores (sad: M = 5.27, SD = 0.83; humoristic: M = 5.25, SD = 1.06; $t(58) = 0.078$, $p = 0.938$).

3.4 Demographics

Finally, it was evaluated whether the decision to interact with the avatar (2nd error) differs according to demographic variables and participants' previous experience. An Independent samples t-test was done to compare mean age of participants who interact and not interact with the chatbot. There was not a significant difference in the mean age of people who interact (M = 35.4, SD = 12.5) and who do not interact (M = 36.6, SD = 10.2) with the chatbot ($t(58) = 0.402$, $p = 0.689$).

Chi-square tests of homogeneity were done to compare the proportion of interactions between males and females and among the familiarity levels. There was not significant difference in the proportion of interactions with the chatbot between males (*prop.* = 0.273) and females (*prop.* = 0.296) groups ($X^2(1, N = 60) = 0.041, p = 1.000$), as well as in the proportion of interactions with the chatbot among familiarity levels ($X^2(3, N = 60) = 1.358, p = 0.814$).

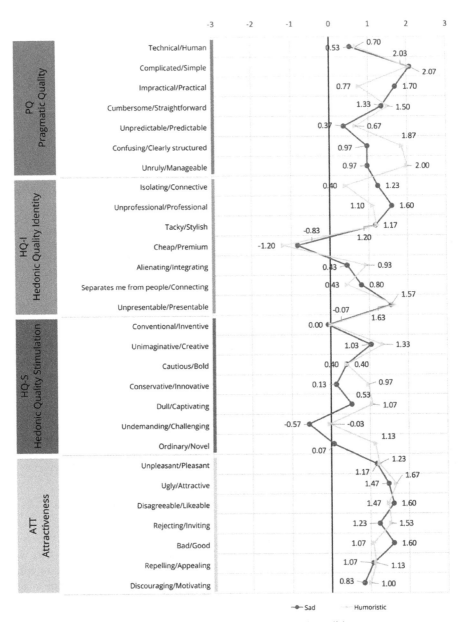

Fig. 6. Attrakdiff results per experimental condition.

4   Discussion

The results suggest that the presence of an avatar, per se, tends to increase interaction with the chatbot and that the inclusion of emotional expression has a significantly positive impact on adherence to chatbot technology, with greater strength in the case of humorous expression compared to sadness.

In turn, the results also suggest that the humoristic version generated more liking. However, these differences do not seem to have been enough to affect UX. However, the humoristic avatar produced differences in the perception of Hedonic Quality, which suggests that this emotion is the one that conveys more innovation, is more challenging and promotes more user interest.

No impact of demographic variables such as gender, age and previous experience was found on intentions to interact with the chatbot.

5   Conclusion

Chatbots are being presented as a technology capable of transforming the way people interact with digital platforms in the future. Although there is plenty of work on how to improve chatbots' communication abilities, there is a lack of empirical research on how to design better solutions to initiate the conversation with the chatbots. This study aimed to explore the use of avatars, expressing emotional states, to boost the interaction with the chatbots during a system failure in an e-commerce platform.

Overall, considering the various results obtained, this study supports the decision to use avatars to initiate interaction with chatbots in error pages and points out advantages in the use of emotional design strategies, namely humour.

However, some limitations should be taken into consideration when interpreting these findings. First, this study used a convenience sample that, therefore, is not representative of the population at large. The participants were mainly familiarized with chatbots, and it is possible that early users have other reactions. Second, the study compared a text-only error screen, without avatar, with two screens with avatars displaying different emotional expressions, i.e., humoristic and sadness. Future studies may benefit from including an emotionally neutral avatar, as well compare other emotions. Further, future work should analyse other aspects of the chatbot design, such as personality, animation and/or sound.

Despite the above-mentioned limitations, these findings can be useful for designing better human-chatbot interaction experiences.

Acknowledgments. National funds financed this work through FCT - Foundation for Science and Technology, I.P., within the scope of the project UIDB/00711/2020 from UNIDCOM/IADE – Unidade de Investigação em Design e Comunicação, Lisboa, Portugal.

References

1. Dale, R.: The return of the chatbots. Nat. Lang. Eng. **22**, 811–817 (2016)

2. Adamopoulou, E., Moussiades, L.: An overview of chatbot technology. In: Maglogiannis, I., Iliadis, L., Pimenidis, E. (eds.) AIAI 2020. IAICT, vol. 584, pp. 373–383. Springer, Cham (2020). https://doi.org/10.1007/978-3-030-49186-4_31

3. Brandtzaeg, P.B., Følstad, A.: Why people use chatbots. In: Kompatsiaris, I., et al. (eds.) INSCI 2017. LNCS, vol. 10673, pp. 377–392. Springer, Cham (2017). https://doi.org/10.1007/978-3-319-70284-1_30

4. Hill, J., Randolph Ford, W., Farreras, I.G.: Real conversations with artificial intelligence: a comparison between human–human online conversations and human–chatbot conversations. Comput. Hum. Behav. **49**, 245–250 (2015)

5. UJET: Critical State of Automation in Customer Experience (2022)

6. Holtgraves, T.M., Ross, S.J., Weywadt, C.R., Han, T.L.: Perceiving artificial social agents. Comput. Hum. Behav. **23**, 2163–2174 (2007)

7. Sproull, L., Subramani, M., Kiesler, S., Walker, J.H., Waters, K.: When the interface is a face. Hum.-Comput. Interact. **11**, 97–124 (1996)

8. Dautenhahn, K., Ogden, B., Quick, T.: From embodied to socially embedded agents – implications for interaction-aware robots. Cogn. Syst. Res. **3**, 397–428 (2002)

9. Jain, M., Kumar, P., Kota, R., Patel, S.N.: Evaluating and informing the design of chatbots. In: DIS 2018: Proceedings of the 2018 Designing Interactive Systems Conference, pp. 895–906 (2018)

10. Lee, O., Shin, M.: Addictive consumption of avatars in cyberspace. Cyberpsychol. Behav. **7**, 417–420 (2004)

11. Suler, J.: The Psychology of Avatars and Graphical Space. True Center Publishing, The Psychology of Cyberspace (2007)

12. Cheng, Y., Qiu, L., Pang, J.: Effects of Avatar Cuteness on Users' Perceptions of System Errors in Anthropomorphic Interfaces (2020)

13. Pellitteri, M.: Kawaii aesthetics from Japan to Europe: theory of the Japanese "cute" and transcultural adoption of its styles in Italian and French comics production and commodified culture goods. Arts **7**, 24 (2018)

14. Mcveigh, B.J.: How Hello Kitty commodifies the cute, cool and camp: 'consumutopia' versus 'control' in Japan. J. Mater. Cult. **5**, 225–245 (2000)

15. Ekman, P.: Emotions Revealed. Recognizing Faces and Feelings to Improve Communication and Emotional Life. Holt Paperbacks (2007)

16. Nilsen, D., McGhee, P., Goldstein, J.: Handbook of Humor Research: Volume 1, Basic Issues. Rocky Mt. Rev. Lang. Lit. **39**, 83 (1985)

17. Betella, A., Verschure, P.F.M.J.: The affective slider: a digital self-assessment scale for the measurement of human emotions. PLoS ONE **11** (2016)

18. Bradley, M.M., Lang, P.J.: Measuring emotion: the self-assessment manikin and the semantic differential. J. Behav. Ther. Exp. Psychiatry **25**, 49–59 (1994)

19. Hassenzahl, M., Burmester, M., Koller, F.: AttrakDiff: Ein Fragebogen zur Messung wahrgenommener hedonischer und pragmatischer Qualität. In: Szwillus, G., Ziegler, J. (eds.) Mensch & Computer 2003: Interaktion in Bewegung, pp. 187–196. Vieweg+Teubner Verlag, Wiesbaden (2003)

Rethinking Interaction with Conversational Agents: How to Create a Positive User Experience Utilizing Dialog Patterns

Marvin Heuer[1]([✉]), Tom Lewandowski[1], Joffrey Weglewski[1], Tom Mayer[1], Max Kubicek[1], Patrick Lembke[2], Simon Ortgiese[2], and Tilo Böhmann[1]

[1] University of Hamburg, Hamburg, Germany
{marvin.heuer,tom.lewandowski,tilo.boehmann}@uni-hamburg.de,
{joffrey.weglewski,tom.mayer,max.kubicek}@studium.uni-hamburg.de
[2] bpc AG, Münster, Germany
{patrick.lembke,simon.ortgiese}@bpc.ag

Abstract. Conversational agents (CAs) are increasingly used as an additional convenient and innovative customer service channel to relieve service employees, as in the studied organization. In the process of analyzing and maintaining the present AI-based agent, however, user satisfaction is low as the CA lacks understanding and offers unsatisfactory solutions to users. Nonetheless, solving the requests and providing a positive user experience is crucial to relieve the service employees' workload permanently. For CAs' improvement, this study followed action design research (ADR) and used design thinking. We identified the central interaction problems (findability, welcome message, dialog control and fallback issues) with a monitoring process and analysis. Afterward, we interviewed users about their expectations and requirements and addressed these problems by creating user-centric mock-ups. Through a quantitative survey, the most popular solutions were implemented in a prototype. Finally, the resulting CA prototype was evaluated, showing a significantly improved user experience afterward, and design guidelines were discovered.

Keywords: conversational agents · chatbot user experience (UX) · fallback strategy · interaction design · artificial intelligence (AI)

1 Introduction

CAs have become increasingly common in organizations as a central channel for customer contact [1, 2]. Organizations introduce CAs in customer service to reduce the workload of customer service employees, leading to cognitive relief and increasing the productivity of entire service units, such as an internal or external information technology (IT) help desk [3]. Unfortunately, dissatisfied users stand out during CA analysis and maintenance. This is mainly due to communication difficulties between the CA and the user, thus leading to unsatisfactory or no solutions. The challenges of today's CAs are that they are learning systems and, initially, are limited [4]. Therefore, CAs

© The Author(s), under exclusive license to Springer Nature Switzerland AG 2023
A. Marcus et al. (Eds.): HCII 2023, LNCS 14033, pp. 283–301, 2023.
https://doi.org/10.1007/978-3-031-35708-4_22

often misunderstand user requests and fail to meet user expectations [5, 6]. Additionally, CAs have problems when a user request cannot be assigned to a learned subject (e.g., intent/entity recognition). Frequently, formulations need to be more variable and holistically designed to reach a successful conclusion [4]. Customers become particularly dissatisfied when the reformulation of their query does not lead to success. In such cases, a successful solution proposal from the CA to the customer may fail. In addition, CAs require continuous improvement, as new use cases are emerging from user queries and need to be included [7, 8].

To tackle this issue, it is necessary to resolve the concerns and create a positive user experience. The goal is to ensure a lasting interaction with the user and always offer a solution. We characterize successful communication as ensuring a permanent interaction between the user and the CA and offering a solution in all cases. Customer satisfaction and the continued use of the CA depend on successful communication. Indeed, interaction problems are a common challenge (Table 1). This paper presents two novel concepts to help keep customer satisfaction and CA usage high.

Table 1. Potential Effort Matrix.

Effort	Potential		
	Small	Medium	High
Small		Message length, Help category	Learning, Text completion, User control
Medium	Response time, sentiment analysis, small talk	Character, Forwarding, UX	Fallbacks
High	Callback, Complaint	Conversation starter, Fallback at greeting	Findability, Buttons, Message variance

The central research question was as follows: "How can a user's CA experience be improved by analyzing, understanding, and optimizing interaction problems?" The sub-questions were "What interaction problems exist between user and CAs, why do they arise, and how are they solved?" and "To what extent can the user experience be improved?" The focus was on users and their perceived usage. The two-level category system and the restructured fallback scheme are explained later.

2 Background

The idea of communicating with computers using natural language (e.g., via voice or text messages) has existed for several decades [9]. Weizenbaum took initial steps toward a text interface between humans and information systems (IS) with *E.L.I.Z.A.* in 1966 [10]. *E.L.I.Z.A.* is an IS that generates responses to text inputs, simulating a psychotherapist in a therapy session [11]. Since then, numerous other CAs have been developed, such as *Parry* [12] or *A.L.I.C.E.* [13, 14], which mainly answered simple rule-based commands and questions, simulating conversations [5, 11]. However, the speech comprehension of these systems was not particularly robust [15], which impaired interaction. They could not hold long conversations with their users or give more than simple and often rule-based responses to the input commands [5]. However, advances in technology in the field of artificial intelligence (AI), specifically in the context of natural language processing and generation (NLP/NLG) [4], are leading to a massive proliferation of these systems in numerous workplaces [16, 17] and support contexts [e.g., 2, 18]. In recent years, this massive technological progress has allowed the development of progressively more intelligent CAs, characterized as AI-based systems, which are (1) user-centric, (2) social and intuitive, (3) learning [9, 19], and as the ChatGPT and large language models (LLM) trend indicates, becoming more (4) aggregative and (5) generative, with the ability to access numerous sources of information in the background and recognize and create new content for users and customers using machine learning (ML) technologies, which also enables interaction.

CAs in the scientific literature are often divided into two subclasses (in taxonomies described with the dimension "communication mode") [20, 21]. The first class of text-based CAs is usually referred to as chatbots, chatterbots, talkbots, or dialogue systems [5, 22]. The second class of speech-based CAs is commonly called virtual, digital, or intelligent assistants as well as digital companions [5]. In many academic publications, however, no distinction is made at all [23]. The distinction is also marginal from a technical perspective because speech-based input can easily be transferred to text-based input and vice versa [20]. Further, combinations of text- and speech-based forms of in- and output approaches exist [15].

This paper defines CAs as text-based and AI-based representations, such as chatbots (see above) [5, 22, 24, 25]. There are two main differences and novelties of this kind of information system (IS) [21]. First, users interact with the system using natural languages like English, German, or Spanish. Second, they rely on "the assistant's knowledgeability and human-like behavior, often summarized as artificial intelligence" [21, p. 2025], which has great potential to assist, solve, augment, or automate user tasks intuitively [7, 20, 26]. A unique characteristic of CAs is their ability to learn and improve through naturalistic interactions [7]. In this paper, the term CA includes all AI-based IS that communicate with users (employees or customers) through a text-based natural language interface enabled by NLP/NLU technologies, such as CA frameworks (e.g., Microsoft LUIS, Google Dialogflow, SAP CAI, or RASA.ai) including an intelligent communication and built-in self-learning component. The actual prototype in this work was developed using SAP CAI.

Currently, CAs are especially adopted in interactive domains, such as customer service and support, marketing, sales and entertainment, teaching and education, and in different workplace applications [15, 20, 23]. CAs have the potential to change the entire interaction and communication channel between customers and service employees [5, 27–29]. As a result, they can transform service provision and value (co)-creation, and thus, entire business models and service systems [30, 31] in the future [5, 32, 33].

CAs facilitate a new form of flexibility, quality, speed, and personalization of the customer relationship [9, 28]. Moreover, they represent a highly scalable and cost-effective solution, saving money by replacing manually executed tasks performed by previously required service employees [34–36]. A transformation towards an innovative, conve-nient, automated, self-learning 24/7 customer service communication and interaction channel available to customers worldwide and multilingually is feasible and could take over initial routine tasks [5, 11, 27]. In addition they offer shorter resolution times and high availability [37].

Based on these findings, particularly the dissatisfaction of users with their interaction with CAs and consequent interaction problems, the need to rethink the design of and interaction with CAs is apparent. Accordingly, we present approaches utilizing user-centered mock-ups and prototypes, which are implemented and allow us to derive design guidelines.

3 Methodology

The goal of this article was to identify problems in interaction design. To achieve our research goal, we followed the ADR approach [38] by combining various sub-steps: Initially, we created user-centered CA solution alternatives (mock-ups) based on expert interviews to solve the identified interaction problems. Subsequently, we selected alter-natives quantitatively through a survey, implemented them as prototypes, and finally evaluated them. An overview of the sub-steps of the methodology is shown in Table 2.

3.1 Action Design Research

As explained by [38], ADR is a research approach for examining and co-creatively solving a specific constellation of problems within an organization. As the name sug-gests, the approach combines action research (AR, [39]) with design science research (DSR, [40]) [41, 42]. This combination aims to create practice-relevant IT artifacts. The approach consists of four stages, starting with the problem formulation phase. The central concept within ADR is the "Building, Intervention, and Evaluation" (BIE) cycle [38]. Generally, an ADR project starts in the first phase by identifying a research gap in practice or theory and formulating initial research questions [38, 41], similar to DSR. The IT artifact idea resembles this BIE cycle, where the artifact is built, put into action within an organization (the AR part), and subsequently evaluated [41]. Thereby, the artifact is improved and refined in a cycle-wise manner [38]. A significant part of the ADR approach involves reflection and the subsequent formalized learning stage. The third and fourth stages lead to an improved IT artifact and aid in the development of design principles and the research outcome [38]. These can take the form of new, initially researched designs or selective improvements of existing designs [38]. Mullarkey and Hevner (2019) [42] propose an "elaborated action design research process model" as a more flexible approach for immersive industry-based projects.

3.2 Data Collection, Analysis, and Procedure

Table 2. Procedure.

Step	Action
1	Interaction problems defined Identified measures for improving the user experience
2	Developed monitoring guide Analyzed logs
3	Potential-effort-matrix defined Prioritizing
4	User-centric solution alternatives created
5	Expert interviews regarding user interaction problems
6	Developed survey for interaction problems and choosing the prototype implementation
7	Focus group setting for evaluating the prototype

As a first step, *interaction problems* were defined and the measures that would improve the user experience were explored. We did this at various levels, i.e., both in the basic design and in the direct interaction. We started to *identify* the CAs' interaction problems so we could solve them and thus improve the user experience. Second, we developed a *monitoring guide* and analyzed the monitoring and chat logs of the current CA [43] and its 443 conversations, allowing us to identify the main problems in the current interaction design. Based on the identified problems, a *potential effort matrix* was derived (see Table 1). We focused on the four areas that offered high potential for improvement combined with comparatively low effort.

To address these four core problems, *user-centric solution alternatives* were created. To improve the user experience, six potential users were involved in the creation process, and an open *interview* was conducted to solicit initial approaches and ideas [44]. These interviews gave us valuable insights on the expectations and requirements regarding the interaction problems of potential users. Next, we enhanced these findings (four interaction problems) with literature review results [45].

As a sixth step, we developed a *survey* with questions about each core problem to elaborate on the identified interaction problems [46, 47]. Eleven questions focused on the findability of the CA, and an additional 14 questions were related to the welcome message. Nine questions addressed issues regarding dialog control, and 11 questions examined the fallback issue. One hundred and twelve people participated in the survey, which gave us a representative view of the issues. With the help of a survey and design thinking techniques [48], alternative solutions were discarded, while the most popular ones were implemented in a prototype. In the seventh step, we evaluated the prototype in a *focus group* setting [49, 50]. The final guideline was created based on the findings of the monitoring, the surveys, and the concrete implementation of improvements in the prototype with subsequent evaluation [51].

3.3 Evaluation

For the evaluation, the prototype was first evaluated, followed by the developed guideline [52]. The evaluation strategy ensured a structured and correct evaluation of the prototype. The goal was to compare the existing CA with the optimized version (i.e., the prototype). The focus was on comparing the change in the user experience and confirming the researched guideline aspects, which were established as explained in the previous subsection.

In order to compare the prototype with the existing CA, we used a between-subjects design [53], which is suitable for such situations. In this evaluation, the prototype and the existing CA were the independent variables, while the subject areas of the scenarios and questions explained below were the dependent variables. The System Usability Score (SUS) score can be used to compare the two variants, i.e., the existing CA and the prototype [54]. Different scenarios were developed so that the prototype could be evaluated in a stepwise manner. The scenarios were created based on the problems identified from the first two steps described above. The problems were selected based on the topics most frequently addressed in the monitoring process. We tackled the interaction problems in the prototype and evaluated its success. Four areas were addressed, and we compared the prototype with the existing CA. For this comparison, we created four scenarios (in connection with the four selected topics), which were to be executed by the test persons for the respective assigned CA. These four scenarios were related to the corresponding problem topic areas. In addition to these topic areas, which were optimized in the prototype, the results of the expert interviews, monitoring, and survey were also used in the implementation of the prototype. These addressed the user experience in general, the fallback scheme, reusability, findability, and the two-level category system.

The design guideline was also evaluated as a summarizing end product. The goal of the guideline was to create helpful knowledge for future projects. For this purpose, a focus group was formed as the first evaluation method to obtain expert feedback on the design guideline [44, 50]. This was a formative evaluation, as it was part of the process of developing the design guideline [55]. Since the evaluation and discussion were carried out directly with those affected (i.e., a focus group) [49], the procedure can be considered a "naturalistic evaluation" [51, 52]. This step of the process aimed to gather suggestions for improving the design guideline. First, we presented the status of the design guideline to the focus group. Then, we discussed the particular content-related topics with the CA team.

Additionally, the structure was discussed. The second evaluation method was a summative "ex post evaluation" [56]. A structured survey with predefined statements [57] was administered to the project owners, who were asked to rate the quality of the guideline on a Likert scale with five values ranging from 1 (strongly disagree) to 5 (strongly agree) [58]. Nine categories were defined and formulated in advance in a Google Forms questionnaire.

4 Results

We started by analyzing the current conversations already happening with the existing CA. It became clear that the CA failed to answer user queries in a satisfactory way. In particular, the CA failed to understand users and therefore did ask them to rephrase their queries. Furthermore, the CA forwarded the user to other contact means (e.g., to a human service employee). As the misunderstanding of the CA and subsequent failure of the conversation were the most pressing issues, we analyzed all conversations with the CA itself. Of the 443 conversations, the CA failed to ask users to reformulate their queries 367 times. Additionally, 181 times the CA suggested categories or topics that the users could check themselves since the CA could not help. On 99 occasions, the CA did not understand the query and answered incorrectly. Further, the CA redirected the user to use other customer service methods 60 times.

In order to differentiate better to improve the user experience with the CA, we isolated the different contexts of the CA. We distinguished between individual queries (249 instances), company-related queries (80 instances), and general queries (85 instances). We regarded 38 further instances as non-relevant, as the users in those cases obviously entered misleading information to mess with the CA. The logs also showed the CA erred in communication by asking multiple queries in one (4 instances) and connecting the greeting with a question (43 instances). Although the CA had a high percentage of dissatisfactory responses, users were tolerant regarding a one-time CA failure. In 96 instances, the CA had to fallback and rephrase one time, but there were only 24 instances with four or more fallbacks. Overall, the CA had 548 single fallbacks.

We focused on the fallback issues and classified them to their contexts. The greatest number of fallbacks were related to individual topics users asked about (255 instances). Another 105 cases resulted in fallbacks regarding general topics, but there were only three instances of company-related topics. Forty-two questions were not classifiable. The main reason behind the fallbacks in 183 instances was that information on the queried topic existed in the CA but was not kept up-to-date. In 77 instances, information on the topic did not exist. Of 273 user reactions to a fallback, the conversation was ended in 74 cases, while in 187 cases the query was reformulated. Only 42 cases were solved after the first fallback, and an additional 145 instances led to another fallback. In total, 97 users left the conversation after the first fallback. Further, 74 left after the second fallback, an additional 30 quit after the third fallback, and 11 left after at least four fallbacks. The data showed that most users quit after the first or second fallback, and thus the design of a fallback handling strategy would be of paramount importance.

To offer help to the user in case of a fallback, topic/category suggestions were offered by the CA 125 times in the hope that they might cover the user's question and solve the problem. However, users took advantage of these suggestions in only 73 cases, of which no solution was found and the problem persisted in 57 cases.

Once the core interaction problems of the CA were defined (see Table 3), the problem understanding and selection phase was considered complete. Then, the solution phase began. In order to find suitable and satisfactory solutions for the problems, alternative solutions had to be designed, from which suitable ones were then selected. Since the context was the design of the interaction and a system, it made sense to involve possible users in the process of generating alternatives as well as in the selection process. The first

Table 3. Procedure.

Interaction problems
Findability
Welcome Message
Dialog control
Fallback issue

step in opening up the solution space was to conduct interviews with six potential users in order to gather initial suggestions for solutions and to open up the solution space. The interviewees were asked openly formulated questions about the central problems.

Regarding findability, the test subjects offered various suggestions. Most preferred an always visible icon on the side of a website. Out of habit, the bottom right was suggested. Placement in a navigation bar was also mentioned occasionally. However, the respondents were relatively divided on the design of the icon; in addition to a speech bubble as an icon, a CA icon was also mentioned several times. There was also disagreement about effects and animations. Some participants were negatively disposed towards them, while others expressed a contrary opinion, for example, related to effects that appear when the website is first loaded (so the CA draws attention to itself). In terms of color, the icon should be adapted to the corporate identity but still stand out somewhat from the rest of the CA and its environment.

The default message at the beginning of a conversation should explain that the chat is a conversation with a CA. After a greeting, a short but friendly and helpful message was expected. In some cases, subjects also mentioned topics or sample questions that the system could answer. A privacy notice in the form of a link was desired in order to not to make the message too long. Concrete language features or humor should be chosen depending on the company context. The respondents preferred a casual approach, but not a humorous one. The message should build trust and express helpfulness, as this is an important basis for the further course of the chat.

Most test subjects preferred free input of their requests in the form of free text. However, there was isolated criticism that many CAs cannot handle this type of input well, which can cause the system to take over and direct the conversation or suggest buttons. Especially when the CA needed feedback to answer the question, some of the control went to the bot. A mix of free text input and buttons thus seemed to make sense to many test subjects. According to the test subjects, buttons were particularly suitable for questions with few but clearly defined answer options (e.g., yes/no questions).

If the CA did not understand a question and made a fallback, there were different opinions from the respondents. Some wanted to be forwarded directly to a real service employee, while others were prepared to rephrase the question or expected similar suggestions from the CA. In such cases, the respondents indicated that they wanted to reformulate once or twice at most. If this still did not lead to a solution, a fallback was inevitable. Direct chat transfer or a contact form via e-mail were preferred as channels, and in some cases, a telephone call or direct callback were also mentioned. Without a fallback, direct forwarding should not be an option. For most of the respondents, the variability of the messages was not very important. Accordingly, slight variations in wording were sufficient, for example, in the fallback context. In general, however, this was a quality feature of a good implementation.

We then conducted a survey. Of the 112 survey participants, only 69 completed questionnaires were used for data analysis. Of these 69 participants, 32 were female, 35 were male, and one was diverse, with one of the participants also not providing gender information. On average, the participants were between 25 and 39 years of age (35 participants). Of the 69 participants, 15 were between 18 and 24 years of age, while 19 participants were between 40 and 59 years of age. None were older than 59. It should also be noted that 65 participants had interacted with a CA before, while only four participants had never interacted with a CA. Regarding the variability in CA responses, 13.04% of the 69 participants stated it is "very important," 39.13% said it was "important," 28.99% were "neutral," 13.04% indicated it was "not important," and 5.80% said it was "not important at all."

Based on the survey results on findability, a disagreement emerged regarding the pages of a website on which a CA should be found. About 45% of the respondents wanted access on every page, while about 41% indicated the contact or customer service page was sufficient. According to the respondents, the reference to the CA should be found on the right edge of the website, 46% preferred the middle, and 39% favored the bottom right side of the website. Regarding the size of the CA icon, a medium size was the most popular (about 59%). The survey results showed that in terms of scrolling behavior, the option of a fixed, ever-visible CA icon was desired by 84% of the respondents. With regard to the color design of a notice, 64% preferred a design matching the color of the website, which nevertheless stands out clearly so that the CA can be found quickly. Approximately 35% of the respondents preferred a design that matches the website and does not stand out strongly. Regarding the shape of the symbol, a square was preferred by 72% of the respondents. However, it was also noted in a comment that the CA design should orient to the design of the website and the corporate design of the company. Similar to the color scheme, the focus should always be on a design that matches the rest of the environment. The graphic symbol of a speech bubble was also popular (72%). Regarding the textual indication of the symbol, the opinions were mixed. About 30% of the respondents stated that no textual reference was necessary, 26% favored "chatbot" as a reference, and about 22% preferred "Ask your question here." The respondents also noted that a textual hint should be as short as possible. Furthermore, 67% of the respondents did not want effects to attract attention. The effect of flying in the CA icon had the most supporters of all the effects shown (12%). Other comments mainly indicated that a CA icon should never overlay content on a website. Intrusive designs were not desired, as they look like advertising. One suggestion was to resize the design depending on which page it is on. Another suggestion was that the icon in the customer service area could be more prominent than on the homepage.

The survey results regarding the default message at the beginning of the conversation showed that the message that is currently used is best received by potential users: "Hello, I am Roberta, your digital assistant. Please ask me your question." Above all, it was emphasized that the brevity of the message is crucial. Based on the survey results, however, a trend was discernible indicating that an optimal default message has not yet been determined. The ratings were mostly in the "like" range (63.77%), while the rest of the responses were "like very much" (21.74%) and "mediocre" (13.04%). If the default message had been optimal, a significant shift to "I like very much" would have been seen in the ratings. It could be concluded that the default message used currently (short, personal, (optional) emojis; welcome formula with introduction of the CA and offer of help) promotes the user experience adequately. With regard to the presentation of the General Data Protection Regulation (GDPR) information, as required within the EU, the button with text content variant was preferred. A total of 84.06% of the respondents found this variant to be at least "average" and predominantly responded "I like" and "I like very much." The previous form of a text block was also rated as "good" by some of the respondents, although the proportion of "bad" ratings was 26.09%. The respondents thought a plain button above the default message seemed unobtrusive in contrast to a larger text block. The information on the GDPR could still be easily accessed. Comments like "one likes to overlook" illustrated the inconspicuousness.

Regarding the dialog design, the majority (57.97%) of the respondents preferred free input. However, some noted that while free input is desirable, it usually does not work well in current CAs, which is why guided CA input is then preferred. Buttons (11.59% of respondents) or quick replies (13.04% of respondents) were almost equally important to the users, which explains why the term button is used synonymously with quick replies in the following. In general, a mix of free text and buttons was preferred (31.88% of respondents for a mix of free text and button or free text and quick replies, i.e., a total of 63.76%), where the use of buttons is independent of the content. The respondents did not differ much in whether the clicked button or "Quick Reply" should be displayed in the user dialog as an answer (34.78% of respondents) or its label or title (37.68% of respondents). Accordingly, a further 17.39% of the respondents indicated that a mix could be used flexibly, and 10.14% of the respondents selected the option "no matter." Buttons should be used after the results, for topic suggestions (63.77% of the asked ones), fallbacks (52.17% of the asked ones), forwardings (68,12% of the asked ones), and yes–no answers (73.91% of the asked ones). In addition, unrestricted free text input was preferred by most of the respondents (82.61%). Text entry was considered the primary input standard (75.36%). Further, intelligent sentence completion was viewed as reasonable as a future feature of CA (13.04% of respondents). Sentence completion automatically displays canned questions for the user to select when entering individual words. As a result, customer satisfaction and comprehension should be improved by correct answers from the CA.

The survey was able to determine a new fallback scheme. Based on the responses, the following formulation was rated as the best: "Sorry, I don't have an answer to that yet. I will be happy to give you the opportunity to speak to a human employee. Your request will be dealt with as soon as possible." A total of 42.03% of the respondents said "I like it a lot," while an additional 40.58% stated "I like it." The subjects generally preferred a transparent response, with the CA disclosing non-knowledge. Compared to rephrasing, a redirect was preferred. In addition, the importance of making an effort to find a solution was conveyed at the end of the message. Based on the survey, the structure of the fallback scheme should be as follows: Make CA limits clear + inspire confidence in the CA + do not blame the user. For fallback 1: Clarify misunderstanding + suggest rewording + give option to forward. In case of fallback 2: Clarify misunderstanding again using a different wording + suggest forwarding. In the formulation of the first fallback, a reformulation option is suggested, while this is omitted in the second fallback. The wording of the second fallback consists of the respondent's request for forwarding, which is reflected in the evaluation of the variant: "Unfortunately, I don't have an answer to this either. My colleagues will take care of it and find a solution. How should the contact be made?" Of the respondents, 71.02% classified this option as "I like" and "I like very much." Compared to other formulations that stood for a second fallback, it was clear that the forwarding option was more appealing. The formulation was intended to produce an optimal scenario for a fallback process. The results of the survey clearly showed that forwarding is desired after only one fallback. This would make it impossible to achieve the goal of relieving the burden on customer service. If a reformulation was suggested to the respondent after one or even two fallbacks, it was rejected in most cases, especially after the second fallback. It can be concluded that the patience of the users is rather low and that a solution should be offered as soon as possible. Meanwhile, category suggestions were a good option. However, categories that are inappropriate and do not offer solutions but rather serve typical FAQs were problematic. Individual concerns characterized the conversations. Forwarding, often chosen in the scenarios, also received a clear vote in the survey regarding the two forms of implementation. While call, QR code, and e-mail were not desired, the respondents felt that a callback option and, above all, chat takeover should be used. Indeed, chat takeover received ratings of "like it a lot" (42.03%) and "like it" (43.48%). Callback received the second-highest rating, with 30.43% of the respondents saying they "like it a lot" and 40.58% saying they "like it." The sales of the other three options were somewhat unclear clear, so they were excluded. Only 5% of the respondents indicated "I like" or "I like very much" in response to the e-mail option.

Table 4. Interaction problems and dialog patterns.

Interaction problems	Solution guideline
Findability	Fixed, visible CA icon
Welcome Message	Short, personal, (optional) emojis; welcome formula with introduction of the CA and offer of help GDPR information as button
Dialog Control	Free text input + buttons
Fallback Issue	Make CA limits clear + inspire confidence in the CA + do not blame the user For fallback 1: Clarify misunderstanding + suggest rewording + give option to forward In case of fallback 2: Clarify misunderstanding again using a different wording + suggest forwarding

Following the evaluation of the survey, the prototype was created. The CA symbol was adapted to make it easier to find, so the image of a speech bubble was included on the website without a textual reference. Some of the aspects collected could only be integrated locally for the evaluation, such as resizing the icon and moving it from the bottom right of the web page edge to a middle position on the right edge of the page. According to the survey, only a small change was required in the welcome message (see Table 4). The final representation of the GDPR notice (see Fig. 1) was removed due to the previous form of a text block.

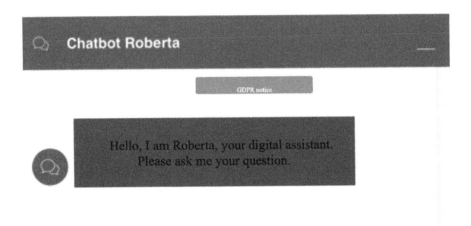

Fig. 1. Welcome message with GDPR (translated to English, design slightly modified).

The topic of dialog design turned out to be appropriate when comparing the results, as many of the results were already used in the CA. The results of the monitoring showed that the topic suggestions were not relevant to the goal. However, this relevance was mainly related to the fallback area where a solution was developed. Intelligent sentence completion was another potential change that emerged from the results. The new fallback scheme was based on the following aspects. First, the wording that the CA sends during a fallback was taken from the survey. Further, the preparation for prototyping revealed a discrepancy between the desire for forwarding after only one fallback and the goal of user relief. This would not have been feasible by forwarding early. Due to this, the fallback was formulated so that a reformulation occurs first, but at the same time there is the option to choose one of the two forwardings. In the case of a second fallback, the reference to a reformulation option is omitted. The forwarding options remain. The new prototype distinguishes the causes of fallbacks. The previously mentioned fallbacks occurred because the CA could not assign a single intent.

In order to exclude missing expressions as a cause, keyword recognition was implemented in the prototype. The feature was declared as a two-level category system. While it is technically supposed to run via the fallback path, visually it looks to the user like query recognition. The CA can recognize specific keywords. If the exact request cannot be assigned to an intent, suitable super-categories are suggested with the help of the recognition. After selecting these categories, questions are displayed in a second stage, which the user can choose. In the case of a wording that matches the query, the user has reached his goal despite the fallback. Unsuitable questions are followed by the option of a redirect. The resulting benefit can be primarily related to improving the UX. The fallback with no prospect of resolution is bypassed, and a second chance is given to process the query. This also prevents premature forwarding and partially relieves customer service. The rate of solved requests cannot yet reach 100% due to the individuality of the requests, which makes forwarding to an employee indispensable for some users. Following prototyping, the prototypes were evaluated. Ten people were interviewed for each variant. The results were positive for all interviewees.

Our results show a significantly improved user experience and a reduced error occurrence without finding a solution. Design guidelines were derived that enable replication of the results. The restructured fallback scheme avoids permanent requests for reformulation and inappropriate category suggestions. A two-level category system intercepts fallbacks and helps to find the user a solution through a topic-specific category set by keyword recognition. Based on the subjects surveyed (>9), the prototype increased the SUS score (interpretation by [54]) of the CA from 67 to 85.25. The first score is acceptable and represents an "OK" usability. The higher score of 85.25 indicates excellent usability and a significant improvement.

The shift in fallback to a new scheme that separates fallbacks according to their state of entry causes a shift in thinking, where fallbacks are no longer primarily to be monitored. Rather, fallbacks do not lead to a solution. This commonly occurring problem [59] could be solved here. The callback option and chat pickup, identified as the most popular redirects, have been widely implemented and meet user expectations (see Fig. 2). General satisfaction could be raised and the CA prototype use was positively evaluated. The core problems arise from frequent errors and a lack of solutions for the user. This has a direct impact on the user experience and is improved by using the prototype's implemented features. A fallback scheme that does not allow permanent rewording but offers specific suggestions minimizes errors and improves the UX. Further, the existing possibility of a redirection ensures recurring use of the CA without a loss of trust. Even so, CAs require constant interaction with the user and thus continuous monitoring and training. The design guideline was also evaluated positively.

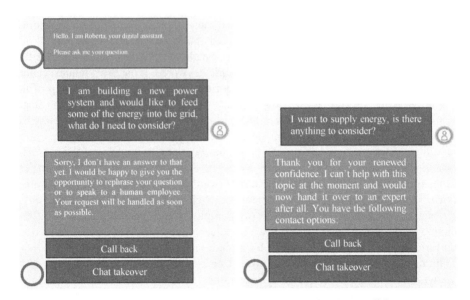

Fig. 2. Twice restructured Fallback-scheme (translated to English).

5 Discussion

Despite the evaluation of the prototype and the design guideline, dissemination of the survey during the COVID-19 pandemic proved problematic but was possible digitally. Evaluation of the prototype was also possible. On-site interviews were extremely helpful for the "Thinking Aloud" method as part of the prototype evaluation. However, it was not possible to ensure that all subjects had the same conditions, so a laboratory experiment was not possible. In addition, the design guideline should have been tested more extensively in practice, which was not done here. The detailed collection of demographic data, both for the survey and the prototype, was not possible in the organization. In this regard, permission for a more detailed collection of demographic data would have been desirable. Other aspect that should be considered critically are the formulation of the prototype as well as design guideline evaluation. During the implementation of both processes, there were queries regarding questions. It may be assumed that questions were interpreted differently, at least in part, which could have influenced the results. There were other organizational challenges in conducting the interviews in general due to the pandemic. Facilitation as well as conducting interviews via video conferencing systems, such as Microsoft Teams, could prove difficult and complicated. However, no such problems arose during the interviews.

Chronologically to the procedure first the extent of the solution ideas is to be mentioned. The interviews with six test persons, each with their own ideas as well as implementations from the literature, do not reflect all possible solutions. Thus, ideas that were not discussed could have resulted in a better UX and more successfully achieved the research objective. Regarding the conduct of the survey, demographic data were included but not considered further in the comparison. Hence, no evaluation of different age groups or genders was made to determine differences in this regard. This approach was sufficient to obtain a general impression of the proposed solutions but could nevertheless lead to differential results. Studies involving diverse industries, different target groups, and a more detailed analysis would be useful. Moreover, no deep analysis of the demographic data was performed in the prototype evaluation.

Of the 69 survey participants, 65 had interacted with a CA before. It would be interesting to survey more people who had not interacted with a CA, which would lead to a better result on user experience. It is possible that this group would have new ideas about CAs, as they would not have a preconceived image of CAs. Furthermore, there might be reasons why this group of people has not yet used a CA. Such information is essential for improving the user experience of a CA. A balanced mix between these two groups (users and non-users) should be ensured in future evaluations so that similarities and differences can be identified, which could then be used to optimize the CA.

In addition, the prototype evaluation does not show perfect statistical significance (requiring 30 test subjects). Thus, the evaluation of the prototype is not sufficient to make a final assessment of the changes. Rather, the guideline aspects must be implemented in a productive environment and monitored over several weeks and then re-evaluated. Above all, the occurrence of fallbacks must be tracked. However, the keyword recognition with the new fallback scheme changes the perspective on fallbacks themselves. A fallback should no longer be regarded as an error. Resolution through the new categories could also lead to a solution, even if the CA technically executes a fallback. The importance of the unresolved request is now the new core aspect to monitor. The UX is significantly dependent on this, as every unresolved request leaves the user dissatisfied.

Overall, the results of this work including the wide range of surveys and user interviews suggest that there has been little research (e.g., [60]) on so-called Dialog Patterns and therefore they offer additional research value. By highlighting interaction problems, new patterns can be identified for the four core problems, which we refer to as *Dialog Patterns*. Little systematic research has been done in this area so far, so this work contributes to it despite its limitations.

6 Conclusion

In summary, optimizing the prioritized problem aspects of the investigated CA show a significant improvement in error occurrence without solution finding and in the user experience. The restructured fallback scheme avoids permanent requests for reformulation and inappropriate category suggestions are avoided. A two-tier category system intercepts fallbacks and gives the user another chance to find a solution via a topic-specific category set with the help of keyword recognition. The change in fallback to a new scheme that separates fallbacks according to their entry status is causing a shift in thinking that fallbacks are no longer primarily to be monitored. Instead, it is fallbacks that lead to no resolution. With the help of the research, the research question: "How can a user's CA experience be improved by analyzing, understanding, and optimizing interaction problems?" can be answered. This paper shows several approaches by means of user-centered mock-ups and prototypes to improve the pressing issue of user satisfaction with the CA interaction, to solve core interaction problems, and shows the need for further research on dialog patterns.

References

1. Castillo, D., Canhoto, A.I., Said, E.: The dark side of AI-powered service interactions: exploring the process of co-destruction from the customer perspective. Serv. Ind. J. **40**(13–14), 900–925 (2020)
2. Zierau, N., et al.: Towards developing trust-supporting design features for AI-based chatbots in customer service. In: International Conference on Information Systems (ICIS). A Virtual Conference (2020)
3. Corea, C., Delfmann, P., Nagel, S.: Towards intelligent chatbots for customer care-practice-based requirements for a research agenda. In: Hawaii International Conference on System Sciences (HICSS). A Virtual Conference, pp. 5819–5828 (2020)
4. Zierau, N., et al.: The anatomy of user experience with conversational agents: a taxonomy and propositions of service clues. In: International Conference on Information Systems. A Virtual Conference (2020)
5. Gnewuch, U., Morana, S., Maedche, A.: Towards designing cooperative and social conversational agents for customer service. In: International Conference on Information Systems (ICIS), Seoul, South Korea (2017)
6. Janssen, A., Grützner, L., Breitner, M.H.: Why do chatbots fail? A critical success factors analysis. In: International Conference on Information Systems, Austin, TX, USA (2021)
7. Lewandowski, T., et al.: Design knowledge for the lifecycle management of conversational agents. In: International Conference on Wirtschaftsinformatik (WI). A Virtual Conference (2022)
8. Meyer Von Wolff, R., Hobert, S., Schumann, M.: Chatbot introduction and operation in enterprises–a design science research-based structured procedure model for chatbot projects. In: Hawaii International Conference on System Sciences (HICSS), Hawaii, HI, USA (2022)
9. Lewandowski, T., et al.: State-of-the-art analysis of adopting AI-based conversational agents in organizations: a systematic literature review. In: Pacific Asia Conference on Information Systems (PACIS). A Virtual Conference (2021)
10. Weizenbaum, J.: ELIZA - a computer program for the study of natural language communication between man and machine. Commun. ACM **9**(1), 36–45 (1966)
11. Brandtzaeg, P.B., Følstad, A.: Why people use chatbots. In: Kompatsiaris, I., Cave, J., Satsiou, A., Carle, G., Passani, A., Kontopoulos, E., Diplaris, S., McMillan, D. (eds.) INSCI 2017. LNCS, vol. 10673, pp. 377–392. Springer, Cham (2017). https://doi.org/10.1007/978-3-319-70284-1_30
12. Colby, K.M.: Artificial Paranoia: A Computer Simulation of Paranoid Processes. Pergamon Press, Oxford (1975)
13. Wallace, R.S.: The anatomy of ALICE. In: Epstein, R., Roberts, G., Beber, G. (eds.) Parsing the Turing Test, pp. 181–210. Springer, Dordrecht (2009). https://doi.org/10.1007/978-1-4020-6710-5_13
14. Shawar, B.A., Atwell, E.: Chatbots: are they really useful? J. Lang. Technol. Comput. Linguist. (Former LDV-Forum) 29–49 (2007)
15. Diederich, S., Brendel, A.B., Kolbe, L.M.: On conversational agents in information systems research: analyzing the past to guide future work. In: International Conference on Wirtschaftsinformatik (WI), Siegen, Germany (2019)
16. Feng, S., Buxmann, P.: My virtual colleague: a state-of-the-art analysis of conversational agents for the workplace. In: Hawaii International Conference on System Sciences (HICSS). A Virtual Conference, pp. 156–165 (2020)

17. Meyer von Wolff, R., et al.: Chatbots at digital workplaces–a grounded-theory approach for surveying application areas and objectives. Pac. Asia J. Assoc. Inf. Syst. **12**(2) (2020)
18. Herrera, A., Yaguachi, L., Piedra, N.: Building conversational interface for customer support applied to open campus an open online course provider. In: IEEE 19th International Conference on Advanced Learning Technologies (ICALT), Maceió, Brazil, pp. 11–13 (2019)
19. Zierau, N., et al.: A review of the empirical literature on conversational agents and future research directions. In: International Conference on Information Systems (ICIS). A Virtual Conference (2020)
20. Diederich, S., Brendel, A.B., Kolbe, L.M.: Towards a taxonomy of platforms for conversational agent design. In: International Conference on Wirtschaftsinformatik (WI), Siegen, Germany, pp. 1100–1114 (2019)
21. Knote, R., et al.: Classifying smart personal assistants: an empirical cluster analysis. In: Hawaii International Conference on System Sciences (HICSS), Hawaii, HI, USA, pp. 2024–2033 (2019)
22. Winkler, R., Söllner, M.: Unleashing the potential of chatbots in education: a state-of-the-art analysis. In: Academy of Management Annual Meeting (AOM), Chicago, USA (2018)
23. Meyer von Wolff, R., Hobert, S., Schumann, M.: How may i help you? – state of the art and open research questions for chatbots at the digital workplace. In: Hawaii International Conference on System Sciences (HICSS), Hawaii, HI, USA, pp. 95–104 (2019)
24. Io, H.N., Lee, C.B.: Chatbots and conversational agents: a bibliometric analysis. In: IEEE International Conference on Industrial Engineering and Engineering Management (IEEM), pp. 215–219. IEEE, Singapore (2017)
25. Vaidyam, A.N., et al.: Chatbots and conversational agents in mental health: a review of the psychiatric landscape. Can. J. Psychiatry **64**(7), 456–464 (2019)
26. Semmann, M., et al.: Intelligent collaboration of humans and language-based assistants (INSTANT). In: International Conference on Information Systems (ICIS), San Francisco, CA, USA (2018)
27. Følstad, A., Nordheim, C.B., Bjørkli, C.A.: What makes users trust a chatbot for customer service? An exploratory interview study. In: Bodrunova, S.S. (ed.) INSCI 2018. LNCS, vol. 11193, pp. 194–208. Springer, Cham (2018). https://doi.org/10.1007/978-3-030-01437-7_16
28. Wilson, J.H.D., Paul, R.: Collaborative intelligence: humans and AI are joining forces. Harv. Bus. Rev. (2018). https://hbr.org/2018/07/collaborative-intelligence-humans-and-ai-are-joining-forces. Accessed 06 Feb 2023
29. Xu, A., et al.: A new chatbot for customer service on social media. In: Conference on Human Factors in Computing Systems (CHI), New York, NY, USA, pp. 3506–3510 (2017)
30. Böhmann, T., Leimeister, J.M., Möslein, K.: Service systems engineering. Bus. Inf. Syst. Eng. **6**(2), 73–79 (2014)
31. Maglio, P.P., et al.: The service system is the basic abstraction of service science. Int. Syst. e-Bus. Manag. **7**(4), 395–406 (2009)
32. Dämon, K.: MEGATREND CHATBOT - Was Chatbots der Wirtschaft bringen. WirtschaftsWoche, 10 July 2017 (2017). https://www.wiwo.de/erfolg/trends/megatrend-chatbot-was-chatbots-der-wirtschaft-bringen/19997318.html. Accessed 06 Feb 2023
33. Tewes, S., Niestroj, B., Tewes, C.: Geschäftsmodelle in die Zukunft denken. Springer Gabler, Wiesbaden (2020). https://doi.org/10.1007/978-3-658-27214-2
34. Wirtz, J., et al.: Brave new world: service robots in the frontline. J. Serv. Manag. **29**(5), 907–931 (2018)
35. Wirtz, J., Kunz, W., Paluch, S.: The service revolution, intelligent automation and service robots. Eur. Bus. Rev. (2021)

36. Oracle. Can Virtual Experiences Replace Reality? (2016). https://www.oracle.com/web folder/s/delivery_production/docs/FY16h1/doc35/CXResearchVirtualExperiences.pdf. Accessed 06 Feb 2023

37. Waizenegger, L., et al.: Conversational agents - exploring generative mechanisms and second-hand effects of actualized technology affordances. In: Hawaii International Conference on System Sciences (HICSS). A Virtual Conference (2020)

38. Sein, M.K., et al.: Action design research. MIS Q. **35**(1), 37–56 (2011)

39. Susman, G.I., Evered, R.D.: An assessment of the scientific merits of action research. Adm. Sci. Q. **23**(4), 582–603 (1978)

40. Hevner, A.R., et al.: Design science in information systems research. MIS Q. **28**(1), 75–105 (2004)

41. Venable, J.R., Pries-Heje, J., Baskerville, R.L.: Choosing a design science research methodology. In: Australasian Conference on Information Systems, Hobart, Australia (2017)

42. Mullarkey, M.T., Hevner, A.R.: An elaborated action design research process model. Eur. J. Inf. Syst. **28**(1), 6–20 (2019)

43. Peras, D.: Chatbot evaluation metrics. In: Economic and Social Development: Book of Proceedings - International Scientific Conference on Economic and Social Development, Zagreb, Croatia, pp. 89–97 (2018)

44. Helfferich, C.: Leitfaden- und Experteninterviews. In: Baur, N., Blasius, J. (eds.) Handbuch Methoden der empirischen Sozialforschung, pp. 669–686. Springer Fachmedien, Wiesbaden (2019). https://doi.org/10.1007/978-3-658-21308-4_44

45. vom Brocke, J., et al.: Reconstructing the giant: On the importance of rigour in documenting the literature search process. In: European Conference on Information Systems (ECIS), Verona, Italy, pp. 2206–2217 (2009)

46. Albers, S., et al.: Methodik der empirischen Forschung, vol. 3. Springer, Wiesbaden (2009). https://doi.org/10.1007/978-3-322-96406-9

47. Nardi, P.M.: Doing Survey Research: A Guide to Quantitative Methods. 4th edn. Routledge, New York (2018)

48. Meinel, C., von Thienen, J.: Design thinking. Informatik-Spektrum **39**, 310–314 (2016)

49. Morgan, D.L.: Focus groups. Ann. Rev. Sociol. **22**(1), 129–152 (1996)

50. Krueger, R., Casey, M.A.: Focus group interviewing on the telephone. State Health Access Data Assistance Center (SHADAC), Minneapolis (2002)

51. Kushner, S.: Naturalistic evaluation: practical knowledge for policy development. Res. Eval. **3**(2), 83–94 (1993)

52. Venable, J., Pries-Heje, J., Baskerville, R.: FEDS: a framework for evaluation in design science research. Eur. J. Inf. Syst. **25**(1), 77–89 (2016)

53. Charness, G., Gneezy, U., Kuhn, M.A.: Experimental methods: between-subject and within-subject design. J. Econ. Behav. Organ. **81**(1), 1–8 (2012)

54. Bangor, A., Kortum, P., Miller, J.: Determining what individual SUS scores mean: adding an adjective rating scale. J. Usability Stud. **4**(3), 114–123 (2009)

55. Scriven, M.: Die Methodologie der Evaluation. In: Wulf, C. (eds.) Evaluation. Beschreibung und Bewertung von Unterricht, Curricula und Schulversuchen, pp. 60–91. Piper & Co. Verlag, Munich (1972)

56. Stockdale, R., Standing, C.: An interpretive approach to evaluating information systems: a content, context, process framework. Eur. J. Oper. Res. **173**(3), 1090–1102 (2006)

57. Phellas, C.N., Bloch, A., Seale, C.: Structured methods: interviews, questionnaires and observation. Research. Soc. Cult. **3**(1), 23–32 (2011)

58. Likert, R.: A technique for the measurement of attitudes. Arch. Psychol. **140**, 44–60 (1932)

59. Diederich, S., Brendel, A.B., Kolbe, L.M.: Designing anthropomorphic enterprise conversational agents. Bus. Inf. Syst. Eng. **62**(3), 193–209 (2020). https://doi.org/10.1007/s12599-020-00639-y

60. Bouguelia, S., Brabra, H., Zamanirad, S., Benatallah, B., Baez, M., Kheddouci, H.: Reusable abstractions and patterns for recognising compositional conversational flows. In: La Rosa, M., Sadiq, S., Teniente, E. (eds.) CAiSE 2021. LNCS, vol. 12751, pp. 161–176. Springer, Cham (2021). https://doi.org/10.1007/978-3-030-79382-1_10

Towards Effective Conversational Agents: A Prototype-Based Approach for Facilitating Their Evaluation and Improvement

Marvin Heuer[1]([✉]), Tom Lewandowski[1], Emir Kučević[1], Jannis Hellmich[1], Michael Raykhlin[1], Stefan Blum[2], and Tilo Böhmann[1]

[1] University of Hamburg, Hamburg, Germany
{marvin.heuer,tom.lewandowski,emir.kucevic,
tilo.boehmann}@uni-hamburg.de, {jannis.hellmich,
michael.raykhlin}@studium.uni-hamburg.de
[2] iteratec GmbH, Munich, Germany
stefan.blum@iteratec.com

Abstract. Using conversational agents (CAs) has become increasingly popular for organizations for various applications, such as customer service and healthcare. However, user satisfaction and engagement with CA adoption stay behind expectations. In this context, quality criteria (e.g., regarding dialog flow or representation) can serve as a basis to evaluate CAs and improve their effectiveness to consequently affect user satisfaction and engagement. Hereby, we contribute to emerging research of quality criteria by proposing a prototype-based approach to facilitate the evaluation and improvement of CAs design and effectiveness. Our approach involves deriving scenarios from synthesized CA criteria from preliminary work, creating prototypes, and evaluating them in expert interviews. By comparing prototypes against each other, the influence on CA effectiveness can be measured. Our results demonstrate an approach for applying the criteria and offer a promising direction towards designing, developing, and operating CAs.

Keywords: conversational agent · chatbot effectiveness · prototyping · evaluation · artificial intelligence (AI)

1 Introduction

Organizations are increasingly implementing conversational agents to help and assist users, and thereby achieving high customer satisfaction. CAs are AI-based IS [1, 2] that are scalable and cost-effective for automating processes and supporting tasks and therefore experience increasing attention in numerous research areas and a variety of practical applications [3]. With their high potential for organizations, much research is conducted on AI-based CAs, primarily focusing on behavior and design [4, 5]. Unfortunately, CA adoption stays behind expectations, especially failing interaction-wise. Moreover, CAs, as intelligent and language-based systems, are prone to errors in operations, and many CAs are discontinued [6, 7]. Several researchers started to evaluate the

A. Marcus et al. (Eds.): HCII 2023, LNCS 14033, pp. 302–320, 2023.
https://doi.org/10.1007/978-3-031-35708-4_23

reasons for the dissatisfactory adoption of CAs in real-world operations [7–9]. In this instance, Lewandowski et al. (2023) [9] present multi-dimensional quality criteria for CA evaluation and improvement to address these challenges, enabling a possibility to evaluate the CA effectiveness and improve CAs in the long-term. In this domain, CA effectiveness can be described as a perceived satisfaction rate to collect user feedback with the CA design and operation, consequently influencing CA adoption [10, 11]. With this background, there is a need for a systematic approach to applying and evaluating criteria in an iterative development process. Therefore, our research question is: *How can a systematic approach be designed and applied to evaluate different versions of a CA in order to identify the most important criteria facilitating an improvement in the design and effectiveness?*

Based on this preliminary work and the research question, we have taken the developed quality criteria [8], and, in this work, we go the step from the concept to expository demonstration, including an instantiation and reflection, and make the impact on CA effectiveness measurable with a systematic variation of design alternatives and thus, enable improving a CA. In an iterative development process, we have developed scenarios and, based on them, created prototypes in a consultancy firm, each contributing by a criterion to CA effectiveness and facilitating improvement of design and operation of CAs. The firm uses an *ExpertBot* to find experts and evaluate and prioritize them. Hereby, the *ExpertBot* is an AI-based, *multi-channel CA listener* integrated into an existing communication channel (e.g., Microsoft Teams) and helps employees to search for internal experts. It suggests suitable experts, which it aggregates from various data sources (e.g., skill database) while listening to proposals and acquisition requests. In these conversations, the CA follows a handover approach when suggesting experts [12, 13]. This shows that in complex CA cases, not only input/output and design play a role (e.g., a focus on social ques [14]), but also further mechanisms (e.g., dialog flow or error handling) must be considered to keep users engaged and achieve a comprehensive user experience (UX). Using this *CA listener* example, we also show, based on scenarios, how this criteria set can help in designing such an *ExpertBot listener.*

To underpin this overall design and evaluation perspective, we developed prototypes for evaluation purposes, provide insights into the prototypes in this paper, and delineated the most relevant quality criteria for CA effectiveness. Based on this, we offer an approach for instantiating criteria, comparing CA versions and showing that incorporating which criteria is important for successful CA adoption and high effectiveness. Thereby, we contribute to facilitating the 'design, development and training' phase as well as the 'operation and improvement' phase of CAs [8] by identifying the most influential quality criteria.

2   Background

2.1   AI-Based Conversational Agents

In recent years, research on AI-based systems has garnered significant attention [15] and transformed from a technical trend to a pervasive phenomenon in our daily lives [16]. Especially chatbots and speech-based assistants, subsumed under the more general term of CAs [17, 18], have seen a surge in interest due to substantial advancements in AI technology [3, 19]. CAs can be defined as *"user interfaces that emulate human-to-human communication using natural language processing, machine learning, and artificial intelligence"* [20].

Thereby, CAs' field of research is highly interdisciplinary and complex: CAs are investigated from multiple perspectives, such as *"informatics, management and marketing, media and communication science, linguistics and philosophy, psychology and sociology, engineering, design, and human-computer interaction"* [21, p. 2916]. At present, CAs find particular use in application domains such as customer service, health, marketing and sales, entertainment, and education [4, 6, 22, 23]. Organizational investments in CAs primarily focus on customer service [9, 21, 24], where CAs are evolving as more and more critical gateways for providing digital services and information [9, 21, 24]. In organizations, they are currently being incorporated into numerous front- and back-end systems, such as websites, corporate wikis, knowledge systems, and instant messengers (e.g., Microsoft Teams or Slack), which have gained massive importance in daily corporate communications since the Covid-19 pandemic.

In this respect, CAs possess numerous advantages. CAs promote new forms of personalization, speed, cost-effectiveness, and automation [9]. Further, CAs can become a transformative technology since users can communicate conveniently, intuitively, and more naturally via a conversational user interface (CUI) instead of a graphical user interface (GUI) [17, 25, 26]. Thereby, CAs can combine and integrate multiple (enterprise) data sources (like databases) from diverse systems globally and 24/7, leading to workload, time and cost reduction [27, 28]. Therefore, they become valuable user interfaces, constituting a central, uniformly, often device-independent and thus time-efficient access point to a system or service landscape with consistent quality [28].

In recent years, research has been resurgent on CAs, particularly since 2016 [21, 29]. This has led to the emergence of various CA technologies and sub-terms, such as conversational UI/AI, chatbots/chatterbots, virtual and smart agents and/or text-based assistants [30]. Gnewuch et al. [6] separate CAs, for example, into text-based CAs, usually referred to as chatbots or speech-based CAs, such as smart personal assistants. This paper utilizes the term "conversational agent" to refer to all text- and AI-based systems, including chatbots, as the CAs investigated in the DSR project were text-based.

CAs have been studied from multiple perspectives. Thereby, studies focus mainly on realizing the potential benefits of CAs, by targeting the design and development of CAs that satisfy user needs and provide rewarding customer experiences [31]. Current studies investigate general CA topics, such as possible application areas [e.g., 27, 32], challenges and requirements to use them auspicious [e.g., 6], as well as technical design aspects, impediments and improvement opportunities, which concern, e.g., the NLP design and functionalities [e.g., 33]. Further, research focuses on designing CAs for better user acceptance [e.g., 24, 34] and user preferences for CAs' visual cues and conversational design [e.g., 14]. Moreover, scholars addressed user attitudes and their acceptance and trust in CAs [e.g., 35, 36].

In this context, CAs are characterized by numerous new characteristics that are gradually apparent during research. CAs depict a novel form of user-centric and socially interactive information systems (IS) characterized by (natural-language-based) intelligence, and an unfinished form of learning IS, leading to, so far, unsolved challenges and many open research questions [30, 37]. Since CAs are still in an unfinished and learning state in companies, there is a need for innovative approaches for managing their implementation, evaluation and improvement throughout their lifecycle because they have limited functionality at the outset and necessitate various interdisciplinary design activities [7, 9, 38].

Although CAs are easy to set up, fueled by diverse CA vendors and frameworks from, e.g., the big tech companies, such as Microsoft Bot Framework (Azure Bot Services), and Google Dialogflow, many CAs fail after their initial rollout due to design and organizational issues [38, 39]. In this context, research on how CAs can be structurally improved in customer service and organizations is scarcely covered in the literature.

Within this context, prior research has been conducted regarding the various impacts of CAs on an individual's perception of trust, enjoyment, and affordance theory [9]. Additionally, research has been conducted in the broader context of IS acceptance theories, including the "Technology Adoption Model" [9]. Furthermore, much fundamental research exists on designing CAs, e.g., regarding design principles and requirements [e.g., 40–42]. As of now, a few studies can be found that provide concrete quality criteria that can be applied to ensure systematic CA improvement and a procedure to apply this criteria set.

We performed an extensive design science research (DSR) project in the preliminary of this study [9], where we combined insights from literature and practical experiences from real-life environments to derive a systemized and synthesized set of CA quality criteria which we will introduce in the following subsection.

2.2 Quality Criteria Set

A set of criteria has been derived in this study's preliminary to assess and enhance the quality of CAs throughout their lifecycle. The set includes 6 meta-criteria, 15 criteria, and 33 sub-criteria. These criteria are presented and discussed in detail in our initial study in [9], covering attributes, implementation suggestions, and constraints. The criteria set is designed to support a cyclical evaluation process at specific intervals during the CAs' lifecycle. The set comprises six meta-criteria: **Input, Output, Dialog Control, Anthropomorphism, Data Privacy,** and **Performance,** as illustrated in Fig. 1.

The **Input** dimension comprises criteria for creating and submitting requests to the CA. This includes determining the available options and methods for submitting requests and designing and evaluating them. A vital factor to consider during evaluation is context awareness. Additionally, it is crucial to reflect, exchange or expand the different channels for communication, such as team collaboration and website frontends, and the necessary control elements, such as buttons, free text, tiles, and carousels.

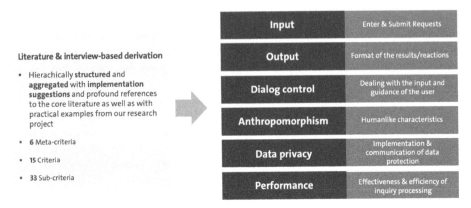

Fig. 1. Final CA Quality Criteria Set - based on [9].

Regarding **Output**, the format of CA responses should be reflected. The responses require selecting a suitable output format for a user- and content-oriented presentation.

Dialog Control is about the evaluation of dialogs regarding the regular operation and failure operation as it deals with the input and guidance of users. In regular operation, the CA proactively avoids error scenarios and, e.g., suggests that the user reformulate his query [43] or asks for more information [44]. In the failure operation, the CA offers various handover actions for solving the user's request nonetheless [13].

The **Anthropomorphism** dimension refers to characteristics like emotions applied to nonhuman objects [14]. As a result, anthropomorphism aspects can positively affect CA usage and can be divided into several aspects.

For **Data Privacy**, data protection must be ensured by communicating and implementing the CA. In contrast, the **Performance** dimension relates to the query processing efficiency in the CA, e.g., the CA-human handover rate.

3 Methodology

To demonstrate our approach, we proceeded in an expository instantiation. For this purpose, we followed an approach using the quality criteria set by Lewandowski et al. (2023) [9] and performed a first reflection based on the Framework for Evaluation in Design Science [45]. The approach first requires an analysis of the criteria to be examined. In a systematic procedure, the criteria must be identified and selected based on different criteria.

In the second step, we developed interaction scenarios from the identified criteria. The focus is on the meaningful design and plausibility of the criteria. Scenarios consisted of a carefully selected set of quality criteria. For example, for an "**Output**" criterion, a scenario may deal with the design of the output in the CA/*ExpertBot*, such as the length of the response or the formulation of the response. We developed these scenarios for each criterion to create new *ExpertBot* versions in step 3. Through these scenarios, design methodological suggestions are offered for initializing the criteria.

The third step is to develop prototypes for these scenarios, which thus transitively instantiate the criteria. The criteria-based prototypes expect an unmodified version of the *ExpertBot* against which the prototype and the respective criterion can be concretely compared.

The fourth step involves reflection by experts on the prototypes for each scenario. We followed the Human Risk & Effectiveness strategy by Venable et al. (2016) [45] to verify decisive criteria for CA effectiveness since many authors focus on CA anthropomorphism and verbal cues [14].

To conduct the expert interviews, we developed an interview guide [46] and created an accompanying presentation. At the interview beginnings, we introduced the expert search (if the experts needed to be made aware of it) and gave explanations on the *ExpertBot listener*. Further, we explained the goal of this project and the upcoming interviews. Afterwards, we asked the experts again about their experience with an expert search. After that, we used the created prototypes as evaluation objects and presented two implementation variants for each scenario. Here, as already mentioned, scenarios 6 and 7 represented an exception. Here, we implemented the criteria of both scenarios in one prototype and compared them to the current state of the *ExpertBot*. After presenting the two variants and the prototypical functionalities, we addressed three questions for each scenario. First, we determined which of the two variants was perceived as more effective in a first view. Secondly, the individual criteria for each scenario were gone through directly afterwards. We asked which implemented criteria had been decisive for the CA effectiveness according to the experts. In this way, we determined for each criterion to what extent it contributes to increased effectiveness. Finally, we determined the weighting for each criterion and each scenario. At the end of the interview, we asked the experts which of the implemented scenarios were the most important across the board and discussed these.

To recruit interview partners, we first contacted the experts for the quality criteria. In addition, we conducted five expert interviews with two people who had already been interviewed beforehand and three new interview partners. Due to their project context, the three newly selected experts were also suitable as interview partners. The average interview length was approximately 32 min. Before the evaluation, we conducted two test interviews to improve and further develop the procedure. For this reason, the test interviews were not recorded or included in the evaluation. We conducted the interviews as a videoconference via Microsoft Teams and recorded them with the consent of the experts. During the interviews, we shared the accompanying presentation, which included the prototypes created. For the evaluation, we noted the interviewees' statements about their activity and contact with the expert search. In addition, we recorded the interviewees' statements about the individual scenarios and the contained criteria. After we completed the evaluation of the individual interviews, the different findings were compiled to check whether the effectiveness of the *ExpertBot* was improved interaction-wise, according to the experts. For this purpose, we checked how many experts listed each criterion among the criteria they considered most influential for facilitating CA evaluation and improvement. Based on the number of these mentions, we created a weighting scale. Since five experts were interviewed (and at least one positive feedback was given for each criterion) and based on the expected answers, we established a scale of one to five, as proposed by [47] and supported a well-founded differentiation. 'Five' meant that the criterion had been highly relevant for CA effectiveness. 'Three' indicated a neutral/moderate relevance, with 'One' indicating a very low relevance.

Table 1. Scenarios, description and related criteria from Lewandowski et al. (2023) [9].

Scenario	Description	Criteria from [9]
Scenario 1	Manageable length of answers Responses description	Output (Content, Format)
Scenario 2	Automatic/Manual forms of contacting	Input (Interaction abilities)
Scenario 3	Query correction	Dialog control (Regular, Failure operation)
Scenario 4	Manual keyword specification	Input (Context awareness)
Scenario 5	Dynamic enable & disable	Input (Interaction abilities)
Scenario 6	Direct learning from user feedback	Performance (Effectiveness), Dialog control (Regular, Failure operation)
Scenario 7	Indirect learning through database expansion	Performance (Efficiency), Output (Content)
Scenario 8	Handling error messages & misunderstandings	Dialog control (Regular, Failure operation)

4   Results

Our prototype-based approach for facilitating CAs' evaluation and improvement had to be concretely implemented as a first step towards the results. In the **Configuration** subsection, we will look at how the approach can work in our organization using a practical example – the *ExpertBot* listener. The **Design & Evaluation** subsection then breaks down the prototypes' design and evaluation.

4.1   Configuration

We took the quality criteria of Lewandowski et al. (2023) [9] to select the criteria for the scenarios. However, we excluded some criteria from the evaluation (Basic design features and Data Privacy) that are important on a meta-level, as they should already be ensured in the background or the basic systems of the CA and not only in the interface of the *ExpertBot*. Data Privacy remains the same issue from version to version as it is ensured on an organizational level. Therefore, we disregarded the criterion in our prototype-based evaluation approach. In addition, the data protection aspect was deemed unproblematic by experts, provided that *"[…] the storage [and processing] of the data takes place on a comparable infrastructure to the chat itself."* Ultimately, sufficient data privacy must be ensured [48], as this is a basic requirement for using IT systems in the EU nowadays[1]. The criterion in the interaction paradigm category was also not reviewed as the organization fixed the paradigm beforehand with the implementation of the *ExpertBot*. The criterion describing the addition of a classic 1:1 CA to the *ExpertBot* had already been implemented and was, therefore, not evaluated. Furthermore, the use case criterion specification of the category request creation (input) was removed from the criteria set beforehand, as *ExpertBot* did not incorporate this functionality.

Once the criteria were selected, in a second step, we developed scenarios, as shown in Table 1. Scenarios consisted of a carefully selected set of quality criteria, which we evaluated in prototype versions of the *ExpertBot*.

However, it was impossible to implement each criterion in a different scenario and thus evaluate the corresponding number of variants. Therefore, we combined several criteria into one scenario instead. The assignment of the scenario to the selected criteria is shown in Table 1. We selected these according to their arrangement in the initial criteria set. However, for Scenarios 6 and 7, we presented and reviewed only one version as the functionality was not yet presented in the current state of the *ExpertBot*.

Based on these steps, we developed criterion-based prototypes for each scenario. It was decided that UI mockups should be created to instantiate the remaining criteria as they stimulate involvement [49]. We used the Figma design tool [50] to create these prototypes based on the current state of the CA. For this purpose, we recreated them within the design application using components to be modified as desired subsequently. To ensure visual consistency with the Microsoft Teams framework application and the current state of the *ExpertBot*, we used a collection of UI components provided by Microsoft in Figma called "Microsoft Teams UI Kit" [51]. However, since the privacy of the employees of the accompanying organization had to be taken into account, we used only fictitious names and profile pictures, for the experts suggested by the *ExpertBot*, within the prototypes. The original *ExpertBot* was compared to a variant of the CA that included the according criterion and was evaluated then in expert interviews. A prototype implements several criteria. The prototypical implementation of the criteria was supported by the derived recommendations from Lewandowski et al. (2023) [9], which, as intended, described what can be expected from an implementation of the respective criterion (even prototypical). Subsequently, we let compare these prototypes to the baseline prototype. We present the prototypes created in detail in the following subsection. We used these prototypes in eight different interaction and usability scenarios for identifying the most influential criteria on the effectiveness of the *ExpertBot* in the next step.

The fourth step involves a reflection by experts on the prototypes for each scenario. We used the Framework for Evaluation in Design Science with the Human Risk & Effectiveness strategy [45] to verify the instantiation and decisive criteria for the effectiveness of the *ExpertBot*, since many authors focus on CA anthropomorphism and verbal cues [14]. The aim was to check whether the quality criteria in instantiated form contribute to CA effectiveness and interaction and facilitate evaluating and improving the expert search process in the CA listener. We conducted expert interviews with staff from the

---

[1] The General Data Protection Regulation requires organizations in the EU and all partner countries to ensure the EU standards on Data Privacy.

accompanying organization based on the prototypes to evaluate the criteria set in the instantiated form.

4.2 Design and Evaluation

This section presents the scenarios developed for answering the research question. The several scenarios were implemented into prototypes and are presented here, as described in the Methodology section.

To begin, we tested different forms of response description. Figure 2 gives an example of how this looked in the prototype and how the experts were interviewed. The first scenario (Fig. 2) included an explanation of the *ExpertBot* and the experience of the offered experts. The value is created by the detailed display of the expert's field and the database because of which this expert was selected. Therefore, the experts rated this prototype design with 1 of 5 points. The experts were not convinced. Although they liked the idea, they did not need an explanation of why the prototype did deliver this solution and rated accordingly.

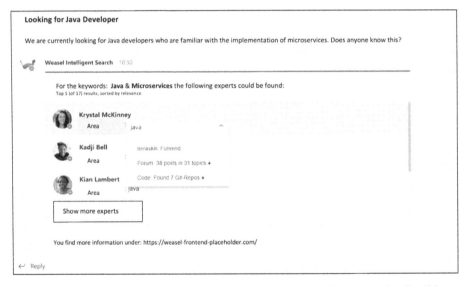

Fig. 2. Prototype for Scenario 1 – Explanation of the expert skills, translated to English.

In contrast, different approaches were linked for scenario 2, as shown in Fig. 3. On the one hand, users were given the option of integrating notifications for suggested experts. On the other hand, the *ExpertBot* icon received a supplementary display and explanation when hovering over the image. The hovering is linked to information that explains to user the scope of the *ExpertBot* and its functionality, which allows the user to get an understanding of the technology. In Fig. 3 one aspect is presented as an example. The scenario 2 reached a score of 3 out of 5 points. The experts deemed the scenario useful as users get informed about the *ExpertBot*, which helps them engage.

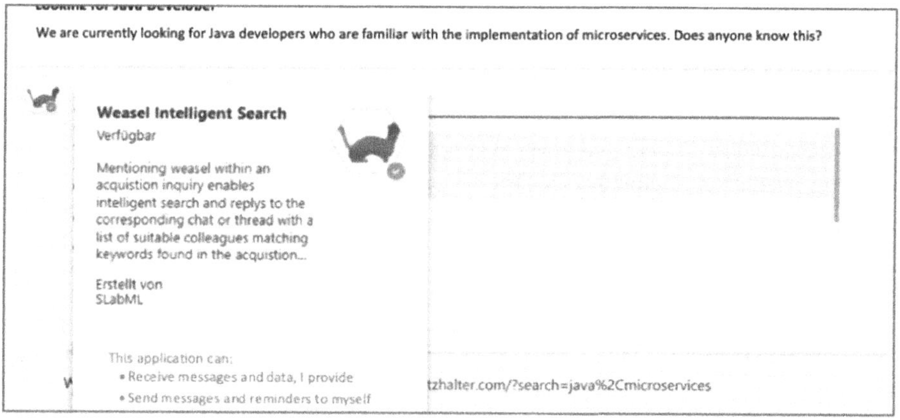

We are currently looking for Java developers who are familiar with the implementation of microservices. Does anyone know this?
Weasel Intelligent Search
Verfügbar
Mentioning weasel within an acquistion inquiry enables intelligent search and replys to the corresponding chat or thread with a list of suitable colleagues matching keywords found in the acquistion...
Erstellt von
SLabML
This application can:
• Receive messages and data, I provide
• Send messages and reminders to myself
tzhalter.com/?search=java%2Cmicroservices

Fig. 3. Prototype for Scenario 2 – Explaining the scope of the CA, translated to English.

For scenario 3, we developed a prototype that incorporates the query correction. In Fig. 4 we added a "Adjust keywords"-button. Further, by clicking on this button, a selection of keywords follows where new keywords can be added or old deselected. The shown scenario was successfully adopted, and the experts rated it as very important. The button helps to activate users to give feedback and contribute to CA improvement and the user experience. The questioned experts acknowledged this scenario with a 5-point score out of 5.

Looking for Java Developer
We are currently looking for Java developers who are familiar with the implementation of microservices. Does anyone know this?
Weasel Intelligent Search 10:00
Krystal McKinney
java, microservices
Kadji Bell
java, microservices
Kian Lambert
java
Adjust keywords
You find more information under: https://weasel-frontend-placeholder.com/
Reply

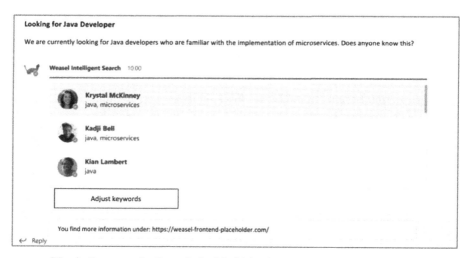

Fig. 4. Prototype for Scenario 3 - Modifying keywords, translated to English.

For the fourth scenario (in Fig. 5), we investigated whether the specific display of the recognized keywords by the *ExpertBot* help the user to engage. Specifically, a discreet bar above the previous results display used the label "Recognized Keywords" to indicate which keywords the CA recognized. Users get a quick and easier overview if the keywords are correct and provide simple, barrier-free feedback and correct them if needed. The experts rated the scenario also as very positive with a score of 5 out of 5.

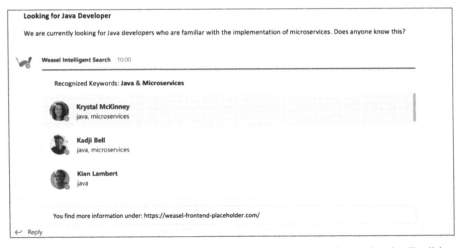

Fig. 5. Prototype for Scenario 4 – Showing the recognized keywords, translated to English.

We identified the switching on and off of the *ExpertBot* as another useful scenario (scenario 5, depicted in Fig. 6). For this purpose, a prototype was used to switch off the *ExpertBot* using an annotation and switch it on again using an annotation. The experts rated this scenario with a 1 out of 5 points.

The *ExpertBot* benefits from user feedback on its answers to improve and provide more accurate answers. Therefore, we used Microsoft Teams emojis for rating answers, which serve as a low-threshold user engagement, even while the *ExpertBot* is turned off. Testing was done in scenario 6 and is shown in the following Fig. 7. Although the experts valued the idea, they rated this scenario with 3 out of 5 points.

Fig. 6. Prototype for Scenario 5 – Switching on/off by annotations in the chat, translated to English.

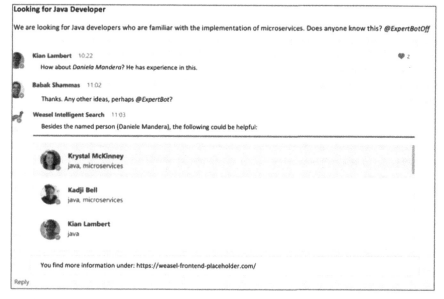

Fig. 7. Prototype for Scenario 6 – Using emojis for feedback, translated to English.

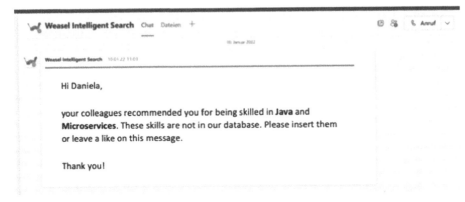

Fig. 8. Prototype for Scenario 7 - Expanding the database, translated to English.

However, the *ExpertBot* learns next from direct user feedback also indirectly through user help in the text and a subsequent database expansion. To this end, in this prototypical scenario 7 (shown in Fig. 8), we tested whether users can be engaged if they are contacted directly in the Teams chat function after other users have suggested to the *ExpertBot* that this person knows a particular domain. This scenario was not rated as positive as the others by the experts and received only 3 out of 5 points.

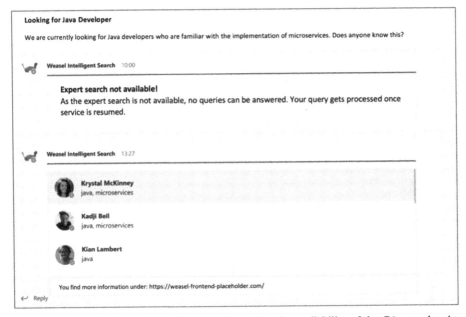

Fig. 9. Prototype for Scenario 8 – Getting informed on the availability of the CA, translated to English.

To achieve a high CA effectiveness and thereby offer an improvement opportunity, the *ExpertBot* must learn to deal with error messages and misunderstandings [52]. We tested and demonstrated with a prototype. In scenario 8 and Fig. 9, the *ExpertBot* is currently unavailable. The experts rated the relevance of this feature with a 5 out of 5 points, as user deemed it very important to get informed on the *ExpertBot* availability.

Table 2. Overview of scenarios, instantiated criteria, and expert rating.

Scenario	Description	Rating
Scenario 1	Manageable length of answers Responses description	1/5
Scenario 2	Automatic/Manual forms of contacting	3/5
Scenario 3	Query correction	5/5
Scenario 4	Manual keyword specification	5/5
Scenario 5	Dynamic enable & disable	1/5
Scenario 6	Direct learning from user feedback	3/5
Scenario 7	Indirect learning through database expansion	3/5
Scenario 8	Handling error messages & misunderstandings	5/5

Generally, the interview analysis showed that several evaluated prototypes had a decisive influence on the effectiveness. Many instantiated criteria contribute to higher effectiveness, as the prototypes that implemented these criteria were rated as more effective than those not implementing them (Table 2). The scenarios "Query Correction", "Recovering from Misunderstandings", "Suggestions Sorting", and "Error Message Handling" most essentially influenced effectiveness. Thus, a criteria-implementing *ExpertBot* has higher effectiveness than an *ExpertBot* not implementing these criteria (or focusing only on, e.g., social cues [53]). Accordingly, for future evaluations of an *ExpertBot*, these prototype implementations help assess the effectiveness and user interaction. However, the expert interviews showed that some criteria (e.g., context awareness) were not as crucial regarding effectiveness.

As a result, we developed a systematic approach for implementing criteria and evaluating versions of the CA in a prototype approach. Here, new versions will be compared with existing versions regarding their effectiveness. CAs must be designed very comprehensively, especially in complex cases. In particular, the prototypes show novel ways of how the criteria set can help designing the complex case of the *ExpertBot*, and how they are essential and let new fields of discussion emerge that have yet to be considered so far.

5   Discussion

Increasingly, IS are becoming more intelligent and user-dependent, promoting communication and collaboration between employees while facilitating sharing of knowledge and ideas. AI-based CAs, such as the *ExpertBot* in this paper, are one form of such IS. However, the effectiveness of CAs also depends on user engagement.

Therefore, the relationship between user engagement and effectiveness is an important consideration when designing prototypes. While a CA can be effective without fostering user engagement, the two concepts are often correlated. This correlation suggests that designers can enhance the CA effectiveness by focusing on user engagement. As CA effectiveness is highly user-relevant [32], investigating this is an essential step for designing and operating user-dependent, collaborative IS to consequently foster their adoption [30].

To offer an approach for investigating the effectiveness, we demonstrated a new approach, created prototypes in scenarios, and evaluated them with experts regarding the criteria most influential for CA effectiveness and, thus, user engagement and contributed to the more general research stream of CAs' quality and effectiveness [1, 9].

Given the lack of satisfaction with the CA adoption [30] and CA failure in general [7], this new approach can demonstrate how to apply quality criteria methodically in an iterative process. This includes a systematic criteria selection, the derivation of scenarios and the creation of prototypes.

The reflection suggests that our approach offers significant value to organizations as it not only integrates the quality criteria in an exemplary way, but also experts corroborate their influence on effectiveness. The approach addresses an existing research gap in CA research with a concrete solution approach and can improve the design and operation of CAs for this purpose. Nonetheless, the prototypes were based on the quality criteria of Lewandowski et al. (2023) [9], continuing their work and demonstrating a concrete prototype-based instantiation while delivering a helpful approach for other researchers. Other quality criteria could lead to other results. Further, the results show that specific criteria have a strong influence (e.g., showing the scope of the CA).

On the other hand, the results provide only a first direction based on a specific set of criteria in a complex CA case. Therefore, further research must investigate how this approach can be refined. In particular, the approach assumes that there are already own design ideas for the prototypes and that an existing version of a CA can be compared against. If a completely new start is made, the approach can only be used to a limited extent, but it does offer a starting point for new research.

Furthermore, we show in this paper how a criteria set can help to design the *ExpertBot* as an example for a complex multi-channel CA. Through the prototypical design, new concepts for developing and designing the complex *ExpertBot* have been tested, which organizations can implement. Especially in the field of complex CA listeners, there exist little research regarding its design, evaluation, and improvement and therefore answers an insufficiently illuminated research space so far. However, since there is no general fixed design specification of CA listeners, these results can only provide a first direction for this and require further research in other constellations and other CAs.

The resulting prototype approach serves as a step for evaluating future CA versions. This approach involves comparing new versions with existing versions to determine their effectiveness. Finally, the approach revealed novel ways of designing CAs to encourage user engagement, which has important implications for developing, designing, and evaluating effective collaborative IS (as CAs) in the future.

6 Limitations and Conclusion

The prototypical approach is a valuable methodology for evaluating the effectiveness of conversational agents (CAs) in facilitating CA improvement. However, it is limited in scope and subject to several potential biases.

One limitation of the prototypical approach is that it is based on a single case study with a specific company and domain-specific experts. As a result, the quality of the results may be influenced, and the study's external validity may be limited. To address this limitation, extending the study with more companies and experts could help leverage the results' quality and increase the study's external validity.

Further, we carried out the evaluation with a few experts, and the participant selection can have a high and limiting influence on the results. Nevertheless, we can assume validity because the interviewed experts have successfully completed CA projects and covered various backgrounds as they originate from a consulting organization.

Despite these limitations, the systematic prototype-based approach presented in this paper provided valuable insights into CA effectiveness by identifying the most influential criteria. In this work, a prototypical effort was conducted based on the criteria set by Lewandowski et al. (2023) [9], which was decomposed into groups of criteria and tested in eight scenarios.

A further in-depth evaluation of different constellations of criteria in real contexts would be useful to refine the prototypical approach further. Additionally, more use case studies can be conducted with the approach in other organizations to achieve more qualitative results.

Finally, the emergence of novel and powerful technologies, such as generative AI (e.g., ChatGPT), presents opportunities for further research into the prototypical approach and its applications. In conclusion, while the prototypical approach has limitations, it remains a valuable methodology for facilitating CA evaluation and improvement.

References

1. Schuetzler, R.M., Grimes, G.M., Giboney, J.S.: An investigation of conversational agent relevance, presence, and engagement. In: Americas Conference on Information Systems (AMCIS), Cancun, Mexico (2018)
2. Lewandowski, T., Grotherr, C., Böhmann, T.: Managing artificial intelligence systems for value co-creation: the case of conversational agents and natural language assistants. In: Edvardsson, B., Tronvoll, B. (eds.) The Palgrave Handbook of Service Management, pp. 945–966. Palgrave Macmillan, Cham (2022). https://doi.org/10.1007/978-3-030-91828-6_45
3. Reinkemeier, F., Gnewuch, U.: Designing effective conversational repair strategies for chatbots. In: European Conference on Information Systems (ECIS), Timisoara, Romania (2022)

4. Diederich, S., Brendel, A.B., Kolbe, L.M.: On Conversational agents in information systems research: analyzing the past to guide future work. In: International Conference on Wirtschaftsinformatik (WI), Siegen, Germany (2019)
5. Zierau, N., et al.: Towards developing trust-supporting design features for AI-based Chatbots in customer service. In: International Conference on Information Systems (ICIS). A Virtual Conference (2020)
6. Gnewuch, U., Morana, S., Maedche, A.: Towards designing cooperative and social conversational agents for customer service. In: International Conference on Information Systems (ICIS), Seoul, South Korea (2017)
7. Janssen, A., Grützner, L., Breitner, M.H.: Why do chatbots fail? A critical success factors analysis. In: International Conference on Information Systems (ICIS), Austin, TX, USA (2021)
8. Lewandowski, T., et al.: Design knowledge for the lifecycle management of conversational agents. In: International Conference on Wirtschaftsinformatik (WI). A Virtual Conference (2022)
9. Lewandowski, T., et al.: Leveraging the potential of conversational agents: quality criteria for the continuous evaluation and improvement. In: Hawaii International Conference on System Sciences (HICSS), Hawaii, HI, USA (2023)
10. Alnefaie, A., et al.: Factors influencing artificial intelligence conversational agents usage in the E-commerce field: a systematic. In: Australasian Conference on Information Systems (ACIS), Sydney, Australia (2021)
11. Moriuchi, E., et al.: Engagement with chatbots versus augmented reality interactive technology in e-commerce. J. Strateg. Mark. **29**(5), 375–389 (2021)
12. Poser, M., Singh, S., Bittner, E.: Hybrid service recovery: design for seamless inquiry handovers between conversational agents and human service agents. In: Hawaii International Conference on System Sciences (HICSS), Hawaii, HI, USA (2021)
13. Poser, M., Wiethof, C., Bittner, E.A.C.: Integration of AI into customer service: a taxonomy to inform design decisions. In: European Conference on Information Systems (ECIS), Timisoara, Romania (2022)
14. Schuetzler, R.M., et al.: Deciding whether and how to deploy chatbots. MIS Q. Exec. (MISQE) **20**(1), 4 (2021)
15. Elshan, E., et al.: Requirements for AI-based teammates: a qualitative inquiry in the context of creative workshops. In: Hawaii International Conference on System Sciences (HICSS), Hawaii, HI, USA (2022)
16. Maedche, A., et al.: AI-based digital assistants. Bus. Inf. Syst. Eng. **61**(4), 535–544 (2019). https://doi.org/10.1007/s12599-019-00600-8
17. McTear, M.F., Callejas, Z., Griol, D.: The Conversational Interface, vol. 6. Springer, Cham (2016). https://doi.org/10.1007/978-3-319-32967-3
18. Feine, J., et al.: A taxonomy of social cues for conversational agents. Int. J. Hum. Comput. Stud. **132**, 138–161 (2019)
19. Meyer Von Wolff, R., Hobert, S., Schumann, M.: Chatbot introduction and operation in enterprises–a design science research-based structured procedure model for chatbot projects. In: Hawaii International Conference on System Sciences (HICSS), Hawaii, HI, USA (2022)
20. Schuetzler, R.M., et al.: The influence of conversational agents on socially desirable responding. In: Hawaii International Conference on System Sciences (HICSS), Hawaii, HI, USA (2018)
21. Følstad, A., et al.: Future directions for chatbot research: an interdisciplinary research agenda. Computing **103**(12), 2915–2942 (2021)
22. Goasduff, L.: Chatbots Will Appeal to Modern Workers, 31 July 2019 (2019). https://www.gartner.com/smarterwithgartner/chatbots-will-appeal-to-modern-workers/. Accessed 24 Feb 2023

23. Gartner: Gartner Says 25 Percent of Customer Service Operations Will Use Virtual Customer Assistants by 2020 (2018). https://www.gartner.com/en/newsroom/press-releases/2018-02-19-gartner-says-25-percent-of-customer-service-operations-will-use-virtual-customer-assistants-by-2020. Accessed 24 Feb 2023
24. Gnewuch, U., et al.: Faster is not always better: understanding the effect of dynamic response delays in human-chatbot interaction. In: European Conference on Information Systems (ECIS), pp. 113–129. Portsmouth, United Kingdom (2018)
25. Dale, R.: The return of the chatbots. Nat. Lang. Eng. **22**(5), 811–817 (2016)
26. McTear, M.: Conversational AI: dialogue systems, conversational agents, and chatbots. Synth. Lect. Hum. Lang. Technol. **13**(3), 1–251 (2020)
27. Meyer von Wolff, R., et al.: Chatbots at digital workplaces–a grounded-theory approach for surveying application areas and objectives. Pac. Asia J. Assoc. Inf. Syst. **12**(2) (2020)
28. Meyer von Wolff, R., Hobert, S., Schumann, M.: How may I help you? – State of the art and open research questions for chatbots at the digital workplace. In: Hawaii International Conference on System Sciences (HICSS), Hawaii, HI, USA, pp. 95–104 (2019)
29. Piccolo, L.S.G., Mensio, M., Alani, H.: Chasing the chatbots. In: Bodrunova, S.S., Koltsova, O., Følstad, A., Halpin, H., Kolozaridi, P., Yuldashev, L., Smoliarova, A., Niedermayer, H. (eds.) INSCI 2018. LNCS, vol. 11551, pp. 157–169. Springer, Cham (2019). https://doi.org/10.1007/978-3-030-17705-8_14
30. Lewandowski, T., et al.: State-of-the-art analysis of adopting AI-based conversational agents in organizations: a systematic literature review. In: Pacific Asia Conference on Information Systems (PACIS). A Virtual Conference (2021)
31. Zhang, J.J., Følstad, A., Bjørkli, C.A.: Organizational factors affecting successful implementation of chatbots for customer service. J. Internet Commer. 1–35 (2021)
32. Laumer, S., et al.: Use cases for conversational agents: an interview-based study. In: Americas Conference on Information Systems (AMCIS), Cancun, Mexico (2019)
33. Adiwardana, D., et al.: Towards a human-like open-domain chatbot. arXiv preprint arXiv:2001.09977 (2020)
34. Bittner, E.A.C., Oeste-Reiß, S., Leimeister, J.M.: Where is the bot in our team? Toward a taxonomy of design option combinations for conversational agents in collaborative work. In: Hawaii International Conference on System Sciences (HICSS), Hawaii, HI, USA (2019)
35. Seeger, A.-M., Pfeiffer, J., Heinzl, A.: When do we need a human? Anthropomorphic design and trustworthiness of conversational agents. In: Proceedings of the Sixteenth Annual Pre-ICIS Workshop on HCI Research in MIS. AISeL, Seoul, South Korea (2017)
36. Go, E., Sundar, S.S.: Humanizing chatbots: the effects of visual, identity and conversational cues on humanness perceptions. Comput. Hum. Behav. **97**, 304–316 (2019)
37. Zierau, N., et al.: A review of the empirical literature on conversational agents and future research directions. In: International Conference on Information Systems (ICIS). A Virtual Conference (2020)
38. Meyer von Wolff, R., Hobert, S., Schumann, M.: Sorry, I can't understand you!–influencing factors and challenges of chatbots at digital workplaces. In: International Conference on Wirtschaftsinformatik (WI). A Virtual Conference (2021)
39. Følstad, A., Brandtzæg, P.B.: Chatbots and the new world of HCI. Interactions **24**(4), 38–42 (2017)
40. Tavanapour, N., Poser, M., Bittner, E.A.: Supporting the idea generation process in citizen participation-toward an interactive system with a conversational agent as facilitator. In: European Conference on Information Systems (ECIS), Stockholm/Uppsala, Sweden (2019)
41. Müller, H.M., Reuter-Oppermann, M.: Chatblood - Towards designing chatbots for blood donors. In: European Conference on Information Systems (ECIS), Timisoara, Romania (2022)
42. Wache, H., et al.: Exploring the abstraction levels of design principles: the case of chatbots. In: International Conference on Wirtschaftsinformatik (WI), Nuremberg, Germany (2022)

43. Diederich, S., Brendel, A.B., Kolbe, L.M.: Designing anthropomorphic enterprise conver-
    sational agents. Bus. Inf. Syst. Eng. **62**(3), 193–209 (2020). https://doi.org/10.1007/s12599-
    020-00639-y
44. Chaves, A.P., Gerosa, M.A.: How should my chatbot interact? A survey on social character-
    istics in human–chatbot interaction design. Int. J. HCI **37**(8), 729–758 (2021)
45. Venable, J., Pries-Heje, J., Baskerville, R.: FEDS: a framework for evaluation in design science
    research. Eur. J. Inf. Syst. **25**(1), 77–89 (2016)
46. Meuser, M., Nagel, U.: Das Experteninterview—konzeptionelle Grundlagen und method-
    ische Anlage. In: Pickel, S., et al. (eds.) Methoden der vergleichenden Politik- und
    Sozialwissenschaft, pp. 465–479. VS Verlag für Sozialwissenschaften, Wiesbaden (2009)
47. Likert, R.: A technique for the measurement of attitudes. Arch. Psychol. **140**(1), 44–60 (1932)
48. Chhetri, T.R., et al.: Data protection by design tool for automated GDPR compliance
    verification based on semantically modeled informed consent. Sensors **22**(7), 2763 (2022)
49. D'Souza, C., et al.: Enabling the generation of web applications from mockups. Softw.: Pract.
    Exp. **48**(4), 945–973 (2018)
50. Figma Inc. (2023). https://www.figma.com. Accessed 24 Feb 2023
51. Figma Inc. Microsoft Teams UI Kit (2023). Accessed 24 Feb 2023
52. Harms, J.-G., et al.: Approaches for dialog management in conversational agents. IEEE
    Internet Comput. **23**(2), 13–22 (2018)
53. Seeger, A.-M., Pfeiffer, J., Heinzl, A.: Texting with humanlike conversational agents:
    designing for anthropomorphism. J. Assoc. Inf. Syst. **22**(4) (2021)

Towards Validating a Chatbot Usability Scale

Samuel Holmes[1]([⊠]), Raymond Bond[1] [iD], Anne Moorhead[1], Jane Zheng[1],
Vivien Coates[2], and Michael McTear[1]

[1] Ulster University, 2-24 York Street, Belfast BT15 1AP, UK
{holmes-w,rb.bond}@ulster.ac.uk
[2] Ulster University, Londonderry BT48 7JL, UK

Abstract. A chatbot usability questionnaire (CUQ) was designed to measure the usability of chatbots. Study objectives: 1) to test the construct validity of CUQ (i.e. does it differentiate between chatbots that we rank as having poor, average or good usability), 2) to assess the intra-rater reliability of CUQ (i.e. do participants provide the same answers/scores when assessing the usability of the same chatbots two weeks apart), and 3) to undertake exploratory factor analysis to study the underlying factors that CUQ measures. Three chatbots were selected by co-authors that were regarded as having good, average and poor usability. Participants used each of the chatbots and completed the CUQ scale for each. Participants repeated this process two weeks later to facilitate the measurement intra-rater variability. Paired t-tests were used to compare CUQ scores from each of the three chatbots. Exploratory factor analysis was used to identify the factors within the CUQ. Paired t-tests and correlation was used to measure intra-rater reliability. There was a total of 156 CUQ survey completions (26 participants completed the CUQ for 3 different chatbots and for 2 rounds: $26 * 3 * 2 = 156$). Intra-rater reliability was supported as there was a good correlation between how participants completed the CUQ for the same chatbot at approximately two weeks apart ($r > 0.7$). As a form of construct validity, the CUQ scores for each of the three chatbots were statistically significant ($p < 0.05$). Factor analysis shows that the CUQ measures four factors 1) personality, 2) user experience, 3) error handling and 4) onboarding of the chatbot.

Keywords: Chatbots · Usability · HCI design and evaluation methods · testing · Conversational user interfaces · User experience

1 Introduction

Chatbots allow people to have human-like conversations with a computer to complete a task, to have a social conversation, or to provide coaching. Given the increasing prevalence of chatbots, it is important to develop new tools, scales and surveys to measure the usability and user experience of chatbots. There are currently numerous tools and scales for measuring system usability. The vast majority of these tools are designed for assessing the usability of traditional 'mouse-and-pointer' systems and thus may not be appropriate for assessing the usability of chatbots. For this reason, we developed

© The Author(s), under exclusive license to Springer Nature Switzerland AG 2023
A. Marcus et al. (Eds.): HCII 2023, LNCS 14033, pp. 321–339, 2023.
https://doi.org/10.1007/978-3-031-35708-4_24

the Chatbot Usability Questionnaire (CUQ). There are very few chatbot usability testing tools available to inform CUQ design, however the ALMA tool [1] informed the CUQ design since it also assesses the following seven aspects of the chatbot usability experience: 'Personality, Onboarding, Navigation, Understanding, Responses, Error Management and Intelligence'. We have described the CUQ questionnaire design in a previous paper [2] and created a website to allow users to download the survey and a CUQ calculation tool (www.ulster.ac.uk/research/topic/computer-science/artificial-int elligence/projects/cuq). The CUQ consists of 16 items (Table 1) in a questionnaire format. However, the CUQ tool requires further validation. According to the literature, there are many aspects to a scale that can be validated. Spector [3] suggests that a good scale should demonstrate both reliability and validity. Scale reliability is a measure of consistency, and there are three main types:

1. Test-retest reliability relates to consistency of a scale over time. If participants ("raters") of a usability test complete the same questionnaire for assessing the same system, each distinct score should be similar in each repetition. This is also known as intra-rater reliability.
2. Internal consistency is concerned with correlation of the items within the questionnaire, and those which measure the same construct (factor) should show strong positive correlation [3]. Ideally a scale will demonstrate both types of reliability, but even one of these will be considered acceptable.
3. Inter-rater reliability, which relates to consistency of scores from different participants [3]. If 100 participants of a usability test complete a questionnaire and it is observed that individual scores are very close, the results may be said to possess inter-rater reliability. In this study, only intra-rater reliability was measured.

Scale validity is the extent to which a scale measures what it is designed to measure. There are several types of validity, the most primitive being face validity. This is the idea that a scale is valid simply because the questions look like they might measure what they are intended to measure according to experts/users [4]. Although face validity results in greater acceptance by respondents, it does not offer conclusive guarantees of technical validity, thus its usefulness is limited [4]. Technical validity is related to the extent to which a scale measures what it is supposed to measure. Three of the most measured types of technical validity are content validity, criterion-related validity and construct validity [5]. This paper only measures a degree of construct validity. Construct validity may be assessed using techniques such as Factor Analysis [6]. Construct validity may be further divided into two types: convergent and discriminant validity. Convergent validity is demonstrated by a correlation between two constructs (factors) which are related to each other. In the context of a chatbot usability questionnaire, for example, two questions assessing the same 'factor' (e.g. personality) will be highly correlated. Discriminant validity, on the other hand, may be demonstrated by the absence of a correlation between two constructs. In other words, if two questions from the questionnaire were selected which relate to different aspects of usability (e.g. personality vs. intelligence), correlation between results for each question would be zero or close to zero. Construct validity can also include testing to see if the summative score from the scale discriminates between chatbots that are agreed by experts to have poor and good usability.

The paper aims to validate the CUQ for measuring the usability of chatbots, namely for construct validity and intra-rater reliability.

Table 1. CUQ question items using a 5-point scale. Where 1 = strongly disagree and 5 = strongly agree.

#	Item/CUQ question
1	The chatbot's personality was realistic and engaging
2	The chatbot seemed too robotic
3	The chatbot was welcoming during initial setup
4	The chatbot seemed very unfriendly
5	The chatbot explained its scope and purpose well
6	The chatbot gave no indication as to its purpose
7	The chatbot was easy to navigate
8	It would be easy to get confused when using the chatbot
9	The chatbot understood me well
10	The chatbot failed to recognise a lot of my inputs
11	Chatbot responses were useful, appropriate and informative
12	Chatbot responses were not relevant
13	The chatbot coped well with any errors or mistakes
14	The chatbot seemed unable to handle any errors
15	The chatbot was very easy to use
16	The chatbot was very complex

2 Methods

Authors (SH, RB, MM) selected three chatbots that they agreed to demonstrate poor, average and good usability. These three chatbots were then used and assessed by participants using the CUQ scale. Participants then performed this task again two weeks later, allowing us to also measure intra-rater reliability. Exploratory factor analysis was also carried out to explore the sub-factors within the CUQ.

2.1 Participant Recruitment

Participants were recruited using convenience sampling, including university staff and students. Inclusion criteria entailed: adults over 18 years who had a reasonable understanding of the English language, basic IT/smartphone skills, and willingness to use a chatbot. A recruitment email was circulated to staff and students at Ulster University via internal mailing lists and an invitation was posted on social media. Participants completed the experiment online, where they had easy access to the Participant Information Sheet (PIS). The consent form and questionnaires were hosted on an online survey platform, Qualtrics. Participants were assigned a randomly generated ID, which they used when completing their CUQs for each chatbot.

2.2 Procedures

Participants completed two rounds of chatbot testing. Round 1: Participants were free to evaluate the three chatbots in any order they liked. Participants selected one of the three chatbots and followed any setup instructions, then spent no more than 5 to 8 min using the chatbot. When finished, they completed the CUQ. They then repeated this process for the other two chatbots. Round 2: Approximately two weeks after completing round one, participants, as for round one, were free to evaluate the chatbots in any order. Participants were able to use the chatbots again if they felt they needed to do so, again spending no more than 5 to 8 min using each one. Participants then completed a CUQ for each of the three chatbots.

2.3 Chatbot Selection

A panel of experts (SH, RB, MM) selected three chatbots using their expertise with the aid of predetermined criteria. The chatbots that were selected were *WoeBot* (a smartphone-based mental health chatbot), *Weight Loss Bot* (a Facebook Messenger-based chatbot for educating users about weight loss), and *FlyBot,* a very rudimentary chatbot flight booking system that was designed by the lead author for the purposes of this research study. Evaluation criteria were developed by the lead author based on areas of assessment used by the ALMA chatbot test tool [1] (Table 2). Each panel member independently ranked the chatbots in order of usability. The panel members then met as a committee to discuss and provide a consensus rating. None of the panel members knew how each member ranked the usability of chatbots, but all agreed that *WoeBot* was considered "good quality", *Weight Loss Bot* was "average quality" and *FlyBot* was "poor quality".

Table 2. Chatbot classification criteria.

UX Aspect	Description	Chatbot Classification		
		Good	Average	Poor
Personality	• Does the chatbot seem friendly? • Is it robotic? • Does the personality fit with its role/purpose?	• Friendly and casual • Personality appropriate to purpose	• Personality is friendly but somewhat limited and robotic	• Personality is very limited, almost robotic • Personality not appropriate to purpose (e.g. inappropriate use of humour)
Onboarding	• Does the chatbot welcome the user and explain how they should use it? • Is the user able to "dive straight in?"	• Chatbot is very welcoming, greeting user by their first name (gets their name and uses it!) • Chatbot explains purpose and functions very well • User can start using chatbot straight away with very little prompting	• Greeting is limited to just a simple "Hello" (no first name use) • Explanation of purpose/function is limited • User needs some prompting before they can use the chatbot	• Chatbot greeting is non-existent • Chatbot does not explain purpose or function • User is unable to "dive straight in" and requires considerable help or instructions for first use
Understanding	• How well does the chatbot understand the user?	• Chatbot understands the user well, and copes well with different variations of responses	• Chatbot sometimes struggles with variations in user response	• Chatbot can only understand user if their responses exactly match expected inputs
Answering	• How does the chatbot answer the user? • Are its responses varied? • Are they relevant?	• Chatbot's answers are varied, interesting and relevant, with a good mix of humour (if appropriate), and multimedia (e.g. GIFs)	• Chatbot answers are relevant but a little dull • Limited use of multimedia or relevant humour	• No variability in answers • Answers are not relevant or are confusing • No humour (or inappropriate humour) or multimedia in responses

(*continued*)

Table 2. (*continued*)

UX Aspect	Description	Chatbot Classification		
		Good	Average	Poor
Navigation	• How quickly can the user get what they need from the chatbot? • Does the user know where they are and what they are doing?	• Chatbot is very easy to navigate • User always knows where they are, how they got there, and what they need to do	• Chatbot is navigable, but user sometimes gets lost or needs reminded about what they need to do	• Chatbot is too complex • User finds that they get lost easily, or is left wondering what to do
Error Management	• How does the chatbot respond to errors? • Does it become confused? • If it does, can it recover? • Does it ask the user to clarify what they meant?	• Chatbot handles and responds to all errors, notifying the user that something went wrong (e.g. "I didn't understand that") and trying to repair the error (e.g. by asking the user to clarify what they meant)	• Chatbot error handling is only very basic and offers limited options for recovery	• Poor error handling - chatbot either crashes when an error occurs (leaving the user wondering what has just happened) or generates a cryptic error message
Intelligence	• Is the chatbot intelligent? • Can it remember things? • Can it manage conversation context?	• Chatbot seems to be intelligent • Chatbot remembers the user's name and manages the context of the conversation (e.g. remembering information it has been given)	• Chatbot seems intelligent but only has limited memory capabilities	• Chatbot intelligence very limited • Chatbot is unable to remember user's name (or does not use it) • Chatbot forgets information the user has already given it

2.4 Data Analysis

Data from the CUQ completions were exported from Qualtrics as CSVs and imported into Microsoft Excel. Scores were calculated out of 100 using the following formula. The mean CUQ score and standard deviation were calculated for each of the three chatbots. A breakdown of CUQ score calculations are detailed below:

1. For each question, assign a score from 1 to 5 based on the level of agreement with the statement in the question (i.e. "Strongly agree" is worth 5 points, "Neutral" is worth 3 points, "Strongly disagree" is worth 1 point).
2. Calculate the sum of all the **odd-numbered** questions (questions with a positive connotation).

3. Calculate the sum of all the **even-numbered** questions (questions with a negative negative).
4. Subtract 8 from the score from *step 2*.
5. Subtract the score from *step 3* from 40.
6. Add the scores from *steps 4 and 5*. This gives a score out of 64.
7. Divide the score from *step 6* by 64 and multiply the answer by 100. This gives a score out of one hundred.

Test-retest reliability (or intra-rater reliability) was measured using paired t-tests to compare mean CUQ scores at each round. Pearson correlation tests were also used to determine correlation between chatbot scores at each round. Test-Retest reliability was measured at question level by calculating the mean score per question for each chatbot and using Spearman correlation tests to determine correlation between question responses (ratings) at each round. Construct validity was measured by using paired t-tests to compare CUQ scores of each of the three chatbots. Statistical significance for t-tests was assumed where $p < 0.05$. Correlation was assumed strong when $r > 0.7$.

Exploratory Factor Analysis was used to identify the factors within the CUQ, and determine which questions were strongly correlated with each factor. Findings from the factor analysis were used to determine which questions could be removed from the CUQ in order to reduce its size and increase its efficiency. McCaffrey [7] suggested that identified factors are only significant if the sum of squares loadings for each factor are greater than 1.0, thus a cut-off point of 1.0 was used to determine which factors were significant.

2.5 Ethics

The study received ethical approval from Ulster University School of Communication and Media Filter (research ethics) Committee in compliance with the Ulster University Code of Practice for Professional Integrity in the Conduct of Research and the Policy for the Governance of Research Involving Human Participants. The study was designed to comply with the five core principles of beneficence, non-maleficence, honesty and integrity, confidentiality and informed consent. Personal data collected during usability tests were collected in compliance with GDPR 2018 and the Data Protection Act 2018.

3 Results

There was a total of 156 CUQ survey completions (26 participants completed the CUQ for 3 different chatbots and for 2 rounds: 26 * 3 * 2 = 156). There were more female participants (15, 58%) than male (11 participants, 42%). Participant ages ranged from 18–25 years to over 50 years, and mode age range was 31–40 years (6 participants, 23%). Most participants (22, 85%) reported that English was their first language. Most participants ranked their technical ability with mobile devices as either 3 or 4 out of 5 (9 participants, 35%). Mean technical ability was 3.8 ± 0.90, the median and mode were 5 (where 5 = high technical ability).

3.1   Intra-rater Reliability

Mean CUQ scores and standard deviations are shown in Table 3. Boxplots and scatter plots of CUQ scores are presented in Figs. 1, 2 and 3. The differences in CUQ scores across the two rounds are not statistically significant. Moreover, all correlations are strong ($r > 0.7$) suggesting a high degree of intra-rater reliability. Individual CUQ question scores per round were also compared (Fig. 4). Inspection of the bar plots at question level per round, shows strong similarity in ratings per round. mean CUQ question scores were analysed to determine the percentage differences between scores for each round (Fig. 5). The largest percentage differences were found in Question 8 (*Weight Loss Bot*, 21.4%), Q10 (*Weight Loss Bot*, 17.3%) and Q4 (*Weight Loss Bot*, 16.1%).

Table 3. Comparison of chatbot CUQ scores by round

Chatbot	Round	Score	T-Test	Correlation
WoeBot	1	72.4 ± 17.9	0.29	0.74
	2	74.9 ± 13.6		
Weight Loss Bot	1	69.2 ± 16.9	0.14	0.84
	2	66.4 ± 16.3		
FlyBot	1	57.3 ± 16.9	0.33	0.81
	2	59.4 ± 17.7		

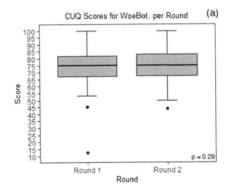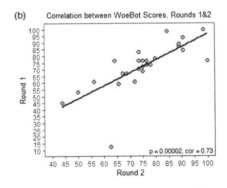

Fig. 1. WoeBot CUQ Scores, per round (a) Boxplot (b) Scatterplot. Error Bars represent SD.

A boxplot of CUQ scores per chatbot is presented in Fig. 6. There is a statistically significant difference between CUQ scores between each chatbot ($p < 0.05$) providing construct validity.

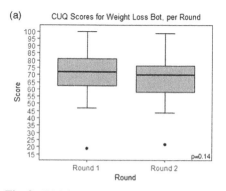

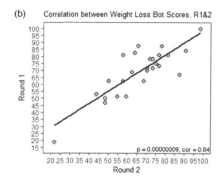

Fig. 2. Weight *Loss Bot* CUQ Scores, per round (a) Boxplot (b) Scatterplot. Error Bars represent SD.

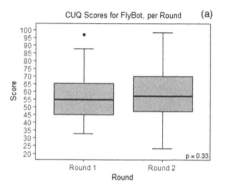

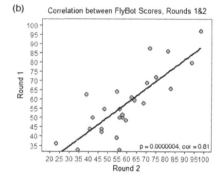

Fig. 3. FlyBot CUQ Scores, per round (a) Boxplot (b) Scatterplot. Error Bars represent SD.

3.2 Factor Analysis

The scree plot from principal component analysis (Fig. 7) suggested a maximum of five factors in the CUQ and perhaps a minimum of three.

Factor analysis using five factors suggested that the sum of square loadings of four factors were greater than 1.0, thus significantly influenced the variance, while the sum of square loading of the fifth factor was less than 1.0, thus was not significant as shown in Table 4. Factor analysis using four factors suggested that the sum of square loadings of four factors were significant (greater than 1.0). Using a cut-off point of 0.5, factor loadings were analysed to identify which questions were closely correlated with each factor. Factors and their correlated questions are summarised in Table 5. Factors were identified based on correlated questions. Factors were named based on their correlated questions (Table 6). From this table, there are four factors being measured by the CUQ, including Personality, User Experience, Error Handling and Onboarding. The only question that did not suitably match the suggested factor name was Q9, correlated with Factor 1 (Personality).

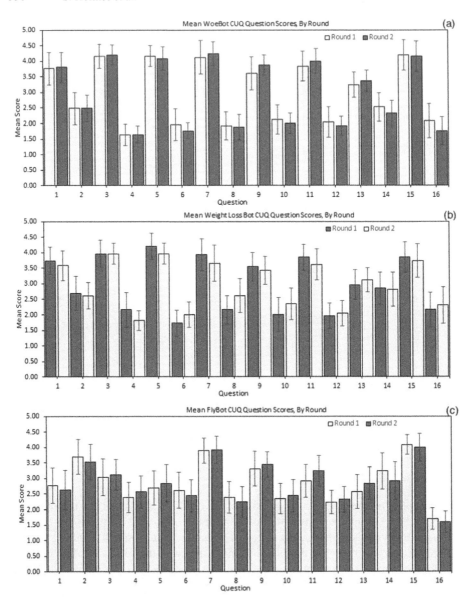

Fig. 4. Mean CUQ Question Scores, per chatbot, per round. (a) *WoeBot* (b) *Weight Loss Bot* (c) *FlyBot*. Error Bars represent SD.

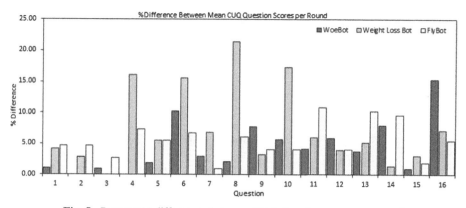

Fig. 5. Percentage differences between CUQ Question scores per round

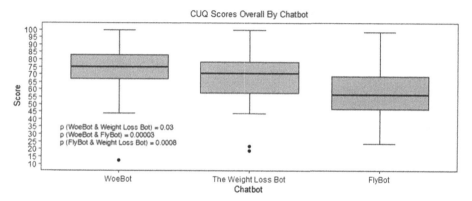

Fig. 6. Chatbot CUQ scores, per chatbot

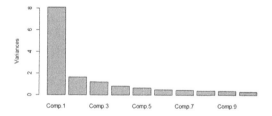

Fig. 7. Scree Plot for CUQ Principal Component Analysis

Following factor analysis, a heuristic for excluding questions was developed. The heuristic is a simple three-step process, 1) identify and remove any questions which do not correlate with any factor, 2) identify and remove any questions which do not relate to their correlated factor and 3) identify and remove, as appropriate, questions from factors which are correlated with more than two questions. Thus, six questions were identified as potentially excludable from the CUQ (Table 7). Removal of questions

Table 4. Sum of square loadings: 5-Factor and 4-factor analysis

SS Loadings	Factor 1	Factor 2	Factor 3	Factor 4	Factor 5
5 factors	3.09	3.06	2.19	1.98	**0.97**
4 factors	3.33	3.25	2.20	1.97	

Table 5. Factors and correlated questions, with loadings

Factor	Question	Loading
1	Q1	0.74
	Q2	−0.78
	Q3	0.65
	Q4	−0.52
	Q9	0.57
2	Q7	0.82
	Q8	−0.70
	Q15	0.86
	Q16	−0.60
3	Q13	0.82
	Q14	−0.78
4	Q5	0.88
	Q6	−0.59

based on this table reduces the CUQ to either 10 or 12 items (Tables 8 and 9). One question (Q9) was excluded because it correlated with a factor (personality) which it was not related to. Question 9 is somewhat ambiguous and is more likely to be related to chatbot understanding. Three questions (Q10, Q11 and Q12) were excluded because they were not correlated with any of the four factors. Two factors (Personality and User Experience) were correlated with more than two questions, and in order to maintain the balance between positive aspect (odd-numbered) and negative aspect (even-numbered) questions, it was determined that two questions should be excluded from one of these two factors. The "User Experience" factor was selected; however, it would have been equally justified to exclude questions from the "Personality" factor instead. Using the same data for all three chatbots, the construct validity of the 10- and 12-item questionnaires proposed above was measured. Boxplots of CUQ scores for 10- and 12-item questionnaires are found in Fig. 8. There is a statistically significant difference between chatbot scores ($p < 0.05$).

Table 6. Suggested factor names, based on correlated question text.

Factor	Q	Text	Suggested Factor Name
1	Q1	The chatbot's personality was realistic and engaging	Personality
	Q2	The chatbot seemed too robotic	
	Q3	The chatbot was welcoming during initial setup	
	Q4	The chatbot seemed very unfriendly	
	Q9	The chatbot understood me well	
2	Q7	The chatbot was easy to navigate	User Experience
	Q8	It would be easy to get confused when using the chatbot	
	Q15	The chatbot was easy to use	
	Q16	The chatbot was very complex	
3	Q13	The chatbot coped well with any errors or mistakes	Error Handling
	Q14	The chatbot seemed unable to cope with any errors	
4	Q5	The chatbot explained its scope and purpose well	Onboarding
	Q6	The chatbot gave no indication as to its purpose	

Table 7. Questions to exclude from CUQ

Question to Exclude	Rationale	New Questionnaire Size
Q9	Q9 only correlates with "Personality" factor (Factor 1), but it does not measure personality	12-item
Q10	Not correlated with any factor	
Q11		
Q12		
Q15	Correlated with "User Experience" (Factor 2), which is already correlated with Q7 and Q8	10-item
Q16	Correlated with only User Experience/Factor 2, which is already correlated with Q7 and Q8	

Table 8. Proposed 12-item CUQ

Question		Question Text	Linked Factor	
Old Number	New Number		Number	Name
	Q1	The chatbot's personality was realistic and engaging	1	Personality
	Q2	The chatbot seemed too robotic		
	Q3	The chatbot was welcoming during initial setup		
	Q4	The chatbot seemed very unfriendly		
	Q5	The chatbot explained its scope and purpose well	4	Onboarding
	Q6	The chatbot gave no indication as to its purpose		
	Q7	The chatbot was easy to navigate	2	User Experience
	Q8	It would be easy to get confused when using the chatbot		
Q13	Q9	The chatbot coped well with any errors or mistakes	3	Error Management
Q14	Q10	The chatbot seemed unable to cope with any errors		
Q15	Q11	The chatbot was easy to use	2	User Experience
Q16	Q12	The chatbot was very complex		

4   Discussion

There were no statistically significant differences between chatbot scores between rounds, and correlation coefficients are all strong (greater than 0.7). This suggests that test-retest reliability of the CUQ tool. It may be observed that while correlation coefficients for *Weight Loss Bot* and *FlyBot* are greater than 0.8, the correlation coefficient for *WoeBot* is less than 0.8 but greater than 0.7. This is due to the presence of an outlier, visible on Fig. 1(b). For this participant, the *WoeBot* CUQ score for Round 1 was 12.5, but was 62.5 for Round 2. It is unknown why this participant scored the chatbot more highly during Round 2, however the difference in scores has reduced the correlation

Table 9. Proposed 10-item CUQ

Question		Question Text	Linked Factor	
Old Number	New Number		Number	Name
	Q1	The chatbot's personality was realistic and engaging	1	Personality
	Q2	The chatbot seemed too robotic		
	Q3	The chatbot was welcoming during initial setup		
	Q4	The chatbot seemed very unfriendly		
	Q5	The chatbot explained its scope and purpose well	4	Onboarding
	Q6	The chatbot gave no indication as to its purpose		
	Q7	The chatbot was easy to navigate	2	User Experience
	Q8	It would be easy to get confused when using the chatbot		
Q13	Q9	The chatbot coped well with any errors or mistakes	3	Error Management
Q14	Q10	The chatbot seemed unable to cope with any errors		

coefficient slightly. Test-retest reliability also exists at the question level (Fig. 4), which shows only a small difference between mean question scores per round for each chatbot without statistical significance. Figure 6 provides support for construct validity where the difference between each of the three chatbots *WoeBot, Weight Loss Bot,* and *Fly-Bot can be seen.* T-test p-values for chatbot scores demonstrate statistical significance which are consistent with the decision of the expert panel. A difference is also observed between mean question scores for each chatbot showing the construct validity exists at the question level. Results from the correlation analysis of individual question scores across chatbots suggested that correlation between individual question scores per chatbot was generally weak, which was expected. For any given question, it is unlikely that the mean score for a supposedly *good* quality chatbot (such as *WoeBot*) would be the same as the mean score for a supposedly *average* or *poor* quality chatbot (such as *Weight Loss Bot* and *FlyBot*), thus would be unlikely that specific question means would correlate across chatbots.

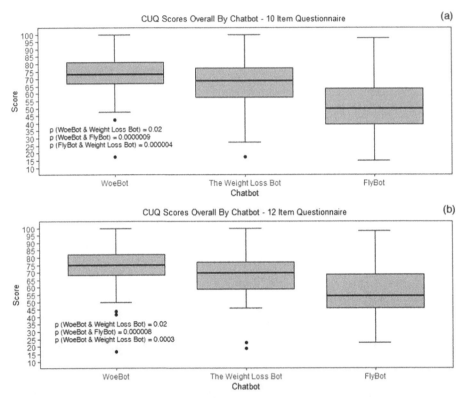

Fig. 8. Chatbot CUQ scores, per chatbot. (a) 10-item CUQ, (b) 12-item CUQ. Error Bars represent SD.

Twelve questions showed percentage differences of >5% between mean scores at each round of questionnaires. The most unreliable questions were Q8, Q10 and Q4 in order from greatest percentage difference to least percentage difference. Q8 was "It would be easy to get confused when using the chatbot, Q10 was "The chatbot failed to recognise a lot of my inputs", and Q4 was "The chatbot seemed very unfriendly". All three of these questions relate to negative aspects of the chatbot User Experience (UX). Differences between question round scores for Q6 and Q16 were >5% for all three chatbots. Q6 was "The chatbot gave no indication as to its purpose", and Q16 was "The chatbot was very complex". Both questions are also related to negative aspects of chatbot UX. Most (n = 9) of the unreliable CUQ questions showed greatest percentage differences in scores between rounds. This may suggest that negative aspects of chatbot UX are more difficult to measure consistently than positive aspects.

Principal component analysis of the CUQ identified a maximum of five possible factors. Factor analysis of five factors showed that the sum of square loading of the fifth factor was less than 1.0. Based on [7], it may be assumed that a factor is only significant if its sum of square loading is greater than 1.0, thus it was determined that there were at most four factors in the CUQ. This was confirmed using factor analysis of four factors. Based on CUQ question topics, these four factors were identified as *Personality, User*

Experience, Error Management and *Onboarding*. Excluding questions from the CUQ based on these identified factors meant the CUQ could potentially be reduced to either 12 or 10 items. It was desired to reduce the CUQ to 10 items if possible, as the questionnaire is intended to be comparable to the System Usability Scale (SUS) which is also a 10-item scale [8]. The new 10- and 12-item questionnaires were tested for construct validity using data for each of the three chatbots and a significant difference was observed between chatbot scores. Thus, it may be determined that the CUQ exhibits construct validity with no more than 10 items.

Martín et al. [1] suggested that chatbot UX may be measured using seven different aspects. The CUQ measures only three of the aspects proposed by Martín et al. [1] (Personality, Error Management and Onboarding). However, the "User Experience" factor of the CUQ covers questions relating to navigation and ease of use, thus it is reasonable to suggest that the "Navigation" aspect is being measured by the CUQ.

4.1 Study Limitations

There were specific limitations to this CUQ validation study. Firstly, the number of participants are limited (n = 26). It may be argued however that in this CUQ validation study, statistical significance was already achieved with n = 26 participants. Other limitations concern the number and type of chatbots. Only three chatbots were selected for this research study and categorised into "good", "average" and "poor" quality, and two of these were health related – *WoeBot* is for mental health, and *Weight Loss Bot* is for weight loss. Although differences in chatbot scores were significant across the three chatbots, it would have been useful to select multiple types of chatbot for each of the three categories, in order to compare differences in scores across different types of chatbot. It was intended that participants would complete round 2 questionnaires approximately 2 weeks after Round 1, however it was not always possible to do this. As the research study ran during summer 2019, some participants were on holiday and were unable to complete round 2 until they returned. Other participants forgot to complete round 2 questionnaires and were sent a reminder. Despite participants not completing both rounds within exactly 2 weeks of each other, CUQ scores and mean question scores were not significantly different. A further limitation is that perhaps missing from CUQ is measuring the quality of the chatbot's responses, e.g. whether they address the user's concerns. The study addresses specific types of bots with limited functionalities and does not include open domain chatbots.

4.2 Future Work

Results from this preliminary validation of the CUQ suggests that the questionnaire demonstrates construct validity and test-retest reliability (also known as *intra-rater* reliability). However there are several types of reliability and validity. The CUQ will be more reliable as a validated instrument for measuring chatbot usability if other types of reliability and validity. Inter-rater reliability of CUQ scores could also be measured using Fleiss' Kappa, and internal consistency may be measured using Cronbach's alpha.

4.3 CUQ Benchmarking

SUS and UEQ have a clear advantage over the present CUQ in that their reliability and validity are based on *benchmarks*. The SUS average score of 68.0 is based on a benchmark of around 500 tests involving more than 5000 users [9]. The UEQ benchmark is based on data from 20,190 participants in 452 evaluations as of 2019 [10]. CUQ validity is currently limited by the number and type of chatbots used. Only three chatbots were used during the study, one for each quality category (good, average and poor). To improve the reliability and validity of the CUQ a benchmark could be established using many chatbots for each quality category, with different chatbot types included in each category. The CUQ validation study is also limited by the number of users (n = 26) who completed the study, for an effective benchmark to be established it would be necessary to include larger numbers of participants in order to be comparable with SUS and UEQ.

5 Conclusion

Chatbot usability testing does not easily follow conventional principles, thus it is necessary to adapt conventional tools for use with chatbots. The CUQ validated in this study is based on the ALMA chatbot test tool [1] and designed to be comparable or equivalent to SUS [8]. Findings from this validation study suggest that the CUQ possesses construct validity and test-retest reliability in its native 16-item form but may also be reduced to a 10-item questionnaire akin to SUS without sacrificing validity, and thus may be deployed in chatbot usability testing scenarios either in conjunction with or as an alternative to SUS. Further validation would determine the extent of content and criterion validity and determine inter-rater validity. Establishment of a benchmark would improve the reliability and validity of the CUQ, and this may be achieved by conducting extensive tests of large numbers of chatbots using large numbers of participants. This CUQ has construct validity and test-retest (intra-rater reliability), and is therefore a useful tool for measuring usability of chatbots. As a validated instrument comparable in procedure to the most popular SUS scale, the CUQ scale will be highly desirable to researchers and business organisations wishing to conduct credible usability tests on chatbots.

References

1. Martín, J., Muñoz-Romero, C., Ábalos, N.: chatbottest - Improve your chatbot's design. chatbottest.com (2017). https://chatbottest.com/. Accessed Mar 2019
2. Holmes, S., Moorhead, A., Bond, R., Zheng, H., Coates, V., McTear, M.: Usability testing of a healthcare chatbot: can we use conventional methods to assess conversational user interfaces?. In: Proceedings of the 31st European Conference on Cognitive Ergonomics, pp. 207–214 (September 2019)
3. Spector, P.E.: Summated Rating Scale Construction. Sage Publications Inc., Iowa (1992)
4. Holden, R.R.: Face validity. In: Weiner, I.B., Craighead, W.E. (eds.) The Corsini Encyclopedia of Psychology, vol. 2, pp. 637–638. Wiley, New Jersey (2010)
5. DeVellis, R.F.: Scale Development: Theory and Applications. SAGE Publications, California (1991)

6. Preedy, V., Watson, R.: Handbook of Disease Burdens and Quality of Life Measures. Springer, New York (2009). https://doi.org/10.1007/978-0-387-78665-0
7. McCaffrey, J.: Revealing Secrets with R and Factor Analysis. Irvine, California: Converge 360 (2017). https://visualstudiomagazine.com/articles/2017/03/01/revealing-secrets-r-factor-statistics.aspx. Accessed Sep 2019
8. Brooke, J.: SUS: a 'quick and dirty' usability scale. In: Jordan, P.W., Thomas, B., McClelland, I.L., Weerdmeester, B. (eds.) Usability Evaluation in Industry, pp. 189–194. CRC Press (1996)
9. Sauro, J.: Measuring Usability with the System Usability Scale (SUS). Colorado: MeasuringU (2011). https://measuringu.com/sus/. Accessed Mar 2020
10. Schrepp, M.: User Experience Questionnaire Handbook, 4th edn. (2019). https://www.ueq-online.org/Material/Handbook.pdf. Accessed Mar 2020

Exploring Active and Critical Engagement in Human-Robot Interaction to Develop Programming Skills: A Pilot Study

Deepti Mishra[1]([⊠]) [ID], Yavuz Inal[3] [ID], Karen Parish[2] [ID], Guillermo Arroyo Romero[1], and Rumi Rajbhandari[1]

[1] Department of Computer Science, Norwegian University of Science and Technology, Gjøvik, Norway
deepti.mishra@ntnu.no
[2] Inland Norway University of Applied Sciences, Hamar, Norway
Karen.Parish@inn.no
[3] Department of Design, Norwegian University of Science and Technology, Gjøvik, Norway

Abstract. Humanoid robots can help improve the spatial programming skills of children by making abstract concepts playful, tangible, concrete, and thereby understandable. However, active and critical engagement with robots creates its own challenges, originating from participants or robots. In this study, we explored to what extent programming a humanoid robot is engaging when the robot helps visualize the coding, instructions, and outcome of the process. The results of the study showed that a teaching session before the experiment was helpful, even though participants had previous experience programming with robots. The participants found programming the robot more enjoyable when compared to programming on a PC. They believed that robots could be useful as learning companions under the guidance of a regular teacher to improve their programming skills.

Keywords: Programming · Humanoid Robots · Human-robot Interaction · Educational Robotics · Engagement · Experiential Learning Theory

1 Introduction

The use of humanoid robots has been a widespread practice for years to help children construct logical reasoning and computational thinking. Children can acquire new knowledge and develop cognitive, conceptual, language, and collaborative skills through interacting with robots [7, 28]. Humanoid robots can spark their interest in coding as they are able to make the robot function [14]. Children program the robot to control its behaviors so that the robot can move, speak, and perform various tasks given by the program. The robot provides children with physically concrete learning experiences as they receive instant visual feedback after programming the robot and discovering their mistakes.

The role of robots in educational settings has been seen as a tutor [3, 31], peer [12, 31], learning companion [20], and co-player [1]. Previous research has found that the role of humanoid robots has an effect on children's learning outcomes in terms of improving the basics of programming skills [12] and engagement [31]. For instance, Diyas et al. [12] investigated the role of humanoid robots (peer vs. teacher) on the learning outcomes of children while they were playing a maze game with a robot. The goal was to help the robot exit the maze, and the children were introduced to the basics of programming to achieve this goal. The authors found that the children finished the task faster in a peer-like interaction. In contrast, a teacher-like interaction was more effective at improving the basics of programming skills. In another study, Zaga et al. [31] studied the effect of different social characteristics of robots (peer vs. tutor) on children's task engagement. Children showed better performance in the peer condition compared to the tutor-like character condition. The peer-like character condition was more effective at engaging children, and they had longer attention spans towards the robot and the task and solved the puzzles faster.

Children's perceptions and expectations of robots might change as a result of their reciprocal experience in interacting with robots [3, 13, 19]. In a study by Alves-Oliveira et al. [3], children interacted with an educational robot in their school, and at the end of the interaction, they were asked to assign a role to the robot. The authors found that the perception of the robot's role changed over time. At the beginning of their interaction, children perceived the robot as a tutor, but they assigned the robot the role of a classmate at the end. Similarly, Manzi et al. [19] studied the psychological effect of NAO and Pepper robots. Two groups of young adults were recruited to interact with the robots. The authors found that participants' expectations are shaped by the interaction irrespective of the type of robots. However, negative attitudes towards robots were not influenced by the interaction with robots.

Humanoid robots can help improve the spatial programming skills of children by making abstract concepts playful, tangible, and concrete, thereby making them more understandable and engaged. They might equip children with the skills necessary for active and critical engagement, encouraging them to move beyond their own perceptions about a certain topic and find out more. Arthur [5] states that "When children are really engaged in learning, they show concentration, persistence and eagerness in their inquiry. They have a positive attitude towards tasks and expect to succeed" [p. 1].

However, improving programming skills through active and critical engagement with robots poses challenges. These challenges can arise from either the participants or the robots [2, 16, 29]. For instance, when the robot is more social, it might be distracting and cause children to focus less on tasks [17]. Moreover, the role of robots, children's experiences, perceptions, and expectations of robots, their level of programming skills, and the difficulty of tasks when programming the robot might affect the active and critical engagement of children. To this end, in this research, we investigated the use of humanoid robots as learning companions for introducing children to the basics of programming. We also analyzed to what extent the experiential learning approach with the robot is engaging, especially when it helped them visualize the coding, instructions, and outcome of the process.

2 Methods

This pilot study involved K6 students, specifically those aged 10–13 years old, who learned to program a humanoid robot (NAO by Softbank Robotics) using the AskNAO Blockly software suite. The programming activity required participants to write programming instructions using blocks to make NAO move along particular paths, produce different speech, change eye color, and use the NAO head sensor.

Early in the experiment's design, it became apparent that there were some obvious differences when NAO was given a position or angle to move to. This problem was evaluated to determine the best course of action, and some conclusions were reached. Due to the limitations of block programming, it was not possible to make an adjustment or provide feedback on the position through programming. The platform used also did not allow for the use of some of NAO's advanced functions, such as cameras or many sensors. Additionally, NAO did not show consistency in adjusting values that would allow for better performance, such as identifying whether a value other than 90 would enable a 90-degree turn. Ultimately, it was decided to design the maze in a way that was more tolerant of position differences (see Fig. 1).

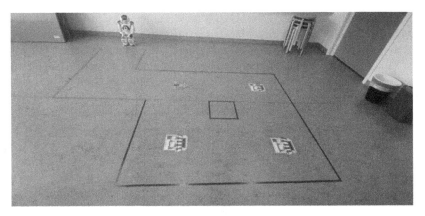

Fig. 1. Experiment setup.

To begin with, it was necessary to define the type of tasks that participants would have to solve. The tasks needed to cover all the basic elements of programming, promote programming interest, and be of an appropriate level of difficulty. Based on these criteria, the programming activity consisted of three tasks that increased in difficulty, and a story was created to frame these tasks. Each child was allowed a maximum of three attempts to complete a task, and we set a time limit of 30 min to work on the three tasks. The three tasks were progressive, with an increase in the difficulty of computational concepts from Task 1 to Task 3. Table 1 presents the details of each task along with the rationale.

2.1 Teaching Session

As programming robot using blocks requires computational thinking skills such as algorithmic thinking, programming concepts, testing, and debugging, we designed a teaching

Table 1. Task description.

Task	Instructions	Visual
#1	Scenario - NAO will walk from its home to its grandmother's home. NAO's grandmother's home is 1 meter ahead and then 1 meter to the side. Step 1: Say "Hello. Nice to meet you" Step 2: Move Nao from his home to his grandmother's home Step 3: Say "Hello Grandma" Step 4: Save the program with your name and the task number Step 5: Inform the researcher Rationale: These simple programming instructions are in correct order, and include actions such as moving straight, turning left 90 degrees, and speaking specific words.	
#2	Scenario - Grandma wants to prepare something to eat, and she asked NAO to buy some groceries. There are three stores in the town, and NAO must visit all of them and then return to its grandmother's home. Step 1: Change the color of NAO's eye LEDs to green Step 2: Say "I will be back soon. Bye" Step 3: Make NAO visit the 3 stores and then return to his grandmother's house Step 4: Say "Here are all the items from the market" Step 5: Change NAO's eye LED color to purple Step 6: Save the program with your name and the task number Step 7: Inform the researcher Rationale: This task builds upon the programming concepts introduced in Task 1, but with the added complexity of using a loop to repeat the instructions for each store. It also introduces the use of simple sensors, such as changing the color of NAO's eye LEDs.	
#3	Scenario - After enjoying all the delicious food that his grandmother has prepared; it is time for NAO to return home. NAO must bid farewell to his grandma and should start walking only when his head was touched. Step 1: Change the color of NAO's eye LEDs to green Step 2: Say "Goodbye. Touch my head if you want me to start walking" Step 3: Make NAO walk from his grandmother's house to his home. NAO will start walking only when his head is touched Step 4: Say "I am tired of walking too much. I am going to bed" Step 5: Change NAO's eye LED color to purple Step 6: Save the program Step 7: Inform the researcher Rationale: This task requires the use of previously used instructions and the implementation of a loop with a condition to ensure that the robot performs specific actions only when a particular event occurs, such as touching its head.	

session in a small group setting that was both informative and entertaining. During the session, participants were introduced to NAO, its capabilities, and how to program it. While NAO can be programmed using Choregraphe, which has a graphical interface, or programming languages such as Python and C++ [26], for this study, AskNao Blockly was chosen because of the simplicity of block programming. Some of the basic concepts that we wanted the participants to incorporate included connections and logic in block programming, logical and sequential thinking, simple movements and actions in the robot, as well as the use of loops, conditions, and sensors.

The pedagogical approach adopted in this study is based on experiential learning theory and the premise that "…knowledge is created through the transformation of experience. Knowledge results from the combination of grasping and transforming experience" [18, p. 41]. This approach allows for a diversity of learning styles in students and acknowledges that, for some, concrete experience helps them grasp, perceive, and gain new knowledge. However, for others, grasping new information happens through symbolic representation or abstract conceptualization. Similarly, some of us process experiences by observing and reflecting on others involved in the experience, while others actively experiment by jumping right in and doing things [22].

This approach was foundational to our planning of the teaching session and tasks, with the aim to motivate participants' interest in both programming and robotics. As a result, we decided not to teach using slides or other types of support materials typically found in a teacher-centered approach to learning. Instead, the session began with an illustration by the teacher, showing an example and guiding the participants on the use of certain functions in the platform. Secondly, each participant would experiment with the use of these functions to complete the task. We aimed for learning through both observation and direct interaction with robots. This also allowed the participants to experiment with different actions that were not even in the original plan of the teachers, and they were encouraged to explore on their own and have fun trying different combinations. By adopting such a pedagogical approach, we propose that programming using a humanoid robot will be engaging.

2.2 Data Collection and Procedure

We collected data using a pre-questionnaire, post-questionnaire, interview, and observations. We created a help sheet to record the time taken by the participants to complete a task in each attempt and whether a help sheet was used. We also saved their code files from each attempt of all three tasks. The experiment was conducted in a laboratory with two researchers present and one researcher observing remotely via Zoom. Both the teaching and task sessions were recorded for observation purposes. Each participant spent approximately 90 min in the experiment.

Upon entering the laboratory, we introduced the aim of the study and carefully explained to the participants what they were being asked to participate in and their rights (in line with our ethical commitment to informed consent). Each participant was asked to fill out a pre-test questionnaire including questions regarding demographics, past experience in programming, and robots. Following this, the participants had a teaching session (see the section Teaching Session). The teaching session lasted for around one hour.

After the teaching session, each participant was given three tasks to work on independently, one after the other. The goal of this task session was to complete the given tasks. At the beginning of each task session, the robot was placed at the starting position by the teacher (NAO's home, see the top left corner of Fig. 1). The interaction followed the following phases:

- We introduced the goal of the task session to the participant and outlined the tasks.
- The task sheet was given, and the participant was informed that they can ask for the help sheet if needed.
- The participant was given control of the computer.
- The participant started with the first task.
- When the participant finished writing the code for a task (programming):

  - They ran the program (testing), where the robot visualized the outcome of their code (output).
  - If there were any mistakes, the participant identified their mistakes using the output and fixed the code (debugging) and ran the program again.

- They repeated the same process with each of the three tasks.
- When the three tasks were finished, we thanked the participant for their work on the tasks.

Following the individual task sessions, participants were asked to fill out the post-test questionnaire. In addition, we conducted a group interview with the participants to obtain detailed data on their improvement in understanding of basic programming, enjoyment, difficulty, and engagement.

3 Results

3.1 Pedagogical Approach

In accordance with our framework for utilizing humanoid robots [22], we created a teaching session based on the experiential learning theory. The participants were encouraged to actively engage during the teaching session, where they practiced using various code blocks. Additionally, they had the opportunity to observe both their peers and teachers. Even though the participants had previous experience programming with robots, they found the teaching session before the task to be helpful. A participant remarked that without the teaching session, *"I wouldn't have been able to do probably any of them (the tasks) and might have barely been able to do the first one because I've done some of this before."*

The participants were provided with instructions on how to locate and utilize various blocks, as well as how to change the values in the blocks. They particularly liked that the teachers not only gave them such information and showed them how to do it, but also let them try it themselves during the session. They thought that by practicing it after they were shown the command blocks, it was easier to remember how to do it when they had to do the task themselves. One of the participants said that *"The thing I liked is how they didn't just give us information, but they let us try after teaching us. After teaching us they actually let us try it to see exactly how it worked. I think if they just gave information, I probably would have forgotten it, but I think that it reinforced the memory of the things I need to do when they told us to do it ourselves."*

3.2 Technical Aspects

Interacting with the Robot. The participants interacted with the NAO robot during the experiment. They seemed more engaged in the activity and seemed generally positive about NAO's responsiveness in terms of speech, walking, turning, hand movements, and touch while performing the tasks. However, during the interviews, when probed further, the participants highlighted many deviations from what they expected. Constraints in terms of the robot's capabilities negatively influenced their expectations and attitudes towards the robot.

For example, the participants reported that the robot was not responsive when they touched its hand, and the sensors on the foot did not work well, yet only the head responded. A participant stated that *"I learned a bit about the NAO... but the NAO robot sometimes wasn't like super responsive like the camera or the touching on the head didn't work. I tried to touch its hand, but it didn't like to pick it up."* Another participant further added that *"Yeah like it would like even though you set it to go straight instead of going at an angle, it went like a rainbow and wonky. So, it sometimes walked out of the maze and didn't get its destination."* The participants believed that the robot's mechanical functionality caused it to go off track.

One reason is that the free version of AskNao Blockly does not provide all the robot's capabilities. All code blocks are available during programming, however, only some of them work, such as the head sensor, even though blocks related to the hand and leg sensors are also available. Secondly, NAO is not very accurate and precise in terms of movement, especially when turning to a certain degree. However, NAO's starting body position, including feet angles, floor surface, slant, and friction, also impacts its directional movement.

AskNao Blockly also has its advantages. During the execution of code blocks, participants can see a specific block (out of many blocks) and the corresponding action by the robot, making it easier for them to see the association between the individual block and the robot's action. This also makes it easier to identify potential blocks that require rework or correction in case the output (robot's actions) is not as expected.

Programming, Performance, Difficulty, and Enjoyment. Participants found programming the robot more enjoyable compared to programming on a PC because the robot was more tactile, and the outcome of the process was visualized by the robot. They were actively during programming the tasks and frequently looked at the robot, apparently trying to visualize the output and spatial movement. This helped to make abstract concepts more tangible and concrete.

The participants were given three attempts for each task. After writing the code (coding), they were asked to run it (testing). If there was an error in the code, the participants could identify it by looking at the robot's actions (debugging - identify mistakes). Then they were given another attempt to correct their code (debugging - correct mistakes). Participants typically took less than a minute to correct their code. It was easy to understand the errors by looking at the output, i.e., the robot's actions in the correct order, and fix them quickly.

Task 1: The participants did not find Task 1 difficult to program. In total, they spent two to three minutes on the first attempt. Only one participant needed another attempt to finish the task because they made a mistake and performed a right turn instead of a left. On the second attempt, they corrected the code in less than one minute and successfully completed the task (see Fig. 2).

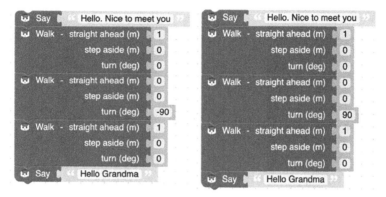

Fig. 2. The example of incorrect (on the left) and corrected (on the right) code of Task 1.

We anticipated, to some extent, the participants' responses regarding their enjoyment and the difficulty level of Task 1. Task 1 involved simple programming instructions in the correct order, such as moving straight, making a left turn of 90°, moving straight again, and making NAO say certain words. Therefore, the participants found it easy and enjoyable. The mistake encountered by one participant was making a right turn instead of a left turn. To make a left turn, the value should be +90° whereas for a right turn, the value should be −90°. We believe it is counter-intuitive because we usually associate positive values with right and negative values with left. The participants also reported finding left and right turns confusing and difficult. A participant stated that "*Because you had to like write the degrees and like right 90° was like minus 90°.*"

Task 2: The participants did not find the programming difficult. In total, they spent five minutes on the first attempt. Similar to the first task, only one participant needed another attempt to finish the task. A left turn was performed instead of a right. On the second attempt, they fixed the code in less than one minute and completed the task (see Fig. 3).

The participants did not find it difficult since it required programming instructions similar to Task 1, however, they used the same blocks multiple times. One of them stated that "*Programming wise the first two levels of the task were quite easy, it wasn't like too easy or too hard. It was quite simple and quite fun. It took some time, but it didn't take forever to do.*" Even though they completed the task successfully, we had expected the participants to use a 'loop' block as this would be more efficient and show progression in their programming skills. However, we did not explicitly instruct them to do so, and

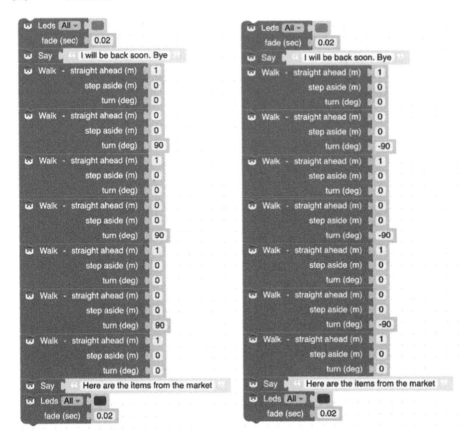

Fig. 3. The example of incorrect (on the left) and corrected (on the right) code for Task 2.

none of them thought about using it. Without the use of a 'loop', this task was simple and just required the same programming blocks such as speech and movements, where the robot was expected to move in square shape maze using 'move forward 1 m' and 'turn −90°' blocks multiple times.

When probed further during interviews, the participants realized they could have used the 'loop' block, however, it did not occur to them when they were doing the task. It appears that the participants viewed Task 2 as a continuation of Task 1 with similar programming blocks and did not think to use other programming constructs, even though they were taught those concepts (e.g., loops) during the teaching session. Another possibility is that they had a choice between solutions with or without using a loop, and they chose a solution that seemed easier and less risky for them.

Task 3: Only one of the participants found Task 3 difficult to program. In total, they spent four to six minutes on the first attempt. Two participants needed another attempt to finish the task. One of them missed the last walk but corrected it in less than one minute. Other one did not wait for its head to be touched. It took less than two minutes for the participant to fix the mistake (see Fig. 4).

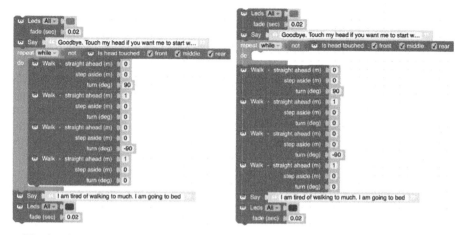

Fig. 4. The example of incorrect (on the left) and corrected (on the right) code of Task 3.

A participant said that "*Task 3 was a bit harder, but I still think that it was fun because it was challenging.*" Another participant further added that "*I think that if it was too challenging then it wouldn't be that fun because then it would just get frustrating after a while if you mess up lots of times.*" This task required some of the previously used instructions along with the knowledge of using a 'loop with condition(s)'. Even though the participants did not use a 'loop' in Task 2, they successfully used a 'loop with condition(s)' in Task 3. This shows that they learned the use of loops and used it when left with no choice, even though loop with condition(s) can be considered more complex than using a simple loop that runs for a certain number of times.

3.3 Psycho-Social Aspects

Awareness. In order to find out participants' awareness of robots, they were asked to describe the robot in their own words. A participant stated that "*a machine that can respond.*" The participants were also aware of the amount of effort needed to program a robot before it can be used in real settings. For instance, a participant said that "*It's a bit of an issue because like if people just want to like do stuff with the robot it can take one hour to program something that will only like last like 3 min.*" Another participant further added that "*So imagine if you wanted the robot to do something like to walk somewhere and do lots of stuff on the way that could take like hours to program.*" The participants had several ideas about how robots could be implemented to be helpful. Using robots for people with special needs was the main goal behind the usefulness of the robots. They also believed that robots could guide people with disabilities to find a location as a tool for wayfinding. They further suggested that the robot could be used with children who have issues managing their feelings and have specific health issues. They proposed that robots could be used instead of service dogs in such cases.

Perception. Programming the robot was enjoyable for the participants. They had positive attitudes toward the implementation of robots in school settings and intended to use them in the future. They found the use of robots in learning the basics of programming both instructive and fun. A participant stated that "*It is quite fun, the possibilities are endless. You can technically program it to do anything.*" However, the participants had concerns about the future of robots. Although they saw robots as effective tools to learn to program, they did not want to imagine a future with robots. A participant clarified the reasons for their concerns, pointing out the issue that there would be lots of machines moving around and taking over human jobs. Another participant further highlighted a specific situation, saying that "*If somehow like the robots try to start programming themselves or something then it might go quite wrong.*" The participants exemplified their feelings about the use of robots in the future with sci-fi movies. For example, a participant stated that "*It's a movie but still in the movie the robot takes over the humans, and also the humans don't get any exercise because they have robots that are just like literally walking them, doing everything for them.*" We observed that the participants' attitudes toward the future of robots influenced their perception of the role of robots in a learning context. They believed that robots could be useful as a learning companion under the guidance of a normal teacher to improve their programming skills. Yet, the robots could only substitute their teacher for a temporary period of time due to illness or injury.

4   Discussion and Conclusion

In this paper, we explored the potential of humanoid robots for introducing children to the basics of programming and discussed to what extent the experiential learning approach is engaging when the robot helped to make programming concepts more concrete and tangible. The participants found the interactive teaching session, with ample opportunity to practice before the task, helpful even though they had experienced programming with robots earlier. The approach taken here incorporates both the possibility to learn through abstract conceptualization or concrete experience, by watching others and/or actively experimenting. This approach enabled engagement with the programming tasks as the participants were able to learn in a way that is appropriate for them.

The participants had no prior experience interacting with NAO robots before the experiment. Previous research shows that after gaining experience interacting with robots, people might change their attitudes and develop a different perception of robots [19], as well as an increased sense of the robot's social presence [13]. Consistent with these arguments, our study found that the teaching session was extremely helpful in aiding participants to become more engaged with the robot and feel more comfortable during the task session.

People prefer a highly humanoid robotic appearance with human-like facial features. Even after a brief interaction with a humanoid robot, the perception of robot's social presence increases [13]. The degree to which a robot's face resembles a human being has a positive impact on people's perception of the robot; the more human-like a robot's face, the more positive the perception [24]. In our study, the participants were generally positive about NAO's responsiveness in terms of speech, walking, turning, hand movements, and touch, however, they also noted several deviations from their expectations.

The NAO robot has specific facial features such as eyes, mouth, and nose, that resemble human beings. In our study, the participants had very positive attitudes toward the robot and found it very cute. They seemed more engaged in the activity during the task session. They believed that robots could be useful as learning companions under the guidance of a teacher to improve their programming skills. These results corroborate the idea that robots may supplement as a learning companion to fill a need that cannot be met solely by human teachers. However, when considering whether robots can substitute for human teachers or other devices, no study indicates that they are more effective than humans, though robots can be more effective than other digital devices [15].

The participants found programming the robot enjoyable because the robot was tactile, and the outcome of the coding process was concrete. Screen-based output may not be ideal for comprehending difficult programming constructs. Providing a tangible object for the programming interface can be an effective way to make difficult programming concepts more understandable for children [25]. This is especially useful for learners with no or little prior experience in programming, as was the case in our study. The learning experience, consisting of programming and controlling robot operations, has been shown to help inexperienced students have a better understanding of the usefulness of computer programming [10]. The reason might be that the use of humanoid robots to learn to program makes the programming output more visible and concrete in the form of the robot's actions e.g., the robots' leg and hand movements, changes in eye color, different speech, and actions related to sensor event such as head/hand/leg touch.

During programming, children frequently looked at the robot, indicating they were trying to visualize the output and the movement in their minds. Similar results were reported by Mioduser and Levy [21] in their study with young children, who found that children could simulate the robot's behaviors by spatially visualizing it before making the robot move, rather than testing its behaviors arbitrarily. The output (such as the robots' leg and hand movements, change in eye color, different speech, actions related to sensor events such as head touch, etc. in correct order) helped children understand errors in the code, making the debugging process faster. Learning to code with tangible systems such as robots helps children develop the ability to correctly sequence and debug their programs [4].

Consistent with prior research [27], the participants enjoyed the programming tasks and generally did not find them difficult. We observed that assigning tasks that built on previous ones was helpful. The level of difficulty of the tasks affected the children's engagement level and experience of flow during the task session, as self-reported challenge is associated with the experience of flow. The level of difficulty should be appropriate for the participants to feel a sense of accomplishment when solving the tasks, but not too challenging as to cause frustration and demotivation.

Regarding the effective use of the basics of programming, the participants in our study did not use the 'loop' block in Task 2 since they had a choice between solution with or without using a loop, whereas they used 'loop with a condition' (considered as more complex) in Task 3. It seems that given a choice in Task 2, they chose a solution that seemed easier and less risky for them. It is not easy for inexperienced programmers to use higher-level abstractions such as loops in their code. Learning loops is an especially difficult concept for novices to understand [23], but as students engage more with the robot, they try more complex programming and take risks [9].

Previous research shows that robots provide active and collaborative learning environments [6, 8]. The use of robots has the potential to promote executive functions [11]. Being able to code and problem-solve with robots and other technologies is an important skill that needs to be developed [30]. Overall, in our study, we observed that, provided there is an active and critical engagement in human-robot interaction, humanoid robots have the potential to improve spatial programming skills by making abstract concepts playful, tangible, concrete, and thereby understandable. The main weakness of this study was the limited number of participants. We conducted this pilot study to explore the challenges in active and critical engagement in human-robot interaction to develop the programming skills of children and to improve the research design of the main study. In the main study, we plan to elaborate further on both the successes and the challenges identified in this study.

References

1. Abe, K., et al.: Toward playmate robots that can play with children considering personality. In: Proceedings of the Second International Conference on Human-agent Interaction, pp. 165–168 (2014). https://doi.org/10.1145/2658861.2658913
2. Ahmad, M.I., Mubin, O., Orlando, J.: Adaptive social robot for sustaining social engagement during long-term children-robot interaction. Int. J. Hum. Comput. Interact. 33(12), 943–962 (2017). https://doi.org/10.1080/10447318.2017.1300750
3. Alves-Oliveira, P., Sequeira, P., Paiva, A.: The role that an educational robot plays. In: Proceedings of the 25th IEEE International Symposium on Robot and Human Interactive Communication (RO-MAN), pp. 817–822 (2016). https://doi.org/10.1109/ROMAN.2016.7745213
4. Angeli, C., et al.: A K-6 computational thinking curriculum framework: implications for teacher knowledge. J. Educ. Technol. Soc. 19(3), 47–57 (2016)
5. Arthur, L.: The early years learning framework: building confident learners. Early Childhood Australia (2010)
6. Benitti, F.B.V.: Exploring the educational potential of robotics in schools: a systematic review. Comput. Educ. 58(3), 978–988 (2012). https://doi.org/10.1016/j.compedu.2011.10.006
7. Benvenuti, M., Mazzoni, E.: Enhancing wayfinding in pre-school children through robot and socio-cognitive conflict. Br. J. Edu. Technol. 51(2), 436–458 (2020). https://doi.org/10.1111/bjet.12848
8. Bers, M.U., González-González, C., Armas-Torres, M.B.: Coding as a playground: promoting positive learning experiences in childhood classrooms. Comput. Educ. 138, 130–145 (2019). https://doi.org/10.1016/j.compedu.2019.04.013
9. Chalmers, C., Keane, T., Boden, M., Williams, M.: Humanoid robots: programing at school. In: Proceedings of the 5th International STEM in Education Conference: Integrated Education for the Real World (2018)
10. Corral, J.M.R., Ruiz-Rube, I., Balcells, A.C., Mota-Macías, J.M., Morgado-Estévez, A., Dodero, J.M.: A study on the suitability of visual languages for non-expert robot programmers. IEEE Access 7, 17535–17550 (2019). https://doi.org/10.1109/ACCESS.2019.2895913
11. Di Lieto, M.C., et al.: Educational robotics intervention on executive functions in preschool children: a pilot study. Comput. Hum. Behav. 71, 16–23 (2017). https://doi.org/10.1016/j.chb.2017.01.018

12. Diyas, Y., Brakk, D., Aimambetov, Y., Sandygulova, A.: Evaluating peer versus teacher robot within educational scenario of programming learning. In: Proceedings of the 11th ACM/IEEE International Conference on Human-Robot Interaction (HRI), pp. 425–426 (2016). https://doi.org/10.1109/HRI.2016.7451788

13. Edwards, A., Edwards, C., Westerman, D., Spence, P.R.: Initial expectations, interactions, and beyond with social robots. Comput. Hum. Behav. **90**, 308–314 (2019). https://doi.org/10.1016/j.chb.2018.08.042

14. Keane, T., Chalmers, C., Boden, M., Williams, M.: Humanoid robots: learning a programming language to learn a traditional language. Technol. Pedagog. Educ. **28**(5), 533–546 (2019). https://doi.org/10.1080/1475939X.2019.1670248

15. Kanero, J., Geçkin, V., Oranç, C., Mamus, E., Küntay, A.C., Göksun, T.: Social robots for early language learning: current evidence and future directions. Child Dev. Perspect. **12**(3), 146–151 (2018). https://doi.org/10.1111/cdep.12277

16. Kanero, J., Oranç, C., Koşkulu, S., Kumkale, G.T., Göksun, T., Küntay, A.C.: Are tutor robots for everyone? The influence of attitudes, anxiety, and personality on robot-led language learning. Int. J. Soc. Robot. **14**(2), 297–312 (2021). https://doi.org/10.1007/s12369-021-00789-3

17. Kennedy, J., Baxter, P., Belpaeme, T.: The robot who tried too hard: social behaviour of a robot tutor can negatively affect child learning. In: Proceedings of the 10th ACM/IEEE International Conference on Human-Robot Interaction (HRI), pp. 67–74 (2015)

18. Kolb, D.A.: Experiential Learning: Experience as the Source of Learning and Development. Prentice-Hall International, Upper Saddle River (1984)

19. Manzi, F., Massaro, D., Di Lernia, D., Maggioni, M.A., Riva, G., Marchetti, A.: Robots are not all the same: young adults' expectations, attitudes, and mental attribution to two humanoid social robots. Cyberpsychol. Behav. Soc. Netw. **24**(5), 307–314 (2021). https://doi.org/10.1089/cyber.2020.0162

20. Michaelis, J.E., Mutlu, B.: Someone to read with: design of and experiences with an in-home learning companion robot for reading. In: Proceedings of the 2017 CHI Conference on Human Factors in Computing Systems, pp. 301–312 (2017). https://doi.org/10.1145/3025453.3025499

21. Mioduser, D., Levy, S.T.: Making sense by building sense: kindergarten children's construction and understanding of adaptive robot behaviors. Int. J. Comput. Math. Learn. **15**(2), 99–127 (2010). https://doi.org/10.1007/s10758-010-9163-9

22. Mishra, D., Parish, K., Lugo, R.G., Wang, H.: A framework for using humanoid robots in the school learning environment. Electronics **10**(6), 756 (2021). https://doi.org/10.3390/electronics10060756

23. Moors, L., Sheehan, R.: Aiding the transition from novice to traditional programming environments. In: Proceedings of the 2017 Conference on Interaction Design and Children, pp. 509–514 (2017). https://doi.org/10.1145/3078072.3084317

24. Prakash, A., Rogers, W.A.: Why some humanoid faces are perceived more positively than others: effects of human-likeness and task. Int. J. Soc. Robot. **7**(2), 309–331 (2014). https://doi.org/10.1007/s12369-014-0269-4

25. Strawhacker, A., Bers, M.U.: "I want my robot to look for food": comparing kindergartner's programming comprehension using tangible, graphic, and hybrid user interfaces. Int. J. Technol. Des. Educ. **25**(3), 293–319 (2014). https://doi.org/10.1007/s10798-014-9287-7

26. Subedi, A., Pandey, D., Mishra, D.: Programming Nao as an educational agent: a comparison between Choregraphe and Python SDK. In: Ben Ahmed, M., Boudhir, A.A., Karaş, İR., Jain, V., Mellouli, S. (eds.) SCA 2021. LNNS, vol. 393, pp. 367–377. Springer, Cham (2022). https://doi.org/10.1007/978-3-030-94191-8_29

27. Sullivan, A., Elkin, M., Bers, M.U.: KIBO robot demo: engaging young children in programming and engineering. In: Proceedings of the 14th International Conference on Interaction Design and Children, pp. 418–421 (2015). https://doi.org/10.1145/2771839.2771868

28. Toh, L.P.E., Causo, A., Tzuo, P.W., Chen, I.M., Yeo, S.H.: A review on the use of robots in education and young children. J. Educ. Technol. Soc. **19**(2), 148–163 (2016)

29. Tokmurzina, D., Sagitzhan, N., Nurgaliyev, A., Sandygulova, A.: Exploring child-robot proxemics. In: Companion of the 2018 ACM/IEEE International Conference on Human-Robot Interaction. ACM, pp. 257–258 (2018). https://doi.org/10.1145/3173386.3177083

30. Turner, S., Hill, G.: Robotics within the teaching of problem-solving. Innov. Teach. Learn. Inf. Comput. Sci. **7**(1), 108–119 (2008). https://doi.org/10.11120/ital.2008.07010108

31. Zaga, C., Lohse, M., Truong, K.P., Evers, V.: The effect of a robot's social character on children's task engagement: peer versus tutor. In: Tapus, A., André, E., Martin, J.C., Ferland, F., Ammi, M. (eds.) Social Robotics. ICSR 2015. Lecture Notes in Computer Science(), vol. 9388. Springer, Cham (2015). https://doi.org/10.1007/978-3-319-25554-5_70

A Comparative Analysis of Real Time Open-Source Speech Recognition Tools for Social Robots

Akshara Pande[1]([envelope]) [iD], Bhanu Shrestha[1] [iD], Anshul Rani[2] [iD], and Deepti Mishra[1,3] [iD]

[1] Education Technology Laboratory, Department of Computer Science (IDI), Norwegian University of Science and Technology, Gjøvik, Norway
{akshara.pande,deepti.mishra}@ntnu.no, bhanus@stud.ntnu.no
[2] Department of Computer Science (IDI), Norwegian University of Science and Technology, Gjøvik, Norway
anshul.rani@ntnu.no
[3] Business Analytics Research Group, Inland School of Business and Social Sciences, Inland Norway University of Applied Sciences, Lillehammer, Norway

Abstract. Social robots are designed to support people through their capabilities such as information gathering, processing, analyzing, and predicting. Social robots play a vital role in various fields such as medical, entertainment, education, and assistance. Speech is a fundamental characteristic of social robots to establish communication with humans. The advancement of artificial intelligence has facilitated speech recognition tools to be substantially effective. It is easier to comprehend the meaning of a speech if it is documented. The speech recognition tools help robots in recognizing human speech. It is supposed that robots can precisely understand what humans are attempting to convey, however it is not achievable every time due to several factors such as constraints in terms of robot functionality or noise in the environment. There are research studies which indicate that speech recognition of children is a challenging problem for robots. The in-built speech recognition capabilities of such robots can be enhanced by integrating it with a more efficient speech recognition tool available in this domain. Therefore, it is necessary to select the appropriate speech recognition tool so that robots can understand human speech in a consistent way. In the present study we are analyzing five real-time speech-to-text recognition tools available from open sources: Google speech recognition, Vosk, CMUSphinx, DeepSpeech and Whisper. Evaluation metrics are generally used to evaluate the performance of speech recognition tools. This analysis will enable us to determine the best real time open-source tool to employ for robot-human interaction.

Keywords: Social robot · speech recognition · Tools · Artificial intelligence · Human-robot interaction · HRI · Real-time

A. Marcus et al. (Eds.): HCII 2023, LNCS 14033, pp. 355–365, 2023.
https://doi.org/10.1007/978-3-031-35708-4_26

1 Introduction

Human robot interaction (HRI) through communication holds substantial opportunity for various domains [1–8]. Speech recognition is one of the features of machine learning that allows machines to interpret different speeches and languages [6]. The speech recognition for HRI is significantly explored in the field of robotics. Erol et al. proposed a smart system where speech recognition can be utilized for identifying human emotions as well [3]. Few studies also showed that robots perform certain tasks and actions based on instructions provided with speech commands [2, 7]. One of the research studies demonstrated robots in the medical field as receptionist robot, nurse assistant and a server with communication being established through speech recognition [4]. Vacher et al. presented a real-time sound analysis system for health smart homes and they also proposed the improvement of speech recognition models for elderly people [8].

Along with various other domains, social robots have been explored for education and entertainment purposes as well. The focus of these studies was mainly on the natural interaction to educate students using speech recognition tools [1, 5]. Real time speech recognition has various advantages including the fact that human accents can occasionally be challenging to understand but speech to text conversion makes it simpler to comprehend spoken words. This can be an important aid in a variety of real-life situations. For example, if students attending a lecture, for some reason struggle to understand the content of the lecture due to some issue with the teacher's voice, they could utilize the speech to text conversion of the teacher's voice, read the text instead and follow along with the lecture in real time. Similarly, with the help of text we can attempt to grasp trembling voice of an elder person or unclear voice of children immediately.

However, embedding speech recognition tools with social robots for educational purposes is not yet explored. Berghe et al. [9] showed that social robots are helpful in studies of language but students might use their native language, and they can be of different age groups. Randall *et al.* demonstrated that social robots could facilitate language acquisition for both native and foreign language therefore enhance inspiration and goal orientation [10]. Though social robots act as supporters for language learning, they still face problems while understanding the spoken language semantics perfectly [11]. Thus, there is a need to embed speech recognition tools with social robots for language learning.

Speech recognition by robots, however, face many challenges. Speech recognition is challenging for social robots as desirable level of accuracy is often not achievable [12–14]. Accuracy can be computed by evaluation metrics [15]. The reasons include the presence of background noise, homophones and language semantics. One of the reports suggest the need to work on child speech recognition as it is not well understood by robots [16]. Another factor that might affect the efficacy of employing speech recognition for robots is the distance between the microphone used by robots and the person that is speaking to the robots which might increase the chances of background noise affecting the speech recognition process [17].

A report on surgical robot mentioned the flaws of speech recognition system as latency, low recognition rate and inadequacy in voice control due to long distance motion [18]. There is, hence, a need to improve the speech recognition capabilities of robots by integrating them with speech recognition tools. Another factor that might affect the efficacy of employing speech recognition for robots is the distance between the microphone used by robots and the person that is speaking to the robots which might increase the chances of background noise affecting the speech recognition process [17]. Past studies indicate that noisy speech may hamper therapy sessions of autistic children as it was found that autistic children's responses were slowed and decreased in presence of noisy environment [19, 20].

In the present study, different open source tools are compared as open-source tools are cost effective [21] and have widespread popularity among scientific communities [22].The aim of the paper is to compare the existing open-source real time speech recognition tools and select the best among them to integrate with a robot for better performance in terms of human-robot interaction. The paper is organized as follows. The methods used have been described in Sect. 2. Section 3 contains the results obtained and related discussions. The conclusions and future directions are summarized in Sect. 4.

2   Methodology

In this study, the same sentences are provided to three users to speak. We have used windows operating system for the study. These sentences are also saved in the computer inside the working folder as a reference text. The speakers speak out loud the sentences through a microphone and have their speech transcribed in real time. The overall pipeline is shown in Fig. 1. We developed a python script to select one of the speech recognition tools among five.

2.1 Open-Source Speech Recognition Tools Used in the Study

We have used Python Package Index (PyPI) to install speech recognition tools. The speech recognition library can work both online and offline and supports a number of engines and APIs [23]. The details of real time open-source speech recognition tools are as follows:

Google Speech Recognition. In order to setup this package, two modules need to be downloaded called speech recognition and pyaudio by using the commands: 'pip install speechrecognition' and 'pip install pyaudio'. Additionally, we also attempted the text to speech conversion, and for this purpose we used the module pyttsx3 which was installed using command 'pip install pyttsx3'. Recognizer instant can be created and Google Web Speech API (recognize_google()) is used to recognize user voice (https://wicg.github.io/speech-api/).

Sphinx. The previously mentioned modules speechrecognition and pyaudio are prerequisites for this speech recognition tool as well. Additionally, one more module is required called pocketsphinx. This can be installed using command 'pip install pocketsphinx'. Here recognize_sphinx() is invoked. The CMU sphinx works offline, which means that no internet connection is needed for speech recognition (https://cmusphinx.github.io/).

DeepSpeech. This open-source tool was proposed in the year 2017 by researchers in Baidu. It uses Google's TensorFlow for implementation [24]. DeepSpeech can

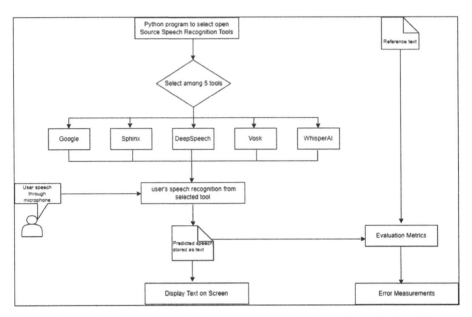

Fig. 1. Pipeline for comparing the five open-source speech recognition tools in real time

be installed using pip command 'pip install deepspeech'. Pre-trained two models 'deepspeech-0.9.3-models.pbmm' and 'deepspeech-0.9.3-models.scorer' are also downloaded for this tool.

Vosk. It is an open-source recognition tool which works offline as well. It is able to recognize 20+ speech languages [25]. It can be installed using command 'pip install vosk'. A pre-trained model 'vosk-model-small-en-us-0.15' is also downloaded. Vosk API works offline.

WhisperAI. This speech recognition model can do multiple tasks and capable of performing multilingual speech languages recognition (https://github.com/openai/whisper). Whisper can be installed using command 'pip install -U openai-whisper'. Other required libraries are numpy, tqdm, more-itertools, ffmpeg, pyaudio, SpeechRecognition, pydub and torch. WhisperAI works offline.

2.2   Evaluation Metrics

Each speech recognition tool predicts the speech of users and displays that on the computer's screen. The text predicted by each of the speech recognition tools is also saved inside the computer folder. To check the performance of speech recognition tool evaluation metrics can be used. These evaluation metrics take the original reference text and the predicted text as inputs and measure the error occurred between the two. We import 'jiwer' python library to evaluate the error measures. The following evaluation metrics used for this purpose.

Word Error Rate. World error rate (WER) is the ratio of number of word insertion (I), number of deletion (D) and num of substitution (S) to the total number of words in original speech (T) (Eq. 1). There is a belief that WER has significant impact on speech analysis [26, 27]. WER calculates the edit distance between spoken word and predicted word by speech recognition tool. In terms of accuracy, WER value should be low.

$$WER = \frac{I + D + S}{T} \qquad (1)$$

Match Error Rate. The possibility that a given match is inaccurate is determined by the Match Error Rate (MER), which is the percentage of I/O word matches [28]. MER can be defined as follows (Eq. 2) [29].

$$MER = \frac{S + D + I}{T + I} \qquad (2)$$

Word Information Lost. Word Information Lost (WIL) represents the proportion of words that are erroneously anticipated between a set of original spoken sentences and the predicted sentences by speech recognition tools [30]. It can be calculated as follows, where Ct is the number of correct words and Pr is the number of words in predicted sentence:

$$WIL = 1 - \frac{Ct}{T} + \frac{Ct}{Pr} \qquad (3)$$

Character Error Rate. Character Error Rate (CER) score represents the proportion of characters for which an inaccurate prediction was made [31]. The speech recognition system performs better with a lower value; a CER of 0 is a perfect result.

3   Results and Discussions

The reference text is presented in Fig. 2, which was selected from Wikipedia about speech recognition [32]. It contains one sentence and total word count was 36. Three speakers were involved in this study, 2 female participants and 1 male participant. The user-friendly commands were included in python so that user can select the desired speech recognition tool (Fig. 3(a)). These speech recognition tools provide an evaluation metrics for each speaker in terms of WER, MER, WIL and CER. The obtained result for each speech recognition tool is illustrated for speaker 1 in Fig. 3. Evaluation measures for each speaker is shown in Table 1.

According to Table1, WhisperAI was predicting best speech as average WER was around 9% which was pretty good. Google speech recognizer was the second best, the average WER obtained was 42.3%. In the past few research studies were done for comparing the speech recognition tools but they did not compare the same research tools which we are using for the present study. Our focus is on real-time open-source speech recognition tools. Këpuska *et al.* compared Microsoft API, Google API and CMU

Fig. 2. Reference text which user is going to speak [32]

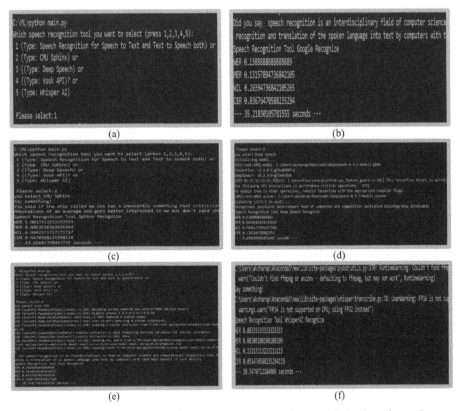

Fig. 3. Output from terminals as evaluation metrics for Speaker 1 (a) Selection of speech recognition tool by user (b) when user selects Google Speech Recognizer (c) when user selects CMU Sphinx Speech Recognizer (d) when user selects DeepSpeech Recognizer (e) when user selects Vosk Speech Recognizer (f) when user selects WhisperAI Speech Recognizer

Sphinx speech recognition tools, they showed Google API was the best among them as WER was smallest for it [33]. Another study demonstrated the experiment with speech recognition tools, Google API provided smallest average error (in terms of WER) than IBM and Wit speech recognition system [28]. As per the Table 1, the third-best tool for speech recognition is Vosk API, however it has WER as 51.7%. The difference between

Google Speech Recognizer and Vosk API is small, but the difference with WhisperAI is large.

Table 1. Evaluation measures for five speech recognition tools

Evaluation Metrics		Google Speech Recognizer	CMU Sphinx	DeepSpeech Recognition	Vosk API	WhisperAI
Speaker1	WER	0.22	1.03	8.08	0.47	0.08
	MER	0.21	0.82	0.94	0.41	0.08
	WIL	0.34	0.96	0.97	0.61	0.13
	CER	0.04	0.61	7.62	0.18	0.05
	Execution Time (Sec)	35.21	43.66	9.70	18.55	30.54
Speaker2	WER	0.86	1.17	9.06	0.89	0.06
	MER	0.86	0.93	0.94	0.64	0.06
	WIL	0.91	0.99	0.97	0.82	0.11
	CER	0.8	0.69	8.69	0.35	0.04
	Execution Time (Sec)	29.54	89.31	7.01	19.64	30.80
Speaker3	WER	0.19	0.58	8.94	0.19	0.14
	MER	0.19	0.46	0.94	0.18	0.13
	WIL	0.26	0.61	0.97	0.27	0.18
	CER	0.1	0.27	8.53	0.04	0.05
	Execution Time (Sec)	34.26	39.99	8.41	18.59	29.84

Besides WER, the other measures were also considered (Table 1). Morris *et al.* proposed that in connected speech recognition (CSR), MER and WIL are more appropriate evaluation measures than WER for assessment of any application where transmitted word information has more weightage than edit cost [34]. In CSR, MER and WIL present evaluation measures in which they can be in range of 0 to 1, where 0 represents absence of errors and 1 represents lack of hits [34]. Wang *et al.* proposed CER measure is more resistant to word segmentation than the conventional word-based ambiguity and exhibits substantially stronger connection in a continuous Chinese speech recognition task with an extensive vocabulary [35]. One of the research compared the effectiveness of speech recognition systems by utilizing the total CER on the data and showed the difference on the basis of gender voice [36].

We found in real-time case scenario that average MER (0.09), WIL (0.14) and CER (0.05) were smallest for WhisperAI recognizer in comparison to other speech recognizer tools (Fig. 4). As per Fig. 5, it is evident that average execution time of WhisperAI speech

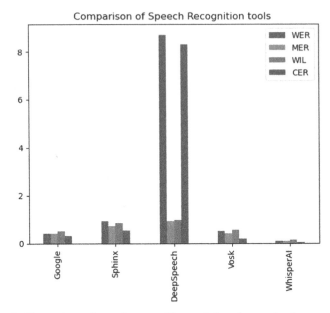

Fig. 4. Comparison of speech recognition tools based on evaluation measures

recognizer was not the smallest. The smallest execution time was for Vosk API. We did not consider DeepSpeech recognizer execution time as smallest because DeepSpeech recognizer stopped before the sentence completion for three of the speakers. WER and CER were also quite high for DeepSpeech recognizer as compared to others (Fig. 4). CMU Sphinx took longer time for execution and obtained displayed output was absurd.

We have suggested the speech recognition tools which could probably enhance speech capabilities of robot so that it will be enabled to interpret spoken language accurately. In order to determine the best speech recognition tools, we focused on its evaluation metrics parameters. In this study we did not get much difference in speech recognition tools based on the gender of the voice used in the experiment. In future, we will attempt to integrate speech recognition tools with social robots, it may require a significant amount of effort and time.

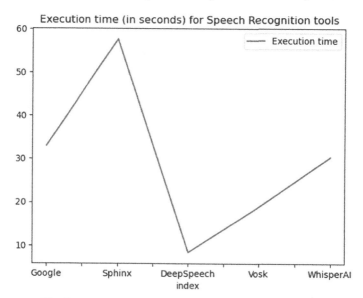

Fig. 5. Average execution time for speech recognition tools

4 Conclusions and Future Work

Our analyses suggest that CMU Sphinx and DeepSpeech recognition tools should be avoided to integrate with social robots since the result of the transcripts when these tools are used produce the highest number of errors. Based on the research, WhisperAI speech recognition tool can be considered the best open-source option amongst the tools chosen for the research to be integrated in a social robot in order to improve speech recognition on it. Similarly, Google speech and Vosk API speech recognition tools could also be considered for integration with the social robots but could be lesser priority than WhisperAI for this purpose. However, user speech used for the experiment was not large, in future longer lines could be incorporated into speech.

While some previous research does exist with regards to the usage of speech recognition for human robot interaction, this paper focused on the viability and possibility of using open-source speech recognition tools with the aim of implementation of these tools for building a better speech recognition medium for human robot interaction. Future research could build on the findings of this research in order to incorporate real-time open-source speech recognition tools with social robots to observe the efficacy of these tools in scenarios where social robots are generally used.

This research has only considered usage of the various open-source speech recognition tools in case of adult voices, but future work could focus on possibly finding if the tools work equally well with children and elderly individuals. Similarly, performances of these tools in terms of speech recognition accuracy could be tested for individuals with speech impairments or with individuals having strong accents or dialects. The performance of these tools for different languages and their ability to correctly predict speech from individuals who are native to the languages and people who use the language as the secondary or learned language could also be an area of future research that could yield productive outcomes.

References

1. Budiharto, W., et al.: EduRobot: intelligent humanoid robot with natural interaction for education and entertainment. Procedia Comput. Sci. **116**, 564–570 (2017)
2. Childers, M., et al.: US army research laboratory (ARL) robotics collaborative technology alliance 2014 capstone experiment. US Army Research Laboratory Aberdeen Proving Ground United States (2016)
3. Erol, B.A., et al.: Toward artificial emotional intelligence for cooperative social human–machine interaction. IEEE Trans. Comput. Soc. Syst. **7**(1), 234–246 (2019)
4. Ahn, H.S., Lee, M.H., MacDonald, B.A.: Healthcare robot systems for a hospital environment: CareBot and ReceptionBot. In: 24th IEEE International Symposium on Robot and Human Interactive Communication (RO-MAN), Kobe, Japan, pp. 571–576 (2015)
5. Hameed, I.A., Strazdins, G., Hatlemark, H.A.M., Jakobsen, I.S., Damdam, J.O.: Robots that can mix serious with fun. In: Hassanien, A.E., Tolba, M.F., Elhoseny, M., Mostafa, M. (eds.) AMLTA 2018. AISC, vol. 723, pp. 595–604. Springer, Cham (2018). https://doi.org/10.1007/978-3-319-74690-6_58
6. Nassif, A.B., et al.: Speech recognition using deep neural networks: a systematic review. IEEE Access **7**, 19143–19165 (2019)
7. Rahat, S.A., Imteaj, A., Rahman, T.: An IoT based interactive speech recognizable robot with distance control using Raspberry Pi. In: 2018 International Conference on Innovations in Science, Engineering and Technology (ICISET). IEEE (2018)
8. Vacher, M., et al.: Complete sound and speech recognition system for health smart homes: application to the recognition of activities of daily living. In: Domenico, C. (ed.) New Developments in Biomedical Engineering, pp. 645–673. In-Tech (2010)
9. van den Berghe, R.: Social robots in a translanguaging pedagogy: a review to identify opportunities for robot-assisted (language) learning. Front. Robot. AI **9**, 958624 (2022)
10. Randall, N.: A survey of robot-assisted language learning (RALL). ACM Trans. Hum.-Robot Interact. (THRI) **9**(1), 1–36 (2019)
11. Taniguchi, T., et al.: Language and robotics. Frontiers Media SA, p. 674832 (2021)
12. Forsberg, M.: Why is speech recognition difficult. Chalmers University of Technology (2003)
13. Mubin, O., Henderson, J., Bartneck, C.: You just do not understand me! Speech recognition in human robot interaction. In: The 23rd IEEE International Symposium on Robot and Human Interactive Communication. IEEE (2014)
14. Shneiderman, B.: The limits of speech recognition. Commun. ACM **43**(9), 63–65 (2000)
15. McCowan, I.A., et al.: On the use of information retrieval measures for speech recognition evaluation. IDIAP (2004)
16. Kennedy, J., et al.: Child speech recognition in human-robot interaction: evaluations and recommendations. In: 2017 12th ACM/IEEE International Conference on Human-Robot Interaction (HRI) (2017)
17. Attawibulkul, S., Kaewkamnerdpong, B., Miyanaga, Y.: Noisy speech training in MFCC-based speech recognition with noise suppression toward robot assisted autism therapy. In: 2017 10th Biomedical Engineering International Conference (BMEiCON). IEEE (2017)
18. Zinchenko, K., Wu, C.Y., Song, K.T.: A study on speech recognition control for a surgical robot. IEEE Trans. Ind. Inf. **13**(2), 607–615 (2017)
19. Ishi, C.T., et al.: A robust speech recognition system for communication robots in noisy environments. IEEE Trans. Robot. **24**(3), 759–763 (2008)

20. Russo, N., et al.: Effects of background noise on cortical encoding of speech in autism spectrum disorders. J. Autism Dev. Disord. **39**, 1185–1196 (2009)
21. Miller, K.W., Voas, J., Costello, T.: Free and open source software. IT Prof. **12**(6), 14–16 (2010)
22. Weber, S., Luo, J.: What makes an open source code popular on Git hub?. In: 2014 IEEE International Conference on Data Mining Workshop (2014)
23. Speech Recognition homepage. https://pypi.org/project/SpeechRecognition/. Accessed 11 Jan 2023
24. DeepSpeech homepage. https://deepspeech.readthedocs.io/en/r0.9/. Accessed 11 Jan 2023
25. Vosk homepage. https://pypi.org/project/vosk/. Accessed 11 Jan 2023
26. Cavazza, M.: An empirical study of speech recognition errors in a task-oriented dialogue system. In: Proceedings of the Second SIGdial Workshop on Discourse and Dialogue (2001)
27. Saon, G., Ramabhadran, B., Zweig, G.: On the effect of word error rate on automated quality monitoring. In: 2006 IEEE Spoken Language Technology Workshop. IEEE (2006)
28. Filippidou, F., Moussiades, L.: A benchmarking of IBM, google and wit automatic speech recognition systems. In: Maglogiannis, I., Iliadis, L., Pimenidis, E. (eds.) AIAI 2020. IAICT, vol. 583, pp. 73–82. Springer, Cham (2020). https://doi.org/10.1007/978-3-030-49161-1_7
29. Match Error Rate homepage. https://torchmetrics.readthedocs.io/en/stable/text/match_error_rate.html. Accessed 11 Jan 2023
30. WORD INFO. LOST homepage. https://torchmetrics.readthedocs.io/en/stable/text/word_info_lost.html. Accessed 11 Jan 2023
31. CHAR ERROR RATE homepage. https://torchmetrics.readthedocs.io/en/stable/text/char_error_rate.html#:~:text=character%20error%20rate%20is%20a. Accessed 11 Jan 2023
32. https://en.wikipedia.org/wiki/Speech_recognition
33. Këpuska, V., Bohouta, G.: Comparing speech recognition systems (Microsoft API, Google API and CMU Sphinx). Int. J. Eng. Res. Appl. **7**(03), 20–24 (2017)
34. Morris, A.C., Maier, V., Green, P.: From WER and RIL to MER and WIL: improved evaluation measures for connected speech recognition. In: Eighth International Conference on Spoken Language Processing (2004)
35. Wang, P., Sun, R., Zhao, H., Yu, K.: A new word language model evaluation metric for character based languages. In: Sun, M., Zhang, M., Lin, D., Wang, H. (eds.) CCL/NLP-NABD -2013. LNCS (LNAI), vol. 8202, pp. 315–324. Springer, Heidelberg (2013). https://doi.org/10.1007/978-3-642-41491-6_29
36. Sarı, L., Hasegawa-Johnson, M., Yoo, C.D.: Counterfactually fair automatic speech recognition. IEEE/ACM Trans. Audio Speech Lang. Process. **29**, 3515–3525 (2021)

It's a Long Way to Neutrality. An Evaluation of Gendered Artificial Faces

Oronzo Parlangeli[1]([⊠]) [ID], Paola Palmitesta[1] [ID], Leonardo Masi[1], Michele Tittarelli[2], and Stefano Guidi[1] [ID]

[1] University of Siena, Siena, Italy
{oronzo.parlangeli,paola.palmitesta,stefano.guidi}@unisi.it,
leonardo.masi@student.unisi.it
[2] Quest-It, Siena, Italy
tittarelli@quest-it.com

Abstract. Implementing gender-neutral virtual agents seems to be one possible solution to the problem of designing technologies which do not represent and convey gender stereotypes. Three tests were structured with the intention of selecting faces of male, female, or neutral gender hypothetical virtual agents. In each of these tests 30 participants assessed the gender and age of 9 hypothetical virtual agent faces by means of an online questionnaire. From the results of these tests, 3 faces were selected, one male, one female and one neutral, which were assessed through an online questionnaire ($N = 83$) with reference to some feminine or masculine characteristics of their personality. The willingness/pleasure to interact with artificial agents having those faces was also assessed. The results highlighted the difficulty in synthesizing faces that are perceived as absolutely neutral. Evaluations of the stimulus characterized by greater gender neutrality were less likely to refer to a female stereotype. The stimulus representing a gender-neutral face resulted also less accepted and liked than the male stimulus in all aspects considered and, in fewer aspects, than the female stimulus as well.

Keywords: virtual agents · gender neutrality · gender stereotypes · acceptability

1 Introduction

The implementation of anthropomorphic artificial agents has been motivated also by the need to facilitate human-technology interaction [1]. In fact, when an artificial agent is envisaged as a human being, it is easier to interact with it by assuming the same mental schemata that are commonly adopted in interactions with people [2]. Bringing the characteristics of the virtual agent closer to those of human beings also implies that the artificial agent is implemented showing external characteristics similar to human beings. Among those characteristics, first and foremost gender cues are frequently adopted [3]. However, it is now well known that even when the technological system with which we interact does not display characteristics that would lead us to classify it according to gender, we will still be inclined to categorize it by reference to gender [4]. This is not the case for all technologies in the same way: while virtual agents tend to be perceived as feminine, in contrast, robots are generally perceived as masculine [4, 5].

© The Author(s), under exclusive license to Springer Nature Switzerland AG 2023
A. Marcus et al. (Eds.): HCII 2023, LNCS 14033, pp. 366–378, 2023.
https://doi.org/10.1007/978-3-031-35708-4_27

Implementing gendered virtual agents means that gender stereotypes related to genders [6] are also transferred to the agent. And therefore the trait of *agency* - the tendency to act affirmatively - should be attributed to technologies perceived as masculine, while that of *communion* - being sensitive and affectionate - to those technologies perceived as feminine. Indeed, recent studies have shown that in the case of artificial systems - in these studies they were robots - the process of anthropomorphization involves referring to them the same stereotypical roles that are referred to humans [5]. It thus becomes possible that in the case of negative stereotypes, some discriminatory attitudes are reinforced [7, 8].

For these reasons, a recent trend is aimed toward the implementation of artificial agents that, although in possession of some human characteristics, do not carry cues that could trigger gender stereotyping, one could say a drive toward neutrality [9–12].

Few studies, however, have attempted to assess how far the pursuit of gender neutrality is an easy way to go and how far the results may satisfy the desire for improved human-virtual agent interaction and the breaking down of gender stereotypes.

1.1 Related Work

It has long been known that even voice cues alone can steer the perception of computers in a direction that makes us perceive them as agents that have a gender, male or female, and activate related stereotypes [13].

The results of a study on a set of artificial voices indicate that none of the voices considered are perceived as exclusively male or female [14]. This result would seem to open up the possibility that the voices are perceived as neutral. In fact, the authors of the study had also included the non-binary category among the response categories. But the item that achieved a higher percentage of categorization as non-binary was only 1.36% as such, and was also the one rated as least human-like.

The Q-voice is a project resulting from the contribution of scholars in various disciplines such as linguistics, sound engineering, and social sciences [9]. Initiated by "Vice", a Copenhagen-based Media Corporation, the project started by considering six natural voices with the intention of synthesizing, from their mixture, a non-binary voice. Underlying this effort was the intent to limit the perpetuation of gender bias through the implementation of gender-neutral technologies. The implementation effort required many iterations with 4,600 evaluators without leading to adequate results. Therefore, in conclusion, the project produced a single voice that was modulated to remain within a certain range.

Focusing more on the appearance of avatars representing virtual agents, [15] used cartoon-style drawings. The creation of an androgynous character required several iterations in the implementation process, especially with regard to haircuts. Their study showed that the androgynous virtual agent suffered less abuse than the female one, but more than the male one. However, it did not induce questions about gender in the interlocutor. And this, according to the authors, leaves the way open towards the possible use of androgynous agents as a tool to mitigate the reference to discriminatory stereotypes.

Again using avatars drawn as cartoons, [10] also had to undergo several iterations of the avatar-making process in order to achieve one that was androgynous. From their results, it appears that, at the level of activating gender stereotypes, there is no noticeable difference between male, female and androgynous avatars.

In a study that considered static images of humanoid social robots, it was found that neutrality was related to the age attributed to the robots: if robots were judged child-like, the likelihood that they were perceived as gender-neutral increased [16].

Instead of focusing on the process of making gender-neutral agents, one study analyzed the results produced by six search engines - Google, Bing, Yahoo, Baidu, Yandex, and DuckDuckGo -. The six search engines were used to identify AI images [17]. For all engines, the Authors used the "com" version of the image search engine (e.g., google.com) which were queried by 200 bots entering the "artificial intelligence" keywords. As a result of the queries, AI images that were gender-neutral or gender-unclassifiable emerged overwhelmingly. In addition, male representations were almost completely absent in the results of Western search engines, whereas they appeared in those of Eastern search engines.

At the moment, also considering that there are not many studies that directly deal with the possible advantage deriving from the use of neutral agents, in the scientific literature it is also possible to find suggestions that urge caution in their use, and that recommend an evaluation of how they are perceived in practice [18].

Altogether, it seems that implementing virtual agents that are perceived as neutral is by no means an easy task. Moreover, the use of gender-neutral virtual agents should still undergo contextual screening for acceptance and effectiveness. Implementation efforts, otherwise, might not achieve, or even mislead, the goals being pursued.

2 The Study

A study was conducted with the aim of testing the possibility of making avatars of virtual assistants that were, although artificial, with a higher level of naturalness than the stimuli adopted in previous studies [10, 15]. This process was designed to answer the research questions below.

Q1: Are neutral virtual agents perceived with stereotypical traits more similar to those of the male gender (agency) or to those of the female gender (communion)?

Q2: From an interaction perspective, do gender-neutral virtual agents generate a good disposition in the user to be perceived as trustworthy, useful, available for interaction, pleasant and realistic?

2.1 Procedure

Stimuli Creation Methodology
In the process of evaluating the perception and acceptance of gender neutrality in digital assistants, we started with a set of 9 visual stimuli, each one representing the face of a digital assistant under implementation. The stimuli were created via a 3D modeling/rendering software called Blender. Among the 9 stimuli, 3 displayed stereotypically male facial features (i.e.: faces with a thick neck, a square jawline, thin lips), 3 were

created to represent a female character (i.e.: faces with thinner neck, a softer bone structure, fuller lips), and 3 were rendered as gender-neutral (their gender was manipulated, using Wrap R3DS, through mashup of the preexisting binary features displayed by male and female stimuli). In order to avoid additional gender biases that could emerge from other gender-related features (such as hair length or hints of cosmetics on eyes and lips), each stimulus was rendered as bald and bearing with a natural appearance, with no facial expression and presented to the user head to shoulders, with no clothes or any other gender-defining hint in their looks. Moreover, their eyes were rendered as staring frontally to the user.

Based on their intended gender, the stimuli were classified as: M1; M2; M3 (men stimuli); W1; W2; W3 (women stimuli); N1; N2; N3 (neutral stimuli, mixed men and women) (see Fig. 1).

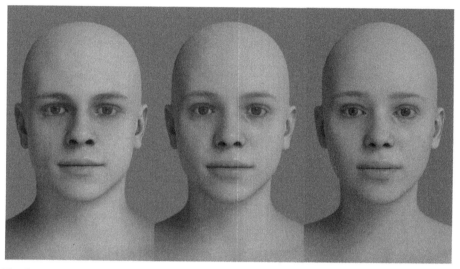

Fig. 1. Examples of the masculine, gender neutral and feminine stimuli evaluated in the Test 1. (3D models by mixamo.com - 3D modeling and rendering QuestIT S.r.l. - 2022).

The process of implementation of comparable stimuli for their degree of masculinity, femininity, neutrality, and age required three iterative tests.

In each test, the 9 stimuli were listed randomly into an online questionnaire that was administered to participants in order to evaluate the degree in which each of them was perceived as masculine, feminine or gender-neutral.

The entire procedure and the questionnaires used to carry out the three tests and the subsequent experiment were approved by the Ethics Committee for Research in the Human and Social Sciences of the University of Siena (Careus act: 72/2022).

Test 1

The first test has been conducted with 30 participants (M = 15, F = 15, age range: 15–60): they were asked to evaluate on a 7 point Likert scale (where 1 corresponds to "definitely not" and 7 to "totally") the degree of masculinity, femininity and neutrality perceived for each stimulus. The subjects were also asked to report the perceived age of each stimulus (in years).

The test resulted in a significant age gap between the male (age range: 25.0–27.7) and the neutral stimuli (age range: 17.9–21.4), thus making it impossible to identify three faces with comparable scores for each parameter (Table 1).

Table 1. Results of the Test 1

Stimulus	Masculinity	Femininity	Neutrality	Age
M1	6.66	1.23	1.20	25.00
M2	6.30	1,43	1.48	27.70
M3	6.56	1.53	1.58	27.20
W1	1.96	6.13	1.76	23.90
W2	1.60	5.76	1.80	22.33
W3	1.70	6.03	1.83	26.40
N1	2.83	3.33	4.90	17.90
N2	3.00	4.03	3.36	21.50
N3	3.03	4.13	4.23	20.90

Table 2. Results of the Test 2

Stimulus	Masculinity	Femininity	Neutrality	Age
M1	6.53	1.50	1.96	25.00
M2	6.20	1.50	1.50	27.70
M3	6.40	1.46	1.80	26.56
W1	2.16	5.93	2.90	21.83
W2	1.80	5.63	3.00	22.83
W3	2.50	5.40	2.60	26.26
N1	3.43	4.30	4.50	19.53
N2	4.06	4.20	4.70	22.53
N3	4.30	3.53	4.36	23.06

Since these results were not helpful to give answers to the experimental questions, a second test was implemented following the same procedure as the first one but with refined stimuli.

Test 2

The second test was submitted to another sample of 30 subjects (M = 15, F = 15,

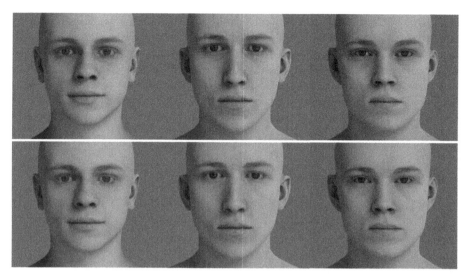

Fig. 2. The three male faces used in Test 2 (bottom row) which were altered from the male faces used in Test 1 (up row). (3D models by mixamo.com - 3D modeling and rendering QuestIT S.r.l. - 2022).

age range: 21–60) after manipulating normal and diffuse textures of the 3D models of the M stimuli using Photoshop. Therefore, M1, M2 and M3's facial features were altered to result in a less stereotypical appearance: eye shadows and circles were deleted, skin details were softened pursuing an ideally younger and less masculine (if not androgynous) look (see Fig. 2).

As a result of these manipulations a reduction of the age gap between M and N stimuli was observed, though this difference was not significant. This may be indicative of how age is often perceived as depending on bone structure, marks and wrinkles on a face, rather than on its gender (Table 2).

However, the age difference between male stimuli and gender-neutral stimuli was still too high to consider these stimuli as suitable for conducting an experiment that could answer the research question.

Test 3

To prevent the perception of gender from being biased by the stimuli's physical features shown in the pictures (such as bald head or broad shoulders), a third questionnaire was created and administered to participants following the same procedure (M = 15, F = 15, age range of 15–70). In this test each stimulus was cropped at the forehead and at the neck base, excluding all of the features that weren't part of the faces themselves (see Fig. 3).

In Table 3 are reported the average gender and age ratings for all the cropped stimuli stimuli. We compared the average age scores for the faces using Linear Mixed-effects Models (LMM) including as fixed effect either face gender or stimulus (in different analyses). The results for the analysis of age ratings showed no significant differences among the faces of different genders ($F_{2,6} = 2.33$, p = .178). The further analyses of the femininity, masculinity and neutrality ratings showed that for all the variables the ratings differed significantly across face genders (Femininity: $F_{2,6} = 72.16$, p < .001; Masculinity: $F_{2,6} = 81.82$, p < .001; Neutrality: $F_{2,6} = 28.65$, p < .001), and in the ways that were expected. Indeed the masculine faces were perceived as most masculine (and least feminine), the feminine faces were perceived as most feminine (and least masculine), and the neutral faces were considered most neutral and intermediate in both femininity and masculinity. The results of all the pairwise comparisons are reported in Table 4.

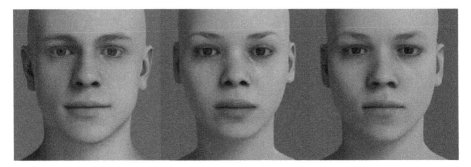

Fig. 3. The three stimuli in the Test 3 that were selected for the experiment (3D models by *mixamo.com* - 3D modeling and rendering QuestIT S.r.l. - 2022).

Table 3. Results of the Test 3

Stimulus	Masculinity	Femininity	Neutrality	Age
M1	6.43	1.33	1.60	23.83
M2	5.63	1.83	2.26	24.83
M3	6.50	1.30	1.86	25.16
W1	2.06	5.60	3.36	22.63
W2	1.96	5.83	2.86	23.66
W3	2.06	5.60	2.70	28.53
N1	3.60	4.00	4.40	19.36
N2	3.56	4.20	3.93	21.53
N3	4.43	2.93	3.73	23.40

Cropping the pictures allowed us the identification of 3 stimuli with comparable enough scores to be considered fully representative of each gender (M1, W2 and N2 were chosen) (see Fig. 3), whereas M1 minimized the age gap with the other two selected stimuli, W2 was the most female face and N2 had acceptable ratings for both neutrality and age.

Table 4. Results of the pairwise comparisons of the mean gender ratings for the different gender faces. P-values were computed approximating the degrees of freedom with Kenward-Roger's method.

Dependent Variable	Fem. - Masc		Fem. - Neut		Masc. - Neut	
	Diff	p-value	Diff	p-value	Diff	p-value
Femininity	4.22	< .0001	2.01	.0030	−2.21	.0018
Masculinity	−4.16	< .0001	−1.83	.0032	2.32	.0009
Neutrality	1.07	.0204	−1.04	.0223	−2.11	.0007
Age	0.333	.9812	3.511	.2037	3.178	.2567

Note. Masc. = Masculine faces, Fem. = Feminine faces, Neut. = Neutral faces. For each dependent variable, p-values for contrast were adjusted with Tukey's method for a family of 3 comparisons

2.2 The Experiment

The 3 representative stimuli were used in a mixed factorial experiment, in which we collected, using an online questionnaire, the ratings about the faces from a sample of 83 participants (41 males; 40 females; 2 identifying themselves as non-binary), all students of the University of Siena. The independent variables were the gender of the avatar face (face gender), which was manipulated within-participants, and the participant gender.

Three different versions of the same questionnaire were structured, varying only the order in which the same three stimuli were presented. In this way, each of the three stimuli was presented in one questionnaire in the first position, in another in the second and in the other questionnaire in the third position.

For each of the three stimuli the participant had to respond to 15 questions which began with "to what extent". Answers were collected on 7 point Likert scales (1 = absolutely not; 7 = absolutely yes). Five questions were a scale aimed at assessing agency, a stereotypical male trait: Do you think this digital assistant could: 1) Behave as a leader?; 2) Advocate their own ideas?; 3) Have a strong personality?; 4) Make important decisions?; 5) Stand their own ground?. Other five questions were a scale on communion, a stereotypical female trait: Do you think this digital assistant could: 1) Show affection?; 2) Feel empathy?; 3) Be tender?; 4) Show compassion?; 5) Be kind?. These 10 questions were derived from the short form of the Bem Sex Role Inventory - BSRI- [19].

The last 5 questions were designed to assess aspects related to the willingness to interact with agents who could present one of the three faces here considered. These were: 1) Trust [20]: Would you trust this digital assistant?; 2) Desirability [21]: Would you like to interact with this digital assistant; 3) Acceptability [22]: Would you like this digital assistant to help you while studying or working?; 4) Beauty [23]: Do you think beauty is a characteristic of this digital assistant?; 5) Realism [24]: Do you think this digital assistant is believable as a real person?.

Each stimulus was presented a second time to the subjects after the first 10 questions, to facilitate its recall without having to scroll repeatedly all the way back to the test's first page before answering the last five questions. The students who participated in the study were contacted in their class and were invited to participate in the study before their class started. Those who voluntarily decided to participate were given a link to fill in the questionnaire anonymously. No reward was provided for the participation in the study. The duration of the test was approximately 10 min.

2.3 Results

Participants had a mean age of 21.5 years (SD = 4.2). 48.2% were women (N = 40), 49.4% men (N = 41) and 2.4% identified as non-binary (N = 2).

Scales Internal Consistency
For each face we computed Cronbach's alpha for the items about female and male traits, and scales had very good internal consistency both for stereotypically female (communion, $\alpha \geq 0.9$), and stereotypically male (agency: $\alpha \geq 0.88$) items. Therefore, we computed the scores for the two scales aggregating the corresponding items, to use in successive analyses.

Effects of Face and Participant Gender
We used linear mixed effects models to compare participants' mean ratings for the different faces. In each model we included face gender (3 levels: M1 Male face, W2 Female face, N2 Neutral face), participant gender (2 levels: man and woman) and their interaction as fixed effects, and participants ratings about a given trait as dependent variable. For each dependent variable a separate model was fit. In each model a random, by-participant, intercept adjustment was included. Given the low number of non-binary participants, the data for this group were not used for the analyses.

In the following Table 5 are reported the results of the tests of all the effects for all the dependent variables considered. For all the dependent variables but Agency, the analysis showed a significant main effect of face gender (all p < .001), indicating significant differences between the mean ratings for the different faces. Moreover, for 3 variables, Agency, Communion, and Beauty, but marginally also for Realism (p = .055), the analyses showed a significant main effect (all p < .01) of participant gender, with higher mean ratings from women than for men. A Face gender x Participant Gender significant interaction was also found for two variables, participants' willingness to interact with the virtual assistant (Desirability), and their degree they would have liked to receive assistance in studying or working (Acceptability).

To understand the main effects of face gender, and the interactions with participants' gender, we conducted a series of paired comparisons of the marginal means for the different faces (averaging across participant gender), adjusting p-values for multiple comparisons with Tukey's method. The results of the comparisons are presented in Table 6 for all the dependent variables.

For all the variables, except Agency, the mean ratings for the neutral assistant (N2) were significantly lower than those for the masculine assistant (M1). For the ratings of Acceptability of assistance, however, the masculine face was preferred over the neutral one only by women.

Table 5. Results of the test of fixed effects in linear mixed effects models. P-value for tests were computed approximating degrees of freedom with Satterthwaite's method.

Dependent Variable	Face gender		Participant Gender		Face gender x Participant Gender	
	$F_{1,158.00}$	p-value	$F_{1,79.00}$	p-value	$F_{1,158.00}$	p-value
Agency	1.33	.266	19.39	**< .001**	0.00	.999
Communion	21.13	**< .001**	14.71	**< .001**	1.31	.272
Trust	13.02	**< .001**	2.76	.101	0.86	.427
Desirability	15.24	**< .001**	2.45	.122	3.04	**.050**
Acceptability	9.61	**< .001**	1.80	.183	4.60	**.011**
Beauty	14.29	**< .001**	8.59	**.005**	0.59	.557
Realism	14.00	**< .001**	3.79	*.055*	0.18	.839

The neutral assistant (N2) was also rated as significantly lower than the feminine assistant (W2) for all the dependent variables but Agency and Acceptability. For the ratings of Willingness to interact, however, this effect was only significant for men.

Lastly, regarding the comparisons between the feminine and the masculine faces, the results of the analyses showed that the masculine assistant (M1) received higher ratings than the feminine one (W2) for Communion, Desirability, and Acceptability. However, for the last two variables, the effect was only significant for women.

3   Discussion

The results obtained deserve a few considerations.

The first has to do with the difficulty of generating stimuli representing faces of virtual agents that are perceived, without uncertainty, as neutral. This difficulty can also be referred to other studies already conducted with the intention of synthesizing neutral voices [9] or of processing visual stimuli of gender-neutral virtual agents [10]. At the moment, however, this difficulty can be attributed to both the designers of these stimuli and the participants. Therefore it would be interesting to address this question directly in an attempt to understand why it is so difficult to follow a design hypothesis of gender-neutral agents. On the other hand, it may be relevant to understand how much the perception of neutrality is facilitated or hindered by cultural factors that can lead to a gender bias in the participants [8, 18].

The second consideration refers to the fact that in this study the male face stimulus is, for almost all the variables considered, the most preferred, while the neutral gender stimulus is the least preferred. It would be unreasonable to formulate general considerations in this regard since these results refer only to three faces. But taken together, the findings provide very consistent clues that suggest closer consideration of the push toward neutrality sometimes invoked to limit reference to discriminatory gender stereotypes [9–12]. Gender neutral stimuli, at least with participants who identify themselves

Table 6. Results of the pairwise comparisons of the marginal means for the judgments about faces for the different variables. P-values were computed approximating the degrees of freedom with Kenward-Roger's method.

Dependent Variable	M1 – W2		M1 – N2		W2 – N2	
	Diff	*p-value*	*Diff*	*p-value*	*Diff*	*p-value*
Agency	−0.034	.9652	−0.207	.2824	−0.173	.4139
Communion	0.647	**.0001**	0.948	**< .0001**	0.300	**.0112**
Trust	0.360	.0958	0.876	**< .0001**	0.516	**.0090**
Desirability	0.524	**.0080**	0.953	**< .0001**	0.429	**.0373**
(women)	0.950	**.0005**	1.150	**< .0001**	0.200	.6956
(men)	0.098	.9150	0.756	**.0062**	0.658	**.0203**
Acceptability	0.786	**.0014**	0.883	**.0003**	0.097	.8992
(women)	1.425	**< .0001**	1.375	**.0001**	−0.050	.9861
(men)	0.146	.8847	0.390	.4213	0.244	.7121
Beauty	0.113	.7982	0.866	**< .0001**	0.754	**.0001**
Realism	0.334	.1859	0.988	**< .0001**	0.653	**.0021**

Note. M1 Male face, W2 Female face, N2 Neutral face. For each dependent variable, p-values for contrast were adjusted with Tukey's method for a family of 3 comparisons

in a binary gender, might not be a good option to limit the reference to gender stereotypes in virtual agents. These kinds of stimuli could be not well accepted at all (Q2).

However, it seems necessary to reflect on these results from another perspective as well. That is, it must be remembered that the face representing the neutral gender had the lowest scores for the stereotypical trait communion (Q1). This could therefore lead to the hypothesis that the neutral stimulus is less able to trigger the negative correlates referable to some gender stereotypes.

4   Limitations

The main limitations of the study refer to the amount of stimuli and to the gender of the participants.

Conducting a study on gender identity of virtual agents with only three stimuli may have led to results with a low level of ecological validity.

Furthermore, the analyses were referred only to participants who declared themselves male or female. The number of non-binary participants was in fact too low. It would be really interesting to continue this study with a higher number of stimuli and with participants who do not recognize themselves in a binary definition of genders.

5   Conclusion

Contrasting gender stereotypes also by trying to design technologies that do not refer to gender representations based on a binary perspective is an objective that must be pursued with greater awareness, both in relation to the most appropriate design processes and considering the different cultures of users.

There is still a long way to go, but the goal makes it worth pursuing.

References

1. Nass, C., Steuer, J., Tauber, E.R.: Computers are social actors. In: Proceedings of SIGCHI 1994 Human Factors in Computing Systems, pp. 72–78. ACM (1994). https://doi.org/10.1145/259963.260288
2. Epley, N., Waytz, A., Cacioppo, J.T.: On seeing human: a three-factor theory of anthropomorphism. Psychol. Rev. **114**(4), 864–886 (2007). https://doi.org/10.1037/0033-295X.114.4
3. Blut, M., Wang, C., Wünderlich, N.V., Brock, C.: Understanding anthropomorphism in service provision: a meta-analysis of physical robots, chatbots, and other AI. J. Acad. Mark. Sci. **49**(4), 632–658 (2021). https://doi.org/10.1007/s11747-020-00762-y
4. Bernotat, J., Eyssel, F., Sachse, J.: The (fe)male robot: how robot body shape impacts first impressions and trust towards robots. Int. J. Soc. Robot. **13**(3), 477–489 (2019). https://doi.org/10.1007/s12369-019-00562-7
5. Parlangeli, O., Palmitesta, P., Bracci, M., Marchigiani, E., Guidi, S.: Gender role stereotypes at work in humanoid robots. Behav. Info. Technol. (2022). https://doi.org/10.1080/0144929X.2022.2150565
6. Eagly, A.H., Nater, C., Miller, D.I., Kaufmann, M., Sczesny, S.:. Gender stereotypes have changed: a cross-temporal meta-analysis of U.S. public opinion polls from 1946 to 2018. Am. Psychol. **75**(3), 301–315. (2019). https://doi.org/10.1037/amp0000494
7. Bracci, M., Guidi, S., Marchigiani, E., Masini, M., Palmitesta, P., Parlangeli, O.: Perception of faces and elaboration of gender and victim/aggressor stereotypes: the influence of internet use and of the perceiver's personality. Front. Psychol. **12**, 561480 (2021). https://doi.org/10.3389/fpsyg.2021.561480
8. Perugia, G., Guidi, S., Bicchi, M., Parlangeli, O.: The shape of our bias: perceived age and gender in the humanoid robots of the ABOT database. In: HRI 2022, Proceedings of the 2022 ACM/IEEE International Conference on Human-Robot Interaction, pp. 110–119. ACM - IEEE Press (2022). https://doi.org/10.1109/HRI53351.2022.9889366
9. Carpenter, J.: Why project Q is more than the world's first nonbinary voice for technology. Interactions **26**(6), 56–59 (2019). https://doi.org/10.1145/3358912
10. Nag, P., Yalçın, Ö.: Gender stereotypes in virtual agents. In: Proceedings of the 20th ACM International Conference on Intelligent Virtual Agents, vol. 41, pp. 1–8 (2020). https://doi.org/10.1145/3383652.3423876
11. Mooshammer, S., Etzrodt, K.: Social research with gender-neutral voices in chatbots—the generation and evaluation of artificial gender-neutral voices with Praat and Google WaveNet. In: Følstad, A., et al. (Eds.) Lecture Notes in Computer Science. Chatbot Research and Design, vol. 13171, pp. 176–191, Springer International Publishing, Cham (2022). https://doi.org/10.1007/978-3-030-94890-0_11
12. Koda, T., Tsuji, S., Takase, M.: Measuring subconscious gender biases against male and female virtual agents in Japan. In: HAI 2022, Proceedings of the 10th International Conference on Human-Agent Interaction, pp. 275–277. ACM, New York (2022). https://doi.org/10.1145/3527188.3563909

13. Nass, C., Moon, Y., Green, N.: Are machines gender neutral? Gender-stereotypic responses to computers with voices. J. Appl. Soc. Psychol. **27**, 864–876 (1997). https://doi.org/10.1111/j.1559-1816.1997.tb00275.x

14. Baird, A., Jørgensen, S.H., Parada-Cabaleiro, E., Cummins, N., Hantke, S., Schuller, B.: The perception of vocal traits in synthesized voices: age, gender, and human likeness. J. Audio Eng. Soc. **66**(4), 277–285 (2018). https://doi.org/10.17743/jaes.2018.0023

15. Silvervarg, A., Raukola, K., Haake, M., Gulz, A.: The effect of visual gender on abuse in conversation with ECAs. In: Nakano, Y., Neff, M., Paiva, A., Walker, M. (eds.) IVA 2012. LNCS (LNAI), vol. 7502, pp. 153–160. Springer, Heidelberg (2012). https://doi.org/10.1007/978-3-642-33197-8_16

16. Ladwig, R.C., Ferstl, E.C.: What's in a name? An online survey on gender stereotyping of humanoid social robots. In: Proceedings of 4th Gender & IT Conference, Heilbronn, Germany (GenderIT2018). ACM, New York (2018). https://doi.org/10.1145/3196839.3196851

17. Makhortykh, M., Urman, A., Ulloa, R.: Detecting race and gender bias in visual representation of AI on web search engines. In: Boratto, L., Faralli, S., Marras, M., Stilo, G. (eds.) BIAS 2021. CCIS, vol. 1418, pp. 36–50. Springer, Cham (2021). https://doi.org/10.1007/978-3-030-78818-6_5

18. Armando, M., Ochs, M., Régner, I.: The impact of pedagogical agents' gender on academic learning: a systematic review. Front. Artif. Intell. **5**, 862997 (2022). https://doi.org/10.3389/frai.2022.862997

19. Choi, N., Fuqua, D.R., Newman, J.L.: Exploratory and confirmatory studies of the structure of the Bem sex role inventory short form with two divergent samples. Educ. Psychol. Meas. **69**(4), 696–705 (2009). https://doi.org/10.1177/0013164409332218

20. Huang, R., Kim, M., Lennon, S.: Trust as a second-order construct: Investigating the relationship between consumers and virtual agents. Telemat. Inform. **70**, 101811 (2022). https://doi.org/10.1016/j.tele.2022.101811

21. Scutella, M., Plewa, C., Reaiche, C.: Virtual agents in the public service: examining citizens' value-in-use. Public Manag. Rev. (2022). https://doi.org/10.1080/14719037.2022.2044504

22. Venkatesh, V., Davis, F.D.: A theoretical extension of the technology acceptance model: four longitudinal field studies. Manage. Sci. **46**(2), 186–204 (2000). https://doi.org/10.1287/mnsc.46.2.186.11926

23. Yuksel, B.F., Collisson, P., Czerwinski, M.: Brains or beauty: how to engender trust in user-agent interactions. ACM Trans. Internet Technol. (TOIT) **17**(1), 1–20 (2017). https://doi.org/10.1145/2998572

24. Strojny, P.M., Dużmańska-Misiarczyk, N., Lipp, N., Strojny, A.: Moderators of social facilitation effect in virtual reality: co-presence and realism of virtual agents. Front. Psychol. **11**, 1252 (2020). https://doi.org/10.3389/fpsyg.2020.01252

Author Index

A

Araújo, Layane   3

B

Banawi, Abdul-Aziz   98
Bande, Lindita   98
Berengueres, Jose Lopez   98
Bi, XiaoLei   154
Blum, Stefan   302
Böhmann, Tilo   283, 302
Bond, Raymond   321

C

Chen, Xiaoshi   262
Chen, Yunfei   24
Chien, Wei-na   39
Coates, Vivien   321
Cortes, Bernardo   273

D

Dong, Jimiao   58
Duarte, Emília   273

E

Emans, Denielle J.   77

G

Galal Ahmed, Khaled   98
Gibson, Michael R.   88
Gong, Shiqi   166
Guidi, Stefano   366

H

Hamdoon, Baraah   98
Hellmich, Jannis   302
Heuer, Marvin   283, 302
Hiyasat, Rund   98

Holmes, Samuel   321
Huang, Lianyu   131

I

Inal, Yavuz   340

K

Kubicek, Max   283
Kučević, Emir   302

L

Lai, Qian   111
Lembke, Patrick   283
Lewandowski, Tom   283, 302
Li, Manhai   131
Li, WenJing   120
Li, Xin   120
Li, Yingxuan   131
Lin, Ziyu   142
Liu, Zhen   142, 166
Liu, Zhichao   262

M

Masi, Leonardo   366
Mayer, Tom   283
McTear, Michael   321
Mishra, Deepti   340, 355
Moorhead, Anne   321
Murdoch-Kitt, Kelly M.   77

N

Nees, Jan P.   154

O

Ortgiese, Simon   283
Owens, Keith M.   88

© The Editor(s) (if applicable) and The Author(s), under exclusive license
to Springer Nature Switzerland AG 2023
A. Marcus et al. (Eds.): HCII 2023, LNCS 14033, pp. 379–380, 2023.
https://doi.org/10.1007/978-3-031-35708-4

P

Palmitesta, Paola   366
Pande, Akshara   355
Parish, Karen   340
Parlangeli, Oronzo   366

Q

Qin, Qianhang   200, 249

R

Rajbhandari, Rumi   340
Rani, Anshul   355
Raykhlin, Michael   302
Romero, Guillermo Arroyo   340

S

Shi, Yuanchun   111
Shrestha, Bhanu   355
Soares, Marcelo M.   3
Sun, Jiahao   58

T

Tan, Jing   58
Tan, Qi   185
Tan, Zhiya   166
Tang, Bo   249
Teles, Júlia   273
Tian, Wenda   200, 249

Tittarelli, Michele   366
Tori, Romero   3

W

Wang, Gengyi   200
Wang, Jian   58
Wang, Min   120
Wang, Tiantian   239
Wang, Ziye   58
Weglewski, Joffrey   283
Wu, Liuyi   239

X

Xie, Yixin   239
Xu, Yingqing   111

Y

Yang, Hai'ou   221
Yang, Qiong   212
Yu, Chun   111
Yu, DanDan   120
Yuan, Xing   239

Z

Zhang, Mang-mang   39
Zhang, Yijing   3
Zhao, Yang   239
Zheng, Jane   321
Zhou, Youtian   249
Zhu, Jixu   262